Mental Health and Benefits Handbook

2nd edition

Child Poverty Action Group

Child Poverty Action Group works on behalf of the more than one in four children in the UK growing up in poverty. It does not have to be like this. We use our understanding of what causes poverty and the impact it has on children's lives to campaign for policies that will prevent and solve poverty – for good. We provide training, advice and information to make sure hard-up families get the financial support they need. We also carry out high-profile legal work to establish and protect families' rights. If you are not already supporting us, please consider making a donation, or ask for details of our membership schemes, training courses and publications.

Published by Child Poverty Action Group
30 Micawber Street
London N1 7TB
Tel: 020 7837 7979
staff@cpag.org.uk
cpag.org.uk

A CIP record for this book is available from the British Library
ISBN: 978 1 915324 28 3

Child Poverty Action Group is a charity registered in England and Wales (registration number 294841) and in Scotland (registration number SC039339), and is a company limited by guarantee, registered in England (registration number 1993854). VAT number: 690 808117

Cover design by Colorido Studios
Internal design by Devious Designs
Typeset by DLxml, a division of RefineCatch Limited, Bungay, Suffolk
Content management system by Konnect Soft
Printed in the UK by CPI Group (UK) Ltd, Croydon CR0 4YY

The authors

Lynsey Dalton is a solicitor and freelance writer on welfare rights.

Daniel Norris is head of welfare rights at CPAG.

The information team at **Mind**.

Acknowledgements

CPAG is proud to be collaborating with Mind on this project. We would like to thank Naomi Jessop, Director of Business at CPAG, and Stephen Buckley, Head of Information at Mind, for making this partnership possible.

Special thanks go to Carri Swann, author of the first edition, and to Tom Messere, author of *The Big Book of Mental Health*, for sharing his expertise and experience.

We are also grateful to the checkers for their invaluable contributions: Liam Bradford, Harriet Chaplin, Carolyn George, Simon Osborne, Samantha Scarlett, Jon Shaw, Martin Williams and the Mind legal team. Thanks to Jo Silcox for her brilliant insights shared on CPAG's Benefits and Mental Health training course.

We would also like to acknowledge Nicola Johnston and Kathy Proctor for editing and managing the production of this *Handbook*, Anne Ketley for updating the index, and Kathleen Armstrong for proofreading.

The law covered in this book was correct on 1 August 2025 and includes regulations laid up to this date.

Contents

Abbreviations

AA	attendance allowance
ACSSL	advanced customer support senior leaders
ADP	adult disability payment
APA	alternative payment arrangement
BDD	body dysmorphic disorder
BMI	body mass index
BPD	borderline personality disorder
BSL	British Sign Language
CA	carer's allowance
CDP	child disability payment
CPN	community psychiatric nurse
DBS	deep brain stimulation
DEA	disability employment adviser
DLA	disability living allowance
DWP	Department for Work and Pensions
ECT	electroconvulsive therapy
ESA	employment and support allowance
HAAS	Health Assessment Advisory Service
HB	housing benefit
HCP	healthcare professional
HMCTS	HM Courts and Tribunals Service
HMRC	HM Revenue and Customs
JSA	jobseeker's allowance
MPTL	managed payment to landlord
NI	national insurance
NMD	neurosurgery for mental disorder
OCD	obsessive compulsive disorder
OCPD	obsessive compulsive personality disorder
PADP	pension age disability payment
PC	pension credit
PIP	personal independence payment
PTSD	post traumatic stress disorder
SADLA	Scottish adult disability living allowance
SCTS	Scottish Courts and Tribunal Service
SMI	Severe mental illness
SSP	statutory sick pay
SSS	Social Security Scotland
TD	tardive dyskinesia
UC	universal credit
VCC	vulnerable claimant champion
VINCYP	Visual Impairment Network for Children and Young People
VNS	vagus nerve stimulation

Part 1

Mental health

Chapter 1

Introduction

This chapter covers:

1. What this *Handbook* covers (below)
2. What are mental health problems (p5)
3. Language used in this *Handbook* (p6)
4. The different types of benefits (p9)
5. How to use this *Handbook* (p10)

1. What this *Handbook* covers

This *Handbook* is a practical guide to social security benefits for people who have a mental health problem or who are struggling with their mental health. It is primarily aimed at advisers helping someone with a mental health problem to apply for benefits. It may also be helpful for people with mental health problems who are making a claim, carers, families and other professionals such as social workers and housing officers.

This book provides advice and guidance for different stages of benefit claims and problems you might encounter during the process. It has been shaped by the experiences and insights of people with lived experience of mental health problems and the benefits system.

Benefit topics included

Part 2 of this *Handbook* focuses on the benefits most commonly claimed by people with a mental health problem. These are:

- employment and support allowance (ESA – see Chapter 4);
- universal credit (UC – see Chapter 5);
- pension credit (see Chapter 6);
- housing benefit (see Chapter 7);
- personal independence payment (PIP – see Chapter 8);
- adult disability payment (in Scotland – see Chapter 9);
- disability living allowance (see Chapter 10);
- child disability payment (in Scotland – see Chapter 11);
- attendance allowance (see Chapter 12);

- pension age disability payment (in Scotland – see Chapter 13);
- benefits for carers (see Chapter 14);
- other financial support (see Chapter 15).

Part 3 covers the evidence you need to support your claim (see Chapter 16) and the assessments for UC, PIP and ESA (see Chapter 17). Chapter 18 sets out the rules about work and benefits and Chapter 19 covers what happens if you are in education or you go into hospital, a care home or prison. If you need to challenge a decision, see Chapter 20. Chapter 21 expains the extra support you should be offered when applying for benefits or carrying out actions to do with your benefits, and what happens if you cannot manage your benefits.

Benefit topics not included

As they are generally unaffected by mental health status, this *Handbook* does not cover:

- most contributory benefits, including new-style jobseeker's allowance;
- severe disablement allowance and incapacity benefit;
- industrial injuries benefits;
- armed forces independence payment;
- statutory sick pay;
- statutory maternity, paternity, adoption and other parental pay;
- maternity allowance;
- bereavement benefits;
- pensions, including private pensions (but see Chapter 6 on pension credit);
- child benefit and guardian's allowance;
- immigration and residence rules, including habitual residence test and right to reside;
- benefit overpayment and deductions;
- fraud, fines and penalties.

For information on these topics, see CPAG's *Welfare Benefits Handbook*. Citizens Advice also has information on many of these benefits and rules (see citizensadvice.org.uk/benefits).

Learning difficulties, learning disabilities and neurocognitive disorders

This *Handbook* focuses on experiences of claiming benefits when someone has a mental health problem. It does not include specific information about claiming benefits when someone has a learning difficulty like dyslexia, or a neurodiverse condition like autism or ADHD. It also does not cover diseases that damage the brain, such as dementia. People with these conditions may also experience mental health problems, so the information about mental health may be useful in these situations. For more specific information about these experiences, visit the Scope,[1] Mencap[2] or Alzheimer's Society[3] websites.

About Mind

Mind works to ensure that people experiencing mental health problems get support and respect. They do this through:
- providing empowering information to help people understand mental health and the choices available to them;
- offering support and signposting through their helplines and online community;
- campaigning on issues that affect people with mental health problems – from benefits to hospital care;
- providing mental health services through a network of local Minds.

You can find out more at mind.org.uk.

About CPAG

Child Poverty Action Group (CPAG) works on behalf of the more than one in four children in the UK growing up in poverty. It works to understand what causes poverty, the impact it has on children's lives, and how it can be prevented and solved.

CPAG collects evidence from families and advisers, and campaigns for achievable and long-term solutions to child poverty. It supports frontline advice workers by providing expert information and advice through:
- books and online information to help advisers navigate the social security system;
- a comprehensive range of training courses about benefits and related topics;
- telephone advice lines for advisers (see Appendix 2);
- legal action to challenge unjust decisions.

You can find out more at cpag.org.uk.

2. What are mental health problems

Mental health problems are when the way you think, feel or act becomes difficult to cope with and has a big impact on your day-to-day life. They can last for a short period or a long time and can happen to anyone. This *Handbook* focuses on symptoms and experiences of mental health problems rather than specific diagnoses.

Mental health problems and disability

Under the Equality Act 2010, a mental health problem is considered a disability if it has a significant and long-term effect on your ability to carry out normal day-to-day activities.[4] This means that any mental health problem can be considered a disability in a legal sense if it affects you enough, even if you do not think of yourself as having a disability.

While the Equality Act 2010 gives a clear definition of a disability,[5] different health-related benefits have different criteria for what they consider enough of an impairment to meet eligibility rules.

For example, to qualify for personal independence payment (see Chapter 8), you must have a mental or physical condition which causes difficulties with certain everyday tasks or getting around, and you must have had (and expect to have) these difficulties for a sufficient length of time.

There are different qualifying conditions for disability living allowance for children (see Chapter 10) and attendance allowance for those over pension age (see Chapter 12).

In this *Handbook,* 'disability' refers to any health conditions and characteristics that are relevant to the benefit being covered.

Severe mental illness

The term 'severe mental illness' (SMI) is sometimes used by the NHS, GPs or local councils, often in reporting and data collection. It refers to some types of mental health problems which are considered to cause significant problems with your day-to-day life and requires ongoing management, even when you are feeling well.[6] It is most commonly used to describe bipolar disorder and schizophrenia.

Your mental health problem can still have a severe impact on your life even if it is not considered to be an SMI by some organisations. In benefit applications, it should not be necessary to state whether your mental health problem is considered an SMI, unless you feel it is relevant. What is important is describing how your mental health problem impacts your life.

3. Language used in this *Handbook*

This *Handbook* uses the term 'mental health problems' because it covers a wide range of experiences. This term may not feel appropriate for you and it is OK to use other terms when talking about your experiences. If you are supporting someone with a mental health problem, it is important to use the language they are comfortable with.

Diagnosis

People have different experiences and views around mental health diagnosis. Not everyone with a mental health problem has a formal diagnosis, and those with a diagnosis might not agree with it. Diagnoses can also change over time.[7] It is important to remember that you do not need a diagnosis to be eligible for benefits, and that no specific diagnosis automatically entitles you to benefits. Benefit entitlements are based on your circumstances and how a particular health problem affects you.

This *Handbook* focuses on symptoms and experiences of mental health problems rather than specific diagnoses.

Diagnosis texts

Some mental health problems are classified differently across medical texts. In the UK, health professionals may refer to these medical texts when making a mental health diagnosis:

- DSM-5-TR is the 5th edition of the *Diagnostic and Statistical Manual of Mental Disorders,* published by the American Psychiatric Association in 2013 and revised in 2022;
- ICD-11 is the 11th edition of the World Health Organisation's *International Classification of Diseases,* published in 2019 and came into effect 2022.

Both are trusted medical sources, but they have differing criteria for which symptoms fit with which mental health problem. For example, schizoaffective disorder has different diagnostic criteria in ICD-11 and the DSM-5-TR.

Even if someone's symptoms appear to fit a diagnostic label given in these texts, they may feel that the diagnosis is not appropriate for them.

Criteria and diagnoses can also change over time. Different editions of the DSM and ICD reflect changes in the understanding of mental health and society. For example, homosexuality was listed as a mental disorder in the first and second editions of the DSM, but was removed in 1973.[8] Therefore, while these texts can be useful, they also reflect the social and medical bias of the times in which they were written.

Controversial diagnoses

Some diagnoses are controversial for the people diagnosed with them and medical professionals. This includes diagnoses like personality disorders.[9]

You may encounter more prejudice and misconceptions because of these diagnoses. This is covered in Chapter 2.

Diagnosis and treatment

Your diagnosis can affect your access to treatments. Some treatments are harder to access unless you have a specific diagnosis. For example, dialectical behaviour therapy (DBT) is a type of therapy offered to some people with borderline personality disorder (also known as borderline pattern personality disorder).[10] In some places, you may not be able to access this treatment through the NHS if you do not have a diagnosis.[11]

Sometimes a diagnosis on its own is not enough to access treatments. For example, some people are denied certain treatments for eating disorders if they are not below a certain body mass index (BMI),[12] even though eating disorders can affect people at any BMI.

Diagnosis and young people

Diagnosis for people under the age of 18 can be complicated. Young people may find it harder to get a diagnosis or their diagnosis may change as they get older. Some diagnoses, such as personality disorder diagnoses, are not usually given to people under 18.[13]

Outdated terminology

Mental health language changes over time. As we learn more about mental health problems, we start to use more accurate and less stigmatising language.

For example, 'dissociative identity disorder' is the up-to-date term for what used to be called 'multiple personality disorder'.[14] 'Bipolar disorder' is the current term for what used to be called 'manic depression',[15] but the term 'mania' is still a valid term for some bipolar disorder symptoms.

However, some people working in the benefit system still use outdated language. If you are supporting someone to claim a benefit, make sure you are using the most up-to-date terms or the terms they prefer. You can politely inform others when they use outdated terms. However, do not correct the person you are supporting if they choose to describe their condition using older terms.

Different perspectives on mental health

Not everyone sees mental health problems the same way – either in themselves and in others. The way we think about mental health depends on many factors, including:[16]

- our experiences in childhood and as adults;
- our cultural background;
- our religion or faith;
- our education, work or hobbies;
- the opinions of people around us.

These influences can affect someone's mental health and the support they seek, including their ability to:

- recognise that they might have a mental health problem;
- talk to others about what they are going through;
- seek treatment that suits their beliefs or experiences;
- describe how they are feeling to others;
- support others who have a mental health problem.

For example, people from different generations may understand and talk about mental health in different ways. Each generation has grown up with different language and social ideas about mental health, which can make it difficult to talk about mental health or speak openly with others, such as, with family members from different generations. Some people might not feel comfortable discussing or seeking help for their mental health, especially if it is not something that is commonly done in their family or community.

Being aware of these differences can help you better understand your needs and be more supportive of others.

It is important to remember that no matter what someone's perspective is, no one should feel guilty or wrong for having mental health problems. They are not something that you cause yourself and they do not make you a bad person.

4. The different types of benefits

There are different types of benefits that you might be entitled to when you have a mental health problem. What you can claim depends on your circumstances – eg, the effects of your condition on your day-to-day life, your support needs, your ability to get out and about, your income, your savings and your work history.

Getting financial support can make a big difference, whether you are managing a short- or long-term mental health problem. Benefits not only provide a regular income but can also open up many other types of support, like help with energy costs or free school meals. The amount of benefit you get might not cover all your costs, but getting benefits can still make a significant difference to your life.

Means-tested benefits

'Means-tested' (or 'income-related') benefits may be available if you have a low (or no) income. Your entitlement is affected by most other types of income and by the amount of savings you have. Your national insurance (NI) contribution record does not matter. The means-tested benefits covered in this *Handbook* are income-related employment and support allowance (ESA – see Chapter 4), universal credit (see Chapter 5), pension credit (see Chapter 6) and housing benefit (see Chapter 7).

Contributory benefits

To qualify for this type of benefit, you must have paid enough NI contributions.

This *Handbook* only covers one kind of contributory benefit: contributory ESA (see Chapter 4). This is the benefit you are most likely to claim if you have paid enough NI contributions and are now unable to work due to a mental health problem. CPAG's *Welfare Benefits Handbook* covers other kinds of contributory benefits and pensions. Citizens Advice has more information on other types of benefits on its website (see citizensadvice.org.uk/benefits).

Disability benefits (non-means tested and non-contributory)

These benefits are to help with the extra costs of having a long-term health problem or disability. They are non-means tested and non-contributory, which means that your NI record, income and savings are not taken into account. You can claim them alongside the other benefits listed above.

The disability benefits covered in this *Handbook* are personal independence payment (see Chapter 8), adult disability payment (see Chapter 9), disability living allowance (see Chapter 10), child disability payment (see Chapter 11), attendance allowance (see Chapter 12) and pension age disability payment (see Chapter 13).

Other types of benefits

There are other types of benefits that might be relevant if you or someone you care for has a mental health problem. For example, you might be eligible for a benefit paid by your employer (eg, statutory sick pay) or for carer's allowance. These benefits are not contributory or means tested but they do have eligibility rules relating to your work history and earnings. They are not all covered in this *Handbook,* but you can find more information about them in CPAG's *Welfare Benefits Handbook.*

Financial help beyond benefits

As well as benefits, there are many other sources of financial help which depend on your location and circumstances – eg, council tax reduction schemes and local welfare assistance schemes. See Chapter 15 for more information.

For help with managing debts, see CPAG's *Debt Advice Handbook* and *Debt Advice Handbook Scotland*. These are available free at cpag.org.uk/handbooks.

5. How to use this *Handbook*

This *Handbook* is divided into two main types of information.

- Chapters deal with various topics related to mental health and relevant benefits. Contents are given at the beginning of each chapter, and there is an index at the end of the book to help you find the information you need. Each chapter has endnote references that give the sources of information. Where an abbreviation is used in the endnotes, the full reference is given in Appendix 4. If you are challenging a benefit decision, you may want to refer to the law.
- Appendices contain supplementary material and information.

There are signposts to other CPAG handbooks which provide more detail on specific topics, such as benefits and debt. Where detailed information is required, such as eligibility criteria for particular benefits, consult the specialist handbook.

Abbreviations are used in the text to save space. The abbreviated term is explained in full the first time it is used in a section, and on pvii there is a list of all the abbreviations used. A glossary of terms used in this book is in Appendix 1.

The information applies to England, Wales and Scotland.

Notes

1. **What this *Handbook* covers**
   1 scope.org.uk/advice-and-support/benefits
   2 mencap.org.uk/advice-and-support/benefits-people-learning-disability
   3 alzheimers.org.uk/get-support/legal-financial/benefits-dementia

2. **What are mental health problems**
   4 ss6 and 15 EA 2010
   5 s15 EA 2010
   6 Public Health England, *Severe Mental Illness (SMI) and Physical Health Inequalities: briefing*, 27 September 2018, at gov.uk

3. **Language used in this *Handbook***
   7 mind.org.uk/information-support/types-of-mental-health-problems/mental-health-problems-introduction
   8 pmc.ncbi.nlm.nih.gov/articles/PMC4695779
   9 mind.org.uk/information-support/types-of-mental-health-problems/personality-disorder/why-is-personality-disorder-controversial
   10 nice.org.uk/guidance/cg78/chapter/Recommendations
   11 mind.org.uk/information-support/drugs-and-treatments/talking-therapy-and-counselling/dialectical-behaviour-therapy-dbt
   12 publications.parliament.uk/pa/cm201719/cmselect/cmpubadm/855/855.pdf, para 13
   13 nice.org.uk/guidance/cg78/ifp/chapter/borderline-personality-disorder
   14 mind.org.uk/information-support/types-of-mental-health-problems/dissociation-and-dissociative-disorders
   15 nhs.uk/mental-health/conditions/bipolar-disorder
   16 mind.org.uk/information-support/types-of-mental-health-problems/mental-health-problems-introduction

Chapter 2

Mental health and benefits

This chapter covers:

Key facts

- Every mental health experience is unique. Even people with the same diagnosis can be affected in very different ways.
- When applying for benefits, focus on how a mental health problem affects you. This gives a clear insight into how your day-to-day life is affected.
- You do not need a formal diagnosis to apply for benefits related to your mental health.
- You may experience stigma from people in the benefits system who have a limited understanding of how mental health works.
- The process of claiming and managing benefits can impact your mental health, even if you do not have a mental health problem. Support is available throughout the benefits process if you need it.

1. How mental health problems can affect you

Poor mental health can affect your day-to-day life. This is true even for those who do not have a mental health problem. Feeling stressed, low or anxious, even for a short period, can make it difficult to be organised, sleep well or concentrate.

Every mental health experience is unique. Even people with the same diagnosis may be affected in very different ways. A certain symptom may cause more difficulty to one person than another, depending on factors like:

- how severe the symptom is;
- how frequently it occurs;
- your physical health;
- your job or daily activities;
- your living situation;

- how much support you have from friends, family or services;
- treatments you may be taking or having;
- whether you have other symptoms or health problems.

When applying for benefits, it is therefore important to clearly explain how your symptoms affect you and your day-to-day life.

Mental health symptoms

Mental health diagnostic labels (such as 'generalised anxiety disorder') are not always the best way to understand mental health problems, as each person can experience the same diagnosis differently. When applying for benefits, focus on how a mental health problem affects you. This gives a clear insight into how your daily life is impacted, rather than relying on a diagnostic label that may not always accurately reflect your full experience or be understood by others.

The impact of your symptoms may also affect the type of support you need during a benefit claim. If you are supporting someone with a mental health problem, do not assume that they need help with everything or that certain symptoms affect them in a certain way. Ask about their capabilities and support needs. There is more information about giving advice in Chapter 3.

Below is an overview of some common mental health symptoms and how they might affect you in the benefits process. These symptoms can apply to a wide range of diagnoses and experiences. This list is not exhaustive, and other symptoms you experience are just as relevant to include in your benefit application. It is also OK if the symptoms listed here affect you differently than outlined.

For some symptoms, certain diagnoses might be particularly relevant. However, not everyone with a particular diagnosis experiences these symptoms. Remember also that not everyone with a mental health problem has a diagnosis (see p6), and some people with a diagnosis might disagree with it.

Compulsions

Compulsions are repetitive behaviours that you feel you have to do to deal with the distress caused by an obsessive or anxious thought. These can be physical actions (like touching things in a particular order) or mental rituals (such as repeating a word or number). Compulsions can be time-consuming and exhausting. They can make it difficult to complete forms, go to new places or interact with people.

When to ask about compulsions

Anyone can experience compulsions, but it might be particularly relevant if someone is diagnosed with:

– anorexia;

- body dysmorphic disorder (BDD);
- hoarding disorder;
- obsessive compulsive disorder (OCD), including perinatal OCD.

Concentration problems

Many mental health problems and treatments can impact concentration levels. You might find it difficult to focus for long periods or you may get easily distracted. You might lack motivation to do things like filling in forms if you know it will need a lot of concentration, or it could take you a long time to complete them. You might also struggle to follow what is being said at appointments or assessments, and you might forget details like claimant commitments or appointment dates.

Delusions

A delusion is a belief that other people do not share and which other experiences or perceptions show cannot be true. However, these delusions can feel completely real to you when you experience them. Delusions may involve false beliefs about yourself or others. For example, you may believe you are a very important person, or that other people are trying to harm you. Delusions can affect your benefit claim in various ways, depending on the specific delusion. If delusions are affecting your claim, it is important to explain this clearly when applying for benefits or asking for adjustments.

When to ask about delusions

Anyone can experience delusions, but it might be particularly relevant if someone is diagnosed with:

- addiction or substance dependency;
- bipolar disorder;
- borderline personality disorder (BPD) (also referred to as borderline pattern personality disorder);
- hoarding disorder;
- psychosis, including postpartum psychosis;
- schizoaffective disorder;
- schizophrenia.

Disorganised thinking and speech

Some mental health problems or treatments can make your thoughts and emotions feel confused and disorganised. Disorganised thinking and speech can lead you to:

- speak very quickly or stumble over words;
- link words by how they sound (eg, rhyming) rather than what they mean;

- repeat words;
- copy what someone else says;
- not finish sentences, either written or verbal;
- change topic very quickly and often;
- split your attention between lots of different things at once.

These symptoms can make it difficult to communicate clearly both verbally and in writing.

When to ask about disorganised thinking and speech

Anyone can experience disorganised thinking and speech, but it might be particularly relevant if someone is diagnosed with:
- bipolar disorder;
- psychosis, including postpartum psychosis;
- schizoaffective disorder;
- schizophrenia.

Dissociation

People experience dissociation in different ways. In general, it is a feeling of disconnection from yourself and the world around you. This normally happens in response to stress or trauma and can last for a short or a long time. Dissociation can create gaps in your memory, both short- and long-term, or make you feel like you are a different person. Some people who dissociate can have difficulty keeping track of what happens in their lives or who they are as a person. This can make it difficult to complete benefit applications, remember appointments or keep track of the progress you have made in a benefit claim.

When to ask about dissociation

Anyone can experience dissociation, but it might be particularly relevant if someone is diagnosed with:
- a dissociative disorder;
- anxiety, including perinatal anxiety;
- bipolar disorder;
- BPD;
- phobias;
- post-traumatic stress disorder (PTSD), including complex PTSD and postnatal PTSD.

Distrust

Distrust can be a symptom of many different mental health problems. It might come from past experiences of being treated badly, from trauma, or it could be due to a delusion. This distrust might make it difficult for you to apply for benefits or ask for help. If something happens with your claim (eg, if you are given a sanction), this may increase your distrust and make it hard to engage with the system.

Eating problems

Eating problems are any relationships with food that you find difficult. They can happen to anyone at any weight. They may involve:

- eating too much;
- eating too little;
- only eating certain types of food, including avoiding certain colours or textures of food;
- purging after eating;
- eating non-food items, such as dirt or soap.

Eating problems can affect your nutrition, which can lead to problems with concentration and overall physical health. You may lack the energy to complete forms or attend appointments, or you may find that stress you experience when applying for benefits triggers eating problem behaviours.

When to ask about eating problems

Anyone can experience eating problems, but it might be particularly relevant if someone is diagnosed with:
– an eating disorder;
– depression;
– premenstrual dysphoric disorder (PMDD);
– specific phobias relating to food or eating.

Flashbacks

A flashback is a vivid experience where you feel as though you are reliving aspects of a traumatic event or that it is happening again in the present moment. Depending on what your flashbacks are triggered by, you might find it very traumatic to recall past events or go to certain places. You may find going to job centre offices upsetting, or find that questions you are asked in benefit forms or in assessments cause flashbacks.

When to ask about flashbacks

Anyone can experience flashbacks, but it might be particularly relevant if someone is diagnosed with:
– a dissociative disorder;
– PTSD, including complex PTSD and postnatal PTSD.

Hallucinations

Hallucinations involve seeing, hearing, feeling or smelling something that other people do not. These can be positive, but they might also be distressing, like hearing voices that are saying horrible things about you. Sometimes people are aware that they are hallucinating and other times they are not. This can make it difficult to know what is real, which can be difficult to explain in benefits forms and assessments. These hallucinations can also be distracting, making it hard to complete forms or concentrate in assessments.

When to ask about hallucinations

Anyone can experience hallucinations, but it might be particularly relevant if someone is diagnosed with:

- addiction or substance dependency;
- bipolar disorder;
- depersonalisation or derealisation disorder;
- psychosis, including postpartum psychosis;
- schizoaffective disorder;
- schizophrenia.

Hoarding

Hoarding is when you have so many things that you cannot manage the clutter where you live and you find it difficult or impossible to throw things away. Hoarding can be experienced as part of another mental health problem or on its own as hoarding disorder. You might find it difficult to keep track of important documents (eg, ID) or judge what is important to keep or throw away.

When to ask about hoarding

Anyone can experience hoarding, but it might be particularly relevant if someone is diagnosed with:

- depression;
- hoarding disorder;
- OCD, including perinatal OCD.

Impulsive actions

Some mental health problems may cause people to act very impulsively. This could include making a big life decision without thinking it through, such as spending a lot of money, quitting a job, or saying things you did not intend to others. It can also include self-harm or other behaviours directed at themselves. Impulsivity can cause disruption in your life and may affect your benefit claim. For example, it might lead to missed appointments or actions that result in sanctions. People working in the benefit system might see these actions as intentional, rather than as a symptom of a mental health problem. If this is the case, it can be helpful to clearly explain how your mental health affects your behaviour.

When to ask about impulsive actions

Anyone can experience impulsive actions, but it might be particularly relevant if someone is diagnosed with:

- addiction or substance dependency;
- a personality disorder with a disinhibition trait;[1]
- binge eating disorder;
- bipolar disorder;
- BPD;
- hoarding disorder;
- impulse control disorders;
- mood and conduct regulation disorders (only applicable to those under 18);[2]
- psychosis, including postpartum psychosis;
- schizoaffective disorder;
- schizophrenia;
- body-focused repetitive action disorders such as trichotillomania and skin picking disorder.

Insecurity, low confidence and low self-esteem

Many mental health problems – and the stigma surrounding them – can cause insecurity, low confidence and low self-esteem. These feelings may prevent someone from applying for benefits altogether if they believe they do not deserve them, even when they are entitled to them. These feelings might make it very hard for someone to advocate for themselves in benefits applications and assessments. They may feel uncomfortable with challenging benefits decisions without support and reassurance.

Intrusive and obsessive thoughts

Intrusive or obsessive thoughts are unwelcome images, urges, worries or doubts that repeatedly appear in your mind. They can be anxiety-inducing and be very hard to manage. These thoughts might focus on a particular situation, such as feeling something bad will happen to you if you go outside, or they might relate to negative thoughts about yourself. They can make it difficult to concentrate, complete forms and interact with other people. They may also affect your self-esteem.

When to ask about intrusive and obsessive thoughts

Anyone can experience intrusive and obsessive thoughts, but it might be particularly relevant if someone is diagnosed with:

- anxiety, including perinatal anxiety;
- BDD;
- hoarding disorder;
- OCD, including perinatal OCD;
- phobias;
- PTSD, including complex PTSD and postnatal PTSD.

Low or lack of insight

Some people with mental health problems might lack insight into how they are acting or feeling. Lacking insight is when we do not recognise or understand something about our mental health. This could include believing things that may not be based on how you usually see the world, or not realising you need support to keep safe. This may prevent someone from applying for benefits or fully explaining how their mental health problem affects them.

When to ask about low or lack of insight

Anyone can experience low or lack of insight, but it is more common with some mental health problems such as:

- hoarding disorder;
- during experiences of psychosis;
- during experiences of mania;
- during experiences of dissociation.

Asking about low or lack of insight can be sensitive. The person might not agree with you about their experience. It is important not to push them or to make assumptions. Instead, reassure them you are available to support them and return to the topic another time. You should only intervene if you believe their low or lack of insight is putting them or others at serious risk of harm (see p333).

Mania or hypomania

Mania and hypomania are periods of overactive and excited behaviour that can have a significant impact on your day-to-day life. Hypomania is milder and lasts for a short period (a few days) and mania is more severe and can last longer. Mania and hypomania may cause a sense of euphoria, excitement and high energy. They can lead to problems concentrating, impulsive behaviour and delusions. During these periods, it can be hard to manage tasks like filling in forms, keeping appointments or meeting deadlines.

When to ask about mania or hypomania

Anyone can experience mania or hypomania, but it might be particularly relevant if someone is diagnosed with:

– bipolar disorder;
– psychosis, including postpartum psychosis;
– schizoaffective disorder.

Memory problems

Many mental health problems – and treatments for them – can affect your memory. You might have problems remembering what someone has told you, or have trouble recalling details from different parts of your life. This can make it difficult to recall important dates or details about yourself that may be required during a benefit claim.

Mood changes

Many mental health problems can lead to shifts in mood. These might be long-term changes (such as periods of feeling low) or might be very rapid mood swings. They may happen at certain times of the year or happen unexpectedly. Low moods can reduce your motivation and self-esteem, making it harder to do a lot of the tasks involved in benefit applications and management. Other moods, like anger or frustration, might make it difficult to interact with others. Very happy or excited moods, such as ones you might experience as part of mania or hypomania, might lead you to downplay how your mental health problem affects you.

Panic attacks

Panic attacks are a type of fear response. They are an exaggeration of your body's normal response to danger, stress or excitement. They have physical symptoms that can feel like a heart attack, such as a racing heart, feeling faint and sweating. They can occur at different times for each person and may be triggered by specific situations. Some people may have panic attacks during assessments or appointments, or have a panic attack just thinking about having to do those things.

When to ask about panic attacks

Anyone can experience panic attacks, but it might be particularly relevant if someone is diagnosed with:
– anxiety, including perinatal anxiety;
– BPD;
– OCD, including perinatal OCD;
– OCPD;
– phobias;
– PTSD, including complex PTSD and postnatal PTSD;
– PMDD.

Paranoia

Paranoia is when you think or feel you are being threatened in some way, even if there is no evidence of this that other people can see. It is similar to some forms of delusions. You may think that you are being watched, that people are intentionally trying to upset you, or that people are trying to steal from you. These feelings can make it very difficult to trust others and engage with services that support people with benefit applications and with the benefit system itself. Paranoia can be based in a real past event. For example, if someone was turned down for benefits or sanctioned in the past, they may believe that the system is against them personally.

When to ask about paranoia

Anyone can experience paranoia, but it might be particularly relevant if someone is diagnosed with:

- bipolar disorder;
- BPD;
- psychosis, including postpartum psychosis;
- schizoaffective disorder;
- schizophrenia.

Physical health problems

Many mental health problems – and treatments for them – can have physical health effects. This can range from aches and pains to fainting and disruptions to the menstrual cycle. These physical health effects can make it harder to complete day-to-day tasks or interact with others for long periods, depending on their nature and severity.

Self-harm

Self-harm is when you hurt yourself as a way of dealing with very difficult or intense feelings, painful memories or overwhelming situations and experiences. Self-harm is not always easily identifiable and can include behaviours like over-exercising. Someone who is self-harming may be particularly vulnerable in stressful situations such as benefits assessments or reviews. Some people are asked about their self-harm in very insensitive ways during assessments, which can be very unsafe. See p264 if you are asked about self-harm in an assessment.

Self-neglect

Self-neglect is when you are living in a way that puts your wellbeing or health at risk. This can include problems with:[3]

- eating reguarly or enough;
- looking after your personal hygiene;
- getting help for medical problems;

- keeping your home clean and safe;
- managing essential tasks such as paying bills.

Self-neglect can happen for a range of reasons, including:
- not being able to look after yourself because of your mental health problem;
- not realising you are neglecting yourself because of your mental health problem;
- not having enough money to look after yourself;
- not having the care and support you need to look after yourself.

If someone is neglecting themselves, they might find it difficult to attend appointments or keep track of paperwork. Be kind and understanding – people who neglect themselves often face stigma or judgement from others. In some cases, self-neglect can be a safeguarding concern (see p333).

When to ask about self-neglect

Anyone can experience self-neglect, but it might be particularly relevant if someone is diagnosed with:
- addiction or substance dependency;
- bipolar disorder;
- depression;
- hoarding disorder;
- psychosis, including postpartum psychosis;
- seasonal affective disorder (SAD);
- schizoaffective disorder;
- schizophrenia.

Sleep problems

Many mental health problems – and treatments for them – can impact sleep. You might sleep too much, sleep too little or have very disrupted sleep. Some people wake up multiple times in the night, have nightmares or struggle to get out of bed in the morning. Sleep problems can impact concentration and memory and make it very difficult to navigate the benefit system.

Suicidal thoughts and feelings

Suicidal feelings can range from having abstract thoughts about ending your life or feeling people would be better off without you, to having clear plans to end your life. These feelings can be frightening and hard to manage – they can last for a short or long time. Suicidal thoughts and feelings can affect your daily life. You might lack motivation, making it hard to attend appointments or complete forms. Issues such as a delay in benefits, miscalculation or a change in circumstances might increase suicidal feelings. People experiencing these feelings can be very vulnerable, and those working in the benefit system do not always fully understand this, nor how their tone or behaviour can unintentionally cause harm. See p264 if you are asked about suicidal thoughts and feelings in a benefit assessment.

In an emergency

If you feel like you might attempt suicide or have seriously harmed yourself:

– call 999 for an ambulance or go straight to A&E, if you can;

– call your local crisis team, if you have the number.

If you cannot do this by yourself, ask someone to help you.

Mental health treatments

Treatments for mental health problems can have side effects that make it difficult to engage with the benefits process. Some of these are outlined below. This list is not exhaustive, and there may be many other experiences that are not covered here which are just as relevant to explain in your benefits application.

It is also important to be aware that not everyone with a mental health problem is getting treatment for it. They may be able to manage the symptoms on their own, or there may be a waiting list for treatment. Waiting lists for mental health support can be very long, and support supplied by the NHS might not last for a long time, so some people may have finished their treatment but are still struggling.

Medications

There are different types of medication someone might take to help with their mental health problem.[4] These can include:

- antidepressants;
- antipsychotics;
- sleeping pills;
- mood stabilisers.

All of these medications have side effects, which range from mild to severe. Some people may stop taking their medications because of the side effects. Common side effects of these kinds of medication can include:

- nausea;
- suicidal thoughts or feelings;
- hypomania or mania;
- drowsiness or decreased alertness;
- heart, liver and eye problems;
- sexual and hormonal problems;
- confusion and memory problems.

The side effects can make it harder to complete forms, remember important dates, or interact with other people.

Harry's experience

'I think not wanting to take medication can often be viewed with suspicion. Like if you aren't willing to take something with serious side effects and consequences, you are considered untreated and therefore contributing to the condition you need benefits for, whereas you may have found other ways of managing the issues.'

Tardive dyskinesia

Tardive dyskinesia (TD) is a condition where your face, body or both make sudden, irregular movements that you cannot control. Some people might call these tics. Some forms of TD are mild, while others can be severe and disruptive, making it difficult to hold objects securely, walk without support or carry out everyday tasks. TD is a side effect of certain antipsychotic medications that may be prescribed for psychosis, schizophrenia, bipolar disorder or severe depression.

TD does not start right away. It can take months or even years for symptoms to show, and they can happen even after you have stopped taking the medication. Not everyone who takes antipsychotic medication will experience TD.

TD may affect the support someone needs with the physical process of applying for benefits.

Talking therapy

Talking therapies are treatments where you speak with a trained professional about your thoughts, feelings and behaviour. They are also known as counselling or psychotherapy, and there are many types. As therapy involves exploring complicated feelings and experiences, the process can make people feel vulnerable. Someone having therapy might feel more anxious or worried just before or after a therapy session, or they may experience heightened feelings over the course of therapy. These feelings can impact their motivation, concentration and ability to interact with others.

Hospital procedures

In very rare cases, some mental health problems are treated with hospital procedures. These include:

- **vagus nerve stimulation (VNS):** an operation to install an electrical device in your chest which sends an electrical pulse to the vagus nerve;
- **deep brain stimulation (DBS):** brain surgery to install a stimulator that sends electric pulses through your brain;
- **electroconvulsive therapy (ECT):** a treatment that involves sending an electric current through your brain;

- **neurosurgery for mental disorder (NMD):** surgery where small areas of your brain are destroyed.

For VNS and DBS, possible side effects can include headaches and sleep problems. For ECT and NMD, side effects can include memory loss, confusion, trouble learning new information and difficulty concentrating. Someone experiencing these side effects may need additional support and reasonable adjustments to help manage a benefit claim.

Sectioning

Being sectioned means you are legally kept in hospital for assessment or treatment because there is a risk to your health and safety or that of others. In England and Wales, this must be done within the rules set out by the Mental Health Act 1983. In Scotland, this must be done under the Mental Health (Care and Treatment) (Scotland) Act 2003.

There are different types of sections with different rules. You must be assessed before you can be sectioned.

For information on sectioning in England and Wales, see Mind's guide to sectioning.[5] For information on sectioning in Scotland, see the Mental Welfare Commission for Scotland's information on the Mental Health Act.[6]

While you are in hospital, your benefits might be stopped or reduced. See Chapter 19 for what happens to your benefits when you are in hospital. Being sectioned might also make it difficult to communicate with organisations managing your benefits, such as the DWP. After being discharged from hospital, you might need to claim benefits for the first time.

2. Stigma and misconceptions

Mental health problems are often misunderstood, which can lead to stigma – ie, negative or inaccurate beliefs. Misconceptions and stigma may be about a specific mental health problem, or they may be about mental health in general. Staff in job centres, assessment centres or the DWP may not be consistently trained about mental health, and may have stigmatising views and misconceptions. You may also encounter stigma and misconceptions from people supporting you with your benefits claim, including friends, family and advisers. You may also have some misconceptions about your mental health and your right to claim benefits.

Types of stigma

During the benefits process, you may encounter stigma because of your mental health problems. This can include, but is not limited to, the following.

- **Trivialising:** this is when your experience is made to seem less important or meaningful than it actually is. This can include people thinking mental health problems are not 'real', or not taking them seriously.
- **Perceptions of violence or danger:** some people assume people with mental health problems are violent or dangerous. This can affect the way they treat you, including how they interpret your tone, words or body language.
- **Stereotypes:** there are many incorrect ideas about how certain mental health problems should 'look'. For example, some people might think that eating problems only affect women or that people with anxiety cannot make eye contact when speaking. Stereotypes can hinder getting the support you need.
- **Not recognising mental health problems as health problems:** even people with mental health problems may not always see their experience as a health problem in the same way they may view physical health problems. They might find it uncomfortable to identify with terms like 'disability', or even feel they are not entitled to health-related benefits.
- **Internal causes of mental health problems:** some people believe that mental health problems happen because of something you have done, or that they are easy to fix. For example, some people feel that people with depression just need to 'cheer up'. Some people may see a mental health problem as a punishment for doing something bad.

There are many more types of stigma and misconceptions you might face in everyday life. No matter what stigma you encounter, remember you have the right to apply for benefits if your mental health affects your life. You are entitled to be treated fairly and with respect.

Intersectionality

Often people experience more than one kind of stigma at the same time. This could be related to your race, class, gender, sexual orientation or health. The way these parts of your identity work together is known as intersectionality. Intersectionality helps us understand that people's experiences of stigma and discrimination are not all the same.

People who experience multiple types of prejudice often experience worse mental health, as well as barriers to recovery. For example, misconceptions about violence and mental health problems can combine with racist stereotypes. Some people wrongly believe that some mental health problems make someone dangerous.[7] There is also a racist stereotype of Black men being dangerous.[8] When someone believes both these things, they may have a very inaccurate view of what someone's behaviour means. This can create bias in how someone is treated for a mental health problem.

Stigma and misconceptions in the benefit system

Staff working in the benefit system have varying levels of knowledge about mental health problems. This can significantly affect your experience at every stage of the benefits process.

If you encounter staff with little knowledge or understanding of mental health, it may lead to:

- being given the wrong information about what benefits you can apply for;
- being put in the wrong work-related groups or given unrealistic work-related requirements;
- having reasonable adjustment requests ignored;
- being sanctioned inappropriately;
- being asked inappropriate or harmful questions during assessments;
- receiving less benefit than you are entitled to, or not getting benefit at all.

It can be hard to recognise when a decision is unfair or wrong, or to know how to challenge it. Organisations like Mind have advisers with in-depth knowledge of benefits and mental health. They can help you understand why decisions have been made, and help you challenge them.

Informal observations

Where assessments are required for benefits such as personal independence payment (PIP), assessors make informal observations of how applicants present themselves (see p265). These observations can influence the outcome of your claim – sometimes unfairly. Sometimes, observations are based on misconceptions about mental health problems, including assumptions that:

- because someone can answer a phone, travel or make eye contact that they do not have anxiety;
- symptoms of depression are easy to overcome and are more reflective of laziness;
- if someone is well dressed or well presented that they are not unwell or struggling with their mental health.

It can be very hard to convey how your mental health problem affects you to someone who has a stereotyped view of mental health problems.

You can request a recording of your assessment (you must usually ask in advance) or, in some cases, can make a recording yourself. There is more information on p261. You can also request a copy of the assessor's report, which is based on notes made by an assessor during an assessment. If an assessor has made inaccurate observations, you can challenge the decision made about your benefit (see Chapter 20).

Priyanka's experience

Priyanka told us about the stigma she experienced when applying for PIP.

'I applied for PIP on the advice of my psychiatrist, my counsellor, my care worker and GP. I had letters from all of my care providers, and at the time, I was under the mental health team after having a breakdown. I was initially dealt with by the crisis team and had crisis help daily in my home.

'My husband came with me to the appointment, and I cried for the whole duration, which was one and a half hours.

'My results came back saying that I was presentable, well dressed, clean. I had points deducted because of this and because I could use a bank card. [The assessor] never once mentioned the distress I was in or any of the information provided by my care providers. At this time, my husband was giving me my meds, feeding me and being my full-time carer.'

Inappropriate questions

Assessors sometimes ask for details about suicidal thoughts, self-harm, trauma or symptoms of psychosis. These questions are not usually necessary in determining whether someone is eligible for benefits.[9] There is more information on p264.

You have a right to ask why a question is relevant. You can also complain about the way an assessor has treated you (see p308). You have a right to bring someone to an assessment with you for support, as well as asking for reasonable adjustments that might make you more comfortable handling certain questions. Chapter 17 has more information about assessments, including about reasonable adjustments and being accompanied.

Challenging stigma and misconceptions

It should not be your responsibility to educate other people about your mental health problem. Unfortunately, you may find yourself in this position. Advocacy services are available to support you, and you can direct others to websites with reliable mental health resources, such as those provided by Mind.[10]

Discrimination

Being treated unfairly because of certain characteristics is illegal under the Equality Act 2010. This kind of unfair treatment is called discrimination. The Equality Act 2010 says you cannot be treated differently or unfairly because of:[11]

- age;
- disability (which can include mental health problems);
- gender reassignment;
- marriage and civil partnership;
- pregnancy and maternity;
- race;
- religion or belief;

- sex;
- sexual orientation.

Discrimination can be unintentional, but it is still illegal. The discrimination could be a one-off action from one person, or the result of a rule or policy. It includes not putting reasonable adjustments in place when they are needed.

The Equality and Human Rights Commission website has more information on disability discrimination and how to challenge it.[12]

Alex, Jo, Benni and Caroline's experiences

Alex, Jo, Benni and Caroline told us about their experiences of applying for benefits. Their experiences show how different the benefit system can be for individuals with mental health problems, depending on the kinds of prejudice they face in the process.

Alex has severe anxiety and obsessive compulsive disorder (OCD), which can be triggered by situations where she feels embarrassed or judged. Alex told us this makes it difficult for her to speak to people over the phone or in person.

'I overhear people in public slating people who claim benefits because of mental health issues, saying they're making it up because they are lazy and saying "we've all got problems but we work". It makes you feel incredibly insignificant not being understood.'

For Alex, this stigma was not just from members of the public. She also saw it reflected in the people managing her benefits when she applied for universal credit (UC).

'I got the impression when talking to professionals about my claim that they didn't believe me. They wanted more evidence and asked me a lot of personal questions. It's very nerve wracking for someone who has an anxiety disorder.'

Jo gets UC and PIP and had very different experiences with each service based on how much they understood her mental health needs.

'Universal credit were amazing with my application. I spoke to multiple different people and they were all really understanding and helped me apply. The work capability section took a long time, but I was awarded it based on the application and contact with my GP. It was great not having to have an interview as that would have set off my anxiety.'

Jo felt that the people handling her UC claim were 'more compassionate about mental health struggles' than she experienced when applying for PIP.

'Honestly, applying for PIP for mental health was horrible and very stressful... they don't understand how much mental health impacts physically as well as mentally. PIP is a very long process.'

Jo had to appeal her PIP decision as many things the assessor wrote were incorrect or they had misunderstood Jo's answers.

Benni is also on UC and found her experience was different in different parts of the country.

'I had support with setting up universal credit as it's quite complicated. I've found universal credit where I applied in the Midlands to be really understanding – they haven't yet put me

through a formal assessment as they judged my capability to work based on the form and information about my PIP. Even before they officially judged my capabilities, they just asked me to do more of the same simple tasks that I was already doing, such as attending groups. I found that universal credit teams where I applied further north did not want to help with anything that was not immediately in their remit.'

Caroline had a very positive experience applying for both UC and PIP. Her experience shows how well the benefits process works when you have support and when the people within the system understand mental health.
'I had an assessment for universal credit which said I didn't have to work if I didn't want to due to my mental health and physical health. With PIP, I just sent in all the paperwork, and they spoke with my CPN [community psychiatric nurse], and I didn't need a further assessment. It was accepted at enhanced rate for both daily living and mobility.'

3. Mental health and the benefit system

The benefit system can be very difficult to understand. It can be difficult to know which rules or benefits apply to you, what reasonable adjustments you may be able to ask for, or how the system should treat you. When you have a mental health problem, these problems can be even more difficult to overcome.

The process of applying for and managing benefits can affect your mental health, even if you do not have a mental health problem. The application process, claimant commitments, appointments, deadlines and budgeting on the low income that benefits provide can lead to poor mental health. If you already have a mental health problem, this process can make it worse.

The benefits system is not well designed for people with mental health problems. This section highlights some core issues identified by people with lived experience, along with suggestions from people with lived experience on how to overcome these issues.

Tips from experience
'Find a buddy. Don't do it alone. You might have a lot of guilt, we all do, but you have the right to be ill and pay your bills comfortably.'

Eligibility

Knowing whether you are eligible for benefits when you have a mental health problem can be difficult. Many people find that the language used in benefits forms and assessments seems more relevant to physical health. It can be hard to know how your experience fits the questions.

To understand which benefits you are entitled to, you may need to use an online benefits calculator or get help from an independent advice service (see advicelocal.uk). Eligibility conditions are set out in each of the benefit chapters of this *Handbook*.

Inflexible systems

The process of applying for benefits and managing a claim can feel inflexible.

You can ask for reasonable adjustments and additional support (see Chapter 21), but the process of getting these changes can be rigid and you may be required to provide evidence.[13]

Repeating information

Over the course of a benefit claim, you might have to explain your mental health problem many times. It can be draining and retraumatising to have to explain your situation over and over again. This can prevent some people from claiming additional benefits or trigger mental health symptoms due to the stress of having to repeat a story.

Hayley's experience

Hayley gets personal independence payment (PIP) and employment and support allowance (ESA). When she goes for a review, she has to repeat her story in full, every time.

'I wish they would look historically at your trail. Because when you go to a person again to see them they don't know anything about you. And they don't link. Like I'm on two benefits – ESA and PIP – and instead of calling me in independently for each one why don't you just link and do it as one?'

Form filling

Many symptoms of mental health problems can make completing forms difficult, but the forms themselves can often be hard to understand. For benefits such as disability living allowance (DLA) and attendance allowance, many questions use wording and examples related to physical health. Despite the fact that mental health problems are relevant for these benefits, the questions might not always seem to reflect your experiences or the variability you might have in your condition. Benefit forms make it difficult to explain how changeable some mental health problems can be.

Without guidance on how the questions relate to a mental health problem, you might not feel you can convey the extent of your problem. This could lead to you being awarded the wrong amount of benefit or no benefit at all.

For advice and tips about filling in a form for a particular benefit, see the chapter about that benefit in this *Handbook*.

Tips from experience

'Ask family or friends for help filling in forms, or a professional. They know how to phrase things better.'

'Take lots of time to consider the questions on the forms and if necessary complete them over several days. It doesn't have to be done all at once.'

'Keep copies of all the forms you send off so that you can refer back to your answers if you need to attend an assessment.'

Evidence requirements

Health-related benefits require supporting evidence. This can be hard to get for a mental health problem, especially if you do not have a diagnosis or are on a waiting list for treatment. Although evidence such as statements from people close to you is also accepted, this is not always made clear. The focus on medicalised evidence can make proving the extent of your mental health problem very difficult and does not reflect the reality of getting help for a mental health problem, where long waiting lists and short treatment times are common.

Chapter 16 has more information and tips about supporting evidence.

Communication

The benefit system has default forms of communication. Universal credit (UC) claims are online, unless requested otherwise, and many other benefits involve sending letters. These communication methods may be changed as a reasonable adjustment (see p328), but it is not always obvious. If you are new to the benefits system or are experiencing a mental health problem that makes it hard to ask for help, you may end up with a form of communication that increases your distress.

Chapter 21 has more information about support.

Tips from experience

'If your condition makes it hard to go out, you can ask for phone appointments instead [of in person appointments].'

'Get a trusted advocate so they can talk/write to the DWP staff if you are unable to.'

Appointments and assessments

Assessments can sometimes be distressing. Whether they are in person, by video or over the phone, they can put a lot of pressure on someone with a mental health problem to explain what they are going through, often to someone who has limited knowledge of mental health problems. The applicant may be asked very triggering and upsetting questions that can be a potential safeguarding issue.

Chapter 17 has more information and tips about assessments.

Tips from experience

'Never be afraid to query any questions asked and make sure you take the opportunity to say everything you want, regardless of how your interviewer reacts or tries to curtail your appointment.'

'Take someone with you who is aware of your health issues.'

Martin's experience

'The assessor asked weird questions. I tried to tell her about my extreme OCD [obsessive compulsive disorder], but all the questions were about which hand I write with. In her report, she wrote that I was clean and did not look malnourished. This triggered me. I was thinking I must be fat. It made me feel so ill and watch my food intake.'

Deadlines

The benefit system involves many deadlines – such as when forms need to be submitted or when changes to your situation must be reported. This can make you feel very pressured. Some people experience constant fear about missing a deadline or being sanctioned, even when no immediate deadline exists.[14] Deadlines can sometimes be extended quite easily by asking, but people often do not know about this.

For information about deadlines and extensions for a particular benefit, see the chapter about that benefit in this *Handbook*.

What advisers say: dealing with deadlines

'Fear can take over and get in the way. In one case, someone was so desperate to get away from worry that they posted a reply straightaway before talking it through with an adviser. In another, with everything worked out with an adviser, there was a fear of letting go of the form and allowing it to drop into the letter box.'

Work-related requirements

People with mental health problems are sometimes placed in the wrong work-related requirement group for benefits such as UC. This can happen due to professionals' prejudice or because the person was not able to fully explain how much their mental health problem affects them. As a result, someone who needs time to get well may be expected to search for work or take a job that worsens their mental health. Stigma and misconceptions around mental health might mean staff misunderstand this as a lack of effort, rather than a symptom of a mental health problem.

Chapter 18 has information about work-related requirements, including about getting these changed.

Tip from experience

'Be honest and open about your struggles to the job coach. Let them know just how much you struggle.'

Reassessments and reviews

Benefits such as PIP and DLA are usually reviewed or reassessed based on the length of your award. For some people, this can be an upsetting process, particularly if their initial assessment was not a good experience. You may be required to revisit traumatic details and face the uncertainty of whether your award will continue. The stress of the assessment can be overwhelming.

Each benefit chapter in the *Handbook* has information about reviews and reassessments for that benefit.

Sanctions

The threat of benefit sanctions is stressful for most people, but for those with mental health problems, worrying about sanctions can significantly affect their lives. A sanction may be the difference between just getting by financially and being unable to stay safe, posing a serious risk. Information about sanctions is often bluntly worded in letters or UC journal messages. This can be upsetting, especially if the message is unexpected and the person receiving it is already in a vulnerable state.

Chapter 18 has information about sanctions and how to challenge them.

Appeals and mandatory reconsiderations

Being turned down for benefits or getting a lower award than expected can be upsetting. Although many mandatory reconsiderations and appeals are successful, the process can still feel overwhelming. An initial rejection may make you feel like there is no point continuing, and you might need encouragement and support to carry on with the process, if that is what you decide to do.

Chapter 20 has more information about challenging benefit decisions, including tips for writing a mandatory reconsideration request and preparing for an appeal.

Tip from experience
'If you disagree with a decision, you can [usually] appeal it. This may be stressful, but you can ask family, friends and services to help you through this.'

4. Getting support

When Mind asked people with lived experience of mental health problems and the benefit system what their advice would be to someone claiming benefits for the first time, most said the same thing: get support.

The support could be from an independent advice service (see advicelocal.uk) or from a friend or family member. See Appendix 2 for advice and support organisations. The support you need depends on many factors, so it is important to find what works best for you. People with lived experience told us the kind of support they find helpful includes the following.

- Help with research, such as:
  - looking up what benefits they might be entitled to;
  - finding what professional support is available.
- Help with questions on forms, such as:
  - reading through the questions with them;
  - helping them understand the questions;
  - writing answers to questions for them;
  - proof reading forms they have completed themselves.
- Help during interviews, such as:
  - providing emotional support;
  - advocating for their needs;
  - acting as proof that the person needs support.
- Help with evidence, such as:
  - writing a statement that can act as evidence;
  - helping them contact professionals for evidence;
  - helping them figure out what kind of evidence they need.
- Help with practical tasks, such as:
  - making phone calls;
  - opening letters;
  - organising forms;
  - reminding them of appointments or when to update details.
- Emotional support throughout the process.

The support someone needs is very individual. If you are seeking support, it is OK to be clear and upfront about which tasks you need help with most. If you are supporting someone else, make sure they feel comfortable telling you what they find helpful and do not make assumptions about what they can or cannot do.

Having support to make a benefits claim and throughout the benefits process can make a big difference in the success of your claim and your wellbeing.

There is more information about support in Chapter 21.

If you are an adviser supporting someone with a mental health problem, see Chapter 3 too.

Notes

1. **How mental health problems can affect you**
   1 mind.org.uk/information-support/types-of-mental-health-problems/personality-disorder/diagnosing-personality-disorder
   2 American Psychiatric Publishing, *Diagnostic and Statistical Manual of Mental Disorders*, 5th edition, text revised, 2022, doi.org/10.1176/appi.books.9780890425787
   3 coventry.gov.uk/coventry-safeguarding-adults-board/safeguarding-adults-life-stories/11
   4 mind.org.uk/information-support/drugs-and-treatments/medication
   5 mind.org.uk/information-support/legal-rights/sectioning
   6 mwcscot.org.uk/law-and-rights/mental-health-act

2. **Stigma and misconceptions**
   7 mind.org.uk/information-support/types-of-mental-health-problems/mental-health-problems-introduction
   8 mind.org.uk/information-support/tips-for-everyday-living/racism-and-mental-health
   9 Mind, *People, Not Tick-Boxes: a call to rebuild the disability benefits system*, October 2020, at mind.org.uk/media/6483/people-not-tick-boxes-october2020.pdf
   10 mind.org.uk/information-support/guides-to-support-and-services/advocacy
   11 s4 EA 2010
   12 equalityhumanrights.com

3. **Mental health and the benefit system**
   13 CPAG, *Making Adjustments? The experiences of universal credit claimants with mental health problems*, February 2022, at cpag.org.uk/making-adjustments
   14 rethink.org/media/4758/tip-of-the-iceberg.pdf

Chapter 3

Giving advice

This chapter covers:

This chapter is mainly aimed at professionals who give advice about benefits. You may find this chapter useful whether you are a benefits specialist or benefits advice is only a small part of your work. It should be read together with the information in Chapter 21 about being a 'third-party representative'.

Key facts

- Giving good advice is not just about supporting someone with something they have difficulty doing. It is also about identifying what their strengths are and empowering them to use those as much as possible.
- It is important to use up-to-date terms, and the preferred language and communication methods of the person you are supporting.
- Not everyone needs the same type of support for the same things. It is important to allow each individual as much agency as possible when they are making a benefit claim.
- You can set boundaries with the person you are supporting, such as agreeing on times when you will not be available and being clear about what you can and cannot support with.

1. Supporting people with mental health problems

If you are not a benefits professional, the benefit system can be very difficult to understand, whether you have a mental health problem or not. The additional barriers and stigma that people with a mental health problem may face can make dealing with the benefit system distressing.[1] Having someone who understands, supports and advocates can make claiming benefits possible.

Good advice and support should come from a place of understanding. This means not only understanding the benefit system but also how an individual's mental health and personal circumstances influence their interaction with the system. People tend to respond better to someone who can relate to their experiences. You do not necessarily need to have had a mental health problem yourself to support someone who does. Taking the time to know more about someone's individual needs can be just as valuable.

Giving good advice is not just about supporting someone with something they cannot do or have difficulty doing. It is also recognising their strengths and empowering them to use those as much as possible. Remember, you are acting as a guide through the benefit system. Avoid gatekeeping information or creating a situation where someone would feel helpless without your support.

What advisers say: giving advice

'Mental health is incredibly complex and everyone has their own story. The only person who fully understands what they are going through is them. It's important to have empathy and treat everyone you meet with dignity, respect and patience. Benefits are often the only financial support some people have, and they are sometimes the only thing preventing someone from becoming homeless or going hungry. Knowing that you are able to support them to receive help is incredibly rewarding.'

Terminology

Mental health and the benefit system can involve jargon. Both you and the person you are supporting might need to explain terms to each other. Part of your role as an adviser is to help people understand this jargon. Explain, in straightforward language, what certain terms mean.

Using up-to-date terms and the preferred language of the person you are supporting shows the person that you understand and respect them. Ask them what terms they prefer and recognise that they are an expert on their own experience.

Sometimes, you may need to use terms – like 'disability' or specific diagnostic labels – that the person you are supporting does not feel describe them. These words may be used in applications. For example, not everyone knows that mental health problems count as a disability, just like physical health problems. Because of this, some people may miss out on essential financial support. If you need to use terminology that feels uncomfortable or inaccurate to the person, explain why and only use it when absolutely necessary. Outside of official forms or assessments, use the person's preferred terms, even if they are not the most up to date.

It is also important to inform others when they use out-of-date or stigmatising terminology. This could happen during benefit appointments or assessments.

You should do this whether the person you are supporting is present at that time or not. This helps create a respectful environment for everyone.

There is more information about mental health terminology on p6 and details about symptoms and treatments in Chapter 2.

Communication preferences

Knowing how someone prefers to give and receive information can be key to effective support. It is important to identify when these preferences should be communicated to the people working in the benefit system as requests for reasonable adjustments (see p326). Remember that no one communication method is better than another, and just because you prefer one form of communication, it does not mean it is right for everyone.

Be as flexible as possible and respect the communication methods that work best for the person you are supporting. Some people might prefer to send voice notes rather than type a text or email. Others may need things explained in diagrams rather than written words.

Timing is also important in effective communication. Some people may process information better at certain times of day due to medication, certain symptoms or personal routine.

There may be times when someone finds it difficult to communicate – eg, around the time of a big event, such as a holiday, or on the anniversary of a traumatic experience. It may be harder to meet deadlines or attend appointments around these times.

Establishing good communication often takes time. Mental health can be deeply personal, and while some people may be comfortable opening up immediately, others may need more time. You may not get the full picture from one conversation.

Finding a suitable place to talk is also important. Some people may prefer a private space where they feel safe to speak without being overheard, while others may prefer to meet in a less formal setting such as a cafe or in a familiar place. Some may prefer to meet online. Try to be flexible to arrange appointments in ways and places that best suit the person's needs.

Support needs

Not everyone needs the same type of support for the same things. It is important to allow each individual as much agency as possible when making a benefit claim. It is better to support someone to understand and manage the process themselves, rather than taking over – unless they have explicitly asked you to do so. Even if you are taking on a substantial supportive role, keep a simple, clear record of what has been done and what steps come next.

Remember that support needs can change over time and with variation in someone's mental health problem. It is helpful to check regularly whether these needs have changed.

The person you are supporting may need your help to request appropriate support within the benefit system – eg, from the job centre or the tribunal. Chapter 21 has more information.

Suicidal feelings and self-harm

Some advisers are uncomfortable talking about suicidal feelings and self-harm, often worrying that mentioning them will make things worse. If you ask these questions respectfully and in a safe way, it is very unlikely to cause harm. Many people experiencing suicidal feelings and self-harm may want to talk about it, but do not feel able to unless you bring up the topic first. These topics can be difficult to talk about, and someone might not bring them up themselves if they do not feel they can trust you. Mind has information on how to talk about suicidal feelings and self-harm, which might help you have these conversations.[2]

Even though having these conversations can be beneficial, take care to ask relevant questions and only explore what is necessary. Make sure you have plans in place to support someone afterwards if they feel vulnerable.

It is important not to overreact or assume that all suicidal feelings and self-harm need urgent medical attention. While these experiences and feelings are serious and indicate that the person is in a vulnerable place, they may have their own safety measures and ways of managing. Make sure you fully listen to what they have to say before taking any next steps.

There is information about answering questions about suicidal feelings and self-harm during an assessment on p264. There are also tips on p334 for advisers and supporters with safeguarding concerns.

Getting needs recognised in the benefit system

As someone with knowledge of the benefit system, you have a key role in helping ensure the person you are supporting is heard and their needs are understood.

Discussing another person's benefits

The DWP, Social Security Scotland, local authorities and other bodies have strict rules about discussing benefit claims with anyone other than the claimant. These policies uphold confidentiality and data protection rules, but they can make it difficult for you to support someone through the benefits system. Chapter 21 has more information about speaking to public bodies on someone else's behalf.

Reasonable adjustments

Some support and communication needs may be considered reasonable adjustments under the Equality Act 2010. As an adviser, you should accommodate these adjustments in your own work, and ensure the person you are supporting knows they have the right to request them from others in the benefit system – eg, from job centres and assessment providers. See p328 for more information about reasonable adjustments.

Alternative payment arrangements

A mental health problem might affect how someone manages their benefit income. Alternative payment arrangements are available for some benefits. These can include:

- splitting a monthly payment into more frequent payments;
- having housing elements paid directly to a landlord, housing association or local authority;
- splitting payments for joint claims between bank accounts.

If the person you are supporting feels that one or more of these options would help them, you can assist them in requesting this change. For more information about alternative payment arrangements for a particular benefit, see the 'Getting paid' section of the chapter on that benefit in this *Handbook*.

Deadline extensions

Deadlines for benefit forms, mandatory reconsiderations and appeals can be stressful. However, there are rules in place to protect individuals who are unable to meet these deadlines. For more information about deadlines and extensions for a particular benefit, see the chapter on that benefit in this *Handbook*.

Rescheduling benefit appointments

Someone may be unable to keep an appointment (eg, at the job centre or for an assessment) due to their mental health. If this happens, let them know the rules about rescheduling and help them to explain their circumstances to the relevant organisation. See Chapter 18 about job centre appointments, Chapter 17 about assessments, and Chapter 20 about appeal hearings.

Work-related requirements and sanctions

Some benefits, such as universal credit, have requirements to look for or prepare for work. However, these requirements do not apply to everyone and should be adjusted to reflect someone's capabilities. People with mental health problems are sometimes placed in the wrong work-related activity group because decision makers do not recognise how their mental health problem affects them. If the person you are supporting is put in the wrong group, explain their options.

If they have been sanctioned (or threatened with a sanction), advise them about their options and the financial support that might be available.

Chapter 18 has information about work-related requirements and sanctions.

Mandatory reconsiderations and appeals

Benefit decisions can usually be challenged. Ensure the person you are supporting is aware of their options if they disagree with a decision. Chapter 20 has more information about challenging decisions. Offer to support them through this process if they are comfortable with this. If you are unable to provide support at any stage on the appeal process, make sure they know who can and support them as much as possible in transferring the relevant information over to the new individual or agency.

Complaining about discrimination

It is unlawful to discriminate against someone because of their mental health problem if it is considered a disability under the Equality Act 2010.[3] This can include failing to make reasonable adjustments. The person you are supporting might not always realise they are experiencing discrimination. The Equality and Human Rights Commission has more information on disability discrimination and how to challenge it.[4] See p308 for details about making a complaint.

Not passing judgement

Some people may feel uneasy about seeking support and talking about their mental health. As an adviser, it is important to be non-judgmental about the person you are supporting. Take time to understand their experience and do further research if necessary. How someone behaves might not always make sense to you, but trying to understand the need behind this behaviour will help you approach these situations with empathy and respect.

Remember that many mental health symptoms are hard or impossible to control, and can make everyday tasks difficult. It is very unlikely that someone is intentionally doing something to impact their benefit claim, like missing a deadline or appointment, even if these things seem simple to you.

Encouragement and realism

Applying for benefits can be a long process, particularly if you need to go through a mandatory reconsideration or an appeal. Once benefits are awarded, they usually need to be managed in the long term, often using an online account. They may involve reassessments or reviews, or reporting on efforts to prepare for or find work. When someone finds this process difficult, try to be encouraging, but also be realistic. Do not promise things you cannot deliver, as this can lead to loss of trust. For example, you cannot guarantee that someone will be awarded the same benefits after a review, but you can encourage them and support them in presenting their case clearly and challenging decisions they are unhappy with.

When supporting someone is challenging

Advisers have a finite number of appointments to offer and a limited amount of time for follow-up work. It can be difficult to know how to respond if the person you support repeatedly misses appointments, fails to respond to calls or emails, or does not complete tasks – eg, providing documents or returning a signed form. Your organisation might have a policy about managing 'dropped contact' or missed appointments. This must be flexible and recognise why someone may struggle to attend appointments or communicate. You should consider reasonable adjustments if someone's challenges are because of their mental health problem. If someone stops engaging with you, and this means they are at risk of losing essential money, this could be a safeguarding concern.

Sometimes distress prompted by a decision or situation is expressed as anger or aggression towards you as the adviser. This is always challenging. Your organisation might have a policy on how to respond, which should be flexible, recognise the underlying reasons and allow reasonable adjustments.

What advisers say: appointments

'I try to see it from their point of view and remain patient. I reassure them that we can always make another appointment and adjust it so that they feel more comfortable. For example, if they prefer face-to-face appointments, make that change so that they are more likely to come to the appointment.'

'We don't book back-to-back appointments. We always have a break between appointments because if something happens or if someone is upset we need time to just be able to sit with them rather than say "I've got another person to see".'

Look after your own needs

There may be times when your role feels particularly challenging and affects your wellbeing. For example, you might feel overwhelmed if someone you are supporting is really struggling with their mental health, or disheartened if their claim has been unsuccessful. It is important to look after your own wellbeing. You could try to:

- set clear boundaries, such as agreeing on times when you will not be available and being clear about what you can and cannot help with. Taking on too much will not help either of you in the long run;
- understand your own stress and needs. You could make a Wellness Action Plan to identify your triggers and strategies for staying well. Talk to your employer about your needs – they may be able to make some changes or offer support;
- use workplace support. Many organisations have employee assistance programmes, which provide free advice and counselling. Others have internal support systems, like mentoring or buddy systems.

2. **The advice journey**

If you are an advice worker, it is likely that you will spend a lot of your time supporting people with the following steps in their benefit claims.

Helping people understand what they might be entitled to

This can be described as a 'benefit check'. Some advice agencies use benefit calculators as a starting point.

- For a brief explanation of the different types of benefits, see p9.
- To understand the basics about the benefits covered in this *Handbook*, see the 'Key facts' list at the start of each chapter.

Starting a claim

Different benefits are claimed in different ways. Even if your advice service does not help people start claims, you may still need to explain the different claims processes and what to do if something goes wrong.

- For how to claim universal credit (UC), see p76.
- For information about moving to UC from other benefits, see p79.
- For how to claim employment and support allowance (ESA), see p56.
- For how to claim personal independence payment (PIP), see p130.
- Information about claiming other benefits can be found in the 'Making a claim' section of the chapter about the relevant benefit.

Completing forms and online applications

This can be one of the most important parts of advice work. The person you are supporting may find it difficult to complete forms due to symptoms or because the forms do not give enough space to fully explain how their mental health problem affects them. Some advice agencies offer access to computers or digital support to help people make and manage benefit claims.

- If you are helping someone to complete a UC50 or ESA50 form, see p81.
- If you are helping someone to complete a PIP form, see p153.
- For help with other forms, see the 'How you are assessed' section of the chapter about the relevant benefit.

Collecting evidence

Supporting evidence about someone's mental health problem and how it affects their life can be crucial in helping them to get the right benefit decision.

For information about different types of evidence that might support your client's claim, and how to get hold of it, see p239.

Assessments

Sometimes, claiming benefits involves having an assessment with a healthcare professional. This is most common for UC, PIP and ESA.

- If someone is going to a PIP or UC/ESA assessment and wants advice, see p251.
- If someone has missed or cannot attend a PIP assessment, see p259.
- If someone has missed or cannot go to a UC/ESA assessment, see p258.

Challenging a decision

Most benefit decisions can be challenged, usually by mandatory reconsideration and appeal. It is often your role to support someone through this process.

- If you are writing a mandatory reconsideration request, see p294.
- If you are helping someone complete an appeal form, see p299.
- If you are helping someone prepare appeal submissions, see p300.
- If you are attending a tribunal hearing with someone, see p301.

Communicating on someone's behalf

It is often important for you to contact other agencies on someone's behalf.

- If you are struggling to get the DWP, Social Security Scotland or a local authority to speak to you as a third-party adviser, see p320.
- If you think that someone may need an appointee, see p325.

Advice appointments

Knowing the benefit system is an important part of giving good advice, but listening and communicating clearly are also crucial.

Advice skills for appointments

- Make the person you are supporting comfortable. Ask if they would prefer an appointment in-person, by video or by phone? What time is best for them? Have you given them the opportunity to bring someone to support them in your appointment? Can you put them at their ease by changing the layout of an appointment room or offering a drink of water?
- Minimise distractions or stressors – eg, interruptions from colleagues or phone alerts.
- In longer appointments, plan breaks.
- Be aware of your body language and tone of voice throughout the appointment.
- Consider a 'script' for the start of the appointment – eg, introducing yourself, explaining your role, and letting the person know they can take a break at any time.
- Explain the nature of your questions. As you may need to ask about what someone cannot do or finds difficult, this can be disheartening. Acknowledge this at the start of the appointment and explain why it is necessary.
- Only ask one question at a time.

- Listen carefully. Avoid 'tuning out' information that does not answer your immediate question. It might still be critical information. Use a notebook to record details.
- Consider using open questions (eg, 'how' or 'when' questions) if the person you are supporting is finding it difficult to open up. Consider asking closed questions (ie, 'yes' or 'no' questions) if you find it difficult to get the precise information you need.
- Be sensitive about difficult questions. Only ask what is strictly necessary. Some people might be happy to open up, but many people can be retraumatised by going into too much detail. If you need to ask a potentially upsetting question, explain why and offer a break if they need it. Discuss with what additional support the person you are supporting may need after a stressful appointment.
- Give advice concisely and without using jargon.
- If the advice is complex, consider the best way to deliver it – eg, verbally with a follow-up letter that sets it out in writing.

3. Difficult times and bad news

Even with good preparation, a benefit claim may not have the outcome that the person hopes for. Decisions are sometimes made that lead to very difficult situations. These can include:

- sanctions, which may leave someone unable to pay for essentials;
- a claim being refused, or a lower award than expected, leading to a mandatory reconsideration or appeal;
- a mandatory reconsideration or appeal not being successful;
- a review or reassessment resulting in a lower award or benefits stopping altogether;
- moving from one benefit to another (eg, due to a change in circumstances), which may make it more difficult to manage or leave someone worse off.

These issues can have a significant impact on someone's mental health.[5] When you are first supporting someone with a benefits issue, it can help to talk about what support or self-care plans they have in place for managing bad news. This could involve speaking to someone they trust, or following a calming routine to help them process the news. It is also helpful to let them know what support is available or where they can find out more about their rights and next steps.

When delivering difficult news, follow the tips starting on p45, including following agreed communication methods and reviewing the person's support needs.

If the person you are supporting is at risk of harm, you may need to take safeguarding action (see p334).

Challenging decisions

Many of the issues above are the result of decisions that can be challenged. Chapter 20 has more information about challenging a benefit decision.

The processes involved in these challenges vary depending on the specific benefit and situation. These processes can take a long time, which may make the person you are supporting feel uncertain about challenging a benefit decision. While you must respect their wishes, make sure they are making an informed decision. Explain the possible outcomes of a challenge, what the process will involve and what support is available. Be realistic about what will be involved so they can make the right decision for them.

When nothing can be done

There are rare occasions when nothing can be done about a benefit decision. Not all decisions are made on challengeable grounds, and sometimes changes to the benefits system leave people worse off. Once an appeal has been heard by a tribunal, it cannot always be taken further, even if you disagree with the outcome.

However, take great care before concluding that a situation is one where 'nothing can be done'. Alternative options like judicial review, complaints and involving an MP might be available (see Chapter 20). Just because a decision is discretionary does not mean that it cannot be challenged (see, for example, p271 about challenging someone's work-related requirements for universal credit, or p256 about asking for a different format/venue for a benefit assessment).

Even when a decision is technically justified based on the rules, it can still have serious impacts – financially, emotionally and on mental health.

Even if there are no steps to challenge the decision, there are still ways to improve the situation. You can, for example, signpost to the financial support that might be available (see Chapter 15).

Notes

1. **Supporting people with mental health problems**
   1 Mind, *People, Not Tick-Boxes: a call to rebuild the disability benefits system,* October 2020, at mind.org.uk/media/6483/people-not-tick-boxes-october2020.pdf
   2 mind.org.uk/information-support/helping-someone-else/supporting-someone-who-feels-suicidal
   3 ss6 and 15 EA 2010
   4 equalityhumanrights.com/en/advice-and-guidance/disability-discrimination

3. **Difficult times and bad news**
   5 Rethink Mental Illness, *Tip of the Iceberg? Deaths and serious harm in the benefits system,* July 2021, at rethink.org/media/4758/tip-of-the-iceberg.pdf

Part 2

Benefits for mental health

Chapter 4

Employment and support allowance

This chapter covers:

Key facts

- Employment and support allowance (ESA) is a benefit for people whose ability to work is limited by a health condition or disability and who are not entitled to statutory sick pay.
- There are two types of ESA: **income-related ESA**, which is means tested, and **contributory ESA**, which is not means tested but relies on you having made enough national insurance contributions and which can be affected by certain pension income.
- Contributory ESA paid under the universal credit (UC) system is called new-style ESA; contributory ESA paid outside the UC system is referred to as old-style ESA. If you make a new claim, or claim UC, you come under the UC system and any contributory ESA you are entitled to is new-style ESA.
- You cannot make a new claim for income-related ESA. If you cannot get income-related ESA, you may claim UC instead. If you are already receiving income-related ESA, you can continue to get it until you are transferred to UC.
- Eligibility for ESA is usually decided using a work capability assessment.
- You can challenge decisions about your eligibility for ESA, including decisions about work capability.

Future changes

From 2028/29, the government is proposing that contributory ESA and new-style jobseeker's allowance be replaced with a single contributory benefit called unemployment insurance.[1]

1. Who can get employment and support allowance

Types of employment and support allowance

There are two types of employment and support allowance (ESA): **income-related ESA**, which is means tested, and **contributory ESA**, which is not means tested but relies on you having made enough national insurance contributions (NI), and can be reduced by certain pension income. You may qualify for one or both types of ESA.

Contributory ESA has two categories. **Old-style contributory ESA** in practice covers awards made before 12 December 2018. **New-style ESA** covers most new claims made on or after 12 December 2018. If you are unsure which type you get, contact the ESA helpline (0800 169 0310; textphone: 0800 169 0314; Relay UK and British Sign Language relay services available).

Basic rules

To qualify for any type of ESA, you must satisfy the basic conditions. These are that:[2]

- you are aged 16 or over and under pension age, which is currently 66 and rising to 67 between 2026 and 2028. (If you are in a mixed-age couple (ie, one of you has reached pension age, but the other has not), see p54); *and*
- you are in (or treated as being in) Great Britain; *and*
- you have limited capability for work (see p57); *and*
- you are not entitled to statutory sick pay (SSP) or new-style jobseeker's allowance; *and*
- you are not doing any work (but there are some exceptions – see p269).

Special rules apply while you are in hospital, living in a care home and in certain other situations (see Chapter 19).

Extra rules for income-related employment and support allowance

To qualify for income-related ESA, you must satisfy extra conditions, such as rules about your income and savings.[3] See CPAG's *Welfare Benefits Handbook* for details.

Income-related ESA is being phased out and replaced by universal credit (UC). Most awards will have been brought to an end by April 2026 (see p79). You cannot make a new claim for income-related ESA, but you may be able to claim UC instead.

If you still get old-style contributory ESA, you can start getting a top-up of income-related ESA without making a new claim for income-related ESA (see p56).

Extra rules for contributory employment and support allowance

You can qualify for contributory ESA if, as well as satisfying the basic rules for ESA on p52:

- for new-style contributory ESA, you accept a claimant commitment (see p273);[4] *and*
- for both old-style and new-style contributory ESA, you satisfy the NI conditions below or fall within very limited exceptions.[5]

The national insurance conditions

The NI conditions relate to the two complete tax years immediately before the relevant benefit year. A 'tax year' runs from 6 April to 5 April the following year. A 'benefit year' starts on the first Sunday in January and runs for 12 months. So, for example, if you claim ESA in 2025, you must satisfy the contribution conditions for the tax years 2022/23 and 2023/24.[6]

Note: if you are unsure whether you have met the NI contributions recently enough, check the linking rules on p60.

The first condition: paid contributions

You must have paid, or be treated as having paid, at least 26 weeks' class 1 or class 2 NI contributions on earnings at or above the lower earnings limit in one of the last two complete tax years immediately before the relevant benefit year. The 26 weeks do not need to have been consecutive.[7] There are limited cases in which this condition does not apply.[8]

Lower earnings limits (weekly)

2022/23: £123
2023/24: £123
2024/25: £123
2025/26: £125

Example

If Sadie makes a new-style ESA claim in 2025, she meets the first condition if she earned at least £123 a week for 26 weeks between 6 April 2022 and 5 April 2023 *or* between 6 April 2023 and 5 April 2024.

The second condition: paid or credited contributions

You must have paid or be treated as having paid class 1 or class 2 NI contributions, or received class 1 credits, on earnings of at least 50 times the lower earnings limit in each of the two complete tax years immediately before the relevant benefit year.[9]

This condition cannot be met by reaching this earnings level in fewer than 50 weeks, unless you have paid or are treated as having paid class 1 contributions.

You qualify for class 1 NI credits during certain periods when you are not actually paying NI – eg, while you are getting ESA or SSP.[10] You may get these credits automatically or may need to apply. See CPAG's *Welfare Benefits Handbook* or gov.uk/national-insurance-credits/eligibility.

Example

If Nicholas makes a new-style ESA claim in 2025, he meets the second condition if he paid (or is treated as having paid) contributions on total earnings of at least £6,150 (50 x £123) in 2022/23 *and* in 2022/24, or if he has received class 1 NI credits for 50 weeks in each of those tax years, or if he satisfies the condition through a combination of contributions and credits.

Duration of contributory employment and support allowance

You are entitled to contributory ESA for a maximum of 365 days, unless you are assessed as having limited capability for work and work-related activity (ie, you are in the support group), in which case you can receive it indefinitely.[11] In some circumstances, you can requalify for contributory ESA.[12]

Who can make a new claim for employment and support allowance

Income-related ESA is being phased out and replaced with UC. You cannot make a new claim for income-related ESA.

However, **contributory ESA** is not being replaced with UC. You can still make a new claim for contributory ESA. It will be for new-style contributory ESA (see p57).

Couples

You claim contributory ESA as an individual. Your eligibility is based on your own NI record. Your ESA amount includes a personal allowance paid at the rate for a single person. Your partner's NI contributions (and pension income) are not taken into account. If you and your partner both satisfy the conditions for getting contributory ESA, you can get an award each.

Disqualification

You can be disqualified from getting ESA for up to six weeks in certain circumstances – eg, if you fail without good cause to accept medical treatment.[13] This is rare in practice. See CPAG's *Welfare Benefits Handbook*.

2. The amount of benefit

The amount of income-related employment and support allowance

You cannot make a new claim for income-related employment and support allowance (ESA). See CPAG's *Welfare Benefits Handbook* for how income-related ESA awards are calculated.

The amount of contributory employment and support allowance

Your contributory ESA award is made up of:

- a personal allowance; *and*

Assessment phase	
Under 25	£72.90
25 or over	£92.05
Main phase	
16 or over	£92.05

- a support component or work-related activity component (see p56); *and*
- a transitional addition in some cases when you have moved to ESA from an older benefit.

This amount can be different during the assessment phase or when you get ESA at the appeal rate (see p56).

Your contributory ESA is reduced if you receive certain pension payments of over £85 a week, or if you are a local councillor and your net allowances are more than £195.50 a week. It is reduced by 50 per cent of the amount by which the pension payments exceed £85 or the councillor allowances exceed £195.50.[14] So, for example, if your relevant pension is £185 a week, your contributory ESA is reduced by £50 (50 per cent of £100) a week.

The amount of contributory ESA you are actually paid can be reduced by sanctions (see p274), disqualification (see above), deductions[15] and alternative payment arrangements (see p62).

The support component

A support component of £48.50 a week is included in your ESA if you have been assessed as having limited capability for work and work-related activity (see p57) – ie, placed in the support group.[16]

The work-related activity component

A work-related activity component of £36.55 a week may be included in your ESA if you have been assessed as having limited capability for work (see p57) – ie, placed in the work-related activity group. However, this component was abolished for new claimants of both contributory and income-related ESA from 3 April 2017. You can get the component if your current ESA entitlement started before 3 April 2017 and in other limited circumstances.[17]

The waiting days, the assessment rate and the appeal rate

You are not usually entitled to ESA for the first seven 'waiting days' at the start of your period of limited capability for work.[18] There are exceptions – eg, if you have stopped getting statutory sick pay, or certain other benefits, in the last 12 weeks.

When you are first entitled to either type of ESA, you are in an 'assessment phase' until a decision is made on your limited capability for work.[19] During the assessment phase, you are not usually paid the work-related activity component or the support component of ESA. There are exceptions – eg, if you are regarded as being terminally ill.[20] If you are under 25, you are also paid a lower rate of the standard allowance during the assessment phase.

If the assessment phase lasts longer than 13 weeks, your full award is backdated to the 14th week of your claim.[21] Sometimes, the 13 weeks can count as having started before you claimed ESA (see the linking rules on p60).[22]

If you are appealing a decision that you are fit for work and not eligible for ESA, you may be entitled to get ESA as the 'appeal rate' (see p306) until your appeal is decided.

3. Making a claim

Claiming income-related employment and support allowance

You cannot make a new claim for income-related employment and support allowance (ESA). However, if you still get old-style contributory ESA, you may be able to start getting a top-up of income-related ESA without having to make a new claim.[23] You can request this by calling 0800 169 0310 (textphone: 0800 169 0314; Relay UK and British Sign Language (BSL) relay services available). You usually need to complete an ESA3 form.

Claiming contributory employment and support allowance

You can start a claim for new-style contributory ESA:[24]

- online at gov.uk/how-to-claim-new-style-esa; *or*
- by phone on 0800 055 6688 (textphone: 0800 328 1344; Relay UK and BSL relay services available) – specify that you want to claim new-style contributory ESA.

The date of claim is usually the date you submit a claim online or start a claim by phone.[25]

At the start of your claim, you are usually required to provide a fit note from your GP or other medical professional confirming you are unfit for work. You are then referred for a work capability assessment (see below).

Claiming in advance and backdating

You can claim new-style contributory ESA **in advance**, up to three months before the date on which you qualify for it.[26]

You can ask that your claim for new-style ESA be backdated by up to three months if you met the qualifying conditions during that time. You do not need to have special reasons for backdating.[27] If you might have qualified for ESA more than three months ago but did not claim because you were given the wrong information or misled by the DWP, you could complain and ask for compensation (see p308).

Note: the term 'backdating' is often informally used to mean getting arrears of your benefit going back to a claim or decision date – eg, after winning an appeal. However, in this *Handbook*, we use backdating to mean getting paid benefit for a period before the date you claimed.

Additional support and appointees

If you have (or will have) difficulty with the claims process and need additional support, see Chapter 21. If you cannot manage the claims process at all, you may need an appointee (see p325).

4. How you are assessed

The work capability assessment

To qualify for employment and support allowance (ESA), you must usually have a work capability assessment (WCA).

The WCA is used by the DWP to decide whether:

- you are **fit for work** and are therefore not eligible for ESA; *or*

- you have **limited capability for work** and can be placed in the 'work-related activity group' – ie, you can get ESA without being required actively to look for work, but are considered well enough to do some work preparation activity such as training or work-focused job centre appointments (see p273); *or*
- you have **limited capability for work and work-related activity** and can be placed in the 'support group' – ie, your health condition or disability is considered so severe that, in addition to not being able to work, you are not required to take steps to prepare for work.

As well as affecting your work-related requirements, this decision affects how much ESA you get (see p55).

The assessment process

Most claimants are assessed using the standard WCA rules and processes described on pp81–96. They apply to both ESA and universal credit (UC), except where otherwise stated.

However, in the following circumstances, a decision is made on your work capability without you going through the usual WCA process or meeting the usual conditions.

Treated as having limited capability for work

You are automatically treated as having limited capability for work for ESA in specific circumstances.[28] Many of these relate to physical health or pregnancy. The main circumstances relevant to your mental health are where:

- you are an inpatient in hospital and have been medically advised to stay for at least 24 hours, or are recovering from treatment as an inpatient (and the DWP is satisfied that your condition remains sufficiently serious), including if you are attending a residential drug or alcohol rehabilitation programme;
- you get income-related ESA while in education – ie, because you are getting a qualifying disability benefit;
- for new-style contributory ESA only, you get UC and have already been assessed as having limited capability for work for UC;
- you are applying for ESA and have provided a current medical certificate, but the WCA has not yet been carried out – ie, you are in the 'assessment phase'. However, this does not apply if you are reclaiming ESA after having failed the WCA, unless your condition has significantly worsened or you have a new health condition;
- you are appealing against a decision that you have failed the WCA, and you have submitted a medical certificate. However, this will not apply if you were treated as failing the WCA because you failed to return the ESA50 questionnaire or failed to attend the medical. Unless your current claim for ESA was made before 30 March 2015, this rule only applies if this is the first time you have failed the WCA, or the first time since a previous decision that you satisfied it;

- you are reclaiming ESA and have provided a current medical certificate, after being treated as failing the WCA because you did not return the ESA50 questionnaire or attend the medical. You can get ESA while waiting for your assessment. However, this only applies if:
  - you have now returned the questionnaire; *or*
  - it is more than six months since the decision treating you as not having limited capability for work; *or*
  - your condition has significantly worsened; *or*
  - you now have a new health condition.

Remember that the DWP must follow guidance before deciding that you failed the WCA due to not returning an ESA50 form (see p328) or attending an assessment (see p258). It should not automatically treat you as having failed the WCA.

Note: special rules might also mean you are found to have limited capability for work if, because of your health condition or disability, work poses a substantial risk to your health (see p95).

Examples

Harri has bipolar disorder. He applied for new-style ESA a few months ago but failed the WCA. He is now experiencing a significant depressive episode, so he reclaims new-style ESA, supplying a medical certificate. The DWP accepts that Harri's symptoms have significantly worsened, and so treats him as having limited capability for work and pays him ESA while a new WCA is arranged.

Vivian has a long-term mental health problem. She claims new-style ESA, but does not return the ESA50 form. Despite DWP policy (see p328), she is treated as having failed the WCA and her ESA stops. Vivian is not aware of her right to challenge this decision, and instead reclaims new-style ESA two months later. She is not paid any ESA until she has completed and returned a new ESA50 form.

Treated as having limited capability for work and work-related activity

You are treated as having limited capability for work and work-related activity (LCWRA) for ESA if:[29]

- you are regarded as being terminally ill – ie, you have a progressive illness and it would not be a surprise to your doctors were you to die from it within the next 12 months. This can apply even if there are also realistic expectations that you may live longer; *or*
- you are receiving or recovering from chemotherapy or radiotherapy treatment for cancer, or you are likely to receive such treatment within six months from the date the DWP determines whether or not you have LCWRA, *and* the DWP is satisfied that you have LCWRA; *or*

- you are pregnant and work-related activity would pose a serious risk to your health or your baby's health.

Note: special rules also apply if, because of your health condition or disability, work-related activity poses a substantial risk to your health (see p95).

Treated as *not* having limited capability for work

You are treated as *not* having limited capability for work for ESA if:

- you are asked by the DWP to provide a new fit note after an earlier one runs out, and after six weeks you have still not done so (in this situation, you are treated as not having limited capability for work only if the DWP is satisfied that this is appropriate in the circumstances – ie, not automatically);[30] *or*
- you do not return an ESA50 questionnaire or attend a medical, and you do not have good cause (see p83);[31] *or*
- you work (with some exceptions – see p269);[32] *or*
- you are in prison, in some circumstances;[33] *or*
- you attend a training course and receive a training allowance or premium, unless it was only for travelling or meal expenses;[34] *or*
- you are (or were) a member of the armed forces and the day in question is a day of sickness absence from duty.[35]

Periods of limited capability for work

Different periods of limited capability for work can be linked to form one continuous period for ESA. Different periods are linked if they are not more than 12 weeks apart.[36]

If periods of limited capability for work are linked, it means that:

- the question of whether or not you satisfy the national insurance contribution conditions for contributory ESA may be decided at the beginning of the first period (see p53);[37]
- you may not have to serve further waiting days (see p56) before becoming entitled to ESA because you have already served them;
- you may get one of the additional ESA components straight away rather than waiting out an assessment phase (see p56).

5. Decisions

Work capability decisions

In practice, the DWP makes a decision about your capability for work within four to eight weeks after you attend an assessment. You should get a decision letter by post.

There are three possible work capability decisions:

- that you are fit for work; *or*
- that you have limited capability for work; *or*
- that you have limited capability for work and work-related activity.

There is more information about these outcomes on p57.

If you are found fit for work

If the DWP decides you are fit for work (either after a work capability assessment, or automatically under the rules on p60), then you are not entitled to employment and support allowance (ESA). If you have been getting ESA, your payment stops.

If you disagree with the decision, you can often appeal it without asking for a mandatory reconsideration first (see p295). Note that there are deadlines for appealing decisions.

You can usually continue to get ESA while an appeal about your work capability is pending, if you continue providing fit notes (see p306). If you claim universal credit (UC) while appealing an ESA decision, you cannot later go back on to old-style ESA, even if you win your appeal.

Examples

Jamal stops work because of his mental health, and claims ESA for the first time. His claim is for new-style contributory ESA. While he is waiting for an assessment, he supplies fit notes and is paid ESA at the assessment phase rate (see p56). Following his assessment, he receives a decision that he is fit for work and his ESA stops. Jamal disagrees with the decision and appeals immediately. He also continues sending fit notes to the DWP. Jamal's ESA payments resume and continue until his appeal is decided. He is paid at the 'appeal rate' which is the same as the assessment phase rate he had previously been getting.

If you are found to have limited capability for work

If the DWP decides you have limited capability for work (placing you in the work-related activity group) but you believe you actually have limited capability for work and work-related activity (ie, should be placed in the support group), you can challenge this decision. In this situation, you *do* normally need to ask for a mandatory reconsideration before appealing (see p294). It is usually best to get advice before challenging this kind of decision, as a new decision maker (or the tribunal) will look at the whole decision again and could decide that you are fit for work.

Length of awards

An award of contributory ESA ends after a year if you are not in the support group (see p54). In other circumstances, awards of ESA do not have a fixed length. Your work capability is usually reassessed at a future point (see p63). You cannot appeal a decision about how often you are reassessed, but you may be able to challenge it through judicial review (see p311).

Other decisions

After making a new claim for ESA, you may receive a decision that you cannot get ESA because you do not meet the eligibility conditions listed on pp52–54, such as the national insurance conditions for contributory ESA. You can challenge this decision through mandatory reconsideration and appeal (see Chapter 20), and provide further evidence if necessary.

While getting ESA, you are likely to receive a range of other decisions, including:

- if you are in the work-related activity group, decisions by your work coach about what your work-related requirements will be (see p270). These decisions are not appealable but you may be able to challenge them through a complaint or judicial review (see Chapter 20);
- decisions about whether you have been overpaid ESA and whether an overpayment can be recovered. Overpayments are not within the scope of this *Handbook*. See CPAG's *Welfare Benefits Handbook* for more information.

6. Getting paid

When you are paid

Employment and support allowance (ESA) is usually paid fortnightly in arrears, although it can be paid at different intervals, including at a daily rate.[38]

If you are waiting for a decision on your claim or you are waiting to be paid and you are in financial need, you may be able to get an advance loan of your ESA.[39] This is called a 'short-term advance'.

Note:

- For the rules about whether you can be paid ESA while waiting for a decision on a new claim or while appealing a decision, see p58.
- If you are moving from ESA to universal credit, see p80 for information about ESA run-on.
- It is possible for payment of ESA to be suspended (see p64).

Where your payment goes

ESA is usually paid directly into your bank account. The DWP can alternatively pay all or part of your income-related ESA or old-style contributory ESA to someone else, if this is in your interests.[40] These alternative payment arrangements might be useful if, for example, you want a trusted family member to look after your ESA income because your mental health problem makes it difficult for you to manage money. ESA can also be paid to an appointee (see p325).

If you do not have a bank account, you can ask for your ESA to be paid into someone else's account as above, or you can ask to be considered for DWP's payment exception service.[41]

7. Reviews and reassessments

Your entitlement to income-related or contributory employment and support allowance (ESA) can change after an award has been made. In certain circumstances, the DWP reviews your entitlement or reassesses you.

Work capability

There are no rules on how often your work capability can be reassessed. Usually, the original assessor recommends how long it should be before you are reassessed. You may be reviewed sooner if you report an improvement or a deterioration in your condition. The DWP has stated that if you are assessed as having limited capability for work and work-related activity, have a 'severe, lifelong' disability or condition, and are 'unlikely to ever be able to move into work', you will not be reassessed.[42]

On reassessment, you are likely to go through the same assessment process as when you claimed ESA (see p57).

Change of circumstances

You should report all changes in your circumstances to the ESA section of the DWP as soon as possible. Do not assume that the ESA section already knows something – eg, about changes to the other DWP benefits you claim or about a pension. You can report a change by phone (0800 169 0310; textphone: 0800 169 0314; Relay UK and British Sign Language video relay services available) but it may be better to do it in writing, using the address on your ESA decision letters, so you have a clear record of what you reported and when.

When you notify the DWP of a change of circumstances, it can change the decision on your ESA entitlement, usually by supersession (see p292).

If you still get income-related ESA and your change of circumstances is that you or your partner now get a qualifying disability benefit, you might be eligible for additional amounts in your ESA. For more information about the date that these additional amounts start from, see p293.

Certain changes in your circumstances might end your income-related ESA and trigger a move to universal credit (see p79).

Ongoing evidence requirement

Once you are getting ESA, you may be asked to provide information at any time, and if you fail to do so, your ESA could be suspended or even terminated.[43]

8. Employment and support allowance and other benefits

Means-tested benefits

If you still get income-related employment and support allowance (ESA), you have passported entitlement to maximum housing benefit (see p121) and Scottish child payment. Passported entitlement does not mean you will get these benefits without making a claim for them.

If you are moving from income-related ESA to universal credit (UC), see p79.

If you get contributory ESA, you may be able to get a means-tested benefit to top up your income. If you still get old-style contributory ESA, you may be able to get a top-up of income-related ESA (see p56). If you get new-style contributory ESA, you may be able to get UC to top up your income.

Non-means-tested benefits

Many non-means-tested benefits are taken into account as income when working out the amount of income-related ESA you get. However, disability benefits such as personal independence payment (PIP) and adult disability payment (ADP) are not taken into account and can in fact increase your income-related ESA by making you eligible for premiums.

Contributory ESA is affected by the rules on overlapping benefits, which means that you may not be paid it in full if you are being paid another earnings-replacement benefit – eg, carer's allowance.[44]

The benefit cap

In some cases, there is a limit on your total income from specified benefits (the 'benefit cap'). ESA is one of the specified benefits. You are not subject to the benefit cap if your ESA includes a support component, or if you get certain other benefits – eg, if you get PIP or ADP. See CPAG's *Welfare Benefits Handbook* for more information.

Other sources of financial help

If you qualify for income-related ESA, you are automatically eligible for some health benefits such as free prescriptions. You may also qualify for council tax reduction and a range of other financial help. See Chapter 15 for more information.

Notes

1 DWP, *Pathways to Work: reforming benefits and support to get Britain working Green Paper*, March 2025

1. **Who can get employment and support allowance**

2 ss1 and 20(1) WRA 2007; reg 40(1) and (7) ESA Regs; reg 37(1) and (8) ESA Regs 2013
3 Sch 1 para 6 WRA 2007
4 s1(3)(aa) WRA 2007
5 Sch 1 paras 1-4 WRA 2007
6 s1B and Sch 1 para 3(1)(f) WRA 2007; Sch 2 paras 2 and 15 ESA(TP)(EA)(No.2) Regs; regs 2(1) and 13 ESA Regs; regs 2 and 14 ESA Regs 2013
7 ss6 and 6A SSCBA 1992; Sch 1 para 1 WRA 2007; reg 7 ESA Regs; reg 8 ESA Regs 2013
8 Reg 8 ESA Regs; reg 9 ESA Regs 2013
9 ss6 and 6A SSCBA 1992; Sch 1 para 2 WRA 2007
10 Reg 8B SS(Cr) Regs
11 ss1A and 1B WRA 2007; ss51 and 52 WRA 2012
12 ss1A and 1B WRA 2007; Vol 8 Ch 41, para 41847 DMG; para V2045 ADM
13 s18 WRA 2007; regs 157 and 158 and Sch 5 para 14 ESA Regs; regs 63, 93 and 94 ESA Regs 2013

2. **The amount of benefit**

14 s3 WRA 2007; regs 72-79 and 94(1) ESA Regs; regs 64-72 and 79 ESA Regs 2013
15 Reg 35, Sch 9 and Sch 9B SS(C&P) Regs; regs 59 and 60 and Schs 6 and 7 UC,PIP,JSA&ESA(C&P) Regs
16 ss2(2) and 4(4) WRA 2007
17 ss2(3) and 4(5) WRA 2007; s15 WRWA 2016; Sch 1 Part 1 ESAUC(MA) Regs
18 Reg 144 ESA Regs; reg 85 ESA Regs 2013
19 s2(1)(a) WRA 2007; regs 7 and 67(2) and Sch 4 para 1(1)(b) and (c) ESA Regs; regs 7 and 62(1) ESA Regs 2013
20 Reg 7 ESA Regs; reg 7 ESA Regs 2013
21 Reg 7(38) SS&CS(DA) Regs; reg 35(7) UC,PIP,JSA&ESA(DA) Regs
22 Reg 5 ESA Regs; reg 6 ESA Regs 2013

3. **Making a claim**

23 s6 WRA 2007; *LH v SSWP (ESA)* [2014] UKUT 480 (AAC), reported as [2015] AACR 14
24 Regs 13 and 15 UC,PIP,JSA&ESA(C&P) Regs; gov.uk/employment-support-allowance/how-to-claim
25 Regs 13(5), 14, 15(4) and 16 UC,PIP,JSA&ESA(C&P) Regs
26 Reg 34 UC,PIP,JSA&ESA(C&P) Regs
27 Reg 28 UC,PIP,JSA&ESA(C&P) Regs

4. **How you are assessed**

28 Regs 20, 25, 26, 30, 33 and 35 ESA Regs; regs 16, 21, 22 and 26 ESA Regs 2013; *El v SSWP (ESA)* [2016] UKUT 397 (AAC)
29 Regs 34 and 35 ESA Regs; regs 30 and 31 ESA Regs 2013
30 Reg 32A ESA Regs; reg 28 ESA Regs 2013
31 s19 SSA 1998; regs 21-24 and 36-39 ESA Regs; regs 17-20 and 33-36 ESA Regs 2013
32 Reg 44 ESA Regs; reg 37 ESA Regs 2013
33 Reg 159 ESA Regs; reg 95 ESA Regs 2013
34 Reg 32(2) and (3) ESA Regs; reg 27 (2) and (3) ESA Regs 2013
35 Reg 32(1) ESA Regs; reg 27(1) ESA Regs 2013
36 Regs 2 (definition of 'period of limited capability for work') and 145 ESA Regs; regs 2 and 86 ESA Regs 2013
37 paras 1-3 Sch 1 WRA 2007

6. **Getting paid**

38 Reg 26C SS(C&P) Regs; reg 51 UC,PIP,JSA&ESA(C&P) Regs
39 Regs 5 and 6 SS(PAB) Regs
40 Reg 34(1) SS(C&P) Regs
41 See gov.uk/payment-exception-service

7. Reviews and reassessments

42 DWP, *Employment and Support Allowance and Universal Credit: changes to the work capability assessment from 29 September 2017*, September 2017

43 Reg 32(1) SS(C&P) Regs; reg 17 SS&CS(DA)Regs; reg 38(2) UC,PIP,JSA&ESA(C&P) Regs; reg 45 UC,PIP,JSA&ESA(DA) Regs

8. Employment and support allowance and other benefits

44 Reg 4(5) SS(OB) Regs

Chapter 5

Universal credit

This chapter covers:

Key facts

- Universal credit (UC) is a means-tested benefit for people who are in or out of work, including people with health conditions and disabilities.
- You may be able to get help with your rent and other housing costs through UC.
- If you have a mental health problem that affects your ability to work, you usually have a work capability assessment. This determines whether you are expected to look for, or prepare for, work in order to get UC, and can also affect how much UC you get.
- You can get UC alongside many other benefits, including contributory employment and support allowance (ESA) and disability benefits – eg, personal independence payment or adult disability payment.
- UC is replacing a number of other means-tested benefits including income-related ESA and, for most people, working-age housing benefit (HB). In 2025, all remaining income-related ESA claimants and most working-age HB claimants will be required to move to UC.
- You can challenge decisions about your entitlement to UC and about your work capability.
- Getting UC can mean that you are eligible for other kinds of financial support.

1. Who can get universal credit

Universal credit (UC) is the main means-tested benefit for working-age people. You can claim it whether you are in or out of work, and whether or not you have a health condition or disability. You do not need to have paid national insurance contributions to qualify for UC.

You can qualify for universal credit UC if:[1]

- you are aged 18 or over and under pension age, which is currently 66 and rising to 67 between 2026 and 2028. **Note:** some 16/17-year-olds, and some people over pension age with younger partners, known as mixed-age couples (see p104), can get UC; *and*
- you are not receiving education (unless an exception applies – see p279); *and*
- you satisfy the habitual residence and the right to reside tests, are in (or treated as being in) Great Britain, and are not a person subject to immigration control – see CPAG's *Welfare Benefits Handbook* for more information*; and*
- you have accepted a claimant commitment (see below); *and*
- your income is not too high (see p75); *and*
- your savings and other capital (eg, shares, certain lump-sum payments and most property that is not your main home) are £16,000 or less.

Note:

- Special rules apply when you are in hospital, staying in a care home and in certain other situations (see Chapter 19).
- You may not have to meet all of these conditions if you transfer to UC under the managed migration process (see p79).

If you are a member of a **couple**, you must usually make a joint claim for UC (see p78 for the practicalities of claiming as a couple).[2] Both of you must usually meet the eligibility conditions above and your income and capital are assessed jointly. If one of you does not satisfy the conditions, there are some circumstances in which you can still claim UC.[3]

Mental health and the claimant commitment

To get UC, most people are expected to work or to prepare for and look for work. These expectations are known as work-related requirements (see p270). They are set out in a document called your 'claimant commitment'. If you do not accept your claimant commitment, your eligibility for UC normally ends.

UC rules recognise that having a health condition or disability, such as a mental health problem, can affect your ability to work. If this applies, you are usually referred for a work capability assessment (WCA) to decide what kind of work-related activity (if any) you can be expected to do (see p80).

If it is decided that, despite having a mental health problem, that you are fit for work, you can still receive UC but you are likely to have more work-related requirements (see p270).

If you have work-related requirements but are struggling to meet them because of your mental health problem, you can ask your work coach to change, reduce or stop them, even when you have been found fit for work[4] (see pp271–73).

If you do not meet your work-related requirements, you may be sanctioned (see p274).

2. The amount of benefit

Universal credit (UC) is a means-tested benefit. It is calculated over a monthly assessment period.

Step 1: calculate your monthly maximum amount

Your maximum monthly amount of UC is made up of the total of:

- a standard allowance, based on your age and whether you are a single claimant or claiming with a partner;[5]
- a child element for each child or qualifying young person you are responsible for (see p70), with an additional amount for a disabled or severely disabled child (see p71).[6] (**Note:** you may only be able to get the standard child element for a maximum of two children, depending on when they were born and some other factors,[7] but there is no such limit for the disabled child addition);
- a limited capability for work (LCW) or limited capability for work and work-related activity (LCWRA) element (p70) for some claimants with a health condition or disability;
- a carer element (see p227);[8]
- a housing costs element for people paying rent or service charges (see p72);
- a childcare costs element;[9]
- a transitional element, if you transfer to UC under the managed migration process and your UC is worth less than your old benefits (see p79);
- a transitional severe disability premium (SDP) element if you meet the criteria (see p73) and transfer to UC under the 'natural migration' process.[10]

Universal credit rates 2025/26

Standard allowance		
Single	Under 25	£316.98
	25 or over	£400.14
Couple	Both under 25	£497.55
	One or both 25 or over	£628.10
Elements		
First child (if born before 6 April 2017)		£339.00

First child (if born on or after 6 April 2017), second child and each subsequent child who qualifies		£292.81
Disabled child addition	Lower rate	£158.76
	Higher rate	£495.87
Limited capability for work		£158.76
Limited capability for work-related activity		£423.27
Carer		£201.68
Childcare costs	One child	up to £1,031.88
	Two or more children	up to £1,768.94
	Percentage covered	85%

Children and young people

As a general rule, a child under 16 or a qualifying young person is included in your UC claim if they normally live with you.[11] There are limited exceptions. If you share care with someone else, get independent advice – see advicelocal.uk.

A **'qualifying young person'** is:[12]

- someone aged 16 who has not yet reached the 1 September after their 16th birthday; *or*
- in most cases, someone aged 16 to 19 who has not yet reached the 1 September after their 19th birthday and who is in approved training or non-advanced education for more than 12 hours a week.

Limited capability for work element

If you are assessed as having LCW (see p80), your UC award does not usually include an extra element. However, in limited circumstances, an LCW element of £158.76 a month *is* included.[13] The main situations in which this happens are if:

- you have continuously received UC since before 3 April 2017 and have had either an LCW element or an LCWRA element continuously included in your award since before 3 April 2017; *or*
- you had an employment and support allowance (ESA) award immediately before 3 April 2017, and had been getting ESA continuously from 3 April 2017 until you claimed UC; *or*
- you had national insurance (NI) credits for LCW (see p54) immediately before 3 April 2017, and had been getting these continuously from 3 April 2017 until you claimed UC.

If you are making a joint UC claim with your partner, only one LCW element can be included, even if you both meet the conditions.[14]

Limited capability for work-related activity element

If you are assessed (or treated) as having LCWRA (see p97), an LCWRA element of £423.27 a month is usually included in your UC maximum amount. If you are making a joint UC claim with your partner, only one LCWRA element can be included, even if you both meet the conditions.[15]

Future changes

The government is proposing major changes to the LCWRA element from April 2026.[16] Under current plans, the LCWRA element will be reduced by nearly half for new claimants. Existing claimants entitled to the element, and those who are terminally ill or have severe lifelong conditions with no prospect of improvement, will still be able to get the full rate. These plans are in draft form and are subject to change.

When you start getting the limited capability for work-related activity element

If you qualify for the LCWRA element for the first time, a three-month waiting period usually applies before it is included in your UC. The waiting period usually begins on the day you provide a fit note (or, where it would be unreasonable to require you to provide one, the date you provide other evidence).[17]

You do not have a waiting period if:

- you regarded as terminally ill (you are automatically treated as having LCWRA – see p97); *or*
- you have moved from ESA to UC with no break in entitlement and you were in the work-related activity group or support group for ESA (similar rules apply if you have been getting NI credits for LCW or LCWRA);[18] *or*
- you were entitled to the LCWRA or LCW element in a UC award that ended immediately before your current UC award started, and your previous UC award ended because you became a member of a couple or you stopped being a member of a couple; *or*
- you were entitled to the LCWRA or LCW element in a previous UC award that ended within the six months before your current award started, and your previous UC award ended because your income was too high; *or*
- you have an award of contributory ESA that includes the support component; *or*
- you have been assessed as having LCW and are then later assessed as entitled to the LCWRA element.

Disabled child addition

Your maximum amount of UC includes a disabled child addition if you are responsible for a child who is entitled to disability living allowance (DLA), child disability payment (CDP), Scottish adult disability living allowance (SADLA), personal independence payment (PIP) or adult disability payment (ADP).

You get the **higher rate** if the child is entitled to the DLA/CDP/SADLA care component at the highest rate, the daily living component of PIP/ADP at the enhanced rate, or if they are certified as severely sight impaired or blind.[19] The disabled child addition is still paid for a child even if you cannot get a child element for them because of the two-child limit.[20]

Housing costs element

When you can get a housing costs element

Your UC may include a housing costs element to help with rent and/or service charges. You cannot get the housing costs element to help pay a mortgage, but you may be separately eligible for a support for mortgage interest loan (see p234).

Your housing costs element may not cover your full rent. If you are a private tenant, the amount you get is usually based on a local housing allowance for a home of the size you are considered to need.[21] If you are a social rented tenant, the amount you get may be affected by the bedroom tax (spare-room subsidy) if you are regarded as having too many bedrooms.[22] In either type of housing, your housing costs element could also be reduced if you have a non-dependant living with you.

If you have a shortfall in the amount of help you get to pay the rent, you can apply to your local council for a discretionary housing payment (see p232).

Non-dependants

A non-dependant is someone who usually lives in your home with you but who is not your partner, a child or a qualifying young person – eg, an adult relative or a friend.[23]

As a general rule, people who are classed as non-dependants attract a deduction from your monthly UC, which is known as a **housing costs contribution.** The deduction is a fixed amount of £93.02 a month for each non-dependant, irrespective of their income and what they actually contribute.[24]

Some people who are classed as non-dependants do not attract a housing costs contribution. These include people aged under 21, people responsible for a child under five, people getting pension credit or carer's allowance/carer support payment, and people getting attendance allowance (AA)/pension age disability payment (PADP), the middle or highest rate of the care component of DLA/CDP/SADLA or the daily living component of PIP/ADP.[25]

In addition, you do not have *any* housing costs contributions applied to your UC if you or your partner are entitled to AA/PADP, the middle or highest rate of the care component of DLA/CDP/SADLA, or the daily living component of PIP/ADP.[26]

Supported housing and temporary accommodation

You cannot get a UC housing costs element to cover your rent if you live in specified or temporary accommodation. Specified accommodation covers many kinds of housing with care and support, and certain kinds of refuge, while temporary accommodation covers certain homelessness accommodation.[27] If your housing is provided by the local authority, a housing association or a charity and you moved there to receive care, support or supervision connected with your health, you can usually be confident that you live in specified accommodation.[28]

If this applies to you, instead of getting a UC housing costs element, you need to claim housing benefit (HB – see Chapter 7, and p120 specifically). Although UC is replacing working-age HB for most people, new HB claims are still accepted from people who live in this type of accommodation. HB can be paid alongside your UC.[29]

If you are unsure whether your accommodation is 'specified', or if the local authority and the DWP are in disagreement, ask your landlord to clarify this and/or get independent advice – see advicelocal.uk.

Other rules

There are more details about the housing costs element of UC in CPAG's *Welfare Benefits Handbook*.

Transitional severe disability premium element

If you transfer to UC from a legacy benefit under the natural migration process (see p79), you might be entitled to an extra element in your UC. If an SDP was included in your legacy benefit, you may be eligible for an extra element in your UC maximum amount (a 'transitional SDP element') on moving to UC. This applies if:[30]

- you have not become part of a couple with someone already on UC; *and*
- within the month before your UC entitlement started, you (or your partner) were entitled to income support, income-based jobseeker's allowance or income-related employment and support allowance, and that included an SDP. You cannot get a transitional SDP element amount if you were only entitled to HB, even if this included an SDP; *and*
- you continued to satisfy the conditions for getting the SDP up to and including the first day of your UC entitlement.

If, however, you transfer to UC under the DWP's managed migration process and your UC would be worth less than your legacy benefit, you should instead be entitled to a transitional element in your UC.

Once awarded, the transitional SDP element continues even if you stop satisfying the conditions for the SDP – eg, if someone becomes a carer for you. However, your transitional SDP element can reduce over time ('erode') or stop entirely – see CPAG's *Welfare Benefits Handbook* for more information.[31]

The amount for each UC monthly assessment period is as follows.[32] Note that this amount applies to UC awards starting on or after 8 April 2025. Lower amounts applied in previous years.

	Award starts on or after 8 April 2025
Single claimant, LCWRA element included in UC	£143.37
Single claimant, LCWRA element not included in UC	£340.50
Joint-claim couple, SDP was payable at the single rate (or couple rate, but the £483.88 payment below does not apply), LCWRA element included in UC	£143.37
Joint-claim couple, SDP was payable at the single rate (or couple rate, but the £483.88 payment below does not apply), LCWRA not included in UC	£340.50
Joint-claim couple, SDP was payable at the couple rate and no one is getting (and entitled to) carer's allowance, carer support payment or the carer element of UC for either of you in your first UC monthly assessment period	£483.88

The above amounts are increased if you were entitled to the SDP and were also getting another premium or premiums for disability in your legacy benefit when you migrated to UC – eg, the enhanced disability premium. Get advice if this applies to you.

Step 2: calculate your earnings and how much can be ignored

Work out your total earnings in the relevant assessment period. This can often be straightforward, but refer to CPAG's *Welfare Benefits Handbook* for how to do it. Note that, if you are working for an employer, the DWP gets this information directly from HMRC through a real-time information system. If you are self-employed and your earnings are low, your UC award may be assessed on more earnings than you actually get (this is known as the minimum income floor).[33]

If your earnings are less than your work allowance, they do not reduce your UC. If they exceed your work allowance, your UC is reduced by 55 per cent of the excess amount.[34] This called the taper rate.

Work allowances

A work allowance is the amount you can earn before your earnings start to be taken into account for calculating your UC. You *only* have a work allowance if you are responsible for a child or if you have LCW. There are two rates.[35]

- If your UC includes a housing costs element: £411 a month.
- If your UC does not include a housing costs element: £684 a month.

Why is there a work allowance for claimants with limited capability for work?

Unlike ESA, UC does not have special rules about the amount of work that you can do while claiming. If you are assessed as having LCW due to your mental health problem, but are well enough to do some work, this is allowed and actively encouraged by the DWP. However, the tasks you do for work are usually taken into account in your next work capability assessment and might lead to a decision that you are 'fit for work'.

Step 3: calculate your other income and how much can be ignored

Different types of income can have different effects on UC. Some income is ignored (eg, PIP, ADP, DLA, CDP, AA and PADP), and other income is taken into account (eg, contributory ESA and carer's allowance/carer support payment). For specific rules on how different benefits, student finance, maintenance payments and pensions affect UC, see CPAG's *Welfare Benefits Handbook*.

Step 4: calculate your universal credit entitlement

Deduct your total relevant income (Steps 2 and 3) from your maximum UC (Step 1). This leaves your UC entitlement for that assessment period.

Note: if, after following these steps, you are not entitled to UC, but you would be if your award included an LCWRA element, you may be able to get UC at one pence a month during the LCWRA waiting period (see p71).[36]

Step 5: calculate your universal credit payment

The amount of UC you actually receive may be further reduced by the benefit cap (see p105), sanctions (see p274), deductions (see below) and alternative payment arrangements (see p102).

Deductions

Deductions can be made from your UC to recover advances, overpayments, third-party debts and fines, as well as to cover some ongoing costs like electricity and gas charges. They cannot normally exceed 15 per cent of your UC standard allowance or reduce your UC award to less than a penny.[37] They should not be confused with 'alternative payment arrangements'. CPAG's *Welfare Benefits Handbook* covers UC deductions in more detail. If you feel your deductions are too high, get advice about whether they can be reduced.

3. Making a claim

If you have been told that you need to move from your existing benefits to universal credit (UC), read p79 before starting a claim.

How to claim

Claiming online

UC claims are usually made online at gov.uk/apply-universal-credit. You are asked to set up an online account and provide an email address, username, password and security questions.

If you need help claiming online, you can call the UC helpline. Staff can complete an online form on your behalf or arrange for you to get help at your local job centre. Alternatively, Citizens Advice can help you make a claim through the free Help to Claim service (citizensadvice.org.uk/helptoclaim in England and Wales, cas.org.uk/helptoclaim in Scotland).

If you claim online, your date of claim is usually the date you submit the completed application (but could be earlier if you asked for help from the DWP or Help to Claim – and see p77 about backdating).[38]

Universal credit helpline

Freephone: 0800 328 5644 (textphone: 0800 328 1344; Welsh language: 0800 328 1744), Relay UK available, Monday to Friday 8am to 6pm. There is also a British Sign Language video relay service.

Most UC claimants are required to set up an online UC account, which is used on an ongoing basis to send you messages about your UC, including decisions, payment information, information requests and appointment details. However, this online contact is not suitable for everyone and you may want to consider claiming by phone instead (see below).

Claiming by telephone

If you would have difficulty managing your UC online, you can claim UC by phone instead and receive future contact by letter and phone call. DWP guidance confirms that this option is open to people who would find it difficult to manage an online account because of a mental health problem.[39] To claim by phone, call the UC helpline. **Note:** be clear that you wish to make a 'telephone claim' and do not just want help by phone to make an online claim.

If you claim by telephone, your date of claim is usually the date that you call to start your claim (but see below about backdating).[40]

Switching an online account to a telephone and paper account and vice versa

If you started your UC claim online but are now finding it difficult to manage your online account, you can switch to receiving phone calls and letters instead of online notifications.[41] The switch is done 'clerically': your online account still exists but should no longer be used to contact you. Likewise, if you have claimed by phone but now feel it would be easier to have an online account, you can switch and a new online account is set up for you.

If the DWP refuses your request to switch, get independent advice service. Your adviser can use a CPAG template for challenging the decision by judicial review (email jrproject@cpag.org.uk for details).

Additional support and appointees

If you have (or will have) difficulty with the claims process and need additional support, see Chapter 21. If you cannot manage the claims process at all, you may need an appointee (see p325).

Claiming in advance and backdating

You may be able to claim UC **in advance** – ie, before you have become eligible.[42]

In some cases, your claim can be backdated by up to one month – eg, if you have a disability or health condition which stopped you from claiming sooner. You may need medical evidence to support this. It is best to make a clear request for backdating at the point at which you claim, but the DWP should also consider a request made later.[43] There is no question about backdating in the online application process, but you can make a request via the journal once the claim is submitted, which should be considered as part of the decision on your entitlement.

If you believe you would have claimed earlier but were misled or wrongly advised by the DWP, and your claim cannot be backdated, you could make a complaint asking for compensation (see p308).

Note: the term 'backdating' is often informally used to mean getting arrears of your benefit going back to a claim or decision date – eg, after winning an appeal. However, in this *Handbook*, we use backdating to mean getting paid benefit for a period before the date you claimed.

What you will be asked and how long it will take

When you claim UC, you are asked questions to check your eligibility and how much you might be entitled to receive. See the start of this chapter to get a sense of what you will be asked about. It is usually a good idea to have to hand:

- your national insurance (NI) number, if you have one (if you do not, you can still start a claim for UC, and doing this will prompt the DWP to allocate you an NI number);
- your phone number (you can choose to give the number of someone you trust);
- your bank account details;
- details about your tenancy, including whether you are in private or social rented accommodation, your landlord's details and the amount of your rent and/or service charges;
- details about anyone who lives with you;
- details about any earnings or other income you have;
- details about your savings or capital (capital includes, for example, savings, shares, certain lump-sum payments and most property that is not your main home).

The DWP says that an online claim takes about 20 minutes, but it often takes longer in practice. Phone claims can take longer.

Couples

If you are claiming online as a couple, one of you should usually start and complete the claim first. That partner is given a linking code, which the second partner then uses to complete their own claim and link the two applications. The process may be different if either of you already gets UC as a single person, or if you are claiming by phone.

Evidence to support the claim

After completing a claim, you are asked to provide further information and evidence – eg, proof of your identity, payslips, your rent agreement and bank statements. You may be asked to attend an interview at the job centre to do this.

If you are struggling to supply evidence on time, or if you cannot attend an interview, try to tell the DWP in advance. If you do not comply with a request for further information, the DWP is likely to say that you have made a 'failed claim' and that your claim has been 'closed' (see p100 on how to challenge this).

If you have a health condition or disability

If you mention when you claim (or later) that you have a health condition or disability that limits your ability to work, you should usually be referred for a work capability assessment (WCA). There is more information about the WCA, including the capability for work questionnaire (UC50), on p80.

To begin the WCA process, you are usually required to provide a fit note showing that your GP or another professional has declared you unfit for work. See p81 for more information about fit notes.

Moving to universal credit from other benefits

If you are getting income-related employment and support allowance (ESA) or working-age housing benefit (HB) and you are not living in specified or temporary accommodation (see p120), you will be transferred to UC under the DWP's managed migration process. Under this process, the DWP will send you a migration notice, explaining that your ESA/HB will end, and inviting you to claim UC instead. Other legacy benefits – income support (IS), income-based jobseeker's allowance (JSA) and tax credits – have already been transferred to UC under this process. You can also move to UC even before you have come under the managed migration process, by choosing to claim UC yourself. This is called 'natural migration'.

Note:

- You cannot make a new claim for income-related ESA. Awards combined with child tax credit have already been replaced by UC, and the remaining awards have started to be replaced. If you are still entitled to income-related ESA, it will end when you come under the managed migration process – expected by December 2025 at the latest. You may transfer earlier through natural migration.
- You cannot make a new claim for working-age HB, unless you live in specified or temporary accommodation. Most working-age HB awards – whether combined with IS, income-based JSA and tax credits, or paid alone – have already ended. If you still have a current award combined with income-related ESA, that will end when you come under the managed migration to UC process (unless you are in specified or temporary accommodation).

If you get income-related ESA only, or income-related ESA and HB only, you should receive a migration notice before September 2025. The DWP aims to move all remaining legacy claimants (except some HB-only claimants) to UC by March 2026. See CPAG's *Welfare Benefits Handbook* for details about the transfer process.

Transitional element

If you are transferred to UC under the managed migration process and the amount of your UC is less than you were getting on your legacy benefits, you are likely to be entitled to a transitional element in your UC calculation (see p69). This transitional element is intended to ensure that you are not worse off at the point you transfer to UC, but the extra amount then reduces ('erodes') over time.[44]

See CPAG's *Welfare Benefits Handbook* for more information about how to calculate this element and how erosion works.

Work capability status on moving to universal credit

If you are moving from ESA to UC – whether by natural or managed migration – you can carry over your existing limited capability for work or limited capability for work-related activity status to your new UC award (see p71).

Run-on of legacy benefits

When you make a new claim for UC, your entitlement to income-related ESA and HB ends, but payment of these benefits continues for two further weeks, as long as you would otherwise remain entitled to them. This is known as a 'run-on' payment. You do not have to pay back a run-on payment; it is not taken into account as income for UC and it is ignored for the benefit cap.[45]

4. How you are assessed

The work capability assessment

If you claim universal credit (UC) and tell the DWP that your health condition or disability affects your ability to work, you are usually referred for a work capability assessment (WCA). The WCA is used by the DWP to decide that:

- you are **fit for work**, so you have some **work-related requirements** attached to your UC (see p270); *or*
- you have **limited capability for work** (LCW), meaning you are not required to actively to look for work, but are considered well enough to do some **work preparation** activity, such as training or work-focused jobcentre appointments (see p270); *or*
- you have **limited capability for work and work-related activity** (LCWRA), meaning your health condition or disability is considered so severe that you are not required to work or take steps to prepare for work.

This decision also affects the amount of UC you get (see p69).

Note: the WCA is also used to decide entitlement to employment and support allowance (ESA – see Chapter 4). The WCA rules and processes in this section apply to ESA as well as UC, except where otherwise stated.

Future changes

The government has announced plans to scrap the WCA in 2028/29. In the future, a health element in UC will instead be paid to claimants also getting a qualifying disability benefit.[46] These plans are in draft form and are subject to change.

Who is not assessed

Most claimants are assessed using the standard WCA process described below. However, in some circumstances, you can be 'treated as having' LCW or LCWRA without going through this process (see pp97–98).

There are also limited circumstances where a WCA is simply not offered – eg, if you have previously failed a WCA either for UC or for new-style ESA (see p98).

If you are over pension age and get UC as part of a mixed-age couple (see p104), the DWP might tell you that you cannot have a WCA. This is incorrect, as the basic rule is that *any* UC claimant can be assessed, and the limited situations in which an assessment may not be carried out do not relate to age.[47] A template for advisers to challenge a refusal to carry out an assessment on this basis by judicial review can be obtained by contacting jrproject@cpag.org.uk.

The assessment process

Fit note

To start the WCA process, you usually need to provide a fit note showing that your GP (or other health professional) has declared you unfit for work. You are generally expected to provide continuous fit notes from the date when you declare a health condition or disability until the DWP makes a decision about your capability for work. You can self-certify for the first seven days. If it would be unreasonable to expect you to get a fit note, the DWP can accept alternative medical evidence – eg, if you have been in hospital and can provide discharge papers confirming why and how long you were there.[48]

Getting a fit note

You can request a fit note from a doctor (including a GP or specialist) or from a nurse, occupational therapist, pharmacist or physiotherapist. You may need an appointment, but if the professional is already familiar with your current condition, ask if they can issue a fit note without requiring a new consultation. There is no charge for a fit note which covers a period of more than a week.

The questionnaire (UC50/ESA50)

The DWP should refer you for a WCA within 28 days of you declaring your illness or disability, sometimes sooner.[49] Once referred, the DWP's assessment provider (see p252) usually sends you a questionnaire to complete (UC50 for UC, ESA50 for ESA).

What advisers say: being sent a UC50/ESA50

'If you don't receive the questionnaire, contact the DWP to chase it up – delays in getting the form can delay your assessment and any decision about your fitness for work.'

A decision can be made without a questionnaire if it is considered that there is enough other information,[50] but the assessment provider and DWP decide whether this is the case. If you are sent a form, you must complete and return it (although see p328 for DWP guidance about unreturned forms). Even if you have an online UC account, you are sent a paper copy of the form.

If you need help completing the form, ask someone close to you or an independent advice service – see advicelocal.uk. If you are unable to get help elsewhere, you can call the assessment provider (see p252) and they may be able to help you to complete the form by phone.[51]

Completing the form

1. It may help to draft your answers on a separate piece of paper or type them so that you can correct any mistakes.
2. Read the list of activities starting on p85 to get an idea of what the DWP needs to know about each activity.
3. Consider all of the mental health symptoms listed on pp13–23.
4. If you have good and bad days, explain this (see p84). If possible, give a rough estimate of how often you could perform an activity and how often you could not. You might want to describe occasions when you have attempted the activity unsuccessfully.
5. If you can do something, but only slowly, with difficulty, ineffectively, or not with a reasonable degree of regularity, say so.
6. Make sure to list all your symptoms and all side effects of medication. You could use the blank 'Other information' section at the end of the form. If you later have to appeal, the First-tier Tribunal may be less likely to believe you have symptoms if you did not mention them on the questionnaire.
7. Read the rules about 'substantial risk' on p95. Consider whether, and how, work or work-related activity might be a risk to your health. There is no question on the form that asks you about this, but you can use the blank 'Other information' page to provide details.
8. Compare the draft of your answers with the list of activities beginning on p85 and work out your score. Do not exaggerate, but be careful not to underestimate your difficulties. Give all the details you can.
9. Try to include supporting evidence, such as a prescription list, hospital report, care plan or a statement from a family member. See Chapter 16 for more information about supporting evidence.
10. Ask someone you trust and who knows you well to check your answers.
11. If someone completes the questionnaire for you, explain why and include their details at the end where the form asks about this. If you completed the form yourself but could only do so slowly or with difficulty, explain this.
12. Use the questionnaire as an opportunity to express any needs or preferences you have if you are required to attend an assessment. See p256 for some examples.
13. Keep a copy of your completed questionnaire and ask the Post Office for free proof of posting.

Timescales

You have four weeks from the date the questionnaire is sent to you to return it. If you miss this deadline, the DWP may decide that you do not have LCW, unless you can show that you had good reason for the delay (see below).[52] After returning the form, it may be several months before you are invited to an assessment.

If you are going to be late completing and returning the questionnaire, tell the DWP as soon as possible by phone or through your online account. Still return the form as quickly as you can and explain why it is late (either on the form or in a covering letter). If a decision is made that you did not have a good reason for being late, but you think you did, consider challenging the decision (see Chapter 20).

'Good reason' is not defined for UC. When deciding whether you have good cause for ESA, the DWP must consider all the circumstances,[53] and good cause could include being too unwell or distressed to complete the form on time or participate in the medical. In practice, the same sort of things should be accepted when deciding whether you have 'good reason' for UC.

DWP guidance on complex needs and unreturned forms

There are procedures the DWP should follow if you are considered to be vulnerable or to have complex needs – eg, if you have a serious mental health problem.[54] These procedures are not a legal requirement, but they do require the DWP to take extra steps before treating you as not having LCW. If you think this applies to you, ask whether the procedures were followed in your case, and seek advice. See pp326–32 (and for UC50/ESA50 forms, see p328 in particular).

Medical assessment

As part of the WCA, you are usually asked to take part in a face-to-face, telephone or video assessment with a **healthcare professional**. A decision can be made without an assessment if it is considered that there is enough other information,[55] but the DWP decides whether this is the case, and if you are asked to attend an assessment, you usually need to go.

UC and ESA assessments are carried out on behalf of the DWP by the Health Assessment Advisory Service. Chapter 17 has more information about the practicalities of assessments, including where they can take place, who assesses you, and what to do if you cannot attend.

The assessment criteria

Activities, descriptors and points

The WCA is largely a test of your ability to perform certain **activities**. There are two main lists of activities: physical (see p85) and mental (see p85) activities.

Each activity has a list of statements called **'descriptors'** which describe different levels of difficulty in carrying out the activity.

Every descriptor has a **points** score. You are awarded the highest-scoring descriptor that applies to you in each activity.

Your points largely determine the outcome of your WCA. There are three possible outcomes.

- You are assessed as having **LCW** if you score a total of 15 points or more across all activities. **Note:** you are also assessed as having LCW if work poses a substantial risk to your health (see p95), or in some circumstances you are 'treated as' having LCW without actually undergoing the assessment (see p97).
- You are assessed as having **LCWRA** if you satisfy certain 15-point descriptors. **Note:** you are also assessed as having LCWRA if work-related activity poses a substantial risk to your health (see p95), or in some circumstances you are 'treated as' having LCWRA without actually undergoing the assessment (see p97).
- Otherwise, you are assessed as **fit for work**.

There is more information about these outcomes on p99.

Good days and bad days

Mental health symptoms can fluctuate. Generally, what counts for the assessment is whether you can do things 'the majority of the time'.[56] Your ability to perform an activity with some degree of repetition should be considered and a 'broad-brush' approach applied, rather than just a day-by-day approach.[57] The severity of your condition, the frequency of your good and bad days and the unpredictability of the bad days are all relevant.[58]

If you have long periods of remission, you may be considered capable of work during these periods. This depends on the severity of your condition and on the length of your periods of ill health and your periods of remission.[59]

If you are finding it difficult to score points because your symptoms are too variable or unpredictable or because you do not have symptoms most of the time, the rules on substantial risk (see p95) might still help you to qualify for LCW or LCWRA.

Example

Shane has depression and sometimes has suicidal thoughts. He typically has two bad days a week, when he cannot start and finish tasks, go out or interact with others at all. On other days, he can sometimes do these things, but with difficulty and not repeatedly throughout the day. Sometimes, having to do these things makes Shane exhausted, and distressed and makes it difficult for him to manage his suicidal thoughts. When assessing his capability for work, all of this must be taken into account when considering what he can do 'the majority of the time'. An assessor cannot simply conclude that Shane is fit for work because he has more good days than bad. It would also be appropriatefor the DWP to consider whether work or work-related activity poses a 'substantial risk' to his health.

Sophie has a long-term mental health condition. When her symptoms first began, she was not well enough to work. Over time, she got used to managing her symptoms and found the support she needed to make work possible again. This cycle might happen multiple times during Sophie's life as her mental health changes, as she starts and finishes different treatments, and as her other circumstances change.

Physical health activities

The first 10 activities in the WCA only apply to you if your difficulties are due to a physical health condition or are the side effect of treatment for a physical health condition.[60] You cannot score points for any of these activities based solely on a mental health problem.

The activities are listed here. See CPAG's *Welfare Benefits Handbook* for the points and descriptors.

Physical health activities

1. Physical mobility
2. Standing and sitting
3. Reaching
4. Picking things up and moving them
5. Manual dexterity
6. Making yourself understood
7. Understanding communication
8. Navigating and staying safe
9. Continence
10. Consciousness during waking moments

When mental health affects physical health

Mental and physical health are closely related. Mental health problems can cause physical symptoms like fatigue, nausea, pain or weakness. Mental health medications can also have physical side effects (see p23).

However, physical symptoms which are the result of a mental health problem, or a side effect of mental health medication, can score you points under the headings above *only* if they can be classed as a 'specific bodily disease or disablement' in their own right.

Mental health activities

You can satisfy descriptors in the second part of the WCA if your difficulties result from a 'specific mental illness or disablement', or if they are a side effect of treatment for a 'specific mental illness or disablement'.[61] In the latter case, the treatment must be provided by a registered medical practitioner.

A 'specific mental illness or disablement' is not defined. It is likely to cover a wide range of mental health conditions and symptoms. You do not need a diagnosis, but having one is useful as evidence of your difficulties. If you do not have a diagnosis, it is particularly important to provide other supporting evidence (see Chapter 16).

Note: if you are concerned that you do not score enough points in these categories to qualify for LCW or LCWRA (see p83), remember that you might also qualify if work or work-related activity presents a substantial risk to your health (see p95). There is no question on the UC50 form that asks you about this, so you should use the blank 'Other information' page at the end (or extra sheets of paper) to provide details.

Activity 11: learning tasks

Take note if you have difficulty with: memory; concentration. See pp13–23 for more mental health symptoms that might be relevant.

This is about your ability to learn new tasks. The specified tasks are just examples. If you cannot repeat a task or have to be shown how to do it again, you have not learned it. Guidance suggests that a task with one or two steps is considered 'simple', and a task with three or four steps is 'moderately complex'.[62] Remember the assessor must consider both your mental health problem and the side effects of any medication you take, as well as whether you can do these tasks consistently.

Descriptors and points

(a) Cannot learn how to complete a simple task, such as setting an alarm clock.	15 points*
(b) Cannot learn anything beyond a simple task, such as setting an alarm clock.	9 points
(c) Cannot learn anything beyond a moderately complex task, such as the steps involved in operating a washing machine to clean clothes.	6 points
(d) None of the above applies.	0 points

If you satisfy the 15-point descriptor (a*), you qualify as having LCWRA.

What the form asks

Can you learn how to do an everyday task such as setting an alarm clock? No/ Yes/It varies

Before ticking any box, think about other simple tasks that involve one or two steps. Examples in the DWP's guidance include using basic functions on a TV remote or brushing teeth. Tick 'no' if you cannot learn to do new tasks of this level of complexity for the majority of the time. If your ability changes, tick 'it varies' and explain how often you could learn basic tasks like this. Could you do it repeatedly on the same day? Only on good days, and if so, how often are these? Unpredictably, or only under certain conditions?

Can you learn how to do a more complicated task such as using a washing machine? No/Yes/It varies
Other moderately complex activities to consider before answering this question could include learning to use a microwave, playing a simple computer game or following the steps to make a cup of tea. If you cannot reliably learn tasks like these for the majority of the time, tick 'no'. If your ability varies, describe the pattern – how often you can manage such tasks, and what affects your ability to learn or retain them.

Activity 12: awareness of hazards

Take note if you have difficulty with: attention; concentration; impulse control; insight into your own difficulties. See pp13–23 for more mental health symptoms that might be relevant.

This activity covers 'awareness of everyday hazards (such as boiling water or sharp objects)'. The term 'everyday hazards' is likely to cover road safety, electrical safety and caring for children or pets, but does not cover risks arising in social situations, such as the risk of being taken advantage of because of your condition.[63]

A wide range of symptoms may apply here – eg, symptoms of depression or psychosis that significantly reduce your attention and concentration. This section might also be relevant if you experience self-harm or some types of impulsive behaviour, or if mental health medication reduces your awareness of hazards. However, the official guidance says that someone is unlikely to score points for this activity because of an anxiety disorder.[64] The same guidance states that if you are aware that an activity poses a risk due to your condition and you avoid doing it, you cannot score points in this category.

It may be difficult to answer this question yourself. It is hard for someone to know if they have a reduced awareness of risks, particularly if they experience a lack of insight as part of a mental health problem. Consider speaking to someone you trust and who knows you well about this section.

Descriptors and points

(a) Reduced awareness of everyday hazards leads to a significant risk of: (i) injury to self or others; *or* (ii) damage to property or possessions, such that the claimant requires supervision for the majority of the time to maintain safety.	15 points*
(b) Reduced awareness of everyday hazards leads to a significant risk of: (i) injury to self or others; *or* (ii) damage to property or possessions, such that the claimant frequently requires supervision to maintain safety.	9 points

(c) Reduced awareness of everyday hazards leads to a significant risk of: 6 points
(i) injury to self or others; *or*
(ii) damage to property or possessions,
such that the claimant occasionally requires supervision to maintain safety.
(d) None of the above applies. 0 points

If you satisfy the 15-point descriptor (a*), you qualify as having LCWRA.

What the form asks

Please tick this box if you can stay safe when doing everyday tasks such as boiling water or using sharp objects.
If you tick this box, you will usually score 0 points. Before doing so, think about other activities that are relevant, like road safety, driving, electrical safety, other kitchen hazards and taking care of children or pets.

Do you need someone to stay with you for most of the time to stay safe? No/Yes/It varies
Tick 'yes' if you think you need this supervision, whether or not you actually get it. When explaining your answer, include all risks, even if they seem unlikely or only happen occasionally. It is a good idea to get your answers checked by someone who knows you well, like a family member or friend.

Activity 13: starting and finishing tasks

Take note if you have difficulty with: motivation; mental fatigue; decisiveness; concentration; memory; hallucinations; compulsions. See pp13–23 for more mental health symptoms that might be relevant.

This activity covers 'initiating and completing personal action (which means planning, organisation, problem solving, prioritising or switching tasks)'. Guidance states that this category is intended to reflect the kinds of difficulties faced by people with psychosis, obsessive compulsive disorder or depressive illnesses that result in apathy or severe mental fatigue, as well as the side effects of medication.[65] This category can still be relevant even if you do not have one of these diagnoses.

There is no definition of 'personal action', but it covers everyday tasks like cooking, dressing, washing and brushing your teeth, planning a simple meal, managing finances and attending appointments.[66] You must be able to carry out the personal action reliably and effectively. In one piece of caselaw, someone with obsessive compulsive disorder who took a long time to complete at least two actions was found not to be able to complete them effectively.[67] In an example in the guidance, someone experiencing a period of mania that led them to spend a large amount of money on impulse purchases, leaving no money for essentials, was considered not to be initiating effective personal action. This is despite the fact that they were able to wash and dress themselves independently in preparation for going shopping.

Descriptors and points

(a) Cannot, due to impaired mental function, reliably initiate or complete at least two sequential personal actions.	15 points*
(b) Cannot, due to impaired mental function, reliably initiate or complete at least two sequential personal actions for the majority of the time.	9 points
(c) Frequently cannot, due to impaired mental function, reliably initiate or complete at least two sequential personal actions.	6 points
(d) None of the above applies.	0 points

If you satisfy the 15-point descriptor (a*), you qualify as having LCWRA.

What the form asks

Please tick this box if you can manage to do daily tasks without difficulty. If you tick this box, you are likely to score 0 points. Before ticking it, think about planning, organisation, problem solving, prioritising and switching tasks. If you cannot do all of these things for the majority of the time, do not tick the box.

Can you manage to plan, start and finish daily tasks? Never/Sometimes/It varies

This question may have a long and detailed answer. Use extra sheets of paper as needed. It may also be useful to keep a diary (or for someone who helps you to keep a diary) for a week or longer, describing the activities you attempt and your difficulties, and to attach a copy of this diary to the form. Be clear about whether you can switch between tasks, organise your day or stay focused. Mention any support you need, even if you do not currently receive it.

Activity 14: coping with change

Take note if you experience: stress; anxiety; panic attacks; obsessions or compulsions. See pp13–23 for more mental health symptoms that might be relevant.

Official guidance says that this activity is about your ability to deal with changes in routine, whether temporary or permanent, and that the difficulties described might usually be experienced by people with obsessive compulsive disorder, severe anxiety or psychotic illness, although you do not need a specific diagnosis.[68] Inability to cope could be indicated by a number of responses, including stress reactions and the need for another person to intervene.[69]

The guidance suggests that if you manage to attend an assessment centre alone and cope with the assessment, you are unlikely to score points in this category.

Descriptors and points

(a) Cannot cope with any change to the extent that day-to-day life cannot be managed.	15 points*
(b) Cannot cope with minor planned change (such as a pre-arranged change to the routine time scheduled for a lunch break), to the extent that, overall, day-to-day life is made significantly more difficult.	9 points
(c) Cannot cope with minor unplanned change (such as the timing of an appointment on the day it is due to occur), to the extent that, overall, day-to-day life is made significantly more difficult.	6 points
(d) None of the above applies.	0 points

If you satisfy the 15-point descriptor (a*), you qualify as having LCWRA.

What the form asks

Can you cope with small changes to your routine if you know about them before they happen? For example, things like having a meal earlier or later than usual, or an appointment time being changed. No/Yes/It varies
Before answering 'yes' to this question, first think about what coping means for you. How might you feel and act? How would a change affect the next part of (or the rest of) your day? Can you deal with more than one change in a day? Would the answer be different on good and bad days? Try to explain this in your written answer. Remember to include situations relevant to you and not just the examples given.

Can you cope with small changes to your routine if they are unexpected? This means things like your bus or train not running on time, or a friend or carer coming to your house earlier or later than planned. No/Yes/It varies
Other examples to consider before answering this question might include an appointment being cancelled or moved at short notice, or products being out of stock at the supermarket.

Activity 15: getting about

Take note if you experience: agoraphobia; anxiety; panic attacks; lack of motivation. See pp13–23 for more mental health symptoms that might be relevant.

This activity is about how your mental health affects your ability to go out, rather than physical health reasons. For the purposes of the descriptors below, 'another person' means someone aged 16 or over.[70] 'Being accompanied by another person' includes taking a taxi or having a lift from a friend,[71] but you are unlikely to be seen as 'accompanied' if it is by a bus driver. You are unlikely to score points if, after being dropped off, you can navigate to a further destination alone – eg, an unfamiliar department in a large hospital.[72] If you need someone with you, but do not have anyone reliably available, then as well as you scoring points for this activity, a decision maker should consider whether work or work-related activity poses a 'substantial risk' to your health (see p95).[73]

Descriptors and points

(a) Cannot get to any place outside the claimant's home with which the claimant is familiar.	15 points
(b) Is unable to get to a specified place with which the claimant is familiar, without being accompanied by another person.	9 points
(c) Is unable to get to a specified place with which the claimant is unfamiliar without being accompanied by another person.	6 points
(d) Neither of the above applies.	0 points

You cannot qualify as having LCWRA on the basis of this activity (getting about) even if you satisfy the 15-point descriptor.

What the form asks

Can you leave home and go out to places you know? No/Yes, if someone goes with me/It varies

Do not tick 'yes(...)' unless this applies for the majority of the time. When writing your answer, consider your ability to go to a range of familiar places that a person might reasonably need to visit (eg, shops, GP surgery, dentist or bank), not just the ones you actually manage to go to. If you struggle with some but not all familiar locations, try to explain why.

Can you leave home and go out to places you do not know? No/Yes, if someone goes with me/It varies

Again, do not tick 'yes(...)' unless this applies most of the time. If you manage to do this sometimes, but do not think you could for the majority of the time, try to explain this – eg, if you can only make such journeys on occasional good days, with extra medication, and/or when you have an urgent reason. Consider giving examples of times when you have attempted to go out and were unsuccessful.

Activity 16: coping with social engagement

Take note if you experience: anxiety; low mood; agoraphobia; panic attacks; psychosis. See pp13–23 for more mental health symptoms that might be relevant.

This activity is about difficulties 'coping with social engagement due to cognitive impairment or mental disorder'. Your ability to engage with others must be restricted due to 'difficulty relating to others or significant distress'. Guidance suggests that relevant conditions might include anxiety, depression, agoraphobia, personality disorder and psychosis, but you do not need a diagnosis for your symptoms to be considered.[74] The same guidance is clear that being able to engage socially some of the time or in some specific contexts will not necessarily stop you from scoring points, and that social situations where you need to be accompanied by another person should be disregarded completely.

'Always' in the descriptor does not mean 24 hours a day, seven days a week. If you are only able engage very rarely, and even then with extreme difficulty and because you have little or no choice, then a decision maker should find that you are 'always precluded' from engaging in social contact. [75]

This activity is ultimately supposed to be a test of your ability to engage with others in a working environment, so the quality of your social contact is as important as the frequency. A decision maker should consider factors such as conversational give-and-take, initiation and response.[76]

The decision maker is not limited to looking at face-to-face contact: phone and online social contact are also considered.

If you attend an assessment, the assessor might make informal observations of your social interaction – eg, your ability to make eye contact and respond to questions, your expression, and any visible symptoms like shaking or sweating. The observations are very limited evidence of your ability to engage in social contact. If it has taken preparation, reassurance or extra medication for you to be able to cope at an assessment, say so – ideally at the start or end of the assessment. If you are experiencing suicidal thoughts or self-harm urges, mention them, even if they are not externally visible.

Descriptors and points

(a) Engagement in social contact is always precluded due to difficulty relating to others or significant distress experienced by the claimant.	15 points*
(b) Engagement in social contact with someone unfamiliar to the claimant is always precluded due to difficulty relating to others or significant distress experienced by the claimant.	9 points
(c) Engagement in social contact with someone unfamiliar to the claimant is not possible for the majority of the time due to difficulty relating to others or significant distress experienced by the claimant.	6 points
(d) None of the above applies.	0 points

If you satisfy the 15-point descriptor (a*), you qualify as having LCWRA.

What the form asks

Can you meet people you know without feeling too anxious or scared? No/ Yes/It varies

The question asks about meeting people, but the legal test is about engaging with them. For example, if you are able to sit near someone you know or start a video call but cannot maintain a conversation or respond appropriately, you should explain this clearly. Similarly, the question refers to feeling 'anxious or scared', but these are not the only feelings that are relevant for the legal test – do you feel overwhelmed, detached, panicked, or have other intense emotional reactions? Explain your own feelings in detail. Answer 'no' to this question if you can only engage with familiar people rarely, with extreme difficulty, and because you have little or no choice.

Can you meet people you do not know without feeling too anxious or scared? No/Yes/It varies
All of the points above apply. Mention whether you need to be accompanied by another person to do this, some or all of the time. If you can only engage with unfamiliar people in very specific contexts, explain this too. Be as detailed as possible, especially if you need support, medication or advanced preparation to manage any social interaction at all.

Activity 17: appropriateness of behaviour

Take note if you experience: psychosis; behavioural problems; substance use issues. See pp13–23 for more mental health symptoms that might be relevant.

This activity covers 'appropriateness of behaviour with other people, due to cognitive impairment or mental disorder'. It is enough that there is a mental health problem at the root of your behaviour; it does not have to be diagnosed. However, being disinhibited or angry without an underlying mental health problem is not enough to score points. The key word here is 'uncontrollable': the assessor will consider whether you can realistically manage or prevent your actions. Psychosis is likely to be relevant. Alcohol abuse does not count by itself, but if you are assessed as having alcohol (or drug) *dependency*, the consequences for your behaviour must be considered.[77]

All the descriptors look at whether you have 'uncontrollable episodes of aggressive or disinhibited behaviour which would be unreasonable in any workplace'. The behaviour could include physical action, but also significant verbal aggression.[78]

It is unclear whether emotional responses like uncontrollable tearfulness are 'disinhibited behaviour'. If this is something you experience, consider the other activities above and the 'substantial risk' route (see p95).

Descriptors and points

(a) Has, on a daily basis, uncontrollable episodes of aggressive or disinhibited behaviour that would be unreasonable in any workplace.	15 points*
(b) Frequently has uncontrollable episodes of aggressive or disinhibited behaviour that would be unreasonable in any workplace.	9 points

(c) Occasionally has uncontrollable episodes of aggressive or disinhibited behaviour that would be unreasonable in any workplace. 6 points

(d) None of the above applies. 0 points

If you satisfy the 15-point descriptor (a*), you qualify as having LCWRA.

What the form asks

Please tick this box if your behaviour does not upset other people.

Only tick this box if your behaviour would be reasonable in a typical workplace. If the people you see regularly are not upset by your behaviour because they know you well, this does not mean you need to tick the box. Likewise, if you do not see other people, and therefore have not had the chance to upset anyone, that does not mean you need to tick the box.

How often do you behave in a way which upsets other people? Every day/ Frequently/Occasionally/It varies

This question is about behaviour that would be unreasonable in an average workplace. The DWP guidance uses the example of a call centre. If your behaviour would be seen as aggressive, disinhibited or upsetting in that kind of setting, you should make that clear. It might help to have someone who knows you well check your answer to this question.

Eating and drinking

There are two further assessment categories, related to eating and drinking. You do not score points for these activities, but if one of the descriptors applies to you, you are automatically considered to have LCWRA.

Only descriptors (c) and (d) in each activity refer to mental health. They are relevant if you:

- limit your food intake – eg, some forms of anorexia, food phobia, delusions or hallucinations around food; *or*
- fail to eat unprompted – eg, due to depression, periods of mania, or strong negative symptoms of schizophrenia.

However, the wording of the descriptors means that they do not apply to many other mental health problems relating to food and weight – eg, binge-eating or purging. If your difficulties do not fit the descriptors, consider other point-scoring activities in the WCA, and the rules on substantial risk (see p95). For more information about eating difficulties, see p16.

1. Conveying food or drink to your mouth

You qualify as having LCWRA if:

(a) you cannot convey food or drink to your own mouth without receiving physical assistance from someone else; *or*

(b) you cannot convey food or drink to your own mouth without repeatedly stopping or experiencing breathlessness or severe discomfort; *or*

(c) you cannot convey food or drink to your own mouth without receiving regular prompting given by someone else in your physical presence; *or*

(d) owing to a severe disorder of mood or behaviour, you fail to convey food or drink to your own mouth without receiving:

(i) physical assistance from someone else; *or*

(ii) regular prompting given by someone else in your presence.

2. Chewing or swallowing food or drink

You qualify as having LCWRA if:

(a) you cannot chew or swallow food or drink; *or*

(b) you cannot chew or swallow food or drink without repeatedly stopping, experiencing breathlessness or severe discomfort; *or*

(c) you cannot chew or swallow food or drink without repeatedly receiving regular prompting given by someone else in your presence; *or*

(d) owing to a severe disorder of mood or behaviour, you fail to:

(i) chew or swallow food or drink; *or*

(ii) chew or swallow food or drink without regular prompting given by someone else in your presence.

Substantial risk

Note: these rules apply to both UC and ESA.

If you do not meet any of the points-scoring descriptors in this chapter, you can still be found to have LCW or LCWRA in some circumstances.

- You will be found to have **LCW** if, because of your health condition or disability, there would be a substantial risk to the mental or physical health of any person were you to be found not to have LCW.[79] The substantial risk is one that could arise from the sort of work you may be expected to do, although it is not necessary to go into the detail of individual job descriptions. Substantial risk will not be accepted if any risk could be significantly reduced by reasonable adjustments in your workplace, or by your taking medication prescribed by your doctor (unless not taking your medication is itself a symptom of your condition).[80]

- You will be found to have **LCWRA** if, because of your health condition or disability, there would be a substantial risk to your mental or physical health or to the mental or physical health of someone else if you were found not to have LCWRA.[81] Regarding work, the same considerations apply as in the point above. Regarding work-related activity, you should explain why activities like training, work-focused interviews or CV writing might present a substantial risk to your mental health. If you appeal about this rule, the First-tier Tribunal should be given a list of the types of work-related activity available in your area, indicating the most and least difficult, and which activities the DWP says that you can do without substantial risk.[82]

When explaining the risk, mention:
- the immediate effects of performing an activity – how does stress, pressure or confrontation make you feel right away? For example, the stress response that might result from being required to attend a job interview or appointments at the job centre;[83] *and*
- the cumulative effects – does regular effort, expectation or stress worsen your mental health over time;[84] *and*
- the risks that would follow from not complying with the requirement – what happens if you are pressured to comply with activity or punished for not complying?

A decision maker should also consider the risks of the *journey* to or from work, job interviews or the job centre.[85] They should not ignore the effects of a journey to *work* based on the possibility that you might find a job where you can work from home. However, they *will* consider whether *work-related activities* can be done from home.[86]

Example

Grace has post-traumatic stress disorder directly related to a traumatic experience in a former workplace. She does not generally struggle with tasks at home or in safe environments, but exposure to workplaces or commuting severely worsens her symptoms. She has avoided these places to decrease her symptoms, and since stopping work, she has been able to manage her mental health well. She does not score many points for any of the WCA activities because she does not have major difficulties with any activity for 'the majority of the time'. Her symptoms are environment-triggered, not constant. In her application, she describes how the workplace triggers her symptoms, and she cannot work when experiencing them. She explains that these symptoms have caused her to self-harm in the past. Despite Grace's low points score, the DWP accepts that the workplace environment would pose a substantial risk to her mental health, which could not simply be managed through reasonable adjustments by her employer. She is found to have LCW.

Treated as having limited capability for work

Note: these rules apply to UC only. For the rules for ESA, see p58.

You are sometimes treated as having LCW without having to go through a new WCA. For UC, this applies if:[87]

- you have already been assessed as having LCW for new-style ESA; *or*
- you are transferring to UC from old-style ESA and you were in the work-related activity group for ESA (see p98). Similar rules apply if you have been getting national insurance (NI) credits for LCW;[88] *or*
- you are at least pension age and get adult disability living allowance (adult DLA), Scottish adult disability living allowance (SADLA); personal independence payment (PIP) or adult disability payment (ADP); *or*
- you have recieved official notice not to work due to contact with an infectious disease; *or*
- you are an inpatient in hospital, or are recovering from treatment as an inpatient (and the DWP is satisfied that your condition remains sufficiently serious), including if you are attending a residential rehabilitation for drug or alcohol addiction; *or*
- you are receiving plasmapheresis, weekly haemodialysis for chronic renal failure, or weekly treatment for total parenteral nutrition for severe gut problems, or are recovering from such treatment; *or*
- you have life-threatening disease that is an uncontrolled or uncontrollable.

Treated as having limited capability for work and work-related activity

Note: these rules apply to UC only. For the rules for ESA, see p59.

You are sometimes treated as having LCWRA without having to go through a new WCA. For UC, this applies if:[89]

- you have already been assessed as having LCWRA for new-style ESA; *or*
- you are transferring to UC from old-style ESA and you were entitled to the support component in your ESA (see p98) (similar rules apply if you have been getting NI credits for LCWRA);[90] *or*
- you have reached pension age and are entitled to attendance allowance or pension age disability payment, the highest rate of the DLA/SADLA care component or the enhanced rate of the daily living component of PIP or ADP; *or*
- you are regarded as being terminally ill – ie, you have a progressive illness and it would not be a surprise to your doctors were you to die from it within the next 12 months. This can apply if there are also realistic hopes that you may live longer than that; *or*
- you are receiving chemotherapy or radiotherapy treatment for cancer, or are recovering from that treatment, or you are likely to receive such treatment

within six months, *and* the DWP is satisfied that your cancer treatment has side effects which are likely to limit your ability to do work-related activity; *or*

- you are pregnant and there is a serious risk to your health or to your baby's health if you do not refrain from work and work-related activity.

Are you transferring to universal credit from employment and support allowance?

If you were getting old-style ESA and were in the work-related activity group or support group, but then claim UC, you automatically have LCW or LCWRA so long as there was no gap between your ESA stopping and your UC starting.[91] (See p79 for more information about moving to UC.)

It is not uncommon for the DWP to overlook this rule. If this affects you, do the following.

- Quote the rules.
- If necessary, challenge the decision on your UC entitlement through a mandatory reconsideration request (see p294).
- Point out that if you were getting the support component in your ESA, the LCWRA element should be included in your UC from your first monthly assessment period.[92]
- Point out that, if you were getting the work-related activity component in your ESA and had been for long enough (see p70), the LCW element should be included in your UC from your first monthly assessment period.[93]
- Remember that, despite these rules, the DWP can still choose to reassess you after your UC starts. It is usually still worth getting your status carried over from ESA as this will affect your work-related requirements, your 'work allowance' (see p74), and possibly your UC amount, while you are waiting for reassessment.

Get independent advice if you need help with any of this, or if you are uncertain whether it applies to you.

Treated as *not* having limited capability for work or work-related activity

Note: these rules apply to UC only. For the rules for ESA, see p60.

In some circumstances, you are treated as *not* having limited capability for work or work-related activity (ie, you are treated as **fit for work**) without this being determined in the normal way through a WCA.

For UC, this applies if:[94]

- you previously failed a WCA, either for UC or for new-style ESA, and you ask to be assessed again (this applies unless the previous decision was made in ignorance of, or based on a mistake about, a material fact, or there has been a relevant change in your condition); *or*
- you do not return the UC50 questionnaire or attend an assessment and do not have good reason (see p82) for this; *or*

- you work, earning above a certain threshold[95] and you are not getting a specified disability benefit.

5. Decisions

If you have an online universal credit (UC) account, decision letters should be uploaded there. If you have a non-digital account, you should be sent decision letters by post.

Work capability decisions

The decision on whether you have capability for work may, in practice, be made between four and eight weeks after you attend a work capability assessment (WCA). There are three possible work capability decisions:

- that you are **fit for work**; *or*
- that you have **limited capability for work** (LCW); *or*
- that you have **limited capability for work and work-related activity** (LCWRA).

There is more information about these outcomes on p80.

If you are found fit for work

If a decision is made that you are fit for work (either following a WCA or automatically under the rules on p98), and you disagree with the decision, you can challenge it by making a mandatory reconsideration request and then appealing against the decision if necessary (see Chapter 20). Note that there are deadlines for appealing decisions.

You can continue to get UC while challenging a decision. However, if you have been found fit for work, you are usually placed in the UC **all work-related requirements group**, which means that you must look for work and engage with work-related requirements. There is more information about work-related requirements on pp270–73.

If you are found to have limited capability for work

If the DWP decides that you have LCW, but you believe you should have been awarded LCWRA, you can challenge this decision. It is usually best to get advice before challenging this kind of decision, as a new decision maker (or the tribunal) will look at the whole decision again and may decide that you are fit for work.

For information about work-related requirements if you have been found to have LCW, see p270.

Length of awards

Awards of UC are not fixed term. Your work capability is usually reassessed at a future point (see p103). You cannot appeal a decision about how often you are reassessed, but you may be able to challenge it through judicial review (see p311).

Decisions about your entitlement

A decision that you are not eligible for universal credit

After making a new claim for UC, you may receive a decision that you are not eligible for UC because you do not meet the non-health-related conditions listed on p68 – eg, about your education status, your right to reside or your capital. You can challenge this decision by mandatory reconsideration and appeal (see Chapter 20), providing further evidence if necessary.

'Claim closure', suspension and termination

After making a new claim for UC, you might receive a decision saying that your claim has been 'closed' because you did not attend an initial interview or provide requested information. You can challenge this decision through a mandatory reconsideration request and appeal (see Chapter 20).

After an award of UC has been made, it can be terminated in certain circumstances, after a period of suspension, if you have not provided requested information.[96] Again, you can challenge the decision – eg, if you do not agree that you failed to provide the relevant information.

Monthly payment statement

Your monthly UC payment statement shows how the DWP has calculated your UC entitlement for that period. If you have an online UC account, you can view the statement in the 'Payments' section. If you have a non-digital account, the statement should be sent by post. If you disagree with the DWP's calculation, you can challenge its decision through a mandatory reconsideration request and appeal (see Chapter 20).

Other decisions

While getting UC, you are likely to receive a range of other decisions, including:

- work coach decisions about your work-related requirements (see p270). (These decisions are not appealable but you may be able to challenge them through a complaint or judicial review – see Chapter 20); *and*
- overpayment decisions (overpayments are not within the scope of this book – see CPAG's *Welfare Benefits Handbook* for information).

6. Getting paid

When you are paid

Universal credit (UC) is normally paid monthly, in arrears, seven days after the end of an assessment period.[97] If the payment date falls on a Saturday, Sunday or bank holiday, it is brought forward. You can check the dates and details of your payments on your online UC account, or you should be sent monthly statements by post if you have a non-digital account.

If budgeting is difficult, you can request more frequent payments under an alternative payment arrangement (see p102). If you live in Scotland, you can be paid twice monthly as a matter of course.[98]

In practice, it can take about **five weeks** after claiming to receive your first payment, but it may take longer. If you are in financial need while waiting, you may be able to get a repayable advance payment of UC. See CPAG's *Welfare Benefits Handbook* for more information.

A lump sum of UC arrears (ie, back pay) may be paid to you in instalments, with your consent, if this is necessary to protect your interests.[99]

Note: it is possible for payment of UC to be suspended (see p104).

Where your payment goes

The default is that all your UC, including any amount to cover rent, is paid into your bank account.

Couples

If you are in a couple, you usually receive a single UC payment. You can decide whose bank account this goes into. The DWP can decide that the other partner should be paid instead or can split the payments between you (see p102) if it considers this to be in either partner's interests or in the interests of a child or someone you care for.[100]

Third parties

All or part of your UC can be paid to another person on your behalf if the DWP considers this is necessary to protect your interests (see p102).[101] This is often described as an 'alternative payment arrangement' and is *not* the same as a 'third-party deduction' (see p75).

Relevant third parties could include an appointee (see p325), a trusted friend or family member, or your landlord.

Managed payment to landlord

An example of part of your UC being paid to a third party on your behalf could be having your rent paid directly by the DWP to your landlord, often known as a 'managed payment to landlord' (MPTL). In England and Wales, this must be necessary to protect your interests, or you must have a certain amount of arrears,[102] but in Scotland, anyone can request an MPTL regardless of their circumstances.[103]

You can request an MPTL by putting a message in your journal or calling the UC section of the DWP. Alternatively, your landlord can request it, normally using an online form.

No bank account

You can ask to have your UC paid into a trusted third party's bank account (eg, a friend or family member) or you can ask to be considered for the DWP's payment exception service.[104] The DWP must agree that this protects your interests.

Alternative payment arrangements

Alternative payment arrangements (APAs) for UC are special payment options the DWP can approve to help you manage your finances. These include:

- more regular payments (see p101);
- payments being split between couples (see p101);
- all or part of your UC being paid to a third party (see p101).

Reasons to consider an alternative payment arrangement

You might consider an APA to make your payments more regular if, because of your mental health problem, you are finding it difficult to budget for monthly payments. You might consider a third-party APA if, for example, there is a risk that you will not manage to pay your rent reliably unless it goes straight to your landlord, or because you want a trusted family member to look after your UC income, because your condition makes it difficult for you to manage money.

Getting an alternative payment arrangement

The DWP can usually make an APA when it considers this to be in your or your partner's interests, or (in some cases) in the interests of your dependent child or of a person you receive the carer element of UC for looking after.[105] An APA can be set up at any point, not just at the start of a claim. You can request it by calling the UC helpline, by letter or by using your online UC account. If the APA involves your landlord, they can request it (see p101).

When deciding whether to make an APA, the DWP splits claimants into two tiers: tier one is for those with circumstances with a 'highly likely or probable need' for APAs and tier two for those with 'less likely or possible need'. You are in tier one if you have a mental health problem, including drug, alcohol or other addiction problems.[106]

Example journal entry for alternative payment arrangement request

'Hello, I am requesting an alternative payment arrangement due to my mental health problem. I have difficulty managing money and staying on top of bills and rent. I would like to receive payments fortnightly and have my rent paid directly to my landlord to prevent arrears. I have been advised that this is appropriate due to my tier one status under DWP guidelines. Please let me know what evidence is needed.'

Note: if you live in Scotland, you have more options for getting fortnightly UC payments (see p101) and getting UC paid directly to your landlord (see p101).

7. Reviews and reassessments

Your entitlement to universal credit (UC) can change after an award has been made. In certain circumstances, the DWP reviews your entitlement or reassesses you. This can lead to a supersession (see p292).

Work capability

If there has been a decision that you *do not* have limited capability for work (LCW), you are not reassessed, unless evidence suggests that the decision was made in ignorance of, or based on a mistake about, a material fact, or there has been a relevant change to your condition.[107]

If there has been a decision that you *do* have LCW (or limited capability for work-related activity – LCWRA), there are no rules about how often your work capability can be reassessed. Usually, the length of time before a reassessment is recommended by the original assessor. You may be reviewed sooner if you report an improvement or a deterioration in your condition. The DWP has stated that you will not be reassessed if you are assessed as having LCWRA, have a 'severe, lifelong' disability or condition, and are 'unlikely to ever be able to move into work'.[108]

Change of circumstances

You should report all changes in your circumstances to the UC section of the DWP as soon as possible. Do not assume that the UC section of the DWP already knows something – eg, about changes to the other DWP benefits you claim. You can report a change on your online journal, by letter or by calling the UC helpline. It can be preferable to report a change in writing so that there is a clear record of what you have said and when.

When you notify the DWP of a change of circumstances, it can change the decision on your UC entitlement, usually by supersession. A change that occurs (or is expected to occur) part way through an assessment period is usually treated as if it happened on the first day of the assessment period, meaning that your UC entitlement changes for the whole of that assessment period. However, there are some important exceptions.[109] There is more information about supersessions in Chapter 20.

Reaching pension age

If you are a **single** UC claimant and you reach pension age, your UC stops from the first day of the next assessment period.[110] You are likely to be eligible for pension credit (PC) and/or pension-age housing benefit (HB) from the date you reach pension age. You can claim PC up to four months before that date and you can claim HB from the start of your final UC assessment period – ie, the assessment period during which you reach pension age.[111]

You should receive a full month's UC for your final assessment period. Any PC or HB you receive for the same period should be ignored for the calculation of UC. Similarly, any UC payment should be ignored for the new PC or HB award.[112]

If you are in a **couple** claiming UC and one of you (but not the other) reaches pension age, your UC generally continues. In this situation, you are regarded as a 'mixed-age couple'. There is more information about mixed-age couples in CPAG's *Welfare Benefits Handbook*.

If you are in a mixed-age couple getting UC and the younger partner reaches pension age, your UC stops. The rules (including about claiming PC and pension-age HB) are the same as described above for single people.

Ongoing evidence requirement

After you have been awarded UC, you may be asked to provide further information about things like your housing costs or earnings, to confirm your ongoing eligibility. If you fail to provide this information or evidence when asked, your UC could be suspended or even terminated (see p100).

8. Universal credit and other benefits

Means-tested benefits

If you make a claim for universal credit (UC), you can no longer get income-related employment and support allowance (ESA). (UC has also replaced income support, income-based jobseeker's allowance (JSA) and tax credits). The same applies to working-age housing benefit (HB), except if you are living in specified or temporary accommodation (see p72). If you are in the limited group of people who can get UC alongside HB, your UC entitlement means you automatically qualify for maximum HB (see p122).

In Scotland, UC is a qualifying benefit for Scottish child payment.

Non-means-tested benefits

When you get UC you may be able to claim other benefits, and getting some other benefits may mean you receive more UC.

- You can get new-style JSA or contributory ESA as well as UC. These are taken into account in full as income for UC (and so reduce your UC entitlement) but it is generally still a good idea to claim them.
- You can claim other non-means-tested benefits at the same time as UC – eg, carer's allowance, child benefit, personal independence payment (PIP), adult disability payment (ADP) and statutory sick pay. Some are disregarded when working out your income for UC (see p75) but some reduce your UC entitlement pound for pound.
- Non-means-tested benefits can sometimes increase your UC. For example, if your child gets disability living allowance (DLA) or child disability payment (CDP), you may be entitled to a disabled child addition (see p71).

The benefit cap

In some cases, there is a limit on your total income from specified benefits (the 'benefit cap'). UC is one of the specified benefits. You are not subject to the benefit cap if you have limited capability for work-related activity for UC, or if you get certain other benefits – eg, if you get PIP, ADP, DLA, CDP or attendance allowance). See CPAG's *Welfare Benefits Handbook* for more details.

Other sources of financial help

If you qualify for UC, you may also be eligible for free prescriptions, council tax reduction and a range of other financial help. See Chapter 15.

Notes

1. **Who can get universal credit**
 1 ss3-5 WRA 2012
 2 s2 WRA 2012
 3 Reg 3 UC Regs; reg 9 UC,PIP,JSA&ESA(C&P) Regs
 4 Regs 88 and 97 UC Regs; paras J3160 and J3250-J3270 ADM

2. **The amount of benefit**
 5 Reg 36 UC Regs
 6 Regs 24-24B UC Regs
 7 s10 WRA 2012; reg 24A UC Regs
 8 Regs 29-30 UC Regs
 9 Regs 31-35 UC Regs
 10 s8 WRA 2012; Sch 2 paras 1, 4 and 7 UC(TP) Regs
 11 Regs 4 and 4A UC Regs
 12 Reg 5 UC Regs
 13 ESAUC(MA) Regs
 14 Reg 27(4) UC Regs
 15 Reg 27(4) UC Regs

16 DWP, Green Paper, *Pathways to Work: reforming benefits and support to get Britain working Green Paper*, March 2025; House of Commons, *Hansard*, col 21, 12 May 2025
17 Reg 28 UC Regs; reg 2 SS(ME) Regs. See the official guidance and example in para F5046 ADM.
18 Regs 19 and 21 UC(TP) Regs
19 Reg 24 UC Regs
20 s10(2) WRA 2012; regs 24 and 36 UC Regs
21 Sch 4 paras 25 and 26 UC Regs. See also lha-direct.voa.gov.uk for the current rates in your area.
22 Sch 4 paras 2 and 30 UC Regs
23 Sch 4 para 9(2) UC Regs
24 Sch 4 paras 13, 14(1), 22 and 33 UC Regs
25 Sch 4 para 16 UC Regs
26 Sch 4 para 15 UC Regs
27 Sch 1 paras 3A and 3B UC Regs
28 Sch 1 para 3A(3) and (6) UC Regs
29 Sch 1 para 3(h) and (i) UC Regs; reg 6(8) UC(TP) Regs; art 6(2) WRA(No.21)O; art 7(3) WRA(No.23)O
30 Reg 63 and Sch 2 UC(TP) Regs
31 Sch 2 para 6 UC(TP) Regs
32 Sch 2 para 2 UC(TP) Regs
33 Reg 62 UC Regs
34 Reg 22(1) UC Regs
35 Reg 22(2)-(3) UC Regs. See also reg 5A UC(TP) Regs if you are in temporary accommodation and therefore get HB instead of a UC housing costs element.
36 Reg 28(7) UC Regs
37 s60 and Sch 6 and 7 UC,PIP,JSA&ESA(C&P) Regs; regs 3 and 11 SS(OR) Regs; SS(PAB) Regs; DWP, *Find Out About Money Taken Off Your Universal Credit Payment*, 12 April 2021, at gov.uk/guidance/find-out-about-money-taken-off-your-universal-credit-payment

3. **Making a claim**
38 Reg 10(1)(a) and (b) and (2) UC,PIP,JSA&ESA(C&P) Regs
39 Reg 8 UC,PIP,JSA&ESA(C&P) Regs; DWP, *Universal Credit Guidance*, 'Non-digital relationships', v3.0, House of Commons library deposited papers, at rightsnet.org.uk/universal-credit-guidance
40 Reg 10(1)(c) and (d) and (2) UC,PIP,JSA&ESA(C&P) Regs
41 DWP, *Universal Credit Guidance*, 'Reasonable adjustments and alternative formats', v5.0, House of Commons library deposited papers, at rightsnet.org.uk/universal-credit-guidance
42 s98 WRA 2012; reg 32 UC,PIP,JSA&ESA(C&P) Regs; para A2048 ADM
43 Reg 26 UC,PIP,JSA&ESA(C&P) Regs; *AM v SSWP (UC)* [2022] UKUT 242 (AAC)
44 Regs 48-57 UC(TP) Regs
45 Regs 8(2A), 8A, 8B, 44, 46(1) and 47(2) UC(TP) Regs; reg 5 UC(MMP&MA) Regs

4. **How you are assessed**
46 DWP, Green Paper, *Pathways to Work*, March 2025, at gov.uk
47 Regs 40 and 41 UC Regs
48 Regs 2 and 5 SS(ME) Regs
49 DWP, *Universal Credit Guidance*, 'Health conditions and disabilities – day 1 to day 29', v14.0, House of Commons library deposited papers, at rightsnet.org.uk/universal-credit-guidance
50 **UC** Reg 43 UC Regs
ESA Reg 21 ESA Regs; reg 17 ESA Regs 2013
51 DWP, *Guidance: capability for work questionnaire*, disclosed to CPAG in response to freedom of information request FOI2022/102752, 6 January 2023
52 **UC** Reg 43 UC Regs
ESA Reg 22 ESA Regs; reg 18 ESA Regs 2013
53 Regs 24 and 39 ESA Regs; regs 20 and 36 ESA Regs 2013
54 DWP, *Universal Credit Guidance*, 'Complex needs overview', v18.0, House of Commons library deposited papers, at rightsnet.org.uk/universal-credit-guidance
55 **UC** Reg 44 UC Regs
ESA Regs 23 and 38 ESA Regs; regs 19 and 35 ESA Regs 2013
56 **UC** Reg 40 UC Regs
ESA Reg 34(2) ESA Regs; reg 30(2) ESA Regs 2013
57 *AF v SSWP (ESA)* [2011] UKUT 61 (AAC); *SAG v Department for Social Development (ESA)* [2011] NICom 171
58 CIB/14534/1996
59 CIB/2620/2000
60 **UC** Regs 39(4) and 40(3) UC Regs
ESA Regs 19(5) and 34(6) ESA Regs; regs 15(5) and 30(6) ESA Regs 2013

61 **UC** Regs 39(4) and 40(3) UC Regs
ESA Regs 19(5) and 34(6) ESA Regs; regs 15(5) and 30(6) ESA Regs 2013
62 DWP, *WCA Handbook*, para 3.5.2
63 *RR v SSWP (ESA)* [2018] UKUT 143 (AAC); *WCA Handbook*, para 3.5.3
64 DWP, *WCA Handbook*, para 3.5.3
65 DWP, *WCA Handbook*, para 3.5.4
66 *MP v SSWP (ESA)* [2015] UKUT 458 (AAC); *WCA Handbook*, para 3.5.4
67 *MW v SSWP (ESA)* [2014] UKUT 112 (AAC)
68 DWP, *WCA Handbook*, para 3.5.5
69 *GV v SSWP (ESA)* [2013] UKUT 405 (AAC)
70 DWP, *WCA Handbook*, para 3.5.6
71 *AB v SSWP (ESA)* [2016] UKUT 96 (AAC)
72 DWP, *WCA Handbook*, para 3.5.6
73 *ET v SSWP (UC)* [2021] UKUT 47 (AAC)
74 DWP, *WCA Handbook*, para 3.5.7
75 *LM v SSWP (ESA)* [2013] UKUT 552 (AAC); *WCA Handbook*, para 3.5.7
76 *JC v SSWP (ESA)* [2014] UKUT 352 (AAC), reported as [2015] AACR 6
77 DWP, *WCA Handbook*, para 3.5.8; *DR v SSWP (ESA)* [2014] UKUT 188 (AAC); reported as [2014] AACR 38
78 *WC v SSWP (ESA)* [2014] UKUT 363
79 **UC** Sch 8 para 4 UC Regs
ESA Reg 29 ESA Regs; reg 25 ESA Regs 2013
80 **UC** Sch 8 para 4(2) UC Regs
ESA Reg 29(3) ESA Regs; reg 25(2) ESA Regs 2013
81 **UC** Sch 9 para 4 UC Regs
ESA Reg 35 ESA Regs; reg 31 UC Regs 2013
82 *KS v SSWP (UC)* [2021] UKUT 132 (AAC)
83 *GS v SSWP (ESA)* [2014] UKUT 16 (AAC)
84 DWP, *WCA Handbook*, para 3.8
85 *Charlton v SSWP* [2009] EWCA Civ 42; *JW v SSWP* [2011] UKUT 416 (AAC); *ET v SSWP (UC)* [2021] UKUT 47 (AAC)
86 *SM v SSWP (ESA)* [2014] UKUT 241 (AAC); *CL v SSWP (ESA)* [2015] UKUT 375 (AAC)
87 Reg 39 and Sch 8 UC Regs
88 Regs 19(2) and 21(2) UC(TP) Regs
89 Reg 40 and Sch 9 UC Regs
90 Regs 19(4) and 21(4) UC(TP) Regs
91 Reg 19 UC(TP) Regs
92 Reg 19(4) UC(TP) Regs
93 Reg 19(2) UC(TP) Regs, with savings regarding pre-April 2017 as in the ESAUC(MA) Regs
94 Regs 41, 43 and 44 UC Regs
95 Reg 41(2) and (3) UC Regs

5. **Decisions**
96 Regs 44-47 UC,PIP,JSA&ESA(DA) Regs

6. **Getting paid**
97 Reg 47(2) UC,PIP,JSA&ESA(C&P) Regs
98 UC(CP)(S) Regs
99 Reg 47(6A) UC,PIP,JSA&ESA(C&P) Regs
100 Reg 47(6) UC,PIP,JSA&ESA(C&P) Regs
101 Reg 58 UC,PIP,JSA&ESA(C&P) Regs
102 DWP, *Alternative Payment Arrangements Guidance*, January 2024, at gov.uk
103 UC(CP)(S) Regs
104 See gov.uk/payment-exception-service
105 Regs 47 and 58 UC,PIP,JSA&ESA(C&P) Regs
106 DWP guidance, *Alternative Payment Arrangements*, 17 January 2024, at gov.uk

7. **Reviews and reassessments**
107 Reg 41(4) UC Regs
108 DWP, *Employment and Support Allowance and Universal Credit: changes to the work capability assessment from 29 September 2017*, September 2017
109 Sch 1 paras 20-33 UC,PIP,JSA&ESA(DA) Regs
110 Sch 1 para 26 UC,PIP,JSA&ESA(DA) Regs
111 Regs 4E and 13D SS(C&P) Regs; reg 6A(3) UC(TP) Regs
112 Reg 5(2)(c) UC(TP) Regs; Explanatory Memorandum to The Universal Credit (Persons who have attained state pension credit qualifying age) (Amendment) Regulations 2020 No.655

6

Chapter 6

Pension credit

This chapter covers:

Key facts

- Pension credit (PC) is a means-tested benefit for people who are at least pension age, including people with health conditions and disabilities.
- There are two types of PC: guarantee credit, which ensures you have a minimum level of income, and savings credit, which is intended to 'reward' you for financially preparing for your retirement. Savings credit is only paid if you reached state pension age before 6 April 2016.
- You do not need to have paid national insurance contributions to get PC.
- You can get PC while in or out of work and it can 'top up' state and other pensions.
- You can get PC alongside some other benefits, including housing benefit and disability benefits – eg, attendance allowance, personal independence payment or adult disability payment. Getting PC alongside a disability benefit can increase how much PC you get.
- You can challenge decisions about your eligibility for PC.
- Getting PC can mean that you are eligible for other kinds of financial support.

1. Who can get pension credit

Pension credit (PC) is a means-tested benefit for people on a low income who are at least pension age, which is currently 66 and rising to 67 between 2026 and 2028. To check your pension age, see gov.uk/state-pension-age. Unlike state pension (see p4), you do not have to have paid national insurance contributions to qualify for PC.

You can qualify for PC whether you are in or out of work, and whether or not you have a health condition or disability. There is no requirement to look for work in order to get PC.

There are two types of PC:

- **guarantee credit**, which ensures you have a minimum level of income; *and*
- **savings credit**, which is intended to reward you for making provision for your retirement, such as through savings or an occupational pension. Savings credit is being phased out.

You can be entitled to either guarantee credit, savings credit or both.

Who can get guarantee credit

You qualify for guarantee credit if:[1]

- you are at least pension age. (If you have a partner and make a new claim for PC, both of you must usually be pension age, but there are exceptions for some 'mixed-age couples', see p110);[2] *and*
- you are not a person subject to immigration control, although there are exceptions to this rule;[3] *and*
- you are in Great Britain (except for periods of temporary absence) and satisfy the habitual residence and right to reside tests;[4] *and*
- your partner (if you have one) is not entitled to PC;[5] *and*
- your income is below a certain amount (known as the 'appropriate minimum guarantee' – see p110).

Note: special rules can apply when you are in hospital or prison and in certain other situations. See Chapter 19 for more information.

Who can get savings credit

You can only qualify for savings credit if:[6]

- you and your partner (if you have one) reached pension age before 6 April 2016; *or*
- either you or your partner reached pension age before 6 April 2016, you were entitled to savings credit on 6 April 2016 and you have remained entitled to it.

There are further conditions to qualify for savings credit. See CPAG's *Welfare Benefits Handbook* for details.

Couples

If you are single, you claim PC for yourself. If you are a member of a couple and both you and your partner are pension age, either of you can claim PC for you both. This is not a joint claim, only one of you claims and is awarded the benefit. If you get guarantee credit, the award includes a couple allowance and premiums for both of you, and takes into account your combined income and capital (see below). If you get savings credit, this is calculated using couple rates and based on your combined income.

If you are a member of a couple and you are at least pension age but your partner is not (often called a '**mixed-age couple**'), you cannot usually qualify for PC.[7] There are some exceptions to this rule.[8] If you do not fall within one of the exceptions, you and your partner may be able to claim universal credit instead of PC. There is more information about mixed-age couples in CPAG's *Welfare Benefits Handbook*.

What advisers say: couples

'What counts as living as a couple is not always clear-cut, especially where one person is the carer for another. We sometimes see ex-spouses return to care for their ex-partner, or friends move in together, or we see long-standing couples remain together solely because of one person's disability but have no relationship other than carer/cared for. There is also a question about at what point an existing couple may need to have separate claims if one enters a care home (see p284). If in doubt, get independent advice.'

2. The amount of benefit

You can be entitled to either guarantee credit, savings credit or both types of pension credit (PC).

The amount of guarantee credit

Step 1: calculate your appropriate minimum guarantee

Your maximum amount of guarantee credit is known as the 'appropriate minimum guarantee' and is made up of a standard minimum guarantee and any relevant additional amounts.[9] The amounts below are weekly.

Standard minimum guarantee

Single person	£227.10
Couple	£346.60
Each additional spouse in a polygamous marriage	£119.50

Your appropriate minimum guarantee may be reduced in certain circumstances – eg, if you are in a couple and one of you is sectioned under the Mental Health Act 1983 (see p280).

Additional amounts

Severe disability	£82.90/£165.80 (if both partners qualify)
Carer	£46.40 (for each partner who qualifies – see p228)

You can also get amounts for a child or qualifying young person for whom you are responsible included in your PC.

First child born before 6 April 2017	£78.10
Each subsequent child	£67.42
Addition for child with disability	£36.54
Addition for child with severe disability	£114.12

A **transitional amount** may also be included if you were getting income support (IS), income-based jobseeker's allowance (JSA) or income-related employment and support allowance (ESA) immediately before you first became entitled to PC, to ensure you are not worse off as a result of moving to PC.[10] For information on transitional amounts for previous child tax credit claimants of pension age, see CPAG's *Welfare Benefits Handbook*.

Step 2: calculate your income

This is the amount you have coming in each week – eg, from benefits, state pensions, private pensions and earnings.[11] Some income is disregarded in part or in full. Benefits disregarded in full include personal independence payment (PIP), adult disability payment (ADP), attendance allowance (AA) and pension age disability payment (PADP). If you have more than £10,000 capital, you are treated as having income of £1 for every £500 (or part thereof) over £10,000.[12] For more information about how different kinds of income are treated for PC, see CPAG's *Welfare Benefits Handbook*.

Note: your partner's income and savings are taken into account, but the income and savings of others who live with you, such as adult children, are not.

Step 3: deduct income from appropriate minimum guarantee

The amount of your guarantee credit is your appropriate minimum guarantee (Step 1) minus any relevant income you have (Step 2).[13] If your income is above the appropriate minimum guarantee, you do not qualify for any guarantee credit. You may still qualify for savings credit.

Step 4: calculate your pension credit payment

Consider the effects of deductions[14] and alternative payment arrangements (see p114). These may further reduce the amount of PC you receive.

Examples

Stella (70) is single and gets AA. She lives alone and no one gets carer's allowance (CA), carer support payment or the UC carer element for looking after her. She lives in rented accommodation.

Step 1: her appropriate minimum guarantee is:

Standard minimum guarantee (single person rate) £227.10; *plus*

Severe disability additional amount £82.90

Total £310.00

Step 2: her relevant weekly income is her basic state pension of £176.45. AA is ignored as income.

Step 3: Stella's relevant weekly income of £176.45 is deducted from her appropriate minimum guarantee of £310.00, leaving her entitled to £133.55 guarantee credit. She is also entitled to maximum pension-age housing benefit (HB) and any other passported benefits that may apply (see p116).

Trevor (75) and Vince (77) are a couple. Sally (44), their niece, lives with them and gets CA and universal credit. Trevor gets the enhanced rate of the daily living component of PIP and Vince gets AA. They live in a home they own outright and they have pension income and savings.

Step 1: Trevor and Vince's appropriate minimum guarantee is £346.60. Their appropriate minimum guarantee does not include a severe disability addition because Sally lives with them. It does not include any carer additions because neither Trevor nor Vince is providing care for the other for 35 hours a week (see p228). However, they may be entitled to savings credit (see below).

Step 2: Trevor and Vince's joint weekly income for calculating PC is £380.15, made up of basic state pension of £282.15 (Trevor £105.70, Vince £176.45), occupational pension of £95, and £3 deemed income from £11,500 savings. PIP and AA are ignored as income.

Step 3: they are not entitled to any guarantee credit because their relevant income exceeds their appropriate minimum guarantee of £346.60.

The amount of savings credit

Savings credit is paid at a maximum weekly rate of £17.30 for a single person or £19.36 for a couple.[15] For how to calculate the amount of savings credit, see CPAG's *Welfare Benefits Handbook*.

3. Making a claim

Pension credit (PC) is administered and paid by the Pension Service, which is part of the DWP.

You can claim PC:[16]

- online at gov.uk/pension-credit/how-to-claim. The online service states that you must have already claimed your state pension;
- by phone. Call the Pension Service on 0800 99 1234 (textphone: 0800 169 0133; Relay UK and British Sign Language video relay services are available);
- on the approved form (Form PC1). You ask for the form by calling the number above, or you can print a copy from gov.uk/pension-credit/how-to-claim, or you can get it from a local authority housing benefit office. Keep a copy of your completed form, and if you are sending your form by post, ask the Post Office for free proof of posting.

What advisers say: Pension Service staff

'I have always found staff on the Pension Service telephone line to be especially helpful. They also have direct access to information about someone's state pension, which has been useful where the person does not have that information themselves.'

The date of claim is usually the date you start a claim by phone or submit it online. If you claim on a PC1 form:[17]

- if you requested a form from the Pension Service or from a local authority office, the date of claim is the date of your request, provided you return the completed form within one month (the Pension Service can can extend this one-month deadline if it considers this is reasonable, so if you return the form late, explain why); *or*
- otherwise (eg, if you return a form too late or if you printed your blank form from the internet) the date of claim is the date your completed form is received.

If the Pension Service asks for missing information, you usually have one month to provide it. If you do not, your claim may be rejected as invalid.

Claiming in advance and backdating

You can claim PC **in advance**, up to four months before the date on which you will qualify for it.[18]

You can ask that your claim for PC be **backdated** by up to three months if you met the qualifying conditions during that time. You do not need to have special reasons for backdating.[19] If you might have qualified for PC more than three months ago but did not claim because you were given wrong information or misled by the Pension Service or another part of the DWP, you could complain and ask for compensation (see p308).

Note: the term 'backdating' is often informally used to mean getting arrears of your benefit going back to a claim or decision date – eg, after winning an appeal. However, in this *Handbook*, we use backdating to mean getting paid benefit for a period before the date you claimed.

Additional support and appointees

If you have (or will have) difficulty with the claims process and need additional support, see Chapter 21. If you cannot manage the claims process at all, you may need an appointee (see p325).

4. How you are assessed

Your eligibility for pension credit (PC) is assessed using evidence about your income, capital and other circumstances. It is important that you provide any information required when you claim.

There is no health assessment for PC.

5. Decisions

Once your claim has been decided, you are sent a letter detailing the amount of any award, and the information on which it was based. You are asked to check this and report any omissions or changes. If you disagree with the decision, you can usually apply for a revision or supersession, or appeal against it. There are usually time limits for all of these options. See Chapter 20 for more information on challenging benefit decisions.

6. Getting paid

When you are paid

If you reached the qualifying age for pension credit (PC) on or after 6 April 2010, PC can be paid weekly, fortnightly or four-weekly in arrears. If you reached the qualifying age before 6 April 2010, you are usually paid weekly in advance.[20]

If you are waiting for a decision on your claim or you are waiting to be paid and you are in financial need, you may be able to get an advance loan of your PC.[21] This is called a 'short-term advance'.

If you are moving from universal credit to PC, see the rules on p104 about overlapping payments.

Note: it is possible for payment of PC to be suspended (see below).

Where your payment goes

PC is usually paid directly into your bank account. The DWP can pay all or part of your PC to someone else, if this is in your interests.[22] These 'alternative payment arrangements' might be useful if, for example, you want a trusted family member to look after your PC income because your mental health problem makes it difficult for you to manage money.

If you do not have a bank account, you can ask for your PC to be paid into someone else's account as above, or you can ask to be considered for the DWP's payment exception service.[23]

7. Reviews and reassessments

Change of circumstances

You should report all changes in your circumstances to the Pension Service as soon as possible. Do not assume that the Pension Service already knows something – eg, about changes to the other DWP benefits you claim, or about an occupational pension. You can report a change by phone but it may be better to do this in writing so that there is a clear record of what you have said and when.

In certain cases, if you were already getting pension credit (PC) before 6 April 2016, you might not need to report all changes in your income during a specified period (an 'assessed income period'). See CPAG's *Welfare Benefits Handbook* for more information.

When you notify the DWP of a change of circumstances, it can change the decision on your PC entitlement, usually by supersession (see p292).

If your change of circumstances is that you have become a member of a 'mixed-age couple', you may need to move to universal credit (see p109).

If your change of circumstances is that you, your partner or your dependent child now receive personal independence payment, adult disability payment, disability living allowance, child disability payment, attendance allowance or pension age disability payment (ie, a qualifying benefit), you might be eligible for additional amounts in your PC. For more information about the date that these additional amounts start from, see p293.

Ongoing evidence requirement

Once you get PC, you may be asked to provide information at any time. If you fail to do so, your PC could be suspended or even terminated.[24]

8. Pension credit and other benefits

Means-tested benefits

If you get the guarantee credit of pension credit (PC), you have passported entitlement to:

- maximum pension-age housing benefit (HB) (see p121); *and*
- Scottish child payment.

Note: passported entitlement does not mean you will get these benefits without making a claim for them.

If you are moving from universal credit to PC, see p104.

Non-means-tested benefits

Many non-means-tested benefits are taken into account as income when working out the amount of PC you get. However, others are disregarded. Personal independence payment, adult disability payment, disability living allowance, child disability payment, attendance allowance and pension age disability payment are not taken into account as income and can in fact increase the guarantee credit of PC by making you eligible for additions (see p110).

The benefit cap

In some cases, there is a limit on your total income from specified benefits (the 'benefit cap'). PC is not one of the specified benefits. The benefit cap does not apply if you are over pension age.

Other sources of financial help

If you have a low income, you may be eligible for council tax reduction and a range of other financial help. See Chapter 15 for more information.

If you are entitled to PC, you may also be eligible for, in England and Wales, the winter fuel payment (and a cold weather payment), or in Scotland, a winter heating payment. Also in Scotland, PC may affect your entitlement to pension age winter heating payment.

Notes

1. **Who can get pension credit**
   1 s2 SPCA 2002
   2 s126 and Sch 4 PA 1995; ss1(6) and 4(1A) SPCA 2002
   3 s4(2) SPCA 2002
   4 s1(2)(a) SPCA 2002; regs 2 and 3 SPC Regs
   5 s4(1) SPCA 2002
   6 s3 SPCA 2002, as amended by PA 2014; reg 7A SPC Regs
   7 s4(1A) SPCA 2002
   8 Arts 4 and 7 WRA(No.31)O; Vol 13, para 77035 DMG; HB Circular A9/2019 (10 July 2019)

2. **The amount of benefit**
   9 s2(3) SPCA 2002; regs 5 and 6, and Sch III para 1(5) and Sch IIA SPC Regs
   10 Reg 6(6)(b) and Sch 1 para 6 SPC Regs
   11 s15 SPCA 2002; regs 14-24 SPC Regs
   12 Reg 15(6) SPC Regs
   13 s2(2) SPCA 2002
   14 Reg 35 and Schs 9 and 9B SS(C&P) Regs
   15 s3(7) SPCA 2002; reg 7(1)(a) SPC Regs

3. **Making a claim**
   16 Reg 4D SS(C&P) Regs
   17 Reg 4F SS(C&P) Regs
   18 Regs 4E and 13D SS(C&P) Regs
   19 Regs 6(16) and (18) and 19(2) and (3) SS(C&P) Regs

6. **Getting paid**
   20 Regs 26B and 26BA SS(C&P) Regs; reg 36(6) SPC(CTMP) Regs
   21 Regs 5 and 6 SS(PAB) Regs
   22 Reg 34(1) SS(C&P) Regs
   23 See gov.uk/payment-exception-service

7. **Reviews and reassessments**
   24 Reg 32(1) SS(C&P) Regs; reg 17 SS&CS(DA) Regs

Chapter 7

Housing benefit

This chapter covers:

Key facts

- Housing benefit (HB) is a means-tested benefit for people who pay rent, including people with health conditions and disabilities.
- You may qualify for 'working-age HB' or 'pension-age HB'. Working-age HB is being replaced by universal credit (UC) for most people, meaning very few people under pension age can make a new HB claim.
- HB might not meet the full amount of rent you must pay if a rent restriction scheme applies.
- You do not need to have paid national insurance contributions to get HB.
- You can get HB while in or out of work and alongside many other benefits.
- You do not usually get HB alongside UC, as UC has its own housing costs element. However, you can get UC and HB together if you live in certain types of accommodation.
- Getting HB alongside a disability benefit can increase how much HB you get.
- You can challenge decisions about your eligibility for HB.
- Getting HB can mean that you are eligible for other kinds of financial support.

1. Who can get housing benefit

Note: for most people under pension age, housing benefit (HB) has been replaced by universal credit (UC). If you are under pension age, you cannot usually make a new claim for HB and need to claim UC instead (but check the exceptions on p120). If you are under pension age and already getting HB, you will probably be transferred to UC at some point (see p79).

Pension-age HB is *not* being replaced by UC, which means that you can make a new claim for pension-age HB.[1] However, if you are a member of a 'mixed-age couple' (ie, one of you is at least pension age but not the other), see p120.

HB is a means-tested benefit for people on a low income who pay rent. You do not have to have paid national insurance contributions to qualify for HB.

You can qualify for HB whether you are in or out of work, and whether or not you have a health condition or disability. There is no requirement to look for work in order to get HB.

You can qualify for HB if:[2]

- your income is low enough; *and*
- your capital is worth £16,000 or less (unless you or your partner get the guarantee credit of pension credit – PC);[3] *and*
- the payments you make for your housing can be met by HB, which is usually paid to cover rent on a tenancy, but can also cover other payments – eg, service charges, licence payments as a lodger or in bed and breakfast accommodation, or site rent for a caravan (we use the term 'rent' to cover all of these); HB cannot be paid to cover a mortgage (see p234);[4] *and*
- you or your partner are liable to pay the rent;[5] *and*
- the payments you make are for the home in which you normally live, or you are only temporarily absent from it (the length of time you can be temporarily absent and still get HB depends on why you are absent and whether you are still in Great Britain or have gone abroad);[6] *and*
- you satisfy the right to reside and the habitual residence tests; *and*
- you are not a person subject to immigration control, although there are limited exceptions to this.

In addition, to qualify for:

- **pension-age HB:**[7]
  - you must be at least pension age, which is currently 66 and rising to 67 between 2026 and 2028. To check your pension age, see gov.uk/state-pension-age; *and*
  - you and your partner must not be on UC or income-related employment and support allowance (ESA). You do not have to be getting PC to qualify for pension-age HB;
- **working-age HB:**[8]
  - you must not yet be pension age; *or*
  - if you are at least pension age, your partner is on UC or income-related ESA.

Note: if you are a member of a 'mixed-age couple' (ie, one of you is at least pension age but not the other), the rules can be complex. You may qualify for working-age HB or pension-age HB, or you may qualify for neither and need to claim UC. It is usually best to get independent advice in this situation. There is more information on mixed-age couples in CPAG's *Welfare Benefits Handbook*.

Special rules apply when you are a student or in hospital and in certain other situations. See Chapter 19 for more information.

If you are working age

In most cases, working-age HB has been replaced by UC (see p79). However, you can make a new claim for working-age HB if you live in:[9]

- **specified accommodation**, which covers:
  - housing with care and support provided by a housing association, charity, voluntary organisation or (in England) a county council;
  - non-permanent housing because you have left home due to domestic abuse and the accommodation is provided by a local authority, housing association, charity, voluntary organisation or (in England) a county council;
  - certain supported accommodation known as 'exempt accommodation';
  - certain local authority hostels for homeless people; *or*
- **temporary accommodation**, which means a specific type of homeless accommodation where rent is paid to a local authority or social housing provider.

If you already get working-age HB and do not live in specified or temporary accommodation, you can carry on getting it until you are transferred to UC.

In many cases, you can move to a new home within the same local authority area and continue getting HB – you do not need to make a new claim for UC.

Example

Charlotte lives with her parents and gets UC. She is offered a housing association flat with care and support. She asks the DWP to add a housing costs element to her UC award but is told that she will need to claim working-age HB instead, because her new home counts as specified accommodation. She is worried about doing this, but is reassured that her UC will continue alongside her HB. All of this is correct.

Couples

This is not a joint claim; only one of you claims. The award includes a personal allowance paid at the couple rate and premiums for both of you (see p122). The amount you get takes into account both partners' income and capital.

If you are a member of a mixed-age couple, see above.

2. The amount of benefit

The maximum amount of housing benefit

Housing benefit (HB) does not necessarily cover all of your rent. Your maximum HB is worked out as follows.[10]

- **Step 1: work out your weekly eligible rent.**[11] This can be less than you actually pay. For example, if you are a private tenant, your eligible rent is usually based on a local housing allowance for the size of home you are assessed as needing.[12] If you are a social tenant getting working-age HB, your eligible rent may be reduced by the bedroom tax if you are considered to have one or more spare bedrooms.[13]
- **Step 2: apply non-dependant deductions.**[14] A non-dependant is a member of your household aged 16 or over who is not your partner – eg, an adult daughter or son. Some people who are classed as non-dependants do not attract a non-dependant deduction – eg, people aged 16 or 17, and many people under 25 getting means-tested benefits. Additionally, non-dependant deductions are not made if you or your partner are getting attendance allowance (AA), pension age disability payment (PADP), the care component of disability living allowance, Scottish adult disability living allowance or child disability payment on your own behalf, or the daily living component of personal independence payment or adult disability payment, or in other limited circumstances.
  If no exception applies, a non-dependant deduction is made from your maximum HB. If your non-dependant is not in paid work, or works less than 16 hours a week, a £19.65 non-dependant deduction is made from your maximum HB each week. If your non-dependant works for 16 hours or more each week, the deduction that is made depends on their gross weekly income.

Income bands	Deduction
£577 or more	£126.65
£463–£576.99	£115.45
£348–£462.99	£101.35
£266–£347.99	£62.00
£183–£265.99	£45.15
£0–£182.99	£19.65

  Only one deduction is made for a couple who are both your non-dependants.
- **Step 3: consider the benefit cap** (see p126).

Note: if you need extra financial assistance to meet your housing costs, you can apply for discretionary housing payments from your local authority (see p232).

Will you get the maximum amount of housing benefit?

You automatically qualify for your maximum HB if you also get the **guarantee credit of pension credit, universal credit or income-related employment and support allowance (ESA)**. This is because all of your income and capital are ignored for HB purposes.[15]

If you do not get one of those benefits, follow the steps below to calculate your HB.[16]

- **Step 1: check that your capital is not too high.** Capital includes investments, certain lump-sum payments and property that is not your main home. Your capital is too high if it is over £16,000.
- **Step 2: work out your maximum HB.** See p121.
- **Step 3: work out your applicable amount.** See below.
- **Step 4: work out your income.** This is the amount you have coming in each week – eg, from benefits, state pensions, private pensions and earnings. Some income is disregarded in part or in full – eg, AA and PADP.
- **Step 5: calculate your HB.** If your income is less than or equal to your applicable amount, you qualify for your maximum HB. If your income exceeds your applicable amount, calculate the difference. Your HB is your maximum HB *minus* 65 per cent of the difference between your income and your applicable amount.

The applicable amount

Your applicable amount for HB consists of:[17]

- a personal allowance. There are different levels of personal allowance depending on your circumstances; *and*
- premiums for additional needs:
  - severe disability premium;
  - enhanced disability premium;
  - for working-age HB only, disability premium;
  - carer premium (see p228);
  - family premium, if you were entitled to HB on 30 April 2016;
  - disabled child premium;
  - enhanced disability premium for a child;
- a support component or work-related activity component, if you are also getting one in your ESA (see p55).

There is no pensioner premium in HB. With pension-age HB, you get a higher personal allowance instead.

3. Making a claim

Note: before starting a new housing benefit (HB) claim, check whether you should be claiming universal credit (UC) instead (see p120).

HB is administered and paid by local authorities. A claim for HB must normally be made in writing on a properly completed claim form, but if you are making a claim for pension credit, you can claim HB at the same time without completing an extra form. You might also be able to claim using an online form or by phone if your local authority has made these options available.[18]

The date of claim is usually the date you start a claim by phone, submit an online claim or, if you claim on a paper form:[19]

- if you requested a form from the local authority or the DWP, the date of your request, provided you return the completed form within one month (the local authority can extend the one-month deadline if it considers that this is reasonable, so if you return the form late, explain why); *or*
- otherwise (eg, if you return a form too late or if you printed your blank form from the internet), the date your completed form is received.

If information is missing from your application, you must usually provide it within one month of being told this, or the claim will not be accepted as valid.[20]

Claiming in advance and backdating

You can claim HB in **advance** if you become liable for rent for the first time but cannot move into your accommodation until after your liability begins. If you are due to move from UC to HB on reaching pension age, see p104 for when to claim.

Your claim for working-age HB may be **backdated** for up to one month if you met the qualifying conditions during that time and can show a good reason (known as good cause) for claiming late.[21]

Your claim for pension-age HB may be **backdated** for up to three months if you met the qualifying conditions during that time. You do not need to show good cause for claiming late.[22] **Note:** the term 'backdating' is often informally used to mean getting arrears of your benefit going back to a claim or decision date – eg, after winning an appeal. However, in this *Handbook*, we use backdating to mean getting paid benefit for a period before the date you claimed.

If you might have qualified for HB earlier but did not claim because you were given the wrong information or misled by the local authority or the DWP (eg, you were wrongly told you needed to claim UC instead), you could complain and ask for compensation (see p308).

Additional support and appointees

If you have (or will have) difficulty with the claims process and need additional support, see Chapter 21. If you cannot manage the claims process at all, you may need an appointee (see p326).

4. How you are assessed

Your eligibility for housing benefit (HB) is assessed using evidence about your income, capital and other circumstances. It is important that you provide any information required when you claim.

There is no health assessment for HB.

5. Decisions

Once the local authority has all the information and evidence it needs, it must make a decision on your claim for housing benefit (HB) within 14 days or as soon as is reasonably practicable.[23]

If you disagree with an HB decision, you can usually apply for a revision, or appeal against it. There are usually time limits for these. See Chapter 20 for more information on getting a benefit decision changed. **Note:** you do *not* have to apply for a mandatory reconsideration before you can appeal an HB decision.

6. Getting paid

Where your payment goes

Housing benefit (HB) is usually paid directly into your bank account. The local authority can sometimes pay all or part of your HB to someone else, including directly to your landlord. It can usually make a 'managed payment to landlord' (MPTL) in limited circumstances, including if it is in your interests, or if you have agreed to it, or if you are in eight weeks' worth of rent arrears.[24] This might be useful if your mental health problem makes it difficult for you to manage money.

Examples

Iris is single and over pension age. She gets the guarantee credit of pension credit and pension-age HB. She has bipolar disorder and has difficulty with budgeting. She lives in a privately-rented flat and currently has one month's worth of rent arrears. Iris's sister helps her to contact the local authority HB office and ask it to pay her rent directly to her landlord. The local authority can do this because it has Iris's consent.

Micah (40) is single and lives in supported accommodation run by a housing association. He is currently experiencing psychosis. He has not paid his rent for three months. The housing association applies to the local authority to receive an MPTL. This request is granted without Micah's consent because he has more than eight weeks' worth of arrears. Micah could challenge this decision if he can argue that it is not in his best interests.[25]

When you are paid

HB is usually paid in arrears at intervals of a week, two weeks, four weeks or a month, depending on when your rent is usually due.[26] Different rules apply if HB is paid directly to your landlord.

If you are waiting for a decision on your claim, you are a private or housing association tenant, and the local authority has not assessed your HB within the required time, the local authority must normally make a payment on account (sometimes called an interim payment) while your claim is being sorted out.[27]

If you are moving from universal credit (UC) to HB on reaching pension age, see the rules on p104 about overlapping payments. If you are moving from HB to UC, see p80 for information about HB run-on.

Note: it is possible for payment of HB to be suspended (see p126).

7. Reviews and reassessments

Change of circumstances

You should report all changes in your circumstances to the local authority housing benefit (HB) office as soon as possible.[28] Do not assume that the local authority already knows something – eg, about changes to the DWP benefits you claim, or about your earnings. You can report a change by phone, but it may be better to do it in writing so you have a clear record.

When you notify the local authority of a change of circumstances, it can change the decision on your HB entitlement, usually by supersession (see p292).

Some changes of circumstances mean that your HB award ends. In this situation, you may need to make a new claim for universal credit instead (see p120).

If your change of circumstances is that you, your partner or your dependent child now receive a qualifying benefit (eg, personal independence payment or adult disability payment), you may become eligible for an extra premium in your HB and/or may no longer be subject to non-dependant deductions. For more information about the date that these changes take effect from, see p293.

Ongoing evidence requirement

Once you are getting HB, you may be asked to provide information at any time. If you fail to do so, your HB could be suspended or terminated.[29]

8. Housing benefit and other benefits

Means-tested benefits

If you are entitled to housing benefit (HB) and are also entitled to the guarantee credit of pension credit, universal credit (UC) or income-related employment and support allowance (ESA), you are automatically entitled to maximum HB because all your income and capital are ignored for HB purposes.

If you are moving from UC to HB on reaching pension age, see p104. If you are moving from HB to UC, see p79.

Non-means-tested benefits

Most non-means-tested benefits are taken into account as income when working out the amount of HB you get. However:

- personal independence payment (PIP), adult disability payment (ADP), disability living allowance (DLA), Scottish adult disability living allowance (SADLA), child disability payment (CDP), attendance allowance (AA), pension age disability payment (PADP), guardian's allowance, child benefit, carer support payment, carer's allowance supplement, child winter heating assistance, young carer grant and Scottish child payment are not taken into account;
- it is often still worth claiming non-means-tested benefits that are taken into account (eg, contributory ESA), because this can qualify you for certain extra premiums and components in your HB and increase your income overall.

The benefit cap

In some cases, there is a limit on your total income from specified benefits (the 'benefit cap'). The benefit cap only applies if you are getting UC or working-age HB. Working-age HB is one of the specified benefits, but pension-age HB is not. You are not subject to the benefit cap if you get certain benefits (eg, if you get PIP, ADP, DLA, SADLA, CDP, AA or PADP), or if you get either UC or ESA and have limited capability for work and work-related activity. See CPAG's *Welfare Benefits Handbook* for more information.

Other sources of financial help

If you have been awarded HB, you may also qualify for council tax reduction and a range of other financial help – eg, discretionary housing payments to top up your HB if it does not cover your full rent. See Chapter 15 for more information.

Notes

1. **Who can get housing benefit**
 1 Reg 6A(3), (4) and (5) UC(TP) Regs; art 4 WRA(No.31)O
 2 ss130 and 134 SSCBA 1992; s115 IAA 1999; reg 10 HB Regs; reg 10 HB(SPC) Regs
 3 Reg 26 HB(SPC) Regs
 4 Regs 11(1) and 12(1) HB Regs; regs 11(1) and 12(1) HB(SPC) Regs
 5 Regs 8, 9, 10 and 56 HB Regs; regs 8, 9 and 10 HB(SPC) Regs
 6 s130(1) SSCBA 1992; reg 7 HB Regs; reg 7 HB(SPC) Regs
 7 Reg 5 HB(SPC) Regs
 8 Reg 5 HB Regs
 9 Reg 2(1) and 6A(2) UC(TP) Regs; Sch 1 paras 3A and 3B UC Regs

2. **The amount of benefit**
 10 Reg 70 HB Regs; reg 50 HB(SPC) Regs
 11 Reg s 12 and 12B HB Regs; regs 12 and 12B HB(SPC) Regs; reg 12 HB Regs, as set out in Sch 3 para 5(1) HB&CTB(CP) Regs
 12 Regs 12D, 13C and 13D HB Regs; regs 12D, 13C and 13D HB(SPC) Regs; see lha-direct.voa.gov.uk for the current rates in your area
 13 Reg 12BA HB Regs
 14 Regs 2(1), definition of 'attendance allowance', 3, 6(1), 70 and 74 HB Regs; regs 2(1), definition of 'attendance allowance', 3, 6(1), 50 and 55 HB(SPC) Regs
 15 s130(3)(a) SSCBA 1992; Schs 4 para 12, 5 para 4, and 6 para 5 HB Regs; reg 26 HB(SPC) Regs
 16 s130(3)(b) SSCBA 1992; reg 71 HB Regs; reg 51 HB(SPC) Regs
 17 Sch 3 HB Regs; Sch 3 HB(SPC) Regs

3. **Making a claim**
 18 Regs 83, 83A and Sch 11 HB Regs; regs 64, 64A and Sch 10 HB(SPC) Regs
 19 Reg 83(5) HB Regs; reg 64(6) HB(SPC) Regs
 20 Reg 83(1), (4C)-(4DA), (6)-(7A) and (9) HB Regs; reg 64(2), (5D)-(5EA), (7)-(8A) and (10) HB(SPC) Regs
 21 Reg 83(12) and (12A) HB Regs
 22 Reg 64(1) HB(SPC) Regs

5. **Decisions**
 23 Regs 89 and 90 HB Regs; regs 70 and 71 HB(SPC) Regs; reg 10 HB&CTB(DA) Regs

6. **Getting paid**
 24 Regs 95 and 96 HB Regs; regs 76 and 77 HB(SPC) Regs; Sch 9 SS(C&P) Regs; *R v Haringey LBC ex parte Azad Ayub* [1992] 25 HLR 566 (QBD); CH 3244/2007; *DLT v Eastleigh BC (HB)* [2014] UKUT 242 (AAC); *ST v Sunderland City Council (HB)* [2019] UKUT 33 (AAC), reported as [2019] AACR 20
 25 Reg 95(1)(b) HB Regs; reg 76(1)(b) HB(SPC) Regs
 26 Reg 92(1), (3), (4) and (6) HB Regs; reg 73(1), (3), (4) and (6) HB(SPC) Regs
 27 Reg 93(1) HB Regs; reg 74(1) HB(SPC) Regs; *R v Haringey LBC ex parte Azad Ayub* [1992] 25 HLR 566 (QBD)

7. **Reviews and reassessments**
 28 Reg 88(1) HB Regs; reg 69(1) HB(SPC) Regs; reg 4 SS(NCC) Regs
 29 Reg 86(1) HB Regs; reg 67(1) HB(SPC) Regs; regs 13 and 14(1) HB&CTB(DA) Regs

8

Chapter 8

Personal independence payment

This chapter covers:

Key facts

- Personal independence payment (PIP) is a non-means-tested benefit for adults with a disability or long-term health condition.
- You can get PIP while in or out of work, and you can get it alongside most other benefits. PIP does not count as income for the purposes of means-tested benefits.
- PIP has two components, each of which can be paid at a standard or an enhanced rate. The daily living component reflects your difficulties with day-to-day activities, such as preparing food and getting dressed. The mobility component reflects difficulties with going out and getting around, including for mental health reasons. You can qualify for one or both components.
- Before a decision is made about your eligibility for PIP, you usually need to complete a questionnaire and take part in an assessment.
- You can challenge decisions about your eligibility for PIP.
- Getting PIP make you eligible for other kinds of financial support.
- You can no longer make a claim for PIP in Scotland (see Chapter 9).

1. Who can get personal independence payment

You can get personal independence payment (PIP) if:

- you are 16 or over and under pension age, which is currently 66 and rising to 67 between 2026 and 2028 (some people over pension age can still get PIP – see below); *and*
- you are not a person subject to immigration control and you meet the residence conditions – see CPAG's *Welfare Benefits Handbook*; *and*
- you meet the disability conditions (see p132); *and*
- you have had your difficulties for at least three months and expect to have them for at least nine months more. This is called the 'required period condition'.[1] If you are terminally ill, see p131.

Note:

- If you meet these criteria but live in Scotland, see Chapter 9.
- Special rules apply if you are classed as being terminally ill (see p131) and when you are in hospital, living in a care home, and in certain other situations (see Chapter 19).
- You claim PIP as an individual. If you are in a couple, one or both of you can claim PIP if you meet the criteria.
- You can claim PIP if you are a carer for someone else but have your own disability or health issues too (see p218).

Getting personal independence payment if you are over pension age

There are various exceptions to the general rule that PIP is for people under pension age.

If you were under 65 on 8 April 2013, and either:

- you are entitled to adult disability living allowance (adult DLA) and have been asked by the DWP to claim PIP instead; *or*
- your entitlement to adult DLA ended less than a year ago,

then you can claim PIP even if you are 66 or over.[2]

If you claimed PIP when you were under 66, an award can be made to you despite you having turned 66 since then.[3]

If you are entitled to PIP when you turn 66, your award continues to its end date if you still meet the entitlement conditions. Your award can also be reviewed (see p157) or you can make a renewal claim (see p158) after you turn 66.

If you have been entitled to PIP, you can reclaim it within one year of your previous award ending, even if you are now 66 or over. **Note:** a new or renewal claim must be based on the same disability or health condition(s) as your former award, or a new condition that has developed as a result of the original one(s).[4]

If you cannot get PIP under one of these exceptions, you might be able to get attendance allowance (see Chapter 12).

Even if you can get PIP after pension age, your entitlement to the mobility component might be restricted. See CPAG's *Welfare Benefits Handbook* for more information.

2. The amount of benefit

The daily living component of personal independence payment (PIP) is paid at one of two weekly rates:[5]
- the standard rate is £73.90;
- the enhanced rate is £110.40.

The mobility component of PIP is paid at one of two weekly rates:[6]
- the standard rate is £29.20;
- the enhanced rate is £77.05.

3. Making a claim

How to claim

You should usually make a claim for personal independence payment (PIP) by phone. Call the PIP claims line (0800 917 2222; textphone: 0800 917 7777; Relay UK and British Sign Language video relay services available – see gov.uk/pip/how-to-claim). You may also be able to claim online depending on where you live – check at apply-for-pip.dwp.gov.uk/eligibility/check-if-eligible. If you are unable to claim by these methods, you or someone supporting you can ask for the paper form PIP1 to be sent to you instead.

If you claim by phone, your date of claim is usually the date of your call to the PIP claims line.[7] If you request a paper claim form (PIP1), your date of claim is the date the DWP receives your request (eg, the date of your phone call), as long as the DWP then receives your properly completed form within one month (or longer if reasonable).[8]

If you get PIP already and your award ends within the next year, see p158.

Claiming in advance and backdating

You can claim PIP **in advance** if you do not satisfy the entitlement conditions, but will do within three months of the date your claim is decided.[9] This may be relevant if you do not yet satisfy the required period condition (see p129) when you first claim.

You cannot **backdate** a claim for PIP.[10] If you believe you would have claimed earlier but were misled or wrongly advised by the DWP, and your claim cannot be backdated, ask for compensation (see p308).

Note: the term 'backdating' is often informally used to mean getting arrears of your benefit going back to a claim or decision date – eg, after winning an appeal. This *is* possible for PIP. However, in this *Handbook*, we use backdating to mean getting paid benefit for a period before the date you claimed. As explained above, this is *not* possible for PIP.

Additional support and appointees

If you have (or will have) difficulty with the claims process and need additional support, see Chapter 21. If you cannot manage the claims process at all, you may need an appointee (see p325).

What you will be asked and how long it will take

When you claim PIP, you are asked questions to confirm your identity and check whether you meet the basic eligibility conditions. It is usually a good idea to have to hand:

- your national insurance (NI) number (note that you do not *need* to have an NI number to start a claim for PIP[11]);
- your phone number and other contact details;
- your bank account details;
- the name, address and phone number of your GP surgery.

It is important that you provide any information required when you claim PIP. Until you do, you may not count as having made a valid claim. Provide any missing information as soon as possible or your date of claim may be affected.

After making a claim, you will go through the assessment process (see p132).

Terminal illness

The PIP claims process is different if you are terminally ill. You are regarded as 'terminally ill' if you have a progressive illness and it would not be a surprise to your doctors were you to die from it within the next 12 months. This can apply even if there are also realistic hopes that you may live much longer than that.[12] You should explain that the claim is on the grounds of terminal illness when making it (claims from terminally ill people are widely referred to as 'special rules' claims).[13] Your GP, consultant, specialist nurse or doctor should complete Form SR1, giving details of your condition and prognosis.

If you claim PIP and you are regarded as terminally ill, you are automatically entitled to the enhanced rate of the daily living component.[14] To get the mobility component, you must still satisfy the disability conditions (see p149), but you do not need to satisfy the required period condition (see p129).

4. How you are assessed

Note: this assessment process does not apply if you are regarded as terminally ill.

To get personal independence payment (PIP), you need to meet its 'disability conditions' (see below). The DWP uses a standard assessment process to decide whether you meet those conditions. You are usually required to:

- complete a questionnaire known as Form PIP2 (the 'How your disability affects you' form – see p153); *and*
- take part in an in-person, telephone or video assessment with a healthcare professional (see p155).

The disability conditions

The health-related eligibility criteria for PIP are known as the 'disability conditions'. You can still qualify if you do not consider yourself to have a disability.

Your entitlement to PIP is assessed using a points-based test. You score points based on how your condition affects your ability to perform 12 different activities: 10 **daily living** activities and two **mobility** activities (see pp136–53).[15] Each activity has a list of 'descriptors' (statements which describe different difficulties with the activity or types of help you might need). You are awarded points depending on which descriptor applies to you. The scoring system is explained on p153.

Your difficulties must be due to a 'mental or physical condition'.[16] You can also score points for difficulties that are a side effect of medication.[17]

Most, if not all, mental health conditions are likely to be recognised as 'mental conditions' for PIP. It is relatively unusual for a decision maker to disagree that your condition counts as a mental condition, and more usual for them to have questions about its severity or impact. It is not essential that you have a diagnosis (see p6) or that you have been prescribed medication or therapy for your condition. Nor is it essential that you are taking medication you have been prescribed, although if you are not, it is important to explain why.[18] **Note:** drug or alcohol dependency counts as a mental condition, although drug or alcohol abuse on its own does not.[19]

What advisers say: not taking medication

'If you are not taking prescribed medication or therapy, that's OK, but the DWP may ask why. You can explain things like fear of side effects, poor past experiences or that you're on a waiting list for help.'

Some of the PIP activities might appear to be chosen to test your physical health, but your mental health is equally relevant.

Examples

Daily living activity 1: Preparing food

Do not worry about: needing a physical explanation for your difficulties.

Think about: whether you have the motivation and focus to prepare yourself regular meals from scratch; whether you can safely use hot or sharp kitchen equipment.

Daily living activity 4: Washing and bathing

Do not worry about: your physical ability to get into or out of the shower, wash yourself and get dry.

Think about: whether you have the motivation or awareness to wash as often as you need to; whether you can only wash if someone encourages you to, or if you have something important to do that day.

You might also have physical side effects from medication or as a symptom of your condition – eg, fatigue, dizziness or nausea. These can be considered when looking at your ability to perform the activities.

Interpreting the conditions

When considering the disability conditions for PIP, there are three key concepts to keep in mind.

1. The support you would get in an ideal world

Points are awarded based on what help you reasonably need, not what help you actually get.[20]

Examples

Dean has a long-term mental health problem. He lives alone, and does not have family or close friends to prompt or encourage him to carry out day-to-day activities. Nonetheless, a decision maker recognises that if someone were around, he would reasonably need prompting due to his mental health to undertake several of the daily living activities, and he scores points accordingly.

Ava has a mental health problem and lives with her parents who provide encouragement and prompting for many of the daily living activities. However, a decision maker concludes that Ava does not *need* this help and does not award her PIP. In challenging the decision, Ava provides more medical evidence, and evidence from her family members and friends, about the severity of her mental health problem and its effects on her day-to-day life and she is awarded the daily living component of PIP.

2. Doing things 'safely', 'to an acceptable standard', 'repeatedly' and 'in a reasonable time'

Unless you can manage an activity in all of the following ways, you are treated as not being able to do it.[21]

- **Safely**. This means 'in a manner unlikely to cause harm to [you] or to another person, either during or after completion of the activity'. An activity is not safe for you if there is 'a real possibility that cannot be ignored of harm occurring'. This involves considering both the likelihood of any harm occurring, and the severity of the consequences if it did occur, so a severe consequence that is relatively unlikely to happen is still relevant.[22]
- **To an acceptable standard**. This is not defined in the regulations, and what it means is closely linked to the activity in question. What is an acceptable standard depends to an extent on your experience of doing the activity, making the test a subjective one. As an example, though, if mental health symptoms mean that you can only leave your home at night, you will probably be classed as unable to undertake journeys to an acceptable standard.[23]
- **Repeatedly**. This means 'as often as the activity being assessed is reasonably required to be completed'. In considering how often you 'reasonably' need to undertake an activity, your own choices should generally be respected.[24] You should also be assessed for your ability to perform activities while living a 'normal' daily life, and should not lose points if you can manage to perform certain activities, but only by adopting a significantly sheltered or altered lifestyle – eg, going out only at certain times, or avoiding all noisy environments.[25]
- **Within a reasonable time period**. This means 'no more than twice as long as the maximum period that a person without a physical or mental condition which limits that person's ability to carry out the activity in question would normally take to complete that activity'. Time you spend thinking about the activity (eg, choosing clothes) can be taken into account if the hesitation is due to your condition.[26]

When considering the disability conditions, you should read these factors into each descriptor. For example, descriptor 1a ('can prepare and cook a simple meal unaided') should be read as 'can safely, repeatedly, to an acceptable standard and within a reasonable time period prepare and cook a simple meal unaided'.

The four factors should be considered separately from one another. For example, if you can manage the activity within a reasonable time period as defined, the fact that you are doing it slowly is not relevant to the question of whether you can manage to an acceptable standard.[27]

3. Fluctuating conditions

Many mental health problems have symptoms or effects that fluctuate. This can make it hard to explain your difficulties, and to show which PIP descriptor applies to you. The following rules can help. It may also be helpful for you to keep a diary to show how your condition affects you (see p243).

Good times and bad times

If a scoring descriptor applies to you at any point in the day (ie, 24 hours, starting from midnight), you are usually accepted as satisfying it on that day.[28] So, for example, if you cannot get dressed in the morning, you should score points for Activity 6 even if you can manage to dress in the afternoon.[29]

Good days and bad days

Your difficulties are normally assessed over a one-year period starting from three months before you claim PIP.[30] If a descriptor will apply to you on over 50 per cent of the days in that period, you score points for that descriptor.[31] These do not have to be consecutive days.

If this is not the case, but the total number of days on which you satisfy two or more scoring descriptors totals more than 50 per cent of the days, the scoring descriptor that applies most often is used. For this rule, if two descriptors apply on the same number of days, the highest scoring one is used.

When calculating which descriptor you satisfy under this rule, it is important to think about how the effects of your condition vary, bearing in mind that you may not need to attempt some activities every day. For example, if your mental health condition means you can only go out or make budgeting decisions on good days, a couple of times a week, you can still score points for these activities, even if you manage to do all your shopping and pay your bills on those days. Similarly, the fact that you can sometimes manage activities if there is a specific reason to do so does not mean that you do not need prompting to manage them on most days.[32]

Example

Ryan has depression. When he receives his PIP questionnaire, he is in a period of severe low mood and his wife completes the form for him explaining the significant issues he is having. When he is later invited to an assessment, his symptoms are less severe, and he explains to the assessor that he is not currently having the difficulties described on the questionnaire. A DWP decision maker decides that Ryan does not qualify for PIP because he does not score enough points. However, Ryan successfully challenges this decision by explaining that his regular periods of severe low mood are likely to add up to more than half of the relevant one-year period. He provides supporting written evidence from his community psychiatric nurse (CPN) and from his wife.

The daily living activities

Note: you qualify for the enhanced rate of the daily living component of PIP if you are regarded as being terminally ill (see p131), even if you have no problems with any of the activities.

The test for PIP looks at 10 daily living activities. The following boxes explain some concepts which are used in deciding your score for each activity.

Assistance, supervision and prompting[33]

'Assistance' means 'physical intervention by another person' and does not include speech. It is help to carry out an activity and does not include someone doing the whole activity for you, or, arguably, someone giving you so much help that they are effectively doing the activity for you.[34]

'Supervision' means 'the continuous presence of another person for the purpose of ensuring [your] safety'. You need supervision if there is a 'real risk' of harm while carrying out the activity, considering both the likelihood and seriousness of the harm.[35] This means that you may still score points even if you would not come to any harm most days if left unsupervised.[36] The risk does not need to be caused by doing the activity; it is enough that you need continuous supervision to carry it out.[37] If someone is also supervising other people at the same time, you can still satisfy a supervision descriptor.[38]

'Prompting' means 'reminding, encouraging or explaining by another person'. This may be the sort of help that is most relevant with many mental health issues. You can score points for needing prompting even if you can sometimes manage unaided when there is a specific or urgent need to undertake the activity.[39] The person prompting you does not always need to be in your presence, so prompting by telephone (or, arguably, someone leaving you notes or reminders) can allow you to score points.[40] Prompting to *stop* performing an activity may count.[41]

Aids and appliances

An aid or appliance means 'any device which improves, provides or replaces [your] impaired mental or physical function; and includes a prosthesis'.[42]

Aids and appliances to assist someone who has a mental health condition might include dosette boxes, mobile phone apps, alarms and reminders. The aid need not be something that only people with a mental health problem use,[43] and does not need to be specifically designed to help with the task that you need it for. However, it is not usually seen as an aid or appliance if it is widely used in the same way by people who do not have your difficulties.[44] Note that the rules are different for an 'orientation aid' that helps you to plan or follow a journey (see p150).

Activity 1: preparing food

Descriptors and points

a. Can prepare and cook a simple meal unaided.	0
b. Needs to use an aid or appliance to be able to either prepare or cook a simple meal.	2
c. Cannot cook a simple meal using a conventional cooker but is able to do so using a microwave.	2
d. Needs prompting to be able to either prepare or cook a simple meal.	2
e. Needs supervision or assistance to either prepare or cook a simple meal.	4
f. Cannot prepare and cook food.	8

Definitions[45]

'Simple meal' means a cooked one-course meal for one made using fresh ingredients.

'Prepare', in the context of food, means make food ready for cooking or eating.

'Cook' means heat food at or above waist height.

This is an objective test of your ability to manage the tasks involved in preparing ingredients and cooking a reasonable range of simple meals. It takes no account of your specific dietary needs,[46] religious beliefs or cultural preferences.[47] Similarly, the impact of things such as childcare responsibilities or family size on your ability to prepare a meal is not relevant.[48] Being able to heat a ready meal in the microwave does not necessarily mean you satisfy descriptor 1c because your ability to prepare a simple meal from fresh ingredients must also be considered.[49] For the same reason, making a bowl of cereal does not fit the definition of preparing a simple meal.

If you cannot read, tell the time or use timers because of your condition, this is relevant to whether you score points for this activity. It is also relevant if you can only make one kind of meal, as this may indicate that you cannot perform the activity to an acceptable standard.[50]

Example

Tariq has depression. He lives with his mother, who cooks all his meals. A decision maker applies descriptor 1a to Tariq because the decision maker believes that although Tariq never actually cooks, he *would* be able to do so if he needed to. Tariq challenges this decision and explains that his motivation is so low that he would not be able to prepare a meal from fresh ingredients without encouragement. Tariq provides a statement from his former housemate saying that when Tariq lived away from home, he ate only microwaved ready meals or cereal and rarely ate three meals a day. The decision is changed and descriptor 1d is applied to Tariq.

Mental health and preparing food checklist

- Do you have difficulty making meals from scratch because of, for example, low mood and reduced motivation?
- Can you make a meal from scratch as many times a day as you reasonably need to eat one?
- Can you heat a ready meal in the microwave, but not make a meal from fresh ingredients?
- Does a lack of appetite, an aversion to food or an eating disorder (see p16) stop you from preparing food?
- Can you safely use heavy, hot or sharp kitchen equipment without supervision? Are intrusive thoughts, for example, an issue?
- Can you attend to a cooker or do you get distracted – ie, causing a risk of fire?
- Do you find it hard to co-ordinate things or follow instructions? Do OCD rituals mean you cannot complete tasks within a reasonable time?
- Can you prepare food that is safe to eat (and not, for example, out-of-date or undercooked)?
- Can you make more than one kind of meal?
- Does it take you a long time to prepare food – specifically, does it take more than twice as long as a person without your condition?
- Do side effects from medication (eg, nausea or dizziness) affect your ability to prepare food?
- If you have good and bad days, can you make meals from scratch on the majority of days?
- Do you need prompting, assistance or supervision, even if you do not currently get it?

See pp13–23 for more information about mental health symptoms that might be relevant to this activity.

Activity 2: taking nutrition

Descriptors and points

a. Can take nutrition unaided.	0
b. Needs:	2
(i) to use an aid or appliance to be able to take nutrition; *or*	
(ii) supervision to be able to take nutrition; *or*	
(iii) assistance to be able to cut up food.	
c. Needs a therapeutic source to be able to take nutrition.	2
d. Needs prompting to be able to take nutrition.	4
e. Needs assistance to be able to manage a therapeutic source to take nutrition.	6
f. Cannot convey food and drink to their mouth and needs another person to do so.	10

The nutritious quality of what you eat is not relevant for these descriptors.[51] If your condition means that you need prompting to eat at all, or enough, you may satisfy descriptor 2d.[52] Prompting to *stop* eating may also score points for this activity.[53]

Mental health and taking nutrition checklist

- Do you have the energy and motivation to eat as often as you reasonably need to?
- Do you forget to eat?
- Do paranoia (see p21) or delusions (see p14) affect your eating?
- Does a lack of appetite, an aversion to food or an eating disorder (see p16) affect the amount you eat?
- Is eating likely to lead to harm, either during or after the activity?
- Do side effects from medication (eg, nausea or dizziness) affect your ability to eat?
- If you have good and bad days, can you eat enough on the majority of days?
- Do you need prompting or supervision, even if you do not currently get it?

See pp13–23 for more information about mental health symptoms that might be relevant to this activity.

Activity 3: managing therapy or monitoring a health condition

Descriptors and points

a. Either: (i) does not receive medication or therapy or need to monitor a health condition; *or* (ii) can manage medication or therapy or monitor a health condition unaided.	0
b. Needs any one or more of the following: (i) to use an aid or appliance to be able to manage medication; (ii) supervision, prompting or assistance to be able to manage medication; (iii) supervision, prompting or assistance to be able to monitor a health condition.	1
c. Needs supervision, prompting or assistance to be able to manage therapy that takes no more than 3.5 hours a week.	2
d. Needs supervision, prompting or assistance to be able to manage therapy that takes more than 3.5 but no more than 7 hours a week.	4
e. Needs supervision, prompting or assistance to be able to manage therapy that takes more than 7 but no more than 14 hours a week.	6
f. Needs supervision, prompting or assistance to be able to manage therapy that takes more than 14 hours a week.	8

Definitions[54]

'Manage medication' means take medication, where a failure to do so is likely to result in a deterioration in your health.

'Medication' means medication to be taken at home, which is prescribed or recommended by a registered doctor, nurse or pharmacist.
'Monitor a health condition' means detect significant changes in your condition which are likely to lead to a deterioration in your health, and take action advised by a registered doctor, registered nurse, or health professional who is regulated by the Health and Care Professions Council, without which your health is likely to deteriorate.
'Manage therapy' means undertake therapy, where a failure to do so is likely to result in a deterioration in your health.
'Therapy' means therapy to be undertaken at home which is prescribed or recommended by a registered doctor, nurse or pharmacist, or health professional regulated by the Health and Care Professions Council. It does not include taking or applying, or otherwise receiving or administering, medication (whether orally, topically or by any other means), or any action which falls within the definition of 'monitor a health condition'.

Therapy for a mental health condition can include, for example, talking therapies (see p24) undertaken at home. As the descriptors about therapy refer to the amount of help you need during 'a week', you should not be excluded from scoring points if you only need help with therapy on a minority of days. General supervision provided in supported accommodation is not regarded as 'therapy'.[55]

Monitoring your health condition could include someone checking on how you are – eg, if you have a mental health problem which is normally controlled by medication.

Aids and appliances to help you manage medication could include a dosette box to organise pills, and/or alarms and reminders, if you are forgetful due to your condition.

It is particularly important to consider what you can do 'safely' (see p134). If you could suffer severe harm if you failed to take your medication or while your condition was not monitored, this must be taken into account, even if the chance of this actually happening is relatively small.

Absence of medication does not necessarily mean the health condition is not severe.[56]

Mental health and medication, monitoring and therapy checklist

- Is there a risk that you will not take your medication when you need to – eg, because of poor memory, or because your condition makes you distrust the medication (see p15)?
- Do you need prompting either at the times when you need to take your medication, or ongoing prompting to convince you of the need to take your medication?
- Do you use a dosette box, alarms or reminders to take medication?
- Is there a risk that you will take too much of your medication – eg, because of poor memory, or deliberately?

- What are the likely consequences if you do not take your medication, or take too much?
- Does the nature of your condition mean that you are at risk of significant harm if you are not monitored by another person (even if the likelihood of the harm is relatively small)?
- If you have good and bad days, can you manage to take medication or monitor your condition on the majority of days?
- If you have better and worse times of day, are there times when you cannot take your medication or monitor your condition?
- Do you need help or encouragement to do self-directed therapy at home? Do you have sessions with a therapist at home?
- Do you need prompting, supervision or assistance, even if you do not currently get it?

See pp13–23 for more information about mental health symptoms that might be relevant to this activity.

Activity 4: washing and bathing

Descriptors and points

a. Can wash and bathe unaided.	0
b. Needs to use an aid or appliance to be able to wash or bathe.	2
c. Needs supervision or prompting to be able to wash or bathe.	2
d. Needs assistance to be able to wash either their hair or body below the waist.	2
e. Needs assistance to be able to get in or out of a bath or shower.	3
f. Needs assistance to be able to wash their body between the shoulders and waist.	4
g. Cannot wash and bathe at all and needs another person to wash their entire body.	8

If you are at risk of harm if you bathe alone, whether you are considered to need supervision, depends on the seriousness of the harm and how likely it is.[57]

To wash to an acceptable standard, you should be clean (and, arguably, dry)[58] when you have finished. If it takes you more than twice as long to wash and bathe than the maximum amount of time it would normally take someone without your condition to do the same, you are not doing it 'within a reasonable time period' and you should score points for needing help.

If you can only motivate yourself to have a bath or shower if you have something important to do that day, but would not manage this unprompted on a normal day, it is arguable that you still need prompting to wash or bathe.[59]

Example

Martina has depression. On the day of her PIP assessment, she manages to have a shower without any encouragement. However, she explains to the assessor that she could not have done this on a normal day when she did not have a specific, important reason to do so. A decision maker agrees that Martina cannot wash or bathe unprompted under normal circumstances and awards descriptor 4c.

Mental health and washing and bathing checklist

- Do you have the motivation and awareness to wash as often as you need to?
- Do you only wash if someone encourages you to, or if you have something important to do that day?
- Are you clean and dry after you have washed?
- Does washing or bathing take you more than twice as long as it would for someone without your condition – eg, due to compulsive behaviour (see p13)?
- Do you need prompting to avoid washing too much?
- Does washing or bathing make you distressed, even if you can manage to do it?
- Do side effects from medication (eg, fatigue or dizziness) affect your ability to wash or bathe?
- If you have good and bad days, can you wash or bathe on the majority of days?
- If you have better and worse times of day, can you wash or bathe at a time when you reasonably need to?
- Do you need prompting, supervision or assistance, even if you do not currently get it?

See pp13–23 for more information about mental health symptoms that might be relevant to this activity.

Activity 5: managing toilet needs or incontinence

Descriptors and points

a. Can manage toilet needs or incontinence unaided.	0
b. Needs to use an aid or appliance to be able to manage toilet needs or incontinence.	2
c. Needs supervision or prompting to be able to manage toilet needs.	2
d. Needs assistance to be able to manage toilet needs.	4
e. Needs assistance to be able to manage incontinence of either bladder or bowel.	6
f. Needs assistance to be able to manage incontinence of both bladder and bowel.	8

'Toilet needs' includes cleaning yourself after using the toilet. You can be awarded points for this activity if you have difficulties which are the result of a mental health problem or the side effect of medication – eg, if problems with memory or attention mean that you do not clean yourself reliably or to an acceptable standard after using the toilet. See pp13–23 for more information about mental health symptoms that might be relevant to this activity.

Activity 6: dressing and undressing

Descriptors and points

a. Can dress and undress unaided.	0
b. Needs to use an aid or appliance to be able to dress or undress.	2
c. Needs either: (i) prompting to be able to dress, undress or determine appropriate circumstances for remaining clothed; *or* (ii) prompting or assistance to be able to select appropriate clothing.	2
d. Needs assistance to be able to dress or undress their lower body.	2
e. Needs assistance to be able to dress or undress their upper body.	4
f. Cannot dress or undress at all.	8

Clothes that are loose-fitting, comfortable and easy to put on may count as aids to help you dress, depending on how much your choice of clothes is restricted due to your condition.[60] Selecting appropriate clothing includes choosing the right clothes for the weather, and also not reusing dirty clothes.[61] If you take a long time to choose clothes due to your condition, you may satisfy descriptor 6c.[62]

Example

Zoe has anxiety, depression, anorexia and symptoms of obsessive compulsive disorder. Every day, she spends over an hour getting dressed because she struggles to decide which clothes to wear. A decision maker agrees that these difficulties are the direct result of Zoe's mental health conditions, that this is more than twice as long as the maximum amount of time it would normally take another person without Zoe's conditions to get dressed, and that Zoe therefore cannot complete this activity 'within a reasonable time period'.

Mental health and dressing and undressing checklist

- Does low mood, reduced awareness or lack of motivation mean you do not change your clothes?
- Can you recognise whether clothes are clean and appropriate for the weather and occasion?
- Do you have difficulty undressing, or choosing clothes – eg, because of a condition that affects your body image?
- Does it take you more than twice as long to get dressed as it would take someone without your condition?

- Are you only able to wear a very limited range of clothes due to your condition?
- Do side effects from medication (eg, dizziness) affect your ability to dress?
- If you have good and bad days, can you get dressed and undressed on the majority of days?
- If you have better and worse times of day, can you get dressed and undressed at the times when you might reasonably need to?
- Do you need prompting or assistance, even if you do not currently get it?

See pp13–23 for more information about mental health symptoms that might be relevant to this activity.

Activity 7: communicating verbally

Descriptors and points

a. Can express and understand verbal information unaided.	0
b. Needs to use an aid or appliance to be able to speak or hear.	2
c. Needs communication support to be able to express or understand complex verbal information.	4
d. Needs communication support to be able to express or understand basic verbal information.	8
e. Cannot express or understand verbal information at all even with communication support.	12

Definitions[63]

'Basic verbal information' means information in your native language conveyed verbally in a simple sentence.

'Complex verbal information' means information in your native language conveyed verbally in either more than one sentence or one complicated sentence.

'Communication support' means support from a person trained or experienced in communicating with people with specific communication needs, including interpreting verbal information into non-verbal forms and vice versa.

If you cannot speak, hear or understand speech in certain social situations but you *can* do so in other social settings or with people you know well, then you are unlikely to score points for this activity. You may instead score points for difficulties engaging with people (Activity 9).

If strangers find it hard to understand you because of your condition (eg, because you have very disorganised speech – see p14), you may score points for needing help to communicate to an acceptable standard and within a reasonable time.

Your ability to read, write or send text messages is not relevant, but if you use writing to communicate in the absence of speech, you may satisfy descriptor 7b.[64]

The definition of 'communication support' includes both someone with specialist training and someone who knows you and is experienced in helping you to communicate.[65]

Mental health and communicating verbally checklist

- Are you unable to take in and understand spoken information – eg, because of lack of focus or hallucinations?
- Are you unable to form words at all as a result of your condition or symptoms?
- Do other people struggle to understand you – eg, due to disorganised speech?
- Can you both say and understand one simple sentence, two simple sentences, and/or one complicated sentence (with or without support)?
- If you have good days and bad days, can you communicate verbally on the majority of days?
- If your condition varies throughout the day, are there times of day when you are unable to speak or understand spoken information?
- Do you need communication support, even if you do not currently get it?

See pp13–23 for more information about mental health symptoms that might be relevant to this activity.

Activity 8: reading and understanding signs, symbols and words

Descriptors and points

a. Can read and understand basic and complex written information either unaided or using spectacles or contact lenses.	0
b. Needs to use an aid or appliance, other than spectacles or contact lenses, to be able to read or understand either basic or complex written information.	2
c. Needs prompting to be able to read or understand complex written information.	2
d. Needs prompting to be able to read or understand basic written information.	4
e. Cannot read or understand signs, symbols or words at all.	8

Definitions[66]

'Basic written information' means signs, symbols and dates written or printed in standard size text in your native language.

'Complex written information' means more than one sentence of written or printed standard-size text in your native language.

If your mental impairment means you need help to understand the meaning of written information, you should score points for this activity. If you have never learned to read in English, you only score points for this activity if this is because of your condition.[67] While the standard of reading required is low, to satisfy descriptor 8d (rather than 8e) you must be able to read and understand some words quickly and without any help.[68] If your ability to read is affected so that you satisfy a descriptor at certain times of the day, you should score points even if you can read unaided at other times of the day.[69]

Mental health and reading checklist

- Are you unable to take in or understand the meaning of written information – eg, because of lack of focus, low mood or delusions/hallucinations?
- How much can you read – eg, can you read signs, symbols, dates, one sentence?
- Does reading or understanding what you have read take more than twice as long for you as it would for someone without your condition?
- If you have good and bad days, can you read and take in information on the majority of days?
- If your condition varies throughout the day, are there times of day when you cannot read and take in information?
- Do you need prompting, even if you do not currently get it?

See pp13–23 for more information about mental health symptoms that might be relevant to this activity.

Activity 9: engaging with other people face to face

Descriptors and points

a. Can engage with other people unaided.	0
b. Needs prompting to be able to engage with other people.	2
c. Needs social support to be able to engage with other people.	4
d. Cannot engage with other people due to such engagement causing either: (i) overwhelming psychological distress to the claimant; *or* (ii) the claimant to exhibit behaviour which would result in a substantial risk of harm to the claimant or another person.	8

Definitions[70]

'Psychological distress' means distress related to an enduring mental health condition or an intellectual or cognitive impairment. **Note:** '*overwhelming* psychological distress' is not defined in legislation but caselaw indicates that 'the threshold is a very high one'.[71]

'Social support' means support from a person trained or experienced in assisting people to engage in social situations. For who this might cover, see p147.

This activity looks at your ability to interact with individuals or small groups,[72] and in social situations.[73] You can score points despite being able to engage with people you know (eg, family and friends) or with people you must interact with for a specific and limited purpose – eg, health professionals or the tribunal.[74]

'Engage with other people' means to 'interact with others in a contextually and socially appropriate manner', 'understand body language' and 'establish relationships'.[75] All three factors should be considered.[76] The test is whether you can engage with adults generally, not just with particular groups of people, such as women or young people.[77]

'Establish relationships' does not refer to any particular type of relationship, but means something more than just the ability to respond to questions.[78] Even if you undertake social activities (eg, going to a pub), you may still score points for this activity if you cannot engage with other people without help,[79] or if the social activities you can cope with alone are very specific and limited by your condition.[80]

While the descriptors distinguish between 'prompting' and 'social support', there is some overlap between them. The person prompting or supporting you does not always need to be physically present.[81] For example, they might support you through the interaction either over the phone or by text message.

'Social support' does not need to be provided by a professional, it could also come from someone (eg, a family member or friend) who has significant experience of supporting you.[82] Social support does not have to be provided at the time of the activity or immediately beforehand. If, for example, you have monthly counselling sessions, and this support is necessary for you to engage with other people, you are likely to satisfy descriptor 9c.[83]

If you cannot engage with other people at all, this must be for one of the reasons mentioned in descriptor 9d for you to satisfy it.[84]

Examples

Toni has a long-term mental health problem. She goes to the chip shop every day. She does not speak to other customers or to staff except to place her order. If anyone tries to chat to her or if the chip shop is too crowded, Toni will go straight home. She does not have a support network and always goes to the chip shop alone. A decision maker recognises that Toni's mental health problem has affected her ability to engage with others. The fact that she can go to a place where other people are present and have an extremely brief exchange while placing her order does not amount to 'engaging with other people'.

Zuri has a personality disorder diagnosis. She belongs to a youth club run by a mental health charity that meets once a week. Zuri finds it difficult to engage with the other young people, but does so with prompting from the session leader. Zuri's mother also needs to reassure and encourage her before she attends. A decision maker applies descriptor 9c because it is agreed that the prompting Zuri needs must come from specific people experienced in helping her and/or trained in supporting people with her difficulties.

Mental health and engaging with other people checklist

- What symptoms do you have that affect your ability to engage with other people – eg, anxiety, paranoia, low mood?
- Can you interact with others in a way that is considered socially appropriate, understand body language, and build relationships?
- Is what you are doing actually social engagement or does it fall short of the definition – eg, is a conversation one-way or you are just answering questions?
- Can you only engage with certain people – eg, friends, family, professionals, or other people of your age or gender?
- Can you only engage with less familiar people if you are in certain social contexts – eg, board-game club or mosque?
- Can you engage with other people safely – ie, without being likely to suffer harm or cause harm to another person?
- Do you have difficulty recognising manipulative or abusive behaviour in others?
- If you have good and bad days, can you engage with other people on the majority of days?
- If your condition varies throughout the day, are there times of day when you cannot engage with other people?
- Can you engage with other people repeatedly – ie, as often as you reasonably need to?
- Do you need prompting or social support, even if you do not currently get it?

See pp13–23 for more information about mental health symptoms that might be relevant to this activity.

Activity 10: making budgeting decisions

Descriptors and points

a. Can manage complex budgeting decisions unaided.	0
b. Needs prompting or assistance to be able to make complex budgeting decisions.	2
c. Needs prompting or assistance to be able to make simple budgeting decisions.	4
d. Cannot make any budgeting decisions at all.	6

Definitions[85]

'Complex budgeting decisions' means decisions involving calculating household and personal budgets, managing and paying bills and planning future purchases.

'Simple budgeting decisions' means decisions involving calculating the cost of goods and calculating change required after a purchase.

The descriptors assess difficulty making decisions because of your condition, not poor money management skills unconnected with your condition. If your condition means that you are very impulsive (see p17), you can satisfy descriptor 10b if this prevents you from budgeting effectively.[86] You can score points whatever your intellect, since motivation and other factors can prevent you from carrying out an activity unaided.[87]

Remember that 'complex' and 'simple' budgeting have specific definitions. You should not be considered able to manage complex or simple budgeting unless you can do *all* of the types of budgeting in the relevant definition. If there are things you cannot do even when you have prompting or assistance, this must be taken into account.[88]

Mental health and budgeting checklist

- Are you unable to calculate the cost of something or work out change – eg, because of lack of concentration, low mood, hallucinations or poor memory?
- Do you forget or lack the motivation to pay bills when they are due?
- Do you forget or fail to put money aside for essentials?
- Can you respond to changes to your income or outgoings – ie, adapting your household budget accordingly?
- Is your spending impulsive?
- Have you spent a lot of money on a plan or scheme that may not really work – eg, during a period of mania (see p19)?
- Does distrust (eg, of online spending or financial institutions – see p15) affect your ability to pay bills?
- Does simple or complex budgeting take more than twice as long for you as it would for someone without your condition?
- Do side effects from medication (eg, confusion or memory problems) affect your ability to manage money?
- If you have good and bad days, can you cope with these activities on the majority of days?
- If your condition varies throughout the day, are there times of day when you cannot cope with these activities?
- Does someone else actually manage your finances for you – eg, an appointee, someone with power of attorney, or a friend/family member informally?
- Do you need prompting or assistance to manage money, even if you do not currently get it?

See pp13–23 for more information about mental health symptoms that might be relevant to this activity.

The mobility activities

There are two mobility activities in the assessment.

Mobility activity 1: planning and following journeys

Descriptors and points[89]

a. Can plan and follow the route of a journey unaided.	0
b. Needs prompting to be able to undertake any journey to avoid overwhelming psychological distress to the claimant.	4
c. Cannot plan the route of a journey.	8
d. Cannot follow the route of an unfamiliar journey without another person, assistance dog or orientation aid.	10
e. Cannot undertake any journey because it would cause overwhelming psychological distress to the claimant.	10
f. Cannot follow the route of a familiar journey without another person, an assistance dog or an orientation aid.	12

Definitions[90]

'Assistance dog' means a dog trained to guide or assist a person with a sensory impairment.

'Orientation aid' means a specialist aid designed to assist people with disabilities to follow a route safely. This means that a standard satnav does not count as an orientation aid, although one designed or modified for people with your condition might.[91]

'Prompting' means reminding, encouraging or explaining by another person.

'Psychological distress' means distress related to an enduring mental health condition or an intellectual or cognitive impairment. **Note:** '*overwhelming* psychological distress' is not defined in legislation but caselaw indicates that 'the threshold is a very high one'.[92]

'Unaided' means without the use of an aid or appliance, or supervision, prompting or assistance.

If you need prompting to leave your home as the thought of going out causes overwhelming psychological distress, you can satisfy descriptor 1b even if once you start a journey you do not need to be accompanied by someone else.[93]

Prompting by phone is potentially sufficient if it is needed for you to leave your home.[94] You can argue that you can satisfy descriptor 1b or 1e if you need prompting to, or cannot, go out during *part* of a day, and your 'lifestyle is restricted to more than a trivial extent'.[95]

The use of the words 'follow the route' means that you can satisfy descriptors 1d and 1f if you need someone to help you get to your destination (this could include help with navigation, supervision to keep you safe, or help dealing with unexpected diversions), but not if you only need help to communicate with people you meet during a journey.[96] It is possible to satisfy descriptor 1d or 1f if you sometimes manage a specific journey alone, as long as you generally need one of the kinds of help described.[97]

If you can manage part of a journey (eg, in your car) by yourself, you can still score points if you need someone else with you at the start or end of the journey.[98] Your ability to manage a range of journeys using different types of transport (and not just a short or local journey) should be considered, and DWP guidance states you should only be considered capable of following an unfamiliar journey if you can do so on public transport.[99]

You can only satisfy descriptors 1d and 1f due to anxiety if you need someone with you to avoid overwhelming psychological distress.[100] That person does not need to be taking action to help you if their presence alone is enough to relieve the distress.[101]

DWP guidance suggests that if you satisfy descriptor 1e as you cannot leave the house at all on the majority of days, you cannot also satisfy descriptor 1f.[102] The Upper Tribunal has held that if you satisfy descriptor 1e, whether you also satisfy descriptor 1f should be decided without taking account of any psychological distress that you experience.[103] If you do *not* satisfy descriptor 1e, you may satisfy 1f on the basis of overwhelming psychological distress that you suffer while on a familiar journey without being accompanied.

If you are actively suicidal or considered to be at significant risk of harming others, you are likely to satisfy descriptor 1f.

Example

Lloyd experiences severe anxiety and panic attacks when leaving the house and requires someone to accompany him to provide reassurance and guidance. Lloyd can manage a short, familiar walk to the local corner shop alone because he has done this many times and knows the route and the people who work in the shop. For any other journey, he needs someone with him. Therefore, despite being able to complete one very specific journey alone, he requires support to go out for the majority of the time, and will meet the criteria for descriptor 1f.

Mental health and planning and following journeys checklist

- What symptoms do you have that affect your ability to plan and follow journeys – eg, anxiety, stress response, panic attacks, reduced motivation?
- Are you generally unable to use public transport – eg, because you do not feel comfortable surrounded by other passengers?
- Do you need encouragement or reassurance to leave the house?
- Do you need to be accompanied in order to stay safe when you are out of the house – eg, because of a lack of perception of danger, because you could not cope if you got lost, or because you are at risk of harming yourself?
- Can you cope with unexpected changes when following a journey – eg, diversions or cancelled buses?
- If you can make a journey alone, can you only do so if it is a short or very straightforward journey?

- Do you have difficulty planning a route or navigating – eg, because of anxiety or a lack of concentration?
- Does it take you a long time to plan a route – specifically, does it take you more than twice as long as a person without your condition?
- If you have good and bad days, can you plan or follow journeys on the majority of days?
- If your condition varies throughout the day, are there times of day when you cannot plan or follow journeys, and does this mean that your 'lifestyle is restricted to more than a trivial extent'?
- Do you reasonably need prompting or for someone to accompany you, even if you do not currently get this help?

See pp13–23 for more information about mental health symptoms that might be relevant to this activity.

Mobility activity 2: moving around

Descriptors and points

a. Can stand and then move more than 200 metres, either aided or unaided.	0
b. Can stand and then move more than 50 metres but no more than 200 metres, either aided or unaided.	4
c. Can stand and then move unaided more than 20 metres but no more than 50 metres.	8
d. Can stand and then move using an aid or appliance more than 20 metres but no more than 50 metres.	10
e. Can stand and then move more than one metre but no more than 20 metres, either aided or unaided.	12
f. Cannot, either aided or unaided: (i) stand; *or* (ii) move more than one metre.	12

Definitions[104]

'Aided' means with the use of an aid or appliance, or supervision, prompting or assistance (see also the definitions of these terms on p136).

'Stand' means stand upright with at least one biological foot on the ground. (This means that double amputees are treated as unable to stand and satisfy descriptor 2f.)

'Unaided' means without the use of an aid or appliance, or supervision, prompting or assistance.

Because this activity is about your physical difficulties with walking, your mental health is not normally relevant. If your physical difficulties are caused by psychological distress, this is considered under Mobility activity 1 instead.[105] However, if you experience physical symptoms such as pain, fatigue or dizziness as a result of your mental condition or as a side effect of medication you must take to treat that condition, you may be able to score points for this activity.[106]

Scoring system

For each activity in the daily living and mobility sections, you are awarded points based on the *one* descriptor that applies most to you. The points you score for each daily living activity are added together, and the points you score for the two mobility activities are added together. You qualify for a component at:[107]

- the standard rate, if you score 8 points or more; *or*
- the enhanced rate, if you score 12 points or more.

Example

Rin has depression. They are awarded 2 points for needing prompting to cook (daily living descriptor 1d), 2 points for needing prompting to wash (4c), 2 points for needing prompting to engage with other people (9b), 2 points for needing assistance with complex budgeting decisions (10b), and 4 points for needing prompting to go out (M1b). They score a total of 8 points for the daily living activities and 4 points for the mobility activities. They are awarded the standard rate of the daily living component of PIP but do not qualify for the mobility component.

The questionnaire (PIP2/AR1/AR2)

As part of the assessment process, you are usually sent a questionnaire about your condition(s), any treatment you receive, and how you satisfy the daily living and mobility activities.

- If you are making a new claim, this is a Form PIP2 (the 'How your disability affects you' form).
- If your existing PIP award is being reviewed, it is a Form AR1 (the shorter 'Award Review – how your disability affects you' form).
- If you are nearing or have reached pension age, or if you have a severe, life-long condition with needs expected to stay the same or increase over time and you have been awarded the enhanced rate of both the daily living and mobility components, you will only get a 'light-touch' review (Form AR2) once every 10 years.

They are available as paper forms, and an online version of the PIP2 is also available for most new claimants. You can request the questionnaire in an alternative format (eg, large print, Braille or British Sign Language) by contacting the PIP helpline.

Many advice agencies can help you complete the questionnaire.

The questionnaire asks for contact details of the health professional who best understands how your condition affects you. **Note:** even when it has these details, the DWP does not often contact them, so it is best for you to provide this evidence.

How to complete the questionnaire

1. It may help to draft your answers on a sheet of paper first.
2. Read the list of activities on pp132–53 to get an idea of what the DWP is assessing. Remember that many of the terms in the assessment have special definitions.
3. Consider all of the mental health symptoms listed on pp13–23.
4. If your needs vary day to day, explain how often and in what way (see p134). Avoid ticking the 'sometimes' box for any activity unless you also explain clearly what you mean by this.[108] To give a full picture of your needs, it might be useful for you to keep a diary for a week or a month, to record your symptoms and the help you need (whether you get it or not). Attach a copy to the questionnaire and refer to it in your answers.
5. If you can, ask someone who knows you well to check that your answers fully explain your difficulties. This is particularly important if you do not always have good insight into your condition (see p19).
6. Be sure to mention all your symptoms and any side effects of the medication. You should also say if you do not take any medication and the reasons why. Absence of medication does not mean your condition is not severe as you may not take medication due to its side effects or you may refuse to take medication due to poor compliance.[109] If there is not an obvious place to mention a particular symptom, you can do this in the free text box near the end of the questionnaire. If you have to appeal, the tribunal may be less likely to accept you have that symptom if you did not mention it anywhere on the questionnaire.
7. If you have other information that is relevant to your difficulties with daily living or mobility activities, send a copy of it with the questionnaire, marked with your name and national insurance number. Chapter 16 has more information about supporting evidence.
8. If you have had a previous disability living allowance (DLA) award, ask the DWP to consider evidence from your DLA claim when making a decision on your PIP claim. You might also ask the DWP to look at evidence from a work capability assessment (see p80).
9. Use the form to let the DWP know what needs or adjustments you may need if you are invited to an assessment. See p256 for some examples.
10. If possible, make a copy of the completed questionnaire and any additional documents. If you send it by post, get a free proof of posting from the Post Office.

Timescales

Your completed questionnaire should be received by the DWP within **one month** of the date it was sent to you. You can often get extra time to complete your questionnaire if this is considered reasonable – eg, to allow you time to get help from an advice service.[110] If you need to ask for extra time, call the PIP helpline as soon as possible.

If you have already missed a deadline, contact the DWP straight away. Not returning the questionnaire, without good reason, can lead to your claim being refused (or your existing award ended).[111] There is more information on below.

The assessment

As part of the PIP assessment process, you are usually asked to take part in a face-to-face, telephone or video assessment with a healthcare professional. A decision can be made without an assessment if it is considered that there is enough other information,[112] but the DWP decides whether this is the case, and if you are asked to attend an assessment, you usually need to go.

PIP assessments are carried out on behalf of the DWP by Maximus, Serco, Ingeus and Capita, or in some areas assessments are carried out by the DWP.[113] Chapter 17 has more information about the practicalities of assessments, including where they can take place, who will assess you, and what to do if you cannot attend.

If you fail to complete part of the assessment process

If you do not attend an **assessment**, and the DWP does not accept that you had good reason for the failure, this will result in a new PIP claim being refused,[114] or an existing award being superseded and ended from the date of the superseding decision.[115]

The same can happen if you do not return a PIP **questionnaire**, although the DWP's guidance suggests that this should not happen if you have a 'mental or cognitive impairment' (see p328).

You can ask for a mandatory reconsideration of this kind of decision (see p294), and appeal if the decision is not changed. You should also get advice about making a new claim, in case your challenge is not successful.

Good reason

If you miss an assessment or do not return a PIP questionnaire, the DWP must decide whether you had a good reason. It should consider your health and the nature of your condition, along with any other reasons why you did not do what was required.[116]

A decision maker will take into account a number of factors including the mental health symptoms you were having at the time.[117] The unsuitability of the location at which you were required to take part in a consultation can also amount to a good reason for not attending it.[118]

Guidance suggests that, beyond your health, a number of other factors may amount to good reason, including caring commitments, a bereavement, a domestic emergency, homelessness, or not having received a notification.[119]

If you need additional support

The DWP's guidance states that parts of the PIP application and assessment process have been adapted for claimants who need additional support (AS), including for mental health reasons.[120] The guidance describes an 'AS marker' that can be attached to your PIP records so that the DWP and the assessment provider consistently recognise your needs. If you believe that you have been overlooked for additional support, contact the PIP helpline or the assessment provider. For more information about additional support, see p326.

If you are unable to engage with the application or assessment process at all, you may need an appointee (see p325).

5. Decisions

Getting a decision

You get decisions about personal independence payment (PIP) by letter. Most people get a decision within four to eight weeks of attending an assessment.

If you disagree with a decision about PIP, you can usually challenge it by making a mandatory reconsideration request and then pursuing an appeal if necessary (see Chapter 20). Note that deadlines apply for challenging decisions.

If you challenge a decision, the DWP (or tribunal) can look at all the PIP disability conditions again, not just the ones you disagree with. This means that, following a mandatory reconsideration or appeal, your award could decrease instead of increasing. It is usually best to get advice before challenging a decision.

If you have been awarded PIP but you are challenging the amount, you can continue to get PIP at the rate you have been awarded during the review or appeal process. However, if you have not been given any award of PIP, you will not get any interim payments while waiting for a decision on a mandatory reconsideration or appeal (see p307 for an example).

Length of awards

PIP is normally awarded for a fixed period – eg, two or five years. The length depends on how soon, if at all, your needs are likely to change.

An fixed-term award may have a review date set, meaning that your entitlement is looked at again before the award ends, or it might have no review date, meaning that you need to reclaim PIP if you want to carry on getting it after the end of the fixed term. There is more information on p158.

An indefinite award can be made if your needs are unlikely to change, or if you are being awarded the highest rate of PIP and your needs are only likely to increase. Most indefinite awards are subject to a 'light-touch' review every 10 years.[121]

Regardless of the stated length of an award, the DWP can reduce or stop the award earlier if it has grounds to revise or supersede it (see p158).

6. Getting paid

When you are paid

Personal independence payment (PIP) is usually paid every four weeks in arrears, or if you are classed as terminally ill, weekly in advance.[122] Payment of PIP starts after a decision has been made on your claim.

Note: it is possible for payment of PIP to be suspended (see p159).

Where your payment goes

PIP is usually paid into your bank account. The DWP can pay all or part of your PIP to someone else, if this is necessary to protect your interests.[123] This kind of alternative payment arrangement (APA) might be useful if, for example, you want a trusted family member to look after your PIP income because your mental health problem makes it difficult for you to manage money, or if you do not have a bank account.[124] An APA can be set up at any point, not just at the start of a claim.

Note:

- The enhanced rate of the **mobility component** can be paid directly to Motability (see p160).[125]
- A lump sum of PIP arrears (ie, 'back pay') may be paid to you in instalments, with your consent, if this is necessary to protect your interests.[126]
- Deductions can be made from PIP (or from PIP back pay) to recover an overpayment of another DWP benefit.[127] If you feel your deductions are too high, get independent advice about whether they can be reduced.

7. Reviews and reassessments

Reassessment

Your entitlement to personal independence payment (PIP) can be reassessed at any time.[128] The DWP might reassess you because you have told it that your condition has got worse or better, or that you have a new condition (see p158). It might also reassess you as part of a scheduled 'award review' (see p158). A reassessment can lead to your PIP award being changed or ended, usually by supersession. Chapter 20 has more information about supersessions and about how to challenge a decision that you disagree with.

Award review

If you have a fixed-term award, it may be reviewed by the DWP up to one year before it ends.[129] The DWP's guidance suggests that all awards longer than two years are subject to review in this way, and that awards for two years or less may also have a review scheduled, but that this is at a decision maker's discretion.[130] You can check whether your PIP will be subject to award review by looking at your award letter or calling the PIP enquiry line. **Note:** it is particularly important to check this if your award was made by a tribunal.

The review process is similar to the assessment process for new claims (see p132). As with a new claim, if you do not return the questionnaire or attend an assessment, this may lead to a decision that you cannot get PIP.

Because of delays in processing reviews, the DWP may extend your award by up to 12 months to make sure payments continue.[131]

If your award is not subject to review, it will end automatically when the fixed term expires. If you want to carry on getting PIP, you must make a renewal claim.

Making a renewal claim

A renewal claim is effectively a new claim for PIP. If you already get PIP, you can make a renewal claim up to six months before your award is due to end (even if you are over pension age – see p129).[132] It is usually best to make the renewal claim as soon as possible. You should not need to make a renewal claim if your PIP is subject to award review (see above).

A renewal claim goes through the usual claim process (see p130) and you are assessed in the same way as with a new claim (see p132).

If no decision is made on a renewal claim before the end of your existing award, your PIP stops until a new decision is made. Other benefits or entitlements that rely on your getting PIP can be affected during this period – eg, a carer's entitlement to carer's allowance, or your access to a Motability vehicle. If there is a delay in getting a decision, or you are not sure what is happening, contact the PIP helpline. If you are told that your award is likely to end before an assessment can be carried out, make a complaint (see p308).

Change of circumstances

You should usually report all changes in your circumstances to the PIP section of the DWP as soon as possible. Do not assume that the PIP section of the DWP already knows, for example, about changes to the other DWP benefits you claim. You can report a change by calling the PIP helpline (0800 121 4433; textphone: 0800 121 4493; Relay UK and British Sign Language video relay services available), or in writing, by sending a letter to the address on your PIP award letter.[133] It is best to report changes in writing, so you have a record of what was said and when.

It is usually best to get independent advice before reporting a change in your health that you think might affect your entitlement to PIP.

If there has been a relevant change of circumstances, a decision maker looks at your award again. You may be asked to go through the assessment process again (see p132). The decision maker will make a new decision about your entitlement, usually by supersession. To find out the date from which the new decision takes effect, see p293.

Note: a change of circumstances can include that your needs are now expected to last beyond the end date of a fixed-term award, even if the *level* of your needs is still the same.[134]

Ongoing evidence requirements

Once you are getting PIP, you may be asked to provide information at any time. If you fail to do so, your PIP could be suspended or even terminated.[135]

8. Personal independence payment and other benefits

Means-tested benefits

Personal independence payment (PIP) can be paid alongside means-tested benefits and is not taken into account as income for their means tests.

If you, your partner or your dependent child are entitled to PIP, you may qualify for additional premiums or amounts in your means-tested benefits, and may not be subject to non-dependant deductions. The same rules could mean that you become entitled to a means-tested benefit for the first time. See the chapter of this *Handbook* about the relevant means-tested benefit.

Non-means-tested benefits

PIP may be paid in addition to any other non-means-tested benefits, except that:

- if you are entitled to PIP, you cannot get claim disability living allowance,[136] attendance allowance,[137] child disability payment, adult disability payment, Scottish adult disability payment or pension age disability payment;[138]
- PIP overlaps with (ie, cannot be paid at the same time as) some war pension payments for constant attendance or mobility, and armed forces independence payment;[139]
- PIP daily living component overlaps with constant attendance allowance under the industrial injuries scheme;[140]
- PIP mobility component is not paid if you get a grant for the use of a vehicle from the NHS.[141]

The benefit cap

In some cases, there is a limit on the total amount of specified benefits you can receive (the 'benefit cap'). The benefit cap does not apply if you, your partner or child are entitled to PIP, even it is not paid because the person entitled to it is in hospital or a care home.

Other sources of financial help

If you get PIP, you may be entitled to other passported benefits such as a blue badge parking permit or a concessionary travel card. Contact your local authority for more information.

If you get the PIP mobility component and you or your carer have a car used only by you or for you, your road tax may be reduced. See gov.uk/financial-help-disabled/vehicles-and-transport.

If you have a low income, you may be eligible for free prescriptions, council tax reduction, and a range of other financial help (see Chapter 15).

Motability

Motability is a charity that runs a scheme to help you lease or buy a car, scooter or powered wheelchair. You are eligible if you get the enhanced rate of the PIP mobility component and have 12 months or more left to run on your award. If you use the scheme, your PIP mobility component is paid directly to Motability.[142] You may also have to make extra payments.

Notes

1. Who can get personal independence payment

1 ss81 and 82 WRA 2012; regs 12-14 SS(PIP) Regs; reg 33(1) UC,PIP,JSA&ESA(C&P) Regs
2 Reg 27 PIP(TP) Regs
3 Reg 25(b) SS(PIP) Regs
4 Regs 15, 25(a), 26 and 27 SS(PIP) Regs

2. The amount of benefit

5 Reg 24(1) SS(PIP) Regs
6 Reg 24(2) SS(PIP) Regs

3. Making a claim

7 Reg 12(1)(b) UC,PIP,JSA&ESA(C&P) Regs
8 Reg 12(1)(c) UC,PIP,JSA&ESA(C&P) Regs
9 Reg 33(1) UC,PIP,JSA&ESA(C&P) Regs
10 Reg 27 UC,PIP,JSA&ESA(C&P) Regs
11 para A2148 ADM
12 s82(4) WRA 2012
13 s82(1)(b) WRA 2012; regs 5(2)(c) and 23(2) UC,PIP,JSA&ESA(DA) Regs
14 s82(2) WRA 2012

4. **How you are assessed**

15 ss77-80 WRA 2012; Part 2 and Sch 1 SS(PIP) Regs
16 ss78-9 WRA 2012
17 DWP, *Personal Independence Payment (PIP) Assessment Guide for Assessment Providers*, November 2024, at gov.uk/government/publications/personal-independence-payment-assessment-guide-for-assessment-providers (abbreviated here as PIP AG), para 1.8.4
18 PIP AG, para 1.6.36
19 *SD v SSWP (PIP)* [2017] UKUT 310 (AAC); *DE v SSWP (PIP)* [2021] UKUT 226 (AAC)
20 *MB v SSWP (PIP)* [2016] UKUT 250 (AAC)
21 Reg 4(2A) and (4) SS(PIP) Regs; *TF v SSWP (PIP)* [2015] UKUT 661 (AAC)
22 *RJ, GMcL and CS v SSWP v RJ (PIP)* [2017] UKUT 105 (AAC), reported as [2017] AACR 32
23 *PA v SSWP (PIP)* [2019] UKUT 270 (AAC); *PM v SSWP (PIP)* [2017] UKUT 154 (AAC); PIP AG, para 2.4
24 *PM v SSWP (PIP)* [2017] UKUT 154 (AAC)
25 *PM v SSWP (PIP)* [2017] UKUT 154 (AAC); *EG v SSWP (PIP)* [2017] UKUT 101 (AAC)
26 *ML v SSWP (PIP)* [2017] UKUT 171 (AAC)
27 *KL v SSWP (PIP)* [2016] UKUT 545 (AAC)
28 *TR v SSWP (PIP)* [2015] UKUT 626 (AAC), reported as [2016] AACR 23. This is essentially a question of whether an activity can be undertaken 'repeatedly'.
29 PIP AG, paras 2.1.13-2.1.14
30 Regs 2, 7(3) and 14 SS(PIP) Regs; reg 24 PIP(TP) Regs; *AB v SSWP (PIP)* [2017] UKUT 217 (AAC)
31 Reg 7 SS(PIP) Regs
32 *GG v SSWP (PIP)* [2016] UKUT 194 (AAC)
33 Sch 1 Part 1 SS(PIP) Regs
34 *SSWP v GM (PIP)* [2017] UKUT 268 (AAC); *JT v SSWP (PIP)* [2018] UKUT 101 (AAC); *CP v SSWP (PIP)* [2018] UKUT 5 (AAC)
35 *RJ, GMcL and CS v SSWP v RJ (PIP)* [2017] UKUT 105 (AAC), reported as [2017] AACR 32
36 DWP, *Safety and Supervision: changes to PIP law from 9 March 2017*, 20 September 2021, at gov.uk/government/publications/personal-independence-payment-changes/safety-and-supervision-changes-to-pip-law-from-9-march-2017
37 *SSWP v IM (PIP)* [2015] UKUT 680 (AAC)
38 *LB v SSWP (PIP)* [2017] UKUT 436 (AAC)
39 *GG v SSWP (PIP)* [2016] UKUT 194 (AAC); *PM v SSWP (PIP)* [2017] UKUT 502 (AAC)
40 *SSWP v MMcK* [2017] CSIH 57. The Supreme Court made no comment on this suggestion in the appeal against this decision (*SSWP v MM (Scotland)* [2019] UKSC 34, reported as [2019] AACR 26).
41 *SO v SSWP (PIP)* [2023] UKUT 56 (AAC)
42 Reg 2 SS(PIP) Regs; *MR v SSWP (PIP)* [2017] UKUT 86 (AAC), although the comments were not strictly necessary to the decision in that case
43 *CW v SSWP (PIP)* [2016] UKUT 197 (AAC), reported as [2016] AACR 44; *NA v SSWP (PIP)* [2015] UKUT 572 (AAC)
44 *CW v SSWP (PIP)* [2016] UKUT 197 (AAC), reported as [2016] AACR 44; *AP v SSWP (PIP)* [2016] UKUT 501 (AAC); *MR v SSWP (PIP)* [2019] UKUT 293 (AAC)
45 Sch 1 Part 1 SS(PIP) Regs
46 *SSWP v KJ (PIP)* [2017] UKUT 358 (AAC)
47 *ZI v SSWP (PIP)* [2016] UKUT 572 (AAC), reported as [2018] AACR 1
48 *SC v SSWP (PIP)* [2017] UKUT 317 (AAC)
49 *AI v SSWP (PIP)* [2016] UKUT 322 (AAC)
50 *LC v SSWP (PIP)* [2016] UKUT 150 (AAC)
51 *MM and BJ v SSWP (PIP)* [2016] UKUT 490 (AAC), reported as [2017] AACR 17
52 *JW v SSWP (PIP)* [2018] UKUT 169 (AAC); *TK v SSWP (PIP)* [2020] UKUT 22 (AAC), reported as [2020] AACR 18
53 *SO v SSWP (PIP)* [2023] UKUT 56 (AAC)
54 Sch 1 Part 1 SS(PIP) Regs
55 *DC v SSWP (PIP)* [2016] UKUT 11 (AAC)
56 PIP AG, para 1.6.36, at gov.uk/government/publications/personal-independence-payment-assessment-guide-for-assessment-providers/pip-assessment-guide-part-1-the-assessment-process
57 *SH v SSWP (PIP)* [2018] UKUT 251 (AAC); *RJ, GMcL and CS v SSWP v RJ (PIP)* [2017] UKUT 105 (AAC), reported as [2017] AACR 32
58 *MB v SSWP (PIP)* [2018] UKUT 139 (AAC)
59 *GG v SSWP (PIP)* [2016] UKUT 194 (AAC)
60 *PE v SSWP (PIP)* [2015] UKUT 309 (AAC), reported as [2016] AACR 10
61 *DP v SSWP (PIP)* [2017] UKUT 156 (AAC)
62 *ML v SSWP (PIP)* [2017] UKUT 171 (AAC)
63 Sch 1 Part 1 SS(PIP) Regs
64 *BM v DfC (PIP)* [2019] NICom 33, reported as [2020] AACR 15 (persuasive while not binding outside of Northern Ireland)
65 *TC v SSWP (PIP)* [2016] UKUT 550 (AAC)
66 Sch 1 Part 1 SS(PIP) Regs

Notes

67 *KP v SSWP (PIP)* [2017] UKUT 30 (AAC)
68 *SE v SSWP (PIP)* [2021] UKUT 1 (AAC)
69 *TR v SSWP (PIP)* [2015] UKUT 626 (AAC), reported as [2016] AACR 23
70 Sch 1 Part 1 SS(PIP) Regs
71 *MH v SSWP (PIP)* [2016] UKUT 531 (AAC), reported as [2018] AACR 12
72 *SM v SSWP (PIP)* [2019] UKUT 292 (AAC); *AM v SSWP (PIP)* [2017] UKUT 7 (AAC)
73 *DV v SSWP (PIP)* [2017] UKUT 244 (AAC); *SF v SSWP (PIP)* [2016] UKUT 543 (AAC)
74 *PM v SSWP (PIP)* [2017] UKUT 154 (AAC)
75 Sch 1 Part 1 SS(PIP) Regs; *SF v SSWP (PIP)* [2016] UKUT 543 (AAC); *SSWP v AM (PIP)* [2015] UKUT 215 (AAC). Both decisions held that the definition of 'engage socially' applies to the words 'engage with other people' in the descriptors.
76 *HA v SSWP (PIP)* [2018] UKUT 56 (AAC)
77 *HA v SSWP (PIP)* [2018] UKUT 56 (AAC); *RC v SSWP (PIP)* [2017] UKUT 352 (AAC)
78 *RC v SSWP (PIP)* [2017] UKUT 352 (AAC)
79 *HJ v SSWP (PIP)* [2016] UKUT 487 (AAC)
80 *AC v SSWP (PIP)* [2021] UKUT 216 (AAC)
81 *SSWP v MM (Scotland)* [2019] UKSC 34, reported as [2019] AACR 26
82 *SSWP v MM (Scotland)* [2019] UKSC 34, reported as [2019] AACR 26; *SL v SSWP (PIP)* [2016] UKUT 147 (AAC)
83 *SSWP v MM (Scotland)* [2019] UKSC 34, reported as [2019] AACR 26, as interpreted by the DWP in para 9 ('Example 3') of ADM Memo 22/20: PIP daily living activity 9 – effect of supreme court judgment
84 *JT v SSWP (PIP)* [2020] UKUT 186 (AAC)
85 Sch 1 Part 1 SS(PIP) Regs
86 *DP v SSWP (PIP)* [2017] UKUT 156 (AAC)
87 *PR v SSWP (PIP)* [2015] UKUT 584 (AAC); *JW v SSWP (PIP)* [2018] UKUT 169 (AAC)
88 *SE v SSWP (PIP)* [2021] UKUT 1 (AAC)
89 In 2017, the DWP amended the wording of some descriptors in this activity, but the High Court quashed the changes in *R (RF) v SSWP* [2017] EWHC 3375 (Admin), reported as [2018] AACR 13. The changes are not included in the descriptors, as they never had any effect (see *AH v SSWP (PIP)* [2018] UKUT 262 (AAC)).
90 Sch 1 Part 1 SS(PIP) Regs
91 *SSWP v NF (PIP)* [2017] UKUT 480 (AAC)
92 *MH v SSWP (PIP)* [2016] UKUT 531 (AAC), reported as [2018] AACR 12
93 *AA v SSWP (PIP)* [2018] UKUT 339 (AAC)
94 The definition of 'prompting' does not require the physical presence of the person who is prompting you.
95 *TR v SSWP (PIP)* [2015] UKUT 626 (AAC), reported as [2016] AACR 23; *PM v SSWP (PIP)* [2017] UKUT 154 (AAC); *AA v SSWP (PIP)* [2018] UKUT 339 (AAC). Note that PIP AG Part 2 suggests that this argument may not be accepted, although it does suggest that only being able to go out in darkness is not managing this activity to an acceptable standard.
96 *MH v SSWP (PIP)* [2016] UKUT 531 (AAC), reported as [2018] AACR 12
97 *AA v SSWP (PIP)* [2018] UKUT 339 (AAC)
98 *JB v SSWP (PIP)* [2019] UKUT 203 (AAC); *SB v SSWP (PIP)* [2019] UKUT 274 (AAC)
99 *MC v SSWP (PIP)* [2019] UKUT 264 (AAC); *SSWP v IV (PIP)* [2016] UKUT 420 (AAC); PIP AG, para 2.4
100 *MH v SSWP (PIP)* [2016] UKUT 531 (AAC), reported as [2018] AACR 12, para 48
101 *AA v SSWP (PIP)* [2018] UKUT 339 (AAC)
102 PIP AG Part 2
103 *MH v SSWP (PIP)* [2016] UKUT 531 (AAC), reported as [2018] AACR 12
104 Sch 1 Part 1 SS(PIP) Regs
105 *MH v SSWP (PIP)* [2016] UKUT 531 (AAC), reported as [2018] AACR 12
106 *NK v SSWP* [2016] UKUT 146 (AAC)
107 Regs 5 and 6 SS(PIP) Regs
108 *AW v SSWP (PIP)* 2022 UKUT 316 (AAC)
109 PIP AG, para 1.3.36
110 Reg 8(1) and (2) SS(PIP) Regs; *SNN v SSWP (PIP)* [2018] UKUT 210 (AAC)
111 Reg 8(3) SS(PIP) Regs
112 Reg 9(1) SS(PIP) Regs says that you 'may' be required to attend a consultation.
113 You can find the health assessment provider for your postcode at gov.uk/guidance/find-your-health-assessment-provider
114 s80(4)-(6) WRA 2012; regs 8(3) and 9(2) SS(PIP) Regs
115 Reg 26(2) UC,PIP,JSA&ESA(DA) Regs; *KB v SSWP (PIP)* [2016] UKUT 537 (AAC)
116 Reg 10 SS(PIP) Regs
117 paras P6071-6074 ADM
118 *OM v SSWP (PIP)* [2017] UKUT 458 (AAC); *TC v SSWP (PIP) (No.2)* [2018] UKUT 286 (AAC)
119 para P6111 ADM
120 PIP AG, paras 1.12.3-1.12.6

5. **Decisions**
121 s88(2) and (3) WRA 2012; paras P2062-2065 ADM

6. **Getting paid**
122 Reg 48 UC,PIP,JSA&ESA(C&P) Regs
123 Reg 58(2) UC,PIP,JSA&ESA(C&P) Regs
124 If you do not have a bank account, you can also ask to be considered for the DWP's payment exception service. See gov.uk/payment-exception-service.
125 Reg 62 UC,PIP,JSA&ESA(C&P) Regs
126 Reg 21ZA SS(C&P) Regs
127 Reg 10 SS(OR) Regs; regs 15-17 SS(PAOR) Regs; *SSWP v AS (PIP)* [2017] UKUT 454 (AAC); *GJ v SSWP (PIP)* [2016] UKUT 8 (AAC); *SSWP v MM (Scotland)* [2019] UKSC 34, reported as [2019] AACR 26

7. **Reviews and reassessments**
128 Reg 11 SS(PIP) Regs
129 Reg 33(2) UC,PIP,JSA&ESA(C&P) Regs
130 para P2063 ADM; DWP response to Freedom of Information request FOI2021/13215, 2 March 2021, at whatdotheyknow.com
131 Response to FOIA request FOI2024/45536, at whatdotheyknow.com
132 Reg 33(2) UC,PIP,JSA&ESA(C&P) Regs
133 Reg 44 UC,PIP,JSA&ESA(DA) Regs
134 *PH v SSWP (DLA)* [2013] UKUT 268 (AAC). While this was a DLA case, it is strongly arguable that the reasoning also applies to fixed-term awards of PIP.
135 Regs 44-47 UC,PIP,JSA&ESA(DA) Regs

8. **Personal independence payment and other benefits**
136 Reg 22(1) PIP(TP) Regs
137 s64(1) and (1A) SSCBA 1992
138 s77(4) WRA 2012
139 Sch 1 paras 5 and 5A SS(OB) Regs; reg 61 UC,PIP,JSA&ESA(C&P) Regs
140 Sch 1 paras 5 SS(OB) Regs
141 Reg 61 UC,PIP,JSA&ESA(C&P) Regs
142 Regs 62, 63 and 64 UC,PIP,JSA&ESA(C&P) Regs

9

Chapter 9

Adult disability payment

This chapter covers:

Key facts

- Adult disability payment (ADP) is a non-means-tested benefit for adults with a disability or long-term health condition who live in Scotland.
- ADP has replaced personal independence payment (PIP) in Scotland. You cannot make a new PIP claim in Scotland.
- You can get ADP while in or out of work, as well as most other benefits. ADP does not count as income for means-tested benefits.
- ADP has two components, each of which is paid at a standard or an enhanced rate. The 'daily living component' is for difficulties with day-to-day activities like preparing food and getting dressed. The 'mobility component' is for difficulties going out and getting around, including for mental health reasons. You can qualify for one or both components.
- Before a determination is made about your eligibility for ADP, you must normally complete a long claim form. You may also be asked to take part in an assessment.
- You can challenge determinations about your eligibility for ADP.
- Getting ADP can mean that you are eligible for other kinds of financial support.

1. Who can get adult disability payment

Adult disability payment (ADP) is a non-means-tested benefit for adults, intended to help with the extra costs of having a disability or long-term health condition.

People with mental health problems, with or without a diagnosis (see p6), may be eligible for ADP.

You can get ADP if:[1]

- you are 16 or over and under pension age, which is currently 66 and rising to 67 between 2026 and 2028 (some people over pension age can also get ADP – see below); *and*
- you are ordinarily resident in Scotland; *and*
- you are not a person subject to immigration control and you meet the residence conditions – see CPAG's *Welfare Benefits Handbook*; *and*
- you are not entitled to child disability payment (CDP), disability living allowance (DLA), Scottish adult disability living allowance (SADLA), personal independence payment (PIP), pension age disability payment (PADP), attendance allowance (AA) or armed forces independence payment; *and*
- you meet the disability conditions (see below); *and*
- you have had your difficulties for at least 13 weeks and expect to have them for at least 39 weeks longer (this is called the 'required period condition').

Special rules apply if you are regarded as terminally ill (see p168) and when you are in prison, living in a care home, and in certain other situations (see Chapter 19).

You claim ADP as an individual. If you are in a couple, one or both of you can claim ADP if you meet the criteria.

Getting adult disability payment if you are over pension age

You may be able to make a new claim for ADP after turning 66 if you had a previous award of ADP, SADLA, DLA or PIP that ended less than a year before you claim.[2]

The upper age limit for getting ADP also does not apply if you claimed ADP before turning 66, are already entitled to ADP when you turn 66, or claim ADP while getting SADLA.[3]

If you have reached pension age and do not get a disability benefit, you should claim PADP (see Chapter 13).

Even if you can get ADP over 66, the amount of the mobility component that you can get might be restricted. There is more information in CPAG's *Welfare Benefits Handbook*.

The disability conditions

The health-related eligibility criteria for ADP are known as the 'disability conditions'. You can still qualify if you do not consider yourself to have a disability.

Your entitlement to ADP is assessed using a points-based test. You score points based on how your mental or physical condition affects your ability to perform 12 different activities: 10 **daily living** activities and two **mobility** activities. The points you are given determine whether you get the daily living and/or the mobility component of ADP, and whether you get the standard or enhanced rate(s) of each. The rules are largely the same as those for PIP. See pp132–53 with reference to the list of differences below.

Differences from the personal independence payment conditions

Some of the wording in the ADP regulations is slightly different from the same provisions for PIP but, in practice, your entitlement should still be the same is it would be if you had claimed PIP.[4] Most of the changes either clarify the meaning of the regulations or reflect PIP caselaw (decisions made by the Upper Tribunal and the courts which say how the law must be applied).

If you are claiming ADP with a mental health problem, the following are the main changes that are likely to be relevant.

- For ADP, there is a definition of 'needs' in the regulations to ensure that you are assessed as needing a type of help if you reasonably require it, even if it is not available or not provided to you.[5]
- In deciding whether you can manage an activity 'safely' for ADP, both the likelihood and severity of any harm must be considered.[6]
- In deciding whether you can manage an activity 'to an acceptable standard' for ADP, the impact of carrying out the activity on you must be considered.[7]
- For ADP, you satisfy a descriptor if it applies during some part of the day (midnight to midnight) unless you do so only for a 'minimal or fleeting' time.[8]
- The ADP definition of 'aid or appliance' clarifies that to score points for using an aid or appliance, you must need to use it (rather than choosing to). It also makes it clear that aids and appliances can include things which are not designed for disabled people.[9]
- Daily living activity 3: unlike PIP, the definition of 'medication' for ADP includes medication prescribed or recommended by a 'health professional who is registered by the Health and Care Professions Council' (*not* just doctor, nurse or pharmacist). There is list of the other regulated professions on the Council's website.[10]
- Daily living activity 7: the ADP definition of 'communication support' contains extra words. The person providing support can be 'trained or experienced in communicating with *people in general, or the individual in particular*'.
- Daily living activity 9: the title of the ADP activity and all of the descriptors have an extra word inserted which is not in the PIP assessment. In each case, they refer to your ability to 'engage *socially* with other people'. This reflects PIP caselaw, which has confirmed that the definition of 'engage socially' applies to this activity. The definition of 'social support' also contains extra words. The person providing support can be 'trained or experienced in assisting *people in general, or the individual in particular*'.

- Mobility activity 1: the ADP regulations contain an extra definition that is not included in the PIP regulations. 'Follow the route of a journey' means 'for an individual to navigate and make their way along a planned route to a planned destination'. Descriptor 1b also contains extra words. It reads: 'Needs *the prompting of another person* to be able to undertake any journey to avoid overwhelming psychological distress to the individual.' It appears that the intention is to leave beyond doubt that reminders from something other than a person (eg, reminder notifications set up on a mobile phone) cannot allow you to satisfy this descriptor.

PIP caselaw and ADP

PIP caselaw that has not been incorporated into the ADP rules is still likely to be persuasive in deciding your ADP entitlement. In one case, the Upper Tribunal for Scotland has held that a tribunal may err in law if it does not follow PIP caselaw from before ADP was introduced if the descriptors are worded identically, even though that caselaw is not formally binding.[11]

2. The amount of benefit

The daily living component of adult disability payment (ADP) is paid at one of two weekly rates:[12]

- the standard rate is £73.90;
- the enhanced rate is £110.40.

The mobility component of ADP is paid at one of two weekly rates:[13]

- the standard rate is £29.20;
- the enhanced rate is £77.05.

3. Making a claim

How to claim

Note: the information here does not apply if you claim adult disability payment (ADP) and are terminally ill (see p168 instead).

You can start a claim for ADP:

- online at mygov.scot/adult-disability-payment/how-to-apply; *or*
- by calling 0800 182 2222 to request a paper claim form; *or*
- if you use British Sign Language, via Contact Scotland BSL.

The date of claim is usually the date you submit your full name and date of birth to Social Security Scotland (SSS), as long as you then provide the rest of the required information (see below). If you do not provide all of the required information within the time allowed your date of claim is the date you eventually provide it. You have *not* made a claim for ADP until you complete all of the required parts of your claim, and provide any required evidence to SSS.

Note: if you get child disability payment (CDP) and are aged 15–17, see p198 for information to help you to decide whether to claim ADP.

Claiming in advance and backdating

You can claim ADP **in advance** if you do not satisfy the entitlement conditions, but will do so within 13 weeks.[14] This may be relevant if you do not satisfy the required period condition (see p165) when you first claim.

You cannot **backdate** a claim for ADP, unless you are regarded as terminally ill.[15] If you might have qualified for ADP sooner but did not claim because you were given the wrong information or misled by SSS, you could complain and ask for compensation (see p310). From November 2025, backdating will be available if you get personal independence payment in another part of the UK and move to Scotland.[16]

Note: the term 'backdating' is often informally used to mean getting arrears of your benefit going back to a claim or decision date – eg, after winning an appeal. However, in this *Handbook*, we use backdating to mean getting paid benefit for a period before the date you claimed.

Additional support and appointees

If you have (or will have) difficulty with the claims process and need additional support, see Chapter 21. If you cannot manage the claims process at all you may need an appointee (see p325).

What you will be asked and how long it will take

To start your claim, you must provide SSS with your full name and date of birth. In practice, you are also asked questions about the residence and presence conditions at this point. SSS refers to this as Part 1 of your ADP claim.

Unless you are regarded as terminally ill (see below), you then have eight weeks to complete your claim by providing the rest of the required information (referred to as Part 2). This eight-week period can be extended if there is good reason for the delay.[17] Part 2 relates to how your condition(s) affect your ability to manage the different daily living and mobility activities and is covered in the 'How you are assessed' section of this chapter (see p169).

Terminal illness

The rules about claiming ADP are different if you are terminally ill. You are regarded as 'terminally ill' if it is the judgement of a doctor or nurse who is involved in your care or diagnosis and acting in a professional capacity, that you have a progressive disease that can reasonably be expected to cause your death.[18] You should explain that the claim is on the grounds of terminal illness when making it (claims from terminally ill people are widely referred to as 'special rules' claims). You must provide a judgement that you are terminally ill – either a Benefits Assessment under Special Rules in Scotland (BASRiS) form or a DWP SR1 or DS1500 form completed by a doctor or nurse.[19]

If you claim ADP and you are regarded as terminally ill, you do not have to provide extra information about your care and mobility needs and are automatically entitled to the enhanced rates of both components.[20]

Moving from disability living allowance to adult disability payment

Until 21 March 2025, you could be transferred to ADP if you lived in Scotland, got disability living allowance (DLA) and were aged 16–64.[21] Now, if you still get DLA and are 18 or over, you will be transferred to Scottish adult disability living allowance (SADLA) instead. Once you get SADLA, you can choose to claim ADP, but only if you were born after 8 April 1948. If you do, ADP replaces your SADLA.

What is Scottish adult disability living allowance?

Scottish adult disability living allowance (SADLA) is a benefit introduced on 21 March 2025, which only people who still have an award of DLA and are aged at least 18 can get.[22] If you are in this situation and live in Scotland, you will be transferred to SADLA without needing to claim. It is not possible to make a new claim for SADLA, but if you had an award of either DLA or SADLA that ended less than one year ago, you can ask to be awarded SADLA. See CPAG's *Welfare Benefits Handbook* for details.

4. How you are assessed

Note: this assessment process does not apply if you are regarded as terminally ill (see p168).

To get adult disability payment (ADP), you need to meet the disability conditions set out on p165. Social Security Scotland (SSS) uses a standard assessment process to decide whether you meet those conditions.

Part 2 of the claim form

When you start a claim for ADP, you are asked to provide information about how your condition(s) affects your ability to manage the different daily living and mobility activities. This is known as Part 2 of your claim (see p168). If you do not complete it, or do not complete it in time, you have not made a claim.

You provide the information using an online Part 2 form (if you started your claim online) or on a paper Part 2 form. You can ask SSS to help you complete the form by calling 0800 182 2222. The form is similar to a personal independence payment (PIP) questionnaire, but with more detailed questions about each daily living and mobility activity. You should complete it in the same way as a PIP questionnaire (see p154).

Timescales

You normally have eight weeks to return the Part 2 form.[23] This eight-week period can be extended if there is good reason for the delay.[24] You should contact SSS and ask for an extension as soon as possible if you need more time.

Supporting evidence

You are usually asked to provide supporting evidence – eg, reports from your doctor or other professionals, a letter from someone who knows you well, and/or a diary of symptoms.[25] See Chapter 16 for more information about supporting evidence. Do not delay submitting the claim while waiting for evidence; it can be provided later by post or online at mygov.scot.

If you cannotprovide supporting evidence yourself, you can ask SSS to gather it on your behalf. You are asked about this when completing the Part 2 form.

The assessment

You can be asked to take part in an assessment if SSS believes it is needed to determine your entitlement. SSS refers to this as a 'consultation'. Usually, a consultation takes place by telephone, by video call or in person) and your needs and wishes should be taken into account.[26] A supporter (eg, a family member, friend or adviser) can take part in your assessment, including speaking on your behalf, unless this is considered unreasonable by SSS.[27] The assessment is audio recorded unless you ask for this not to happen.[28]

The advice about what to do at an assessment is similar to that for PIP. For tips on how to prepare for an assessment, see p260.

If you do not take part in an assessment

If you have been asked to take part in an assessment and cannot do so, explain this to SSS as soon as possible and ask for it to be rearranged. If you have already missed it, contact SSS as soon as possible with an explanation. Guidance suggests that if you do not attend an assessment, a determination will normally be made based on the information that SSS already has about you. However, the law also allows SSS to make a determination that you are not entitled to ADP simply because you did not take part in the assessment.[29]

If this happens, you can request a redetermination (see p313). You should make a new claim for ADP as well, in case your challenge is unsuccessful.

5. Decisions

Getting a determination

You get decisions about adult disability payment (ADP) by letter.[30] In the Scottish benefits system, these decisions are known as 'determinations'.

If you disagree with a determination, you can challenge it by asking for a redetermination and then pursuing an appeal if necessary (see Chapter 20). Note that deadlines apply for challenging determinations.

If you challenge a determination, Social Security Scotland (SSS) or a tribunal can look at all the ADP disability conditions again, not just the ones you ask it to reconsider. This means that, following a redetermination or appeal, your award could decrease instead of increasing. It is usually best to get advice before challenging a determination.

You may be able to get interim payments of ADP at the same rate as your previous award while a redetermination request is being considered and while an appeal is pending. This is known as 'short-term assistance' (see p316).

Length of awards

ADP is awarded without a fixed end date. When making an award, SSS can (but does not always) specify a period after which it will review your ADP award, if it thinks that your needs may change. The length of any review period should be based on whether, and how soon, your needs are likely to change. If you get the enhanced rate of both ADP components and your needs are unlikely to change (or only unlikely to increase) you may not be set a review period. If a review period is set, SSS must make a new determination of your entitlement after that period ends (see p172).[31]

SSS can reduce or stop the award earlier if it has grounds to (see p172).

6. Getting paid

When you are paid

Adult disability payment (ADP) is usually paid every four weeks in arrears. If you are regarded as terminally ill, you are paid weekly in advance instead.[32] You will start to be paid ADP after a decision has been made on your claim.

Note: it is possible for payment of ADP to be suspended (see p173).

Where your payment goes

ADP is usually paid into your bank account.

Note:

- Payment of your ADP can be made to another person for your benefit, if Social Security Scotland (SSS) considers this is appropriate.[33] This might be useful if, for example, you want a trusted family member to look after your ADP income because your mental health problem makes it difficult for you to manage money.
- The enhanced rate of the mobility component can be paid directly to Motability (see p173).
- Deductions can be made from ADP to recover an overpayment of another SSS benefit.[34]
- Your ADP payments can be suspended if you fail to provide information when you are asked to (see p173) or if there are issues about the person your benefit is being paid to. SSS must consider your financial circumstances before making a decision to suspend payment.[35]

7. Reviews and reassessments

Scheduled reviews

When Social Security Scotland (SSS) makes an award of adult disability payment (ADP), it may specify a review date when it will make a new determination on your entitlement. SSS calls this a 'scheduled review'. There is more information about how review periods are set on p171.[36]

As part of the review process, you are likely to be asked to complete a form, and may be invited to an assessment, similarly to when you make a new claim for ADP (see p169).

Change of circumstances

You should report changes in your circumstances to SSS as soon as possible.

You can report a change by phone or on the form you can download from mygov.scot/adult-disability-payment-changes/letting-social-security-scotland-know. Check your most recent determination carefully, as it tells you how you must report a change.[37]

It is usually best to get independent advice before reporting a change in your health that you think might affect your entitlement to ADP.

If there has been a relevant change of circumstances, a decision maker looks at the award again and makes a new determination (see p314).[38]

Moving from Scotland

If you move from Scotland to elsewhere in the UK, your ADP entitlement ends 13 weeks after you stop being ordinarily resident in Scotland.[39] **Note**: your ADP may *not* end (but your payment could be affected) if you go into hospital, residential care or prison elsewhere in the UK (see Chapter 19).[40]

For how your benefit is affected if you move out of the UK, see CPAG's *Welfare Benefits Handbook*.

Ongoing evidence requirements

If SSS is reviewing your ADP award, or it thinks that your circumstances may have changed, it can ask you to provide further information.

If you do not provide the information within the time limit SSS sets you to do so, your ADP payments can be suspended.[41] If you need more time to provide the information, contact SSS as soon as possible to request an extension.

8. Adult disability payment and other benefits

Adult disability payment (ADP) interacts with other benefits in the same ways that personal independence payment (PIP) does. There are the same benefit cap exemptions for ADP as for PIP, and the same rules about Motability apply. See p159 for more information.

A child who gets the ADP highest rate care component gets a child winter heating payment.

Notes

1. Who can get adult disability payment

1 s31 and Sch 5 SS(S)A 2018; Parts 2-6 DAWAP(S) Regs
2 Reg 23 DAWAP(S) Regs
3 Reg 24 DAWAP(S) Regs
4 Sch 1 DAWAP(S) Regs
5 Reg 2 DAWAP(S) Regs
6 Reg 7(2)(b) and (3)(a) DAWAP(S) Regs
7 Reg 7(2)(b) and (3)(b) DAWAP(S) Regs
8 Reg 10(2) DAWAP(S) Regs
9 Reg 2 DAWAP(S) Regs
10 hcpc-uk.org/about-us/who-we-regulate/the-professions
11 *SSS v AH, AS, SS and GA* [2024] UT 63

2. The amount of benefit

12 Reg 34(1) DAWAP(S) Regs
13 Reg 34(2) DAWAP(S) Regs

3. Making a claim

14 Reg 35(2) DAWAP(S) Regs
15 Reg 26(4)-(6) DAWAP(S) Regs
16 Reg 9(9) The Social Security (Cross-border Provision, Case Transfer and Miscellaneous Amendments) (Scotland) Regulations 2025 (draft)
17 Reg 35(4) and (6) DAWAP(S) Regs
18 s31(1)(b) and Sch 5 para 1(2)-(3) SS(S)A 2018; reg 26(7), (8) and (10) DAWAP(S) Regs; SSS, *Chief Medical Officer's Guidance for Clinicians Completing a BASRiS Form*

19 SSS, *Special Rules for Terminal Illness: frequently asked questions*
20 Reg 26(1) DAWAP(S) Regs
21 Regs 2 and 3 The Disability Assistance for Working Age People (Transitional Provisions and Miscellaneous Amendment) (Scotland) Regulations 2022 SSI No.217
22 s31 and Sch 5 SS(S)A 2018; regs 3 and 4 DA(SADLA) Regs

4. **How you are assessed**
23 Reg 35(4) DAWAP(S) Regs
24 Reg 35(6) DAWAP(S) Regs
25 SSS DMG *Gathering supporting information for adult disability payment*, paras 2, 8-15 and 32-4
26 s14(a) and (b) SS(S)A 2018; SSS DGM *Consultations for adult disability payment*
27 s59 SS(S)A 2018
28 mygov.scot/adult-disability-payment-consultations/audio-recording-consultation
29 s54(3) SS(S)A 2018; SSS DMG, *Consultations for Adult Disability Payment*, para 17

5. **Decisions**
30 ss37 and 40 SS(S)A 2018
31 Regs 37 and 47 DAWAP(S) Regs; SSS DMG, *Choosing an appropriate review period for adult disability payment*

6. **Getting paid**
32 Reg 36 DAWAP(S) Regs
33 Reg 33(1) DAWAP(S) Regs
34 Reg 44 DAWAP(S) Regs
35 Regs 38 and 39 DAWAP(S) Regs

7. **Reviews and reassessments**
36 Regs 37 and 47 DAWAP(S) Regs; SSS DMG, *Choosing an appropriate review period for adult disability payment*
37 s56(2)(b) SS(S)A 2018
38 Reg 48 DAWAP(S) Regs
39 Reg 53(4) DAWAP(S) Regs
40 Reg 53(2) DAWAP(S) Regs
41 s54 SS(S)A 2018; reg 38 DAWAP(S)Regs

Chapter 10

Disability living allowance

This chapter covers:

Note: this chapter only covers the rules about disability living allowance (DLA) for children.

Key facts

- Disability living allowance (DLA) is a non-means-tested benefit for children with a disability or long-term health condition.
- You can claim DLA for a child alongside most other benefits. It does not count as income for the purposes of means-tested benefits.
- DLA has two components. A child can qualify for one or both. The 'care component' reflects a child's needs for attention or supervision during the day and/or at night, and is paid at one of three rates. The 'mobility component' reflects difficulties going out and getting around, including for mental health reasons, and is paid at one of two rates.
- You can challenge decisions about a child's eligibility for DLA.
- Getting DLA for a child can make you eligible for other financial support.
- You can no longer make a claim for child DLA in Scotland (see Chapter 11).

1. Who can get disability living allowance

Disability living allowance (DLA) is a non-means-tested benefit for children and young people under 16 (we use the term '**children**' in this chapter). DLA is intended to help with the extra costs of having a disability or long-term health condition. Children with mental health symptoms, with or without a diagnosis (see p8), may be eligible.

You can get DLA for a child if the child:[1]

- is under 16 when you claim (they must be at least three to get the higher rate of the mobility component and five to get the lower rate; DLA normally ends when a child is 16); *and*
- meets the residence conditions and is not a person subject to immigration control (although there are some exceptions) – see CPAG's *Welfare Benefits Handbook*; *and*
- meets the disability conditions below; *and*
- has had their needs for at least three months and is expected to have them for at least six months longer (this is called the 'qualifying period condition').

Note:

- If a child meets these criteria but lives in Scotland, see Chapter 11.
- Special rules apply if a child is regarded as being terminally ill (see p183) and in certain other situations (eg, if they are living in a care home – see Chapter 19).

The disability conditions

The health-related eligibility criteria for DLA are known as the 'disability conditions'. Importantly, the child does not need to be considered to have a disability to qualify. In this section, we use the expression 'so severely disabled, physically or mentally'. This is the phrase used in law but, in practice, it just means that a child's difficulties must be the result of a mental or physical health condition or disability.

Disability conditions for the care component

Entitlement to the care component of DLA is about a child's need for **attention** and/or **supervision**. Broadly, 'attention' is active care and 'supervision' is passive care which might never involve intervention.[2] The two categories can overlap, and when completing a DLA form, it is important to emphasise the full extent of a child's needs without limiting information to one category or the other.

'Attention' and mental health

Attention means 'a service of a close and intimate nature... involving personal contact carried out in the presence of the disabled person' and does not need to be physical.[3] Encouragement, stimulation, reassurance or giving verbal instructions may be attention.[4] Attention must be in connection with 'bodily functions'.[5] These include things like eating, washing, dressing and undressing, taking medication, reading, communicating, cognition and sleeping. So, for example, if you need to encourage a child to change their clothes, wash, and take medication, this may be classed as attention.

Decision makers must consider the amount of attention needed to allow a child 'as far as reasonably possible to live a normal life'.[6] Having a social life, recreation and cultural activities are part of normal life. A child's age and interests should be taken into account when deciding what help they reasonably need.[7]

'Supervision' and mental health

To show that a child needs supervision (eg, to prevent them from self-harming), you do not need to show that supervision would completely remove all risk of harm; the test is whether it would result in 'a real reduction in the risk of harm'.[8]

In considering a need for supervision, the decision maker weighs the likelihood of a risk and the seriousness of the potential consequences.[9] For example, the consequences of an unsupervised child acting on suicidal thoughts could be dire, even though the likelihood of this happening might be reasonably low. In this situation it can be argued that the child reasonably requires continual supervision.[10] In assessing the likelihood of danger, the DWP must look at what has happened in the past as well as what may happen in the future.[11]

Lowest rate care component

A child can get the lowest rate care component if, due to their mental or physical health condition or disability, they require attention from another person for a significant portion of the day (whether during a single period or a number of periods) in connection with their bodily functions.[12]

'A significant portion of the day' is often taken to mean about an hour.[13] However, spending less time than that in total but needing to give attention for a number of short periods might qualify. Factors like the amount, importance or effect of the attention may be taken into account.[14] Help at night does not count.[15]

Middle rate care component

A child can get the middle rate care component if they:[16]

- satisfy one of the daytime disability conditions *or* one of the night-time disability conditions (see below); *or*
- undergo renal dialysis, in certain circumstances.

Highest rate care component

A child can get the highest rate care component if they:[17]

- satisfy one of the daytime disability conditions *and* one of the night-time disability conditions (see below); *or*
- are regarded as being terminally ill (see p183).

The daytime disability conditions

The daytime disability conditions are that, as a result of their mental or physical health condition or disability, a child satisfies at least one of the following two requirements.[18]

– They require **frequent attention** from another person throughout the day in connection with their bodily functions. Frequency refers to the number and pattern of times attention is needed over a period of time, and should be considered as a whole.[19] A child may still qualify even if the times when attention is needed are not spread evenly throughout the day.[20] The total amount of time taken up is not relevant.

– They require **continual supervision** throughout the day in order to avoid substantial danger to themself or others. 'Continual' does not mean constant, but it is more than supervision which is required only occasionally or intermittently.[21] The fact that a child may need less supervision in a safe, structured environment, such as school, does not mean that continual supervision is not needed.[22] If it is unavoidable that a child is left alone for a period, they can still qualify if you can show that they are at risk during this time.

The night-time disability conditions

'Night' means 'that period of inactivity' which begins when 'the household... closes down for the night'. This is usually assumed to start at around 11pm and end at around 7am.[23] So if, for example, a child can be understood as having night needs if care is needed at 11pm, even if they do not go to bed until later.

The night-time disability conditions are that, as a result of their mental or physical health condition or disability, a child satisfies at least one of the following two requirements.[24]

– They require **prolonged or repeated attention** from another person at night in connection with their bodily functions. Sleeping is a 'bodily function', so help needed for a child to get (back) to sleep is attention.[25] There is no clear definition of 'prolonged' but it could mean around 20 minutes.[26] 'Repeated' means twice or more.[27] There is no requirement that attention is needed 'most of the time' – eg, on more than half the nights in a week. There should instead be a broad overall judgement of a child's needs.[28]

– They require another person to be awake at night for a prolonged period or at frequent intervals to **watch over** them in order to avoid substantial danger to themself or others. A 'prolonged period' may mean about 20 minutes or more.[29] 'At frequent intervals' is more than twice. The frequent intervals need not be spread throughout the night, but can be concentrated in one part of it.[30]

What else you need to know about the care component

- To get the care component of DLA, a child's need for attention or supervision must be 'substantially in excess of the normal requirements' of a child of the same age.[31]
- The attention or supervision they 'require' is what is *reasonably required* rather than what is *medically required*.[32]
- A child with a mental health problem does not need to have a diagnosis to get the care component. What is important is that they have care needs because of their mental health symptoms.[33] However, medical evidence is usually still important to establish that they have mental health symptoms and what their needs are.[34] Problems can sometimes arise if a child has, for example, behavioural issues that are not clearly linked to a particular mental health

condition. In these cases, decision makers will consider whether a child has the physical or mental power to control their behaviour.[35]

- Refusing medical treatment for a child may affect whether or not they can get the care component. If treatment offered by their doctor would remove the need for help, the attention or supervision a child gets may not be reasonably required. However, it may not be 'reasonably appropriate' for you to agree to the treatment – eg, because of the risks or side effects.[36]

Examples

Ffion (12) has anorexia. Anorexia affects different people in different ways, but for Ffion, it means that she restricts the amount of food she eats, exercises excessively and has compulsive weighing and appearance-checking behaviour. Due to her illness, FFion struggles with her emotions and thoughts. She can be withdrawn around other people and finds it difficult to concentrate.

Because of her condition, Ffion needs more care and support than most children her age. At home, her parents give her lots of reassurance and persuasion to eat meals. She needs help getting dressed, and this takes a long time, due to appearance-checking behaviours. She needs support to take part in social activities and extra encouragement to communicate, especially during counselling sessions. At school, she needs attention at lunch time and extra support to engage with others and focus in lessons.

Ffion is awarded the middle rate of the care component of DLA. This is because she needs frequent attention from another person throughout the day in connection with bodily functions such as eating, dressing, reading and communicating.

Elsie (8) has social anxiety and selective mutism. She experiences significant anxiety in settings like school, after-school clubs and large family gatherings. As a result, she does not speak to teachers, classmates, or others outside her close family. A decision maker awards her the lower rate of the care component of DLA on the basis that she needs another person's help to communicate for a 'significant portion' of the day. However, Elsie's grandmother, who is her DLA appointee, challenges this decision. She argues that the middle rate should be awarded because Elsie actually needs frequent attention throughout the day. She explains that Elsie not only needs help with communicating but, because of her anxiety, with activities like eating her school lunch and getting changed for PE.

Disability conditions for the mobility component

Lower rate mobility component

A child aged five or over can get the lower rate mobility component of DLA if, because of their mental or physical health condition or disability, they cannot use unfamiliar routes outdoors 'without guidance or supervision from another person most of the time'.[37] The need for guidance or supervision must be substantially more than the typical needs of a child of the same age.[38]

'Guidance' and 'supervision' can overlap. It is important to emphasise the full extent of a child's needs without trying to fit them neatly into either category.

'Guidance' can mean physically leading or directing a child, or verbally giving instructions or encouragement. It can include helping to avoid obstacles or places that upset them, or leading or persuading a child when they become disorientated or are anxious.

'Supervision' can be precautionary. For example, it can be monitoring a child's mental or emotional state in case they need more assistance to continue walking, or monitoring the route ahead for places or situations which might upset them. Supervision can also be active, such as encouraging or cajoling a child, or distracting them from fears[39] or possibly alarming situations.[40] Unlike the 'continual supervision' condition for the DLA care component (see p178), the child does not need to require supervision to prevent 'substantial danger'.[41] If they get the care component because they require continual supervision, they may also get the lower rate mobility component, but this is not automatic.[42] It is enough that supervision helps, even if it does not remove risks completely or if a child may not always respond well to the person providing it.[43]

If a child's mental health problem means that they need someone with them to overcome a fear of going outside, they are likely to satisfy the 'guidance or supervision' requirement.[44] If they can just manage a walk into their garden, this could be enough to qualify.[45] If no amount of reassurance can persuade them to go outside, it is possible that they may not qualify.[46]

Higher rate mobility component

A child aged three or over can get the higher rate mobility component if:[47]

- they have a disability from a physical cause that means they are unable, or virtually unable, to walk; *or*
- they are both blind and deaf; *or*
- they are blind or severely visually impaired; *or*
- they were born without feet or are a double amputee; *or*
- they have a 'severe mental impairment' (ie, arrested or incomplete development of the brain which results in severe impairment of intelligence and social functioning), have 'severe behavioural problems' and qualify for the highest rate of DLA care component.[48] This definition is unlikely to apply to children whose only disability or health condition is a mental health problem, but can apply to children with mental health symptoms who also have a developmental condition or autism.

'Unable or virtually unable to walk'

To get the higher rate mobility component due to walking difficulties, those difficulties must have a physical cause.[49] This does not mean that this category is always irrelevant for children with mental health problems. For example, if a child's walking is impaired by physical weakness due to anorexia, the cause is physical and they can meet this criterion.[50]

'Benefit from enhanced facilities for locomotion'

On top of the criteria above, to get the DLA mobility component, a child must be able to 'benefit from enhanced facilities for locomotion'. That means they must be able to make outdoor journeys from time to time.[51] It is not essential that they are interested in or enjoy going out, provided that it would be beneficial for them to do so.

Example

Arthur (15) has severe depression. For Arthur, this means no longer enjoying the things he used to and feeling very low most of the time. He lacks energy or enthusiasm for day-to-day tasks, has a poor appetite and experiences disrupted sleep. For the last three months, Arthur has been unable to go to school because of his condition. He self-harms and has recently been telling his mother that he is having suicidal thoughts.

Arthur needs substantially more help than another 15-year-old without his condition. The attention he needs in the daytime includes encouragement and prompting to wash, change clothes, eat, take medication and communicate with professionals. He also needs continual supervision throughout the day to minimise the risk of self-harming or acting on suicidal thoughts. Arthur's needs are likely to satisfy one or both of the daytime care conditions (he only *needs* to satisfy one).

Arthur often remains awake until 1 or 2 am because he struggles to fall asleep, during which time he experiences particularly difficult thoughts and feelings. His mother regularly spends two hours or more after 11 pm comforting and reassuring Arthur to help him get to sleep. During this time, she is also supervising him to minimise the risk of self-harm. Arthur's needs are likely to satisfy one or both of the night-time care conditions (he only *needs* to satisfy one).

Based on his daytime and night-time needs, Arthur should be awarded the highest rate of the care component of DLA.

Arthur's needs are also likely to satisfy the requirements for the lower rate of the mobility component of DLA. He rarely leaves the house, except to go to medical appointments with his mother. It is unlikely that he could go out without guidance or supervision from another person because of his need for verbal reassurance, encouragement and comforting, as well as the need for supervision to minimise the risk that he will hurt himself or act on suicidal thoughts.

Arthur will not be awarded the higher rate of the mobility component of DLA because he does not have any difficulty with the physical act of walking or with his sight, has both feet and does not have, for example, a developmental condition or autism.

2. **The amount of benefit**

Disability living allowance (DLA) care component is paid at one of three weekly rates:[52]

- the lowest rate is £29.20;
- the middle rate is £73.90;
- the highest rate is £110.40.

DLA mobility component is paid at one of two weekly rates:[53]
- the lower rate is £29.20;
- the higher rate is £77.05.

3. Making a claim

How to claim

A claim for disability living allowance (DLA) is made by an adult on a child's behalf. This person must usually live with the child and is often the child's parent or guardian.[54]

A claim for DLA must be in writing, by completing the approved claim form (DLA1 Child). It is best to request a claim form the DLA helpline (0800 121 4600, textphone: 0800 121 4523, Relay UK and British Sign Language video relay services available). A form you request by phone should arrive date stamped, and if you return it within six weeks, the date you called to request it will be treated as your date of claim. The DWP can extend the six-week deadline if it considers that this is reasonable, so if you return the form late, explain why.[55]

If you do not get a date-stamped form, or if you return a date-stamped form too late, your date of claim will be the date that the DWP receives your completed form. This applies, for example, if you print a DLA1 Child form from the internet.

The claim form asks questions about the child's needs. See p183 for tips on completing the form.

Claiming in advance and backdating

A claim for DLA can be made **in advance**, before a child meets the qualifying conditions on p175, provided you claim no more than three months before the child will actually qualify.[56]

A claim for DLA cannot be **backdated.**[57] If you believe you would have claimed earlier but were misled or wrongly advised by the DWP, you could make a complaint and ask for compensation (see p308).

Note: the term 'backdating' is often informally used to mean getting arrears of your benefit going back to a claim or decision date – eg, after winning an appeal. However, in this *Handbook*, we use backdating to mean getting paid benefit for a period before the date you claimed.

Additional support

If you have (or will have) difficulty with the claims process and need additional support, see Chapter 21.

Terminal illness

The DLA claims process is different if a child is terminally ill. They are regarded as 'terminally ill' if they have a progressive illness and it would not be a surprise to their doctors were they to die from it within the next 12 months. This can apply even if there are realistic hopes that they may live longer than that.[58]

If you are claiming on the basis of a child's terminal illness, you must tick the box on the claim form to say you are claiming under the 'special rules'. The claim will then be fast-tracked. In addition to the claim form, you must provide Form SR1 or DS1500, completed by the child's GP, consultant or specialist nurse.

If a child is regarded as being terminally ill, they are automatically treated as satisfying the conditions for the highest rate of the DLA care component. They do not automatically get DLA mobility component, so if you think they will qualify for this, you must complete the mobility sections of the form. They must satisfy the usual mobility conditions (except the three-month qualifying period).

4. How a child is assessed

Note: this assessment process does not apply if a child is regarded as terminally ill.

To get disability living allowance (DLA), a child must meet the disability conditions, set out on pp176–81. The DWP uses a standard assessment process to decide whether a child meets these conditions.

The claim form

The assessment process starts with the DLA claim form, which asks about the child's needs. If you find it difficult to complete the form, many advice agencies can help, and, in some circumstances, the DWP can send a visiting officer to assist you to complete the form at your home. See Chapter 21 for more information.

Completing the claim form

Before you start, look at the rules on pp176–81 to understand what the decision maker needs to know.

Consider all of the mental health symptoms listed on p13.

Give as much detail as you can. The form has limited space for you to explain a child's difficulties, so it is usually a good idea to use extra sheets of paper to provide more details. You might use one sheet per activity (eg, eating, communicating, going out) as well as one sheet to summarise your child's main symptoms and treatment history.

To give a full picture of a child's needs, it might be useful to keep a diary for a week or a month, recording their symptoms and the help they need and received each day. Attach the diary to the form and refer to it in your answers.

Remember to explain:
- how often help is needed each day (and night);
- how long help is needed for each time;
- what has happened, or could happen, if the child does not get the help they need;
- how many days (and nights) a week help is needed. The child may still get DLA even if they need help on fewer than half of the days in a week. It is not about simply comparing the number of 'good' versus 'bad' days.[59] Explain fully the help needed on bad days, and include the help needed on good days for an overall picture.

Ideally, get someone who knows the child well to check your answers.
Keep a copy of the completed form and ask the Post Office for free proof of posting.

Gathering further information

When you return the DLA form, it is a good idea to enclose supporting evidence – eg, reports from a child's doctor or other professionals, a letter from their teacher or someone else who knows them well, and/or a symptoms diary. Chapter 16 has more information.

DLA can be awarded on the basis of the claim form (and supporting evidence) alone. However, if it needs more details, the DWP may contact you, the child's medical professionals, their school, or someone else you named on the form.

Note: it is generally better to provide information from these people or organisations when you make the claim than to rely on the DWP to contact them for information.

What advisers say: supporting evidence for DLA

'Do read supporting evidence carefully before sending it off. Unfortunately, DLA is about emphasing the restrictions and difficulties a child has [but] quite rightly, for so many reasons, evidence from consultants or schools will emphasise the positives, achievements and way a child contributes. They may not always include the more limited ways that a child might get involved, or detail the extra support or adjustments needed to make that happen. You or an adviser may need to speak to the professional directly about the DLA criteria.'

The DWP can arrange for the child to be given a medical examination by a healthcare professional. This is fairly rare. If you (or an older child) refuse a medical examination without good cause, the claim is likely to be refused.[60]

5. Decisions

Getting a decision

You get decisions about disability living allowance (DLA) by letter. Most people get a decision within about 15 weeks of returning the form.

If you disagree with a decision about DLA, you can usually challenge it by making a mandatory reconsideration request and then pursuing an appeal if necessary. See Chapter 20 for more information. Note that there are deadlines for challenging decisions.

If you challenge a decision, the DWP (or tribunal) can look at all the DLA disability conditions again, not just the ones that you disagree with. This means that following a mandatory reconsideration or appeal, an award could decrease, instead of increasing. It is usually best to get advice before challenging a decision.

If a child has been awarded some DLA, you can continue to get it during the review or appeal process (see p306). However, if a child has not been given any award of DLA, you will not get any interim payments while waiting for a mandatory reconsideration or appeal decision. If the reconsideration request or appeal is successful, any payments owed from the date of claim will be paid at that point.

Length of awards

DLA can be awarded for a fixed period or indefinitely.[61] The length of award should be based on how soon, if at all, the child's needs are likely to change.

Regardless of the stated length of an award, the DWP can reduce or stop the award earlier if it has grounds to revise or supersede it (see p186).

If an award is for a fixed term, you are invited to make a renewal claim up to six months before the award runs out (see p186).

6. Getting paid

Disability living allowance (DLA) is paid to an adult appointee.

DLA is normally paid every four weeks in arrears, on a Wednesday.[62] However, DLA can be paid at shorter intervals in individual cases, and DLA under the special rules for terminal illness can be paid weekly.

Note: it is possible for payment of DLA to be suspended (see p187).

7. Reviews and reassessments

Making a renewal claim

If disability living allowance (DLA) is awarded for a fixed period, you can make a renewal claim up to six months before the fixed term ends. You will be sent a renewal claim form (DLA1A). It is important that you return your completed form well before the existing award ends, as backdating is not possible.

The DWP normally treats a renewal claim as a new claim beginning on the day after an award ends.[63] However, the information you give in the renewal claim may be used to revise or supersede the child's existing award, in which case their entitlement may be changed earlier.[64]

Change of circumstances

You should usually report all changes in a child's circumstances to the DLA section of the DWP as soon as possible. You can report a change by calling the DLA helpline (see p182), or in writing, by sending a letter to the address on the DLA award letter.[65] It is best to report changes in writing so that there is a clear record of what was said and when.

It is usually best to get independent advice before reporting a change in a child's health that you think might affect their entitlement to DLA.

If there has been a relevant change of circumstances, a decision maker looks at the award again. You might be asked to go through the assessment process again (see p183). The decision maker will make a new decision, usually by supersession (see p292).

Note:

- A change of circumstances can include that a child's needs are now expected to last beyond the end date of a fixed-term award, even if the level of their needs is still the same.[66]
- If a child gets DLA and is moving to Scotland, you should notify Social Security Scotland. They will be transferred to child disability payment (CDP – see Chapter 11) automatically without having to make a claim.

Reaching the age of 16

When a child who is getting DLA reaches 16, they are normally invited to claim personal independence payment (PIP). See Chapter 8 for more information.

What advisers say: claiming PIP

'When a young person is assessed for PIP at 16, the first thing DWP will want to know is whether they are capable of handling their own claim or whether someone will still need to be their appointee. You may get a visit or phone call from the DWP and they may want to speak to the 16-year-old to assess that situation. If the young person is not able or willing to

communicate, you will have to explain that to the DWP as being part of the reason why a PIP claim is being made.'

'PIP is a different benefit, with different criteria, so just because a child got a certain rate of DLA it doesn't mean they'll get the equivalent rate of PIP – it may be the same, more, or less.'

Ongoing evidence requirements

You may be asked to provide information at any time after DLA is awarded. If you fail to do so, the child's DLA could be suspended or even terminated.[67]

8. Disability living allowance and other benefits

Means-tested benefits

Disability living allowance (DLA) can be paid alongside means-tested benefits and is not taken into account as income for their means tests.

If your dependent child is entitled to DLA, you may qualify for additional premiums or amounts in your means-tested benefits, and may be exempt from non-dependant deductions. The same rules could mean that you become entitled to a means-tested benefit for the first time. See the chapter of this *Handbook* about the relevant means-tested benefit.

Non-means-tested benefits

DLA can be paid in addition to any other non-means-tested benefits, except that a child cannot get DLA at the same time as personal independence payment or child disability payment.[68]

A child in Scotland who gets the DLA highest rate care component is eligible for a child winter heating assistance payment.[69]

Carers' benefits

If a child gets the middle or highest rate of the DLA care component, you or someone else who regularly looks after them may be entitled to carer benefits. See Chapter 14 for more information.

The benefit cap

In some cases, there is a limit on the total amount of specified benefits you can receive (the 'benefit cap'). The benefit cap does not apply to you if your child is entitled to DLA, even it is not paid because they are in hospital or a care home.

Other sources of financial help

If you get DLA for a child, you may be entitled to a blue badge parking permit or a concessionary travel card. Contact your local authority for more information.

If a child gets the DLA mobility component and their carer has a car used only for the child, the carer's road tax may be reduced. There are details at gov.uk/financial-help-disabled/vehicles-and-transport.

If you have a low income, you may be eligible for free prescriptions, council tax reduction and other financial help. See Chapter 15 for more information.

Motability

Motability is a charity that runs a scheme to help you lease or buy a car, scooter or powered wheelchair. You are eligible if a child gets the enhanced rate of the DLA mobility component and there are 12 months or more left to run on their award. If you use the scheme, the child's DLA mobility component is paid directly to Motability.[70] You may also have to make extra payments.

Notes

1. Who can get disability living allowance

1 ss71(6), 72 and 73 SSCBA 1992; regs 3(3), (4), (4A) and (5B) and 18 PIP(TP) Regs
2 R(A) 3/74; R(A) 2/75
3 Reg 10C SS(DLA) Regs; *R v National Insurance Commissioner ex parte Secretary of State for Social Services* [1981] 1 WLR 1017 (CA), also reported as R(A) 2/80; R(A) 1/06
4 *Mallinson v Secretary of State for Social Security*, 21 April 1994 (HL), reported as R(A) 3/94; CA/177/1988; CDLA/14696/1996; R(DLA) 1/07, tribunal of commissioners
5 *Mallinson v Secretary of State for Social Security*, 21 April 1994 (HL), reported as R(A) 3/94
6 R(DLA) 2/02
7 *Secretary of State for Social Security v Fairey (aka Halliday)*, 21 May 1997 (HL), reported as R(A) 2/98
8 R(A) 3/92
9 *RJ, GMcL and CS v SSWP (PIP)* [2017] UKUT 105 (AAC), reported as [2017] AACR 32. Although this case relates to PIP, the same arguments about the likelihood of harm occurring and the need for supervision to prevent it also apply to DLA.
10 CA/15/1979, approved in R(A) 1/83; R(A) 2/89
11 CA/33/1984
12 ss71(6) and 72 SSCBA 1992
13 CDLA/58/1993
14 CSDLA/29/1994; *Ramsden v SSWP*, 31 January 2003 (CA), reported as R(DLA) 2/03; *SO v SSWP (DLA)* [2019] UKUT 272 (AAC)
15 R(DLA) 8/02
16 s72(4)(b) SSCBA 1992; reg 7 SS(DLA) Regs
17 s72(4)(a) and (5) SSCBA 1992
18 s72(1)(b) SSCBA 1992
19 R(DLA) 5/05
20 CA/140/1985

21 R(A) 1/73
22 *CP v SSWP (DLA)* [2013] UKUT 230 (AAC)
23 *R v National Insurance Commissioner ex parte Secretary of State for Social Services* [1974] 1 WLR 1290 (DC), also reported as R(A) 4/74; R(A) 1/04; CDLA/2852/2002; CDLA/997/2003; *LB v SSWP (DLA)* [2018] UKUT 445 (AAC); R(A) 1/78
24 s72(1)(c) SSCBA 1992
25 R(A) 3/78
26 R(DLA) 5/05
27 R(DLA) 5/05
28 *AD v SSWP (DLA)* [2017] UKUT 29 (AAC)
29 Vol 10 Ch 61, para 61165 DMG
30 Vol 10 Ch 61, para 61164 DMG
31 s72(1A)(b) SSCBA 1992; R(DLA) 1/05; *BM v SSWP (DLA)* [2015] UKUT 18 (AAC), reported as [2015] AACR 29
32 R(A) 3/86; *Mallinson v Secretary of State for Social Security*, 21 April 1994 (HL), reported as R(A) 3/94
33 R(DLA) 3/06, tribunal of commissioners
34 CDLA/4475/04
35 R(DLA) 3/06, tribunal of commissioners
36 CDLA/3925/1997; *HJ v SSWP (DLA)* [2010] UKUT 307 (AAC); R(DLA) 10/02
37 s73(1)(d) SSCBA 1992; R(DLA) 6/03
38 s73(4A) SSCBA 1992
39 R(DLA) 3/04
40 CDLA/42/1994
41 CDLA/42/1994
42 CDLA/42/1994; CDLA/3360/1995; CSDLA/591/1997; CDLA/2643/1998; R(DLA) 4/01
43 *IN v SSWP (DLA)* [2013] UKUT 249 (AAC); R(DLA) 4/01; R(DLA) 6/05
44 CDLA/42/1994; R(DLA) 3/04
45 CDLA/2142/2005
46 CDLA/2364/1995; *KH v SSWP (DLA)* [2015] UKUT 8 (AAC), but see CDLA/42/1994
47 s73 SSCBA 1992; reg 12(1)(b) SS(DLA) Regs
48 *JH v SSWP (DLA)* [2010] UKUT 456 (AAC); *AH v SSWP (DLA)* [2012] UKUT 387 (AAC); *SSWP v MG (DLA)* [2012] UKUT 429 (AAC)
49 Reg 12(1)(a) SS(DLA) Regs; *KS v SSWP (DLA)* [2013] UKUT 390 (AAC)
50 CDLA/1525/2008
51 CM/5/1986; *BP v SSWP* [2009] UKUT 90 (AAC)

2. **The amount of benefit**
52 Reg 4(2) SS(DLA) Regs
53 Reg 4(1) SS(DLA) Regs

3. **Making a claim**
54 Reg 43 SS(C&P) Regs
55 Regs 4(1) and 6(8), (8A) and (9) SS(C&P) Regs; *SNN v SSWP (PIP)* [2018] UKUT 210 (AAC) – although decided on similar rules for PIP, this case considers circumstances that may be reasonable and the discussion is relevant for DLA claims
56 Reg 13A(1) SS(C&P) Regs
57 s76(1) SSCBA 1992
58 ss66(2), 72(5) and 73(9) and (12) SSCBA 1992; regs 3(9)(b) and 6(6)(c) SS&CS(DA) Regs

4. **How a child is assessed**
59 R(A) 2/74; see also *Moyna v SSWP*, 31 July 2003 (HL), reported as R(DLA) 7/03; *DJ v SSWP (DLA)* [2016] UKUT 169 (AAC)
60 s19(3) SSA 1998

5. **Decisions**
61 s71(3) SSCBA 1992; R(DLA) 11/02

6. **Getting paid**
62 Regs 22 and 25 and Sch 6 SS(C&P) Regs

7. **Reviews and reassessments**
63 Reg 13C SS(C&P) Regs
64 CDLA/14895/1996
65 Reg 32(1B) SS(C&P) Regs
66 *PH v SSWP (DLA)* [2013] UKUT 268 (AAC)
67 Reg 32(1) SS(C&P) Regs

8. **Disability living allowance and other benefits**
68 s71(7) SSCBA 1992
69 Reg 10 WHACYP(S) Regs
70 Regs 44, 45 and 46 SS(C&P) Regs

Chapter 11

Child disability payment

This chapter covers:

Key facts

- Child disability payment (CDP) is a non-means-tested benefit for children and young people with a disability or long-term health condition who live in Scotland.
- You can claim CDP alongside most other benefits. It does not count as income for the purposes of means-tested benefits.
- CDP has two components. A child or young person can qualify for one or both. The care component is paid at one of three rates and reflects needs for attention or supervision during the day and/or at night. The mobility component is paid at one of two rates and reflects difficulties going out and getting around, including for mental health reasons.
- You can challenge determinations about eligibility for CDP.
- Getting CDP can make you eligible for other kinds of financial support.

1. Who can get child disability payment

Child disability payment (CDP) is a non-means-tested benefit for children and young people (we use the term 'children' in this chapter). CDP is intended to help with the extra costs of having a disability or long-term health condition. Children with mental health problems, with or without a diagnosis (see p8), may be eligible.

You can get CDP for a child if the child:[1]

- is under 16 when you claim (they must be at least three to get the mobility component and five to get the lower rate; they can keep getting CDP until they turn 18, or 19 in some circumstances); *and*
- meets the residence conditions, and is not a person subject to immigration control – see CPAG's *Welfare Benefits Handbook; and*
- is not getting disability living allowance (DLA), personal independence payment (PIP), adult disability payment (ADP) or armed forces independence payment; *and*
- unless terminally ill (see p195):
  - meets the disability conditions (see below); *and*
  - has had their needs for at least 13 weeks and is expected to have them for at least 26 weeks longer (these are sometimes called the 'the backwards test' and 'the forwards test').

Note: special rules apply in certain situations – eg, if they are living in a care home (see Chapter 19).

The disability conditions

The health-related eligibility criteria for CDP are known as the 'disability conditions'. This does not mean that a child must be considered to have a disability to qualify.

Disability conditions for the care component

The care component of CDP is paid at one of three rates: lowest, middle or highest. The conditions for getting each rate are largely the same as for DLA. See p176 for how they are interpreted for DLA.

A child can get the **lowest rate** care component if:[2]

- due to a mental or physical disability or health condition, they require attention from another person for a significant portion of the day in connection with their bodily functions; *or*
- they are 16 or over and, due to a mental or physical disability or health condition, they cannot prepare a cooked main meal for themself if they have the ingredients.

A child can get the **middle rate** care component if they:[3]

- satisfy one of the daytime conditions *or* one of the night-time conditions (see p192); *or*
- have renal dialysis in certain circumstances.

A child can get the **highest rate** care component if they:[4]

- satisfy one of the daytime conditions *and* one of the night-time conditions (see p192); *or*
- have renal dialysis in certain circumstances; *or*
- are terminally ill (see p195).

To meet these conditions, a child under 16 must need attention or supervision 'substantially in excess of the normal requirements' of a child of the same age.[5]

The daytime and night-time conditions

These conditions are largely the same for CDP as for DLA. See p177 for how they are interpreted for DLA.

The **daytime** conditions are that, due to a mental or physical disability or health condition, a child requires:[6]

- frequent attention throughout the day in connection with their bodily functions; *or*
- continual supervision throughout the day to avoid substantial danger to the child or others.

The **night-time** conditions are that, due to a mental or physical disability or health condition, a child requires:[7]

- prolonged or repeated attention from another person at night in connection with their bodily functions; *or*
- another person to be awake for a prolonged period or at frequent intervals at night to watch over them, to avoid substantial danger to the child or others.

When night-time begins and ends depends on the ordinary routine of the child's household.[8]

Definitions for the care component

The following terms are defined in the rules. Other terms are not, but have been interpreted in a certain way in DLA caselaw (see p176). This DLA caselaw is likely to be persuasive for CDP. However, decision makers and tribunals deciding CDP cases are not bound to follow DLA caselaw in every case, and over time the CDP assessment criteria may be interpreted differently by courts and tribunals, leading to new CDP caselaw.

'Attention' means 'the provision of personal care, prompting or motivation in relation to bodily functions or assistance with communication needs'.[9]

'Bodily functions' means 'the normal actions of any organ of the body, including the brain, or of a number of organs acting together'.[10]

'Require' means 'reasonably require'.[11]

'Significant portion of the day' can be a single period or several periods during the day.[12]

'Supervision' means 'the precautionary or anticipatory presence of another person to monitor an individual's physical, mental or emotional health including monitoring for obstacles or dangerous places or situations'.[13]

Examples

Arran (15) has depression. He needs frequent prompting and motivation throughout the day – eg, to get out of bed, eat meals, participate in lessons and take part in counselling sessions. To support his CDP claim, Arran's father keeps a diary to record of how often and for how long he needs this help.

Georgia (14) has previously tried to take her own life, and has shared with her foster carers her detailed plans for attempting suicide again. She also self-harms, with past incidents resulting in hospitalisation due to the severity of her injuries. Georgia reasonably needs to have someone with her for 24 hours a day to minimise the risk of substantial danger. She can qualify for the higher rate of the CDP care component based on both her daytime and night-time needs. This can apply even if she is rarely awake in the night, because the serious risk of harm if she woke up at night and was not supervised can be weighed against the low likelihood of occurrence (see p177 for related DLA caselaw).

Disability conditions for the mobility component

The mobility component is paid at one of two rates: lower or higher.

The conditions for getting each rate are largely the same as for DLA. See p179 for how the conditions are interpreted for DLA.

A child aged five or over can get the **lower rate** mobility component if:[14]

- as a result of physical or mental impairment, they cannot move around outside, on unfamiliar routes, without requiring supervision or guidance from another person most of the time; *and*
- if they are under 16, the supervision or guidance they need is 'substantially in excess of the normal requirements' of a child of the same age.

Definitions for the mobility component

'**Supervision**' means 'the precautionary or anticipatory presence of another person to monitor an individual's physical, mental or emotional health including monitoring for obstacles or dangerous places or situations'.[15]

'**Guidance**' means 'direction or leading by physical means or verbal suggestion or persuasion'.[16]

A child aged three or over can get the **higher rate** mobility component if:[17]

- they are unable, or virtually unable, to walk, or the (physical) exertion required to walk would lead to a danger to their life or a serious deterioration in their health; *or*
- they have no legs or feet; *or*
- they are both blind and deaf and are 'unable, without the assistance of another person, to walk to any intended or required destination while out of doors'; *or*
- they have a severe visual impairment; *or*

- they are terminally ill (see p195); *or*
- they qualify for the highest rate of the CDP care component, have a 'severe mental impairment' (ie, arrested or incomplete development of the brain which results in severe impairment of intelligence and social functioning), and have 'severe behavioural difficulties'.

Note: a child cannot normally qualify for either rate of the mobility component unless they are 'able, from time to time, to benefit from assistance for movement'.[18]

2. The amount of benefit

Child disability payment (CDP) mobility component is paid at one of two weekly rates:[19]

- the lower rate is £29.20;
- the higher rate is £77.05.

CDP care component is paid at one of three weekly rates:[20]

- the lowest rate is £29.30
- the middle rate is £73.90
- the highest rate is £110.40.

3. Making a claim

How to claim

A claim for child disability payment (CDP) is made by a parent or appointee (see p325) on a child's behalf. You can start a claim for CDP:

- online at mygov.scot/child-disability-payment/how-to-apply; *or*
- by calling 0800 182 2222 to request a paper claim form; *or*
- in British Sign Language, via Contact Scotland BSL.

Claims for CDP are made in two parts.

- **Part 1** registers the claim. You can do this by phone or online. You must provide the name and date of birth of the child to register the claim. In practice, Social Security Scotland (SSS) also asks for other information, such as contact details and the name of the adult with responsibility for the child, where you live and bank details.
- **Part 2** asks about the child's disability or health condition and how it affects them. There is more information about Part 2 on p196.

If you do Part 1 by phone, you are sent a paper form to complete for Part 2. If you do Part 1 online, you set up an account with SSS which you then use to complete

Part 2. **Note:** if the child is terminally ill there is a different claims process (see below).

Your date of claim is the date you complete Part 1, so long as you complete Part 2 of the claim within six weeks of that date. Otherwise, the date of claim is the date SSS receives the Part 2 form.[21] The six-week period can be extended if you can show there is good reason for the delay.[22] If anything is preventing you from completing Part 2, ask for more time as soon as possible.

Claiming in advance and backdating

A claim for CDP can be made **in advance**, before a child has satisfied the qualifying conditions, provided they will meet the condition within 13 weeks of making the claim.[23]

CDP cannot be backdated unless your child is terminally ill. If a child might have qualified for CDP earlier but you did not claim because you were misled or wrongly advised by SSS or the DWP, you could make a complaint and ask for compensation (see p310).

Note: the term 'backdating' is often informally used to mean getting arrears of your benefit going back to a claim or decision date – eg, after winning an appeal. However, in this *Handbook*, we use backdating to mean getting paid benefit for a period before the date you claimed.

Additional support

If you have (or will have) difficulty with the claims process and need additional support, see Chapter 21.

Terminal illness

The rules about claiming CDP are different if a child is terminally ill. For CDP, a child is regarded as 'terminally ill' if it is the judgement of a doctor or nurse involved in the care or diagnosis of the child, and acting in a professional capacity, that the child has a progressive disease that can reasonably be expected to cause their death.[24]

If you are claiming CDP on the basis of a child's terminal illness, you must tick the box on the claim form to say you are claiming under the 'special rules'. The claim will then be fast-tracked. In addition to the claim form, you must provide Form DS1500, SR1 or a Benefits Assistance under Special Rules in Scotland (BASRiS) form completed by a doctor or nurse.[25]

If a child is regarded as terminally ill, you do not have to provide extra information about their care and mobility needs as they are automatically entitled to the highest rate care component and the higher rate mobility component.[26] The care component can be paid from birth, but the mobility component is not payable until the child is three years old.

4. How a child is assessed

Part 2 of the claim form

When you start a claim for child disability payment (CDP), you are asked to provide information about different aspects of the child's needs. This is known as Part 2 of the claim (see p194) and if you do not complete it, or do not complete it in time, you have not made a claim.

You provide the information using an online Part 2 form (if you started your claim online) or on a paper Part 2 form. You can ask Social Security Scotland (SSS) to help you complete the form by calling 0800 182 2222. The form is similar to a disability living allowance (DLA) form, but with more detailed questions about each daily living and mobility activity. You should complete it in the same way as a DLA form (see p183).

Timescales

You usually have six weeks from starting a CDP claim to return the Part 2 form. The six-week period can be extended if you can show there is good reason for the delay.[27] If anything is preventing you from completing Part 2, ask for more time as soon as possible.

Supporting evidence

You are usually asked to provide supporting evidence – eg, reports from a child's doctor or other professionals, a letter from their teacher or someone else who knows them well, and/or a diary of symptoms.[28] See Chapter 16 for more information about supporting evidence. Do not delay submitting the claim while waiting for evidence; it can be provided later by post or online at mygov.scot.

If you cannot provide supporting evidence yourself, you can ask SSS to gather it on your behalf. You are asked about this when completing the Part 2 form.

5. Decisions

Getting a determination

You get decisions about child disability payment (CDP) by letter. In the Scottish benefits system, these decisions are known as 'determinations'.

If you disagree with a determination about CDP, you can challenge it by making a redetermination request and then pursuing an appeal if necessary (see p312). Note that deadlines apply for challenging determinations.

If you challenge a determination, Social Security Scotland (SSS) or the tribunal can look at all the CDP disability conditions again, not just the ones you disagree with. This means that, following a redetermination request or appeal, an award could decrease, instead of increasing. If you have a CDP award, it is usually best to get advice before challenging a determination.

You may be able to get interim payments of CDP at the same rate as a previous award during the redetermination and appeal process. This is known as 'short-term assistance' (see p316).

Length of awards

CDP is awarded without a fixed end date. When making an award, SSS usually specifies a period after which it will review the CDP award. The length of this period should be based on whether, and how soon, a child's needs are likely to change. If their needs are unlikely to change, the review period should be between five and 10 years long. SSS must make a new determination at the end of the reviw period (see below).[29]

SSS can reduce or stop the award earlier if it has grounds to (see below).

6. Getting paid

Child disability payment (CDP) is paid to the person who has made the claim on the child's behalf, or to the child directly once they are 16.

CDP is usually paid every four weeks in arrears. If the child is terminally ill, CDP is paid weekly in advance.[30]

Note: it is possible for payment of CDP to be suspended (see p198).

7. Reviews and reassessments

Scheduled reviews

When Social Security Scotland (SSS) makes an award of child disability payment (CDP), it specifies a review date when it plans to look at the award again and make a new determination on the child's entitlement. SSS calls this a 'scheduled review'.[31] There is more information about how review periods are set above.

As part of the review process, you may be asked to complete a form and provide supporting evidence, similar to when you make a new claim for CDP (see p194).

Change of circumstances

You should report all changes in a child's circumstances to SSS as soon as possible. You can report a change by phone or or on the form you can download from mygov.scot. Check your most recent determination carefully, as it tells you how you must report a change.[32]

It is usually best to get independent advice before reporting a change in the child's health that you think might affect their entitlement to CDP.

If there has been a relevant change of circumstances, a decision maker looks at the award again and makes a new determination (see p314).[33]

Moving to adult disability payment aged 16–18

A child who gets CDP will usually need to apply for adult disability payment (ADP) before turning 18 to avoid a break in payments. They can choose to claim ADP from as early as 13 weeks before turning 16. Get advice to help you and your child decide whether to claim ADP early. The entitlement conditions for ADP are completely different, and they may not qualify for ADP at all or may qualify for a lower award. However, they may also be better off claiming ADP – eg, if they do not have any night-time care needs but would be entitled to the enhanced rate of ADP daily living component. You can use the information in Chapter 9 to work out their likely ADP entitlement and compare this with their CDP award. If an ADP claim is refused, CDP entitlement continues until the child's 18th birthday (and they can try to claim ADP again before then).[34]

Moving from Scotland

If you move from Scotland to elsewhere in the UK, CDP entitlement ends after 13 weeks (unless you tell SSS less than 13 weeks after you moved, in which case it ends 13 weeks after you tell it).[35] **Note:** your CDP may *not* end (but your payment could be affected) if you go into hospital, residential care or prison elsewhere in the UK.[36]

For how your benefit is affected if you move out of the UK, see CPAG's *Welfare Benefits Handbook*.

Ongoing evidence requirements

If SSS is reviewing a child's CDP award, or it thinks that their circumstances may have changed, it can ask you to provide further information.

If you do not provide the information within the time limit SSS sets you to do so, CDP payments can be suspended.[37] If you need more time to provide the information, contact SSS as soon as possible to request an extension.

8. Child disability payment and other benefits

Child disability payment (CDP) interacts with other benefits in the same ways that disability living allowance (DLA) does. There are the same benefit cap exemptions for CDP as for DLA, and the same rules about Motability apply. See p187 for more information.

A child who gets the CDP highest rate care component gets a child winter heating payment.

Notes

1. **Who can get child disability payment**
    1 s31 and Sch 5 SS(S)A 2018; Part 3 DACYP(S) Regs
    2 Reg 11(1)(a)-(b) and (5)(c) DACYP(S) Regs
    3 Regs 11(1)(c)-(d) and (5)(b) and 16 DACYP(S) Regs
    4 Regs 11(1)(c)-(d) and (5)(a), 15(1)(a) and 16(4) DACYP(S) Regs
    5 Reg 11(2) and (4) DACYP(S) Regs
    6 Reg 11(1)(c) DACYP(S) Regs
    7 Reg 11(1)(d) DACYP(S) Regs
    8 Reg 11(6)(a) DACYP(S) Regs
    9 Reg 11(6)(b) DACYP(S) Regs
    10 Reg 2 DACYP(S) Regs
    11 Reg 11(8) DACYP(S) Regs
    12 Reg 11(1)(a) DACYP(S) Regs
    13 Reg 11(7) DACYP(S) Regs
    14 Reg 12 DACYP(S) Regs
    15 Reg 11(7) DACYP(S) Regs
    16 Reg 12(7) DACYP(S) Regs
    17 Reg 13 DACYP(S) Regs
    18 Reg 14 DACYP(S) Regs

2. **The amount of benefit**
    19 Reg 23(2) DACYP(S) Regs
    20 Reg 23(1) DACYP(S) Regs

3. **Making a claim**
    21 Reg 24(5) DACYP(S) Regs
    22 Reg 24(4) and (6) DACYP(S) Regs
    23 Reg 24(2) DACYP(S) Regs
    24 Sch 5 para 1 SS(S)A 2018; reg 15(6)-(9) DACYP(S) Regs
    25 SSS, *Special Rules for Terminal Illness: frequently asked questions*
    26 Reg 15(1) DACYP(S) Regs

4. **How a child is assessed**
    27 Reg 24(4) and (6) DACYP(S) Regs
    28 SSS DMG *Gathering supporting information for adult disability payment*, paras 2, 8-15 and 32-4

5. **Decisions**
    29 Regs 26 and 30 DACYP(S) Regs; SSS DMG, *Review periods for child disability payment*

6. **Getting paid**
    30 Reg 25 DACYP(S) Regs

7. **Reviews and reassessments**
    31 Regs 26 and 30 DACYP(S) Regs; SSS DMG, *Review periods for child disability payment* and *scheduled reviews for child disability payment*
    32 s56 SS(S)A 2018
    33 Reg 31 DACYP(S) Regs
    34 Reg 4(1) DACYP(S) Regs – being refused ADP does not affect your award of CDP
    35 Reg 36(4) DACYP(S) Regs
    36 Reg 36(2) DACYP(S) Regs
    37 s54 SS(S)A 2018; regs 26A-26F DACYP(S)Regs

Chapter 12

Attendance allowance

This chapter covers:

Key facts

- Attendance allowance (AA) is a non-means-tested benefit for people over pension age who have a disability or long-term health condition.
- You can get AA whether you are in or out of work, and you can get it alongside most other benefits. AA does not count as income for the purposes of means-tested benefits.
- AA is paid at two rates. Which rate you get depends on your needs for attention or supervision during the day and at night.
- You can challenge decisions about your eligibility for AA.
- Getting AA can make you eligible for other kinds of financial support.
- AA usually stops being paid if you are in hospital or residential care for more than 28 days.
- You can not make a claim for AA in Scotland and will need to claim pension age disability payment instead.

1. **Who can get attendance allowance**

Attendance allowance (AA) is a non-means-tested benefit for people over pension age, intended to help with the extra costs of having a disability or long-term health condition. People with mental health symptoms, with or without a diagnosis (see p6), may be eligible.

You can get AA if you:[1]

- are pension age or over (which is currently 66 and rising to 67 between 2026 and 2028; check your pension age at gov.uk/state-pension-age); *and*
- meet the residence conditions, and are not a person subject to immigration control (although there are some exceptions) – see CPAG's *Welfare Benefits Handbook*; *and*
- are not entitled to personal independence payment (PIP), adult disability payment (ADP), pension age disability payment (PADP) or the care component of disability living allowance (DLA); *and*
- meet the disability conditions below; *and*
- have had your needs for at least six months (sometimes called the 'qualifying period' condition).

Note:
- AA has replaced in Scotland by PADP and it is no longer possible to claim AA.
- If you are getting PIP, ADP or DLA and reach pension age, you can carry on getting that benefit rather than having to switch to claiming AA. Check the chapter of this *Handbook* about the relevant benefit for any rules that apply when you reach pension age.
- Special rules apply if you are regarded as being terminally ill (see p204) and in certain other situations – eg, if you are in hospital or living in a care home (see Chapter 19).

The disability conditions

The health-related eligibility criteria for AA are known as the 'disability conditions'. Importantly, you do not need to consider yourself disabled to qualify. In this section, we avoid using the expression 'so severely disabled, physically or mentally'. This is the phrase used in law but, in practice, it just means that your difficulties must be the result of a mental or physical health condition or disability.

What advisers say: not just for severe disability

'Please do not be put off by the legal jargon. The conditions apply across a wider range of difficulties than you might first think when considering the legal wording. AA is not just for people who see themselves as "severely disabled" – awards are made to people living with perhaps less severe sounding, but still really limiting, conditions like anxiety and depression.'

AA is paid at one of two rates.

You get the **lower rate** of AA if you satisfy one of the daytime disability conditions *or* one of the night-time disability conditions.[2] You may also get the lower rate of AA if you undergo renal dialysis.[3]

You get the **higher rate** of AA if you satisfy one of the daytime disability conditions *and* one of the night-time disability conditions.[4] You also get the higher rate of AA if you are regarded as terminally ill (see p204).

The daytime and night-time disability conditions

The **daytime disability conditions** are that, as a result of your mental or physical health condition or disability, throughout the day you need:[5]

- frequent attention from another person in connection with your bodily functions; *or*
- continual supervision in order to avoid substantial danger to yourself or others.

The **night-time disability conditions** are that, as a result of your mental or physical health condition or disability, at night you need:[6]

- prolonged or repeated attention from another person in connection with your bodily functions; *or*
- another person to be awake for a prolonged period or at frequent intervals to watch over you in order to avoid substantial danger to yourself or others.

The daytime and night-time disability conditions are the same as those for DLA (see p176). You can argue that DLA caselaw about the meaning of these conditions, including about the meanings of 'bodily functions' (p176), 'attention' (p176) and 'supervision' (p177), ought to be followed in your AA case.

Examples

Hazel (68) has depression and struggles with daytime activities like changing clothes, washing, taking medication and eating enough. She is also the main carer for her son who has a physical disability. Hazel sees herself as a carer, not as a person needing care, and assumes that she cannot qualify for AA. However, her adviser explains that what matters is the help she reasonably needs, not the help she actually gets (see p178 and p218). If Hazel reasonably needs frequent attention from another person in the daytime in connection with her bodily functions, she may qualify for the lower rate of AA.

Jerry (77) experiences hallucinations, delusions and disordered thinking. He needs frequent attention during the day and prolonged attention at night for support with bodily functions like cognition, communication, taking medication and getting to sleep. This means that he should qualify for the higher rate of AA. When completing his AA claim form (see p204), Jerry's appointee (his daughter) includes a diary of the symptoms Jerry has experienced over the last month, including the help he has needed from family members each day, and what has happened when that help was not available.

Note: in both examples, getting an award of AA might also mean becoming entitled to pension credit, or getting a greater amount. See Chapter 6.

2. The amount of benefit

Attendance allowance is paid at one of two weekly rates:[7]

- the lower rate is £73.90;
- the higher rate is £110.40.

3. Making a claim

How to claim

A claim for attendance allowance (AA) must be in writing, using the approved claim form (AA1). It is best to request a claim form by calling the AA helpline (0800 731 0122, textphone: 0800 731 0317, Relay UK and British Sign Language video relay services available). A form you request by phone should arrive date stamped, and if you return it within six weeks, the date you called to request it will be treated as your date of claim.[8] The DWP can extend the six-week deadline if it considers that this is reasonable, so if you return the form late, explain why.[9]

If you do not get a date-stamped form, or if you return a date-stamped form too late, your date of claim will be the date that the DWP receives your completed form. This applies, for example, if you print an AA1 form from the internet.

The claim form asks a lot of questions about your needs. There are tips for completing it on p204.

What advisers say: getting a paper form

'When you call the AA helpline, the recorded message tells you to go online and download a claim form instead of waiting on hold. You do not have to do this – even if you are very computer literate. Getting through to a telephonist and getting a form posted out to you is best. It means your claim starts from the date of the phone call (so long as you get the form back in time).'

Claiming in advance and backdating

You can claim AA **in advance**, before you meet the qualifying conditions on p200, provided you claim no more than six months before you will actually qualify.[10]

AA claims cannot be **backdated**.[11] If you might have qualified for AA earlier but you did not claim because you were misled or wrongly advised by the DWP, you could make a complaint and ask for compensation (see p308).

Note: the term 'backdating' is often informally used to mean getting arrears of your benefit going back to a claim or decision date – eg, after winning an appeal. However, in this *Handbook*, we use backdating to mean getting paid benefit for a period before the date you claimed.

Additional support and appointees

If you have (or will have) difficulty with the claims process and need additional support, see Chapter 21. If you cannot manage the claims process at all, you may need an appointee (see p325).

Terminal illness

The AA claims process is different if you are terminally ill. You are regarded as 'terminally ill' if you have a progressive illness and it would not be a surprise to your doctors if you were to die from it within the next 12 months. This can still apply even if there are realistic hopes that you may live longer.[12] When you claim, make it clear that the claim is on the grounds of terminal illness (these are known as 'special rules' claims).[13] Your GP, consultant or specialist nurse should complete Form SR1 or DS1500, giving details of your condition and prognosis.

If you are regarded as terminally ill, you are automatically entitled to the higher rate of AA.[14]

4. How you are assessed

Note: this assessment process does not apply if you are regarded as terminally ill (see above).

To get attendance allowance (AA), you must meet the disability conditions set out on p201. The DWP uses a standard assessment process to decide whether you meet these conditions.

The claim form

The assessment process starts with the AA1 form, which asks about your needs. If you find it difficult to complete the form, many advice agencies can help, and in some circumstances, the DWP can send a visiting officer to assist you complete the form at your home. See Chapter 21 for more information.

Completing the claim form

Before you start, look at the rules on p201 to understand what the decision maker needs to know. Also, consider all of the mental health symptoms listed on p13.

Give as much detail as you can. The form has limited space for you to explain your difficulties, so it is usually a good idea to use extra sheets of paper to provide more details. You might use one sheet per activity (eg, eating, communicating, night-time care needs) as well as one sheet to summarise your main symptoms and treatment history.

To give a full picture of your needs, it might be useful to keep a diary for a week or a month recording your symptoms and the help you needed and received each day. Attach the diary to the form and refer to it in your answers.

Remember to explain:

– what help you need, even if you do not actually get it;
– how often help is needed each day and night;
– how long help is needed for each time;
– what has happened or could happen if you do not get the help you need;
– how many days (and nights) a week help is needed. You may still get AA even if you need help on fewer than half of the days in a week. It is not about simply comparing the number of good versus bad days.[15] Explain fully the help you need on bad days, but include the help needed on good days for an overall picture.

Ideally, get someone who knows you well to check your answers.

Keep a copy of your completed form and ask the Post Office for free proof of posting.

What advisers say: completing the AA claim form

'Think outside the boxes. Do not be contained by the examples or to the types of difficulties as listed on the form.'

'Take it slowly and be kind to yourself. For every page, take time to congratulate yourself on what you do manage, but do think about how any help from someone else could make a difference. It can be very upsetting describing all these difficulties and limitations to get a full picture over on the form. Take breaks, do it over several sessions, get help and plan something cheerful for afterwards.'

'There is some flexibility about how long you have to return the form, no matter what date might be stamped on it (see p203).'

Gathering further information

When you return the AA form, it is a good idea to enclose supporting evidence – eg, reports from your doctor or other professionals, a letter from someone who knows you well and/or a symptoms diary. Chapter 16 has more information.

AA can be awarded on the basis of the claim form (and supporting evidence) alone. However, if it needs more details, the DWP may contact you, your GP or someone else you named on the form. **Note:** it is generally better to provide information from these people or organisations when you make the claim than to rely on the DWP to contact them for information.

The DWP can arrange a medical examination by a healthcare professional. For AA, this is very rare in practice. If you refuse a medical examination without good cause, the claim is likely to be refused.[16]

5. Decisions

Getting a decision

You receive decisions about attendance allowance (AA) by letter. Most people get a decision in about eight weeks after returning the claim form.

If you disagree with a decision about AA, you can usually challenge it by making a mandatory reconsideration request and then pursuing an appeal if necessary (see Chapter 20). Note that deadlines apply for challenging decisions.

If you challenge a decision, the DWP (or tribunal) can look at all parts of your claim, not just the part you disagree with. This means that following a mandatory reconsideration or appeal, the award could decrease, instead of increasing. It is usually best to get advice before challenging a decision.

If you have been awarded the lower rate of AA and challenge this decision, you can continue to get the lower rate during the review or appeal process. However, if you have not been given any award of AA, you will not get any interim payments while waiting for a decision on a mandatory reconsideration or appeal. See p306 for more information.

Length of awards

AA can be awarded for a fixed period or indefinitely.[17] The length of award should be based on how soon, if at all, your needs are likely to change.

Regardless of the stated length of an award, the DWP can reduce or stop the award earlier if it has grounds to revise or supersede it (see p207).

If an award is for a fixed term, you will be invited to make a renewal claim up to six months before the award runs out (see p207).

6. Getting paid

When are you paid

Attendance allowance (AA) is normally paid every four weeks in arrears, on a Monday. In some cases, it can be paid at shorter or longer intervals in arrears, or weekly in advance.[18]

If you leave a care home and expect to return there within 28 days, AA can be paid at a daily rate for days at home.[19]

Note: it is possible for payment of AA to be suspended (see p207).

Where your payment goes

AA is usually paid into your bank account. Some or all of your AA can be paid to someone else on your behalf if this is in your interests.[20] This might be useful if, for example, you want a trusted family member to look after your AA income because your mental health problem makes it difficult for you to manage money.

7. Reviews and reassessments

Making a renewal claim

If attendance allowance (AA) is awarded for a fixed period, you can make a renewal claim up to six months before this period ends. You will be sent a new claim form. It is important that you send back your completed form well before the existing award ends, as no backdating is possible.

The DWP normally treats a renewal claim as a new claim beginning on the day after an award ends.[21] However, the information you give in the renewal claim may be used to revise or supersede your existing award, in which case your entitlement may be changed earlier.[22]

Advice from advisers: renewal claims

'Give as much information on the renewal form as you gave on the first claim form. Don't assume that "the DWP knows that already about me".'

Change of circumstances

You should usually report all changes in your circumstances to the AA section of the DWP as soon as possible. You can report a change by calling the AA helpline, or in writing by sending a letter to the address on the AA award letter.[23] It is best to report a change in writing so there is a clear record of what you have said and when.

It is usually best to get independent advice before reporting a change in your health that you think might affect your entitlement to AA.

If there has been a relevant change of circumstances, a decision maker looks at the award again. You might be asked to go through the assessment process again (see p204). The decision maker will then make a new decision, usually by supersession (see p292).

Ongoing evidence requirements

Once you are getting AA, you may be asked to provide information at any time. If you fail to do so, your AA could be suspended or even terminated.[24]

8. Attendance allowance and other benefits

Means-tested benefits

Attendance allowance (AA) can be paid alongside means-tested benefits. It is not taken into account as income for their means tests.

If you are entitled to AA, you may qualify for additional premiums or amounts in your means-tested benefits and may be exempt from non-dependant deductions. The same rules could mean that you become entitled to a means-tested benefit for the first time. See the chapter of this *Handbook* about the relevant means-tested benefit.

Non-means-tested benefits

AA can be paid in addition to many other non-means-tested benefits. However, you cannot claim AA if you are entitled to personal independence payment, adult disability payment, pension age disability payment or the care component of disability living allowance.[25] AA also overlaps with (ie, cannot be paid at the same time as) armed forces independence payment and constant attendance allowance under the industrial injuries scheme or war pensions scheme.[26]

The benefit cap

In some cases, there is a limit on the total amount of specified benefits you can receive (the 'benefit cap'). The benefit cap does not apply if you are entitled to AA, even if it is not paid because you are in hospital or a care home. If you are not entitled to AA, the benefit cap does not apply anyway if you are over pension age and single (or if you have a partner and you are both over pension age).

Other sources of financial help

If you have a low income, you may be eligible for free dental treatment, council tax reduction and other financial help. See Chapter 15 for more information.

Notes

1. **Who can get attendance allowance**
   1 ss64, 65 and 66 SSCBA 1992; reg 2 SS(AA) Regs
   2 s65(3) SSCBA 1992
   3 s65(2) SSCBA 1992; reg 5 SS(AA) Regs
   4 s65(3) SSCBA 1992
   5 s64(2) SSCBA 1992
   6 s64(3) SSCBA 1992

2. **The amount of benefit**
   7 Sch 4 Part III SSCBA 1992

3. **Making a claim**
   8 Reg 6(8), (8A) and (9) SS(C&P) Regs
   9 Reg 6(9) SS(C&P) Regs; *SNN v SSWP (PIP)* [2018] UKUT 210 (AAC) – although decided on similar rules for PIP, this case considers circumstances that may be reasonable and the discussion is relevant for AA claims
   10 s65(6) SSCBA 1992
   11 s65(4) SSCBA 1992
   12 s66(2)(a) SSCBA 1992
   13 Regs 3(9)(b) and 6(6)(c) SS&CS(DA) Regs
   14 s66(1) SSCBA 1992

4. **How you are assessed**
   15 R(A) 2/74; see also *Moyna v SSWP*, 31 July 2003 (HL), reported as R(DLA) 7/03; *DJ v SSWP (DLA)* [2016] UKUT 169 (AAC) – although about DLA, the discussion is also relevant for AA
   16 s19(3) SSA 1998

5. **Decisions**
   17 s65(1)(a) SSCBA 1992

6. **Getting paid**
   18 Reg 22 and Sch 6 SS(C&P) Regs
   19 Reg 25 SS(C&P) Regs
   20 Reg 34(1) and (2) SS(C&P) Regs

7. **Reviews and reassessments**
   21 Reg 13C SS(C&P) Regs
   22 CDLA/14895/1996
   23 Reg 32(1B) SS(C&P) Regs
   24 Reg 32(1) SS(C&P) Regs

8. **Attendance allowance and other benefits**
   25 s64(1) and (1A) SSCBA 1992
   26 Sch 1 paras 5 and 5a SS(OB) Regs

Chapter 13

Pension age disability payment

This chapter covers:

Key facts

- Pension age disability payment (PADP) is a non-means-tested benefit for pension-age adults with a disability or long-term health condition who live in Scotland.
- Attendance allowance claimants living in Scotland are being transferred to PADP.
- PADP is paid at one of two rates, depending on your level of difficulty/needs.
- You can get PADP whether or not you work, and you can get it alongside other benefits. PADP does not count as income for means-tested benefits.
- You can challenge determinations about your eligibility for PADP.
- Getting PADP can mean that you are eligible fo other kinds of financial help.

1. Who can get pension age disability payment

Pension age disability payment (PADP) is a non-means-tested benefit, intended to help with the extra costs of having a disability or long-term health condition. People with mental health symptoms, with or without a diagnosis (see p6), may be eligible.

You can get PADP if:[1]

- you have reached pension age, which is currently 66 and rising to 67 between 2026 and 2028; *and*
- you are ordinarily resident in Scotland; *and*
- you are not a person subject to immigration control and meet the other residence conditions (see CPAG's *Welfare Benefits Handbook*); *and*
- unless terminally ill, you meet the disability conditions (see below); *and*
- unless terminally ill, you have had your difficulties for at least 26 weeks (this is called the 'required period'), but see below if you had a previous award of PADP or attendance allowance (AA); *and*
- you are not entitled to AA, adult disability payment (ADP), personal independence payment (PIP), disability living allowance (DLA), Scottish adult disability living allowance (SADLA) or armed forces independence payment. There is an exception if you are transferred from AA to PADP and an increased award of PADP is backdated because you are terminally ill.

Special rules apply if you are regarded as terminally ill (see p213) and when you are in prison, living in a care home, and in certain other situations (see Chapter 19).

Have you previously had a pension age disability or attendance allowance award?

If you claim PADP within two years of a previous award to PADP or an award of AA ending, you do not have to satisfy the required period condition providing the new award is at the same level or less than the previous award.[2] If you were previously entitled to the lower rate of PADP or AA, you have to satisfy the required period condition to be entitled to the higher rate.

The disability conditions

The health-related eligibility criteria for PADP are known as the 'disability conditions'. You can still qualify if you do not consider yourself to have a disability.

PADP is paid at a lower or higher rate depending on your attention and supervision needs.[3] You get the lower rate of PADP if you satisfy at least one of the daytime disability conditions *or* at least one of the night-time disability conditions, or have dialysis in some circumstances.[4] You get the higher rate of PADP if you satisfy at least one of the daytime disability conditions *and* at least one of the night-time disability conditions.[5] You also get the higher rate of PADP if you are terminally ill (see p213). The rules are the same as those for AA – see p201.

2. The amount of benefit

Pension age disability payment is paid at one of two weekly rates.[6]

- The lower rate is £73.90.
- The higher rate is £110.40.

3. Making a claim

How to claim

You can start a claim for pension age disability payment (PADP) online at mygov.scot/pension-age-disability-payment/how-to-apply, by calling 0800 182 2222 to request a paper form or, if you use British Sign Language, via Contact Scotland BSL.

The date of claim is usually the date you give your full name and date of birth to Social Security Scotland (SSS), as long as you then provide the rest of the required information. If you do not provide all the required information within the time allowed, your date of claim is the date you eventually provide it. You have not made a claim for PADP until you complete all of the required parts of your claim, and provide any required evidence to SSS.

Note: if you live in Scotland and get attendance allowance (AA), you do not need to claim PADP, as you will be transferred to it.

Claiming in advance and backdating

You can claim PADP **in advance** if you do not satisfy the entitlement conditions but will do within 26 weeks in advance.[7] This may be relevant if you do not satisfy the required period condition (see p211) when you first claim. Your entitlement begins on the date you meet all the requirements.

You cannot **backdate** a claim for PADP, unless you are regarded as terminally ill (see p213).[8] If you might have qualified for PADP sooner but did not claim because you were misled or wrongly advised by SSS, you could complain and ask for compensation (see p312).

Note: the term 'backdating' is often informally used to mean getting arrears of your benefit going back to a claim or decision date – eg, after winning an appeal. However, in this *Handbook*, we use backdating to mean getting paid benefit for a period before the date you claimed.

Additional support and appointees

If you have (or will have) difficulty with the claims process and need additional support, see Chapter 21. If you cannot manage the claims process at all you may need an appointee (see p325).

What you will be asked and how long it will take

To start your claim, you must provide SSS with your full name and date of birth. In practice, you are also asked questions about the residence and presence conditions at this point. SSS refers to this as 'Part 1' of your PADP claim.

Unless you are regarded as terminally ill (see below), you then have eight weeks to complete your claim by providing the rest of the required information (referred to as 'Part 2'). This eight-week period can be extended if there is good reason for the delay.[9] Part 2 relates to how your condition(s) affect your ability to manage the disability conditions (see p211).

Terminal illness

The rules about claiming PADP are different if you are terminally ill. You are regarded as 'terminally ill' if it is the judgement of a doctor or nurse who is involved in your care or diagnosis and acting in a professional capacity, that you have a progressive disease that can reasonably be expected to cause your death.[10] You should explain that the claim is on the grounds of terminal illness when making it (claims from terminally ill people are widely referred to as 'special rules' claims). Your GP, consultant or specialist nurse should complete Form DS1500, SR1 or a Benefits Assistance under Special Rules in Scotland (BASRiS) form,[11] giving details of your condition and prognosis.

If you claim PADP and you are regarded as terminally ill, you do not have to provide extra information about your care needs and are automatically entitled to the higher rate.[12]

Transfers to pension age disability payment

If you live in Scotland (or in a European Economic Area state and have a 'genuine and sufficient' link to Scotland – see CPAG's *Welfare Benefits Handbook*) and you get AA, you will transfer to PADP. This is expected to happen during 2025. You will be notified in writing that you are being transferred to PADP and that your AA will end when your PADP starts.[13] Unless you are terminally ill, you are awarded the same rate of PADP as your previous award of AA.[14]

4. How you are assessed

Note: this assessment process does not apply if you are regarded as terminally ill (see above).

To get pension age disability payment (PADP), you need to meet its 'disability conditions', set out on p211. Social Security Scotland uses an assessment process to decide whether you meet those conditions.

Timescales

You usually have eight weeks from starting a PADP claim to return the Part 2 form. The eight-week period can be extended if you can show there is good reason for the delay.[15] If anything is preventing you from completing Part 2, ask for more time as soon as possible.

Supporting evidence

You are usually asked to provide supporting evidence – eg, reports from your doctor or other professionals, a letter from someone who knows you well, and/or a diary of symptoms. See Chapter 16 for more information about supporting evidence. Do not delay submitting the claim while waiting for evidence; it can be provided later by post or online at mygov.scot.

If you cannot provide supporting evidence yourself, you can ask SSS to gather it on your behalf. You are asked about this when completing the Part 2 form.

5. Decisions

Getting a determination

You get decisions about pension age disability payment (PADP) by letter.[16] In the Scottish benefits system, these decisions are known as 'determinations'.

If you disagree with a determination, you can challenge it by asking for a redetermination and then pursuing an appeal if necessary (see Chapter 20). Note that deadlines apply for challenging determinations.

If you challenge a determination, Social Security Scotland (SSS) or a tribunal can look at all the PADP disability conditions again, not just the ones that you disagree with. This means that, following a redetermination or appeal, your award could decrease instead of increasing. If you have an award of PADP, it is usually best to get advice before challenging a determination.

You may be able to get interim payments of PADP at the same rate as your previous award during the redetermination or appeal process This is known as 'short-term assistance' (see p316).

Length of awards

PADP is awarded without a fixed end date. When making an award, SSS normally specifies a period after which it will review the PADP award. The length of this period should be based on whether, and how soon, your needs are likely to change. If your needs are unlikely to change, the review period should be between five and 10 years long. SSS must make a new determination at the end of the review period (see p215).

SSS can reduce or stop the award earlier if it has grounds to (see p207).

6. Getting paid

When you are paid

Pension age disability payment (PADP) is usually paid every four weeks in arrears. If you are regarded as terminally ill, you are paid weekly in advance instead.[17] You will start to be paid PADP after a determination has been made on your claim.

Note: it is possible for payment of PADP to be suspended (see p173).

Where your payment goes

PADP is usually paid into your bank account. Some or all of your PADP can be paid to someone else on your behalf if this is in your interests.[18] This might be useful if, for example, you want a family member to look after your PADP income because your mental health problem makes it difficult for you to manage money.

7. Reviews and reassessments

Scheduled reviews

When Social Security Scotland (SSS) makes an award of pension age disability payment (PADP), it may specify a review date when it plans to look at the award again and make a new determination on your entitlement. SSS calls this a 'scheduled review'. There is more information about how review periods are set on p214.[19]

As part of the review process, you are likely to be asked to complete a form, similarly to when you make a new claim for PADP (see p213).

Changes of circumstances

You must report any changes in your circumstances to SSS as soon as possible.[20] You can report a change by phone or on the form you can download from mygov.scot.

If you report a change that may affect the amount of your PADP, SSS makes a new determination.

Ongoing evidence requirements

Once you are getting PADP, you may be asked to provide information at any time. If you fail to do so, your PADP payments could be suspended.[21] If you need more time to provide the information, contact SSS as soon as possible to request an extension.

8. Pension age disability payment and other benefits

Pension age disability payment (PADP) interacts with other benefits in the same ways that attendance allowance (AA) does. There are the same benefit cap exemptions for PADP as for AA. See p208 for more information.

Notes

1. **Who can get pension age disability payment**
   1 s31 and Sch 5 SS(S)A 2018; Parts 2-7 DAOP(S) Regs
   2 Reg 8 DAOP(S) Regs
   3 Reg 6(1) DAOP(S) Regs
   4 Regs 5, 6(2) and 7 DAOP(S) Regs
   5 Regs 5 and 6(3) DAOP(S) Regs

2. **The amount of benefit**
   6 Reg 26(1) DAOP(S) Regs

3. **Making a claim**
   7 Reg 27(2) DAOP(S) Regs
   8 Reg 27(4)-(6) DAOP(S) Regs
   9 Reg 27(4)-(6) DAOP(S) Regs
   10 s31(1)(b) and Sch 5 para 1 SS(S)A 2018; reg 18(6)-(9) DAOP(S) Regs; SSS, *Chief Medical Officer's Guidance for Clinicians Completing a BASRiS Form*
   11 SSS, *Special Rules for Terminal Illness: frequently asked questions*
   12 Reg 18(1) DAOP(S) Regs
   13 Sch para 8 DAOP(S) Regs
   14 Sch para 9(4) DAOP(S) Regs

4. **How you are assessed**
   15 Reg 27(4)-(6) DAOP(S) Regs

5. **Decisions**
   16 ss37 and 40 SS(S)A 2018

6. **Getting paid**
   17 Reg 28 DAOP(S) Regs
   18 Reg 25 DAOP(S) Regs

7. **Reviews and reassessments**
   19 Regs 29 and 39 DAOP(S) Regs; SSS, *Decision Making Guide: choosing an appropriate review period for pension age disability payment*, at socialsecurity.gov.scot
   20 s56 SS(S)A 2018
   21 s54 SS(S)A 2018; reg 30 DAOP(S) Regs

Chapter 14

Carers' benefits

This chapter covers:

Key facts

- Many different kinds of care, support and assistance can be considered when deciding whether you are a carer for benefit purposes. You do not need to be a professional carer, a relative, or live with the person you are supporting.
- The main carer benefit in England and Wales is carer's allowance, and in Scotland is carer support payment. These are non-means-tested benefits, but you cannot qualify if you earn more than £196 a week.
- Being a carer can increase the amount of means-tested benefits (eg, universal credit or pension credit) that you receive.
- Before claiming carer benefits, it is important to check how they will affect any other benefits that you and the person you are supporting receive.

1. Who is a carer

The term 'carer' means different things in different contexts.

- **Paid carer:** also called a 'care worker'. This means that you are employed to provide care. You are likely to care for people you do not know personally, possibly in a place such as a care home. You are not entitled to claim carer benefits for this type of work.
- **Unpaid carer:** this is when you care for a friend or relative and are not paid to do so. You might care for this person most of the time, or you might only do this occasionally. You do not need to live with someone, or be related to them, to count as a carer.

- **Carer for benefits purposes:** if your caring role meets specific criteria (see below), you may be able to claim the carers' benefits mentioned in this chapter.

What is 'caring'

People often think of caring as involving physical and practical tasks for someone. However, caring also includes support related to emotional and mental needs.

These might include the following.

- keeping someone company or supervising them to ensure their safety;
- helping them to go out and/or to take part in social activities;
- providing emotional support when needed;
- helping them to cook and clean;
- prompting and encouraging them to dress, wash or eat;
- helping someone seek help for their mental health problem, including reminding them to take medication, helping them make GP appointments, or attending appointments with them;
- advocating for them when they interact with other services, like banks, schools or the DWP;
- shopping for them or with them;
- helping with benefits, bills and budgeting.

You might feel that these actions are just part of your relationship, particularly if the person you are supporting is your child, partner or another close relative. This might mean that you do not consider yourself a carer. However, you can qualify for carers' benefits if you meet the criteria set out in this chapter.

Carers with a health condition or disability

Many carers have physical or mental health conditions or their own care needs. This does not automatically prevent them from qualifying for carer benefits.

You may want to get advice before claiming carer benefits if you get health- or disability-related benefits for yourself. Tasks you do as a carer are likely to be considered when you have a benefit assessment and could potentially affect your entitlement. This depends on the kinds of difficulties you have and the help you are giving to someone else. For example, if you have difficulty walking due to a physical health condition, this would not affect your ability to provide emotional support and budgeting assistance to someone else.

2. Where to start with carers' benefits

Before claiming any carers' benefits, it is a good idea to **get independent advice,** because some carers' benefits can affect your other benefits or the benefits of the person you are supporting. Use advicelocal.uk to find advice services in your area.

- As a carer looking for financial support, you often start by claiming **carer's allowance** (CA) in England and Wales (see p220) or **carer support payment** (CSP) in Scotland (see p223). These are the main benefits for carers. There are rules about how much you can earn, how many hours of caring you must do to qualify, and the disability benefits that the person you look after must be getting.
- If you live in Scotland, are aged 16–18, and cannot get CSP or CA (eg, because you are at school), you may be able to claim a **young carer grant** instead (see p228). In some situations, you can claim both.
- If you get universal credit (UC), you can declare your caring responsibilities to receive the **carer element of UC** (see p227). The eligibility criteria are broadly the same as for CA, but unlike CA, there is no earnings limit. If you are eligible for both, it generally makes sense to apply for CA *and* get the UC carer element. Although CA reduces your UC pound for pound, there are advantages to having CA in the background, such as retaining some income during gaps in UC eligibility. It is particularly advantageous in Scotland, where getting CSP or CA can mean that you also get extra carer's allowance supplement payments which are disregarded as income for UC (see p225).
- If you get a means-tested benefit other than UC (eg, pension credit) and are entitled to CA, you can get a **carer premium or addition** (see p228).
- While getting CA you receive **national insurance (NI) credits.**[1] If you care for someone who gets a qualifying disability benefit, but do not provide care for enough hours to make you eligible for CA, you may still be able to apply for NI credits as a carer. The same might apply if you have recently finished, or will soon start, qualifying for CA.[2] Before applying, check that you do not already get sufficient NI credits from another source.
- Outside the benefits system, there is **other support available for carers** (see p229).

Example

Amy (24) has a long-term mental health problem. Her working-age parents provide day-to-day care for Amy between them. Her parents both work and they do not currently get any benefits. They want advice about claiming carers' benefits. Their advice worker explains the different types of benefits and their eligibility conditions. They discuss which member of the couple – if either – would be best to claim. They also check whether claiming a carers' benefit(s) will affect Amy's own benefits.

3. Carer's allowance

Who can get carer's allowance

If you live in England and Wales, you qualify for carer's allowance (CA) if you satisfy the following conditions.[3]

You must be caring for someone for 35 hours a week or more

You do not have to live with this person or be related to them. Caring can include supervision as well as assistance. It usually covers activities that you do in the person's presence, but might also include some time spent on tasks like shopping for them, organising their affairs, preparing for them to come to stay with you or clearing up after they visit.[4] See p218 for more about what 'caring' can mean.

As long as you care for 35 hours a week, it does not matter if these hours are not spread evenly throughout the week – eg, you might provide all 35 hours of care at the weekend. However, you cannot average out the hours if you provide care for more than 35 hours in some weeks and fewer than 35 in others.[5] In some circumstances, you can take a temporary break from caring and continue to qualify for CA.[6]

Note: only one person can qualify for CA for caring for the same person. If you cannot agree on who this should be, the DWP decides. If you care for two or more people at the same time, you can only get CA for supporting one of them.[7]

The person you care for must get a qualifying benefit

The person you care for must get a qualifying benefit.

Qualifying disability benefits

Attendance allowance (AA), pension age disability payment (PADP), the highest or middle rate of the care component of disability living allowance (DLA), Scottish adult disbility living allowance (SADLA) or child disability payment (CDP), either rate of the daily living component of personal independence payment (PIP) or adult disability payment (ADP), armed forces independence payment or constant attendance allowance of £90.20 a week or more paid with an industrial injuries benefit or war disablement pension.[8]

CA stops if the qualifying disability benefit of the person for whom you are caring stops because they are in hospital or a similar institution (see p280).[9]

If the person you are caring for has claimed a disability benefit but has not yet had a decision (or is appealing a refusal), you cannot claim CA yet but may be able to make a backdated claim once they have a decision awarding them benefit (see p222).

You must earn no more than £196 a week

This includes net earnings from employment[10] and net profits from self-employment.[11]

Note:

- There are some other amounts that can be disregarded from your earnings – eg, income tax refunds or a loan/advance from an employer.[12]
- If your earnings from employment fluctuate, your weekly earnings may be calculated as an average.[13] If you are self-employed, your weekly earnings are usually averaged over a year.[14]
- When calculating earnings from employment or self-employment, the cost of paying someone else to look after the person you care for (or to look after a child under 16 for whom you are getting child benefit), up to a maximum amount, can often be deducted from your earnings figure.[15]

You must not be in full-time education

Usually, you are regarded as being in full-time education and cannot get CA if:[16]

- your course is described as full-time by your university, college or school; *or*
- you are attending the course for 21 hours a week or more.

You are treated as still being in full-time education during vacations and any temporary interruption of the course, but not if you have agreed a non-temporary absence such as a year out.[17]

You can get CA if you are classed as being in part-time education.

You must be over compulsory school age

You can claim CA from the last Friday in June if you will have turned 16 by the end of the summer holidays.

There is no **upper age limit** for CA. However, because of the overlapping benefit rules, if you receive state pension you may not be paid CA even if you qualify (see p223). Even if you are not paid CA, your underlying entitlement may mean that you get a carer element if you are entitled to universal credit (UC – see p227) or a carer premium or carer addition in your other means-tested benefit (see p228).

You must meet the immigration and residence conditions

You cannot get CA if you are a person subject to immigration control or if you do not satisfy the residence conditions. See CPAG's *Welfare Benefits Handbook* for more information.

The amount of benefit and getting paid

CA is paid at a weekly rate of £83.30.[18] You are paid weekly in advance or four-weekly in arrears, usually on a Monday.[19]

If you live in Wales, you may be eligible for a grant from the Carers Support Fund Wales to top up your CA – see carers.org/around-the-uk-our-work-in-wales/carers-support-fund-wales-programme.

Making a claim

You can claim CA online at gov.uk/carers-allowance or on paper form DS700 (DS700(SP) if you get a state pension). You can download form from gov.uk or request one by calling the Carer's Allowance Unit (0800 731 0297; textphone: 0800 731 0317; Relay UK and British Sign Language video relay services are available).

Note: before claiming, you should be aware of how CA affects your entitlement to means-tested benefits and the means-tested benefit entitlement of the person you care for (see p223).

Additional support

If you have (or will have) difficulty with the claims process and need additional support, see Chapter 21.

Claiming in advance and backdating

You can claim CA **in advance**, up to three months before you qualify.[20]

A claim for CA can usually only be backdated for a maximum of three months.[21]

It can sometimes be backdated further.[22]

- If you claim CA within three months of a decision (including a tribunal decision) to award a qualifying benefit to the person you are caring for, your CA is usually backdated to the first day of the benefit week in which the qualifying benefit is payable.
- If your CA stopped because the person you care for had their qualifying benefit reduced or stopped, and you make a further claim within three months of the decision to reinstate/resume payment of the qualifying benefit, your CA is backdated to the date your last CA award ended or the date from when the qualifying benefit was re-awarded/resumed in payment, whichever is later.

Note: the term 'backdating' is often informally used to mean getting arrears of your benefit going back to a claim or decision date – eg, after winning an appeal. However, in this *Handbook*, we use backdating to mean getting paid benefit for a period before the date you claimed.

Decisions and changes of circumstances

CA awards are usually made for an indefinite period.[23] Once you are awarded CA, you should report all changes in your circumstances to the Carer's Allowance Unit as soon as possible. Do not assume that the Carer's Allowance Unit already knows something – eg, about changes to your income or to the qualifying benefit of the person you care for. You can report a change by phone, letter or at gov.uk/carers-allowance.[24] It is preferable to report a change in writing so that there is a clear record of what you have said and when.

Carer's allowance and other benefits

Means-tested benefits

If **you** are entitled to CA and a means-tested benefit:

- your CA is taken into account as income and reduces your benefit pound for pound. It is still generally worth claiming CA alongside UC (see p218);
- you may get a carer element included in your UC (see p227) or a carer premium or carer addition included in your other means-tested benefit (see p228);
- you do not have any work-related requirements (see Chapter 18).[25]

If **the person you care for** gets a means-tested benefit that includes a severe disability premium/addition, that premium/addition is removed if you get CA for looking after them. Get independent advice before claiming CA.

Non-means-tested benefits

You can get CA at the same time as disability benefits such as PIP, ADP, DLA, CDP and AA. CA does not affect the amount of the disability benefit and vice versa. However, any tasks you do as a carer are likely to be considered when you are assessed for a disability benefit and might affect your future entitlement (see p218).

There are other non-means-tested benefits that CA overlaps with, meaning you cannot be paid both in full – eg, state pension or contributory employment and support allowance (ESA). If you have claimed CA successfully but are not paid it because of these **overlapping benefit rules**, you are said to have an 'underlying entitlement' to CA.

The benefit cap

In some cases, there is a limit on the total amount of specified benefits you can receive (the 'benefit cap'). The benefit cap does not apply if you or your partner get CA or have an 'underlying entitlement' to it under the overlapping benefit rules above.

4. Carer support payment

Who can get carer support payment

In Scotland, you qualify for carer support payment (CSP) if you satisfy the following conditions.[26]

Note:

- Special rules may apply if you are in hospital and in certain other situations (see Chapter 19).
- If you live in England or Wales, claim carer's allowance (CA) instead (see p220).
- You can usually qualify for CSP if you are a student, but may not be eligible if you are aged 16–19 on a non-advanced, full-time course or approved training.[27]

You must be caring for someone for 35 hours a week or more

The rules are the same as for CA (see p220).

The person you care for must get a qualifying benefit

This means they get one of the disability benefits listed on p220.[28]

CSP stops if the qualifying disability benefit of the person for whom you are caring stops because they are in hospital or a similar institution (see p280).

If the person you are caring for has claimed a disability benefit but has not yet had a decision (or is appealing a refusal), you cannot claim CSP yet but may be able to make a backdated claim once they have a decision awarding them benefit (see p225).

You must earn no more than £196 a week

This includes net earnings from employment and net profits from self-employment.[29] The rules are the same as for CA (see p221), but note the following differences.

- Social Security Scotland (SSS) has discretion about how to average your earnings over a period of up to 26 weeks, if they vary in different weeks and you have provided payslips.[30]
- If you are an employee, SSS can usually get information about your earnings from HMRC. However, you should not rely on this and should tell SSS if your earnings increase, as otherwise you may be overpaid.

You must be 16 or over

You must be aged 16 or over to get CSP, but if you are still at school you can only get CSP in limited situations.[31] See CPAG's *Welfare Benefits Handbook* for more information. (If you are aged 16 to 18, you may be able to get a young carer grant – see p228.)

There is no **upper age limit** for CSP. However, because of the overlapping benefit rules, if you receive state pension you may not be paid CSP even if you qualify (see p226). Even if you are not paid CSP, your 'underlying entitlement' may mean that you get a carer element in your universal credit (UC – see p227) or a carer premium or carer addition in your other means-tested benefit (see p228).

You must meet the immigration and residence conditions

You cannot get CSP if you are a person subject to immigration control or if you do not satisfy the residence conditions. See CPAG's *Welfare Benefits Handbook*.

The amount of benefit and getting paid

CSP is paid at a weekly rate of £83.30.[32] You are usually paid four-weekly in arrears.[33]

If you are paid CSP, you can get a **carer's allowance supplement.**[34] This is paid in two lump-sum payments each year. The payments in 2025 are £293.50 each and will be made in June (to those who were getting CA or CSP on the qualifying date of 14 April) and December (to those who were getting CA or CSP on 13 October). SSS pays CA supplement automatically. CA supplement is disregarded as income for means-tested benefits.

Note:

- Scottish carer supplement will replace CA supplement for people getting CSP from late 2025, and be paid alongside CSP.
- The Scottish government plans to make increased payments to CSP claimants caring for more than one disabled person.[35]

Making a claim

You can claim CSP online at mygov.scot/carer-support-payment/how-to-apply, or by phone on 0800 182 222, in writing on the approved form or, if you use British Sign Language, via Contact Scotand BSL.

Note: before claiming, you should be aware of how CSP affects your entitlement to means-tested benefits and the means-tested benefit entitlement of the person you care for (see p226).

If your CSP ends but you become entitled again within 26 weeks of it ending, in some circumstances, your entitlement can be determined again without you needing to make another claim.[36]

Additional support

If you have (or will have) difficulty with the claims process and need additional support, see Chapter 21.

Claiming in advance and backdating

Advance claims for CSP are expected to be possible from late 2025.[37]

A claim for CA can usually only be backdated for a maximum of 13 weeks.[38]

In extremely limited situations, you may be able to get extra backdating if you are in education or have lived in the UK for less than two years.[39] See CPAG's *Welfare Benefits Handbook* for more information.

If you claim CSP within 13 weeks of a decision (including a tribunal decision) to award a qualifying benefit to the person you are caring for, your CSP can be backdated to the first day of the benefit week in which the qualifying benefit is payable if you met the entitlement conditions on that date.[40]

Note: the term 'backdating' is often informally used to mean getting arrears of your benefit going back to a claim or decision date – eg, after winning an appeal.

However, in this *Handbook*, we use backdating to mean getting paid benefit for a period before the date you claimed.

Decisions and changes of circumstances

Once you are awarded CSP, you should report all changes in your circumstances to SSS as soon as possible. Do not assume that SSS already knows something – eg, about changes to your income or to the qualifying benefit of the person you care for. You can report a change online, in writing on the form you can download from mygov.scot/carer-support-payment-change-of-circumstances-form, or by phone.[41] It is preferable to report a change in writing so that there is a clear record of what you have said and when.

Carer support payment and other benefits

Means-tested benefits

If **you** are entitled to CSP and a means-tested benefit:

- your CSP (but not carer's allowance supplement) is taken into account as income and reduces your benefit pound for pound. It is still generally worth claiming CSP alongside UC (see p218);
- you may get a carer element included in your UC (see p227) or a carer premium or carer addition included in your other means-tested benefit (see p228);
- you do not have any work-related requirements (see Chapter 18).[42]

If **the person you care for** gets a means-tested benefit that includes a severe disability premium/addition, that premium/addition is removed if you get CSP for looking after them. Get independent advice before claiming CSP.

Non-means-tested benefits

You can get CSP at the same time as disability benefits such as ADP, PIP, SADLA, DLA, CDP, PADP and AA. CSP does not affect the amount of the disability benefit and vice versa. However, any tasks you do as a carer are likely to be considered when you are assessed for a disability benefit and might affect your future entitlement (see p218).

There are other non-means-tested benefits that CSP overlaps with, meaning you cannot be paid both in full – eg, contributory employment and support allowance or state pension. If you have claimed CSP successfully but are not paid it because of these **overlapping benefit rules**, you are said to have an 'underlying entitlement' to CSP.

The benefit cap

In some cases, there is a limit on the total amount of specified benefits you can receive (the 'benefit cap'). The benefit cap does not apply if you or your partner get CSP or have an 'underlying entitlement' to it under the overlapping benefit rules above.

5. Carer element of universal credit

A carer element of £198.31 a month is included in your maximum amount of universal credit (UC – see p69) if:[43]

- you are an unpaid carer; *and*
- you satisfy the eligibility conditions for carer's allowance (CA – see p220) or carer support payment (CSP – see p223); *or*
- you would satisfy the CA/CSP eligibility conditions but for the fact that your earnings are too high.

You do not claim a carer element – it should be included in your UC calculation when you have declared your caring responsibilities. You may need to prompt the DWP to add the carer element, and check that it has been added from the correct assessment period. Get independent advice if you are not sure.

You do not need to have claimed CA/CSP to get a carer element of UC. If you get both CA/CSP and UC, your UC is reduced pound for pound by your CA/CSP. There can still be good reasons for claiming CA while getting UC (see p218).

If you get the carer element of UC, you do not usually have any work-related requirements (see Chapter 18).[44] At the same time, there is no fixed limit on how much you can work or earn while getting a carer element of UC (unlike CA/CSP).

You cannot get the carer element at the same time as you are getting the limited capability for work or limited capability for work-related activity element of UC (the **LCW/LCWRA element** – see p70 and p71). You are paid the element with the higher value. If you claim UC with a partner, one of you can get the carer element while the other gets the LCW/LCWRA element.[45]

Getting a new carer element in your UC could erode a **transitional severe disability premium element** (see p73) or **transitional protection element** (see p79).

If you are claiming UC as a single person, only one carer element can be included, even if you care for more than one person. If you are making a **joint UC claim**, you can get two carer elements if both you and your partner are carers who meet the conditions, provided you are not caring for the same person. If you are both caring for the same person, you get one carer element. Similarly, if someone other than your partner is caring for the same person, only one of you can get the carer element of UC.[46]

Note: if the person you care for gets a means-tested benefit that includes a severe disability premium/addition, that premium/addition will be removed if you get the carer element of UC for looking after them. Bear in mind that the severe disability premium/addition is worth more than the carer element of UC. It is usually a good idea to get independent advice before declaring your entitlement to a carer element.

Example

Jade claims UC after stopping work to become a full-time carer for her son Zayn. Zayn has a mental health condition and receives the middle rate of the care component of disability living allowance. Jade meets all the eligibility conditions to get a carer element in her UC. However, it is not automatically included in her UC award. Jade challenges this by asking for a mandatory reconsideration (see p294) and succeeds in having the carer element added from her first assessment period.

Jade does not claim CA, because she understands this is not necessary for her to get the carer element in her UC, and has been told that CA would reduce her UC pound for pound so she would be financially no better off.

6. Carer premium and carer addition

If you get a means-tested benefit other than universal credit, and you or your partner are entitled to carer's allowance (CA – see p220) or carer support payment (CSP – see p223), you can qualify for an extra amount in your means-tested benefit. This is known as a carer premium, or as a carer addition for pension credit (PC).[47]

The premium/addition is worth £46.40 a week, or £92.80 if both you and your partner get CA/CSP. To see how the premium/addition affects the calculation of your benefit, see p121 for housing benefit, p110 for PC and p55 for income-related employment and support allowance.

You do not 'claim' the premium/addition but should notify the relevant means-tested benefit office that you are entitled to CA. You can get a carer premium/addition if you have an 'underlying entitlement' to CA but do not get payments of CA because of the overlapping benefit rules (see p223).

7. Young carer grant in Scotland

Who can get a young carer grant

A young carer grant is a single annual payment of £390.25 which can be claimed by some unpaid carers aged 16–18 living in Scotland. It is expected to be extended to include 19-year-olds in late 2025. You can qualify for a young carer grant if you care for one or more people who get a qualifying disability benefit throughout the 13 weeks before you claim (the qualifying benefits are the same as for carer's allowance (CA) – see p220). You must provide care for sufficient hours during this 13-week period: a total of at least 208 hours of caring, spread over at least 10 of the 13 weeks. You can add together hours of care you provide for up to three people so long as they each get a qualifying benefit throughout the qualifying period.

There are also immigration and residence conditions for getting a young carer grant. See CPAG's *Welfare Benefits Handbook* for details.

Note:

- If the person you care for claimed a disability benefit more than 13 weeks ago and has not yet been awarded it, you can still claim a young carer grant. Your claim will be refused now, but if the disability benefit is later awarded, you may be able to get the young carer grant for the date when you claimed.[48]
- If someone else has received a young carer grant in respect of a person you care for within one year before the date of your claim, you cannot usually get a young carer grant for caring for that person.[49] However, it does not matter if someone else gets CSP, CA or the carer element of universal credit (UC) for supporting someone that you care for – you can still get a young carer grant.

Making a claim

You can claim a young carer grant online at mygov.scot/young-carer-grant/how-to-apply, by phone on 0800 182 222, in writing on the form downloadable from mygov.scot/young-carer-grant-paper-form or, if you use British Sign Language, via Contact Scotand BSL.

You can get a young carer grant once a year. If you have previously received a young carer grant, claim again one year after the date of your last claim.[50]

Young carer grant and other benefits

You cannot qualify for a young carer grant if you are entitled to **CSP** or **CA** on the date of your claim or at any point in the 13-week qualifying period, or if you have claimed CSP, unless your claim has been refused.[51]

Note:

- A young carer grant does not count towards the benefit cap and does not count as income or capital for means-tested benefits.
- If you are a young carer living in Scotland, you can get a package of support (whether or not you can get a young carer grant) from Young Scot. There is more information at young.scot. You may also be able to get help, support and services from your local authority – ask for a young carer's assessment.

8. Other support for carers

Not all unpaid carers are eligible for carers' benefits. You might not care for the person enough hours in the week to qualify, the person might not get a qualifying benefit or you might be earning too much money in another job. This does not mean there is no support available. You might also need these extra forms of support if you are a carer and have a health condition or disability yourself. **Note:** Chapter 15 has information about other financial support.

Carer's assessment from social services

Anyone caring for another person can ask to have a carer's assessment completed by their local social services. The assessment considers what support the local authority can offer you – eg, respite care (see below), financial help, or putting you in touch with local support networks for carers. You can request an assessment by contacting your local authority's child or adult social services department (depending on the age of the person you care for).

Respite care

Respite care is any arrangement that provides a temporary break from your caring responsibilities. This could be in the form of a holiday, a short stay for the person you are caring for in a place like a care home or day centre, or getting a replacement carer for a short time. If you care for someone regularly, you may be entitled to some forms of respite care whether or not you get a carers' benefit. It is available from your local authority and some charities. You need to have a carer's assessment from your local authority to know if you are eligible (see above). Rethink Mental Illness has more information at rethink.org/advice-and-information/carers-hub.

Flexibility at work

Many workers have statutory rights to request flexible working and take time off in emergencies involving a dependant. Your workplace might also have additional benefits for carers, such as carer's leave. Carers UK provides information at carersuk.org/help-and-advice/work-and-career/your-rights-in-work.

Emotional support

National and local charities for carers run support groups, online forums and may have other practical support available for unpaid carers. They are there to support your wellbeing as a carer. You can find information about these from Carers UK online at carersuk.org/help-and-advice.

Notes

2. **Where to start with carers' benefits**
1 Reg 7A SS(Cr) Regs; regs 26 and 29 SP Regs
2 s23A(2) and (3)(c) SSCBA 1992; regs 5(1)(b)-(c) and 7 SS(CCPC) Regs; regs 27, 37(1) and (2)(a)-(b) and 38(1)(a)-(c) and (2) SP Regs

3. **Carer's allowance**
3 s70 SSCBA 1992; regs 4-9 SS(ICA) Regs
4 Reg 4(1) SS(ICA) Regs; CG/6/90
5 R(G) 3/91
6 Reg 4(2) SS(ICA) Regs
7 s70(7) SSCBA 1992; reg 4(1A) SS(ICA) Regs
8 s70(2) SSCBA 1992
9 *SSWP v Pridding* [2002] EWCA Civ 306
10 Reg 8 SS(ICA) Regs; regs 2(1), 9 and 10(4) SSB(CE) Regs; CIS/521/1990; R(IS) 9/95; CIS/743/1992; *Minter v Kingston Upon Hull CC and Potter v SSWP* [2011] EWCA Civ 1155
11 Reg 8 SS(ICA) Regs; regs 11(2), 13 and 14 SSB(CE) Regs; R(IS) 13/91; R(FC) 1/91; CTC/26/1989
12 Sch 1 SSB(CE) Regs
13 Reg 8(3) SSB(CE) Regs; CG/4941/2003
14 Regs 4(1) and (3), 11(1) and 12(1) SSB(CE) Regs and R(IB) 7/03, disapplying reg 4(2) of these Regs
15 Regs 10(3) and 13(3) and Sch 3 SSB(CE) Regs
16 Reg 5 SS(ICA) Regs; *SSWP v Deane* [2010] EWCA Civ 699
17 *SM v SSWP* [2016] UKUT 406 (AAC)
18 Sch 4 SSCBA 1992
19 Reg 22(1) and (3) and Sch 6 SS(C&P) Regs
20 Reg 13 SS(C&P) Regs
21 Reg 19 SS(C&P) Regs
22 Reg 6(16)-(22), (33) and (34) SS(C&P) Regs
23 Reg 17 SS(C&P) Regs
24 Reg 32ZA SS(C&P) Regs
25 s19(2)(b) WRA 2012

4. **Carer support payment**
26 s28 and Sch 2 SS(S)A 2018; Part 3 CA(CSP)(S) Regs
27 Reg 13 CA(CSP)(S) Regs
28 Regs 2 and 5(1) CA(CSP)(S) Regs
29 Reg 14(1) CA(CSP)(S) Regs
30 Sch 2 para 7(3)(b) CA(CSP)(S) Regs
31 Regs 4 and 13 CA(CSP)(S) Regs
32 Reg 16(1) CA(CSP)(S) Regs
33 Reg 22 and Sch 1 para 7 CA(CSP)(S) Regs
34 s81 SS(S)A 2018
35 The Carer's Assistance (Young Carer Grant and Carer Support Payment) (Miscellaneous Amendment and Saving Provision) (Scotland) Regulations 2025 (draft)
36 Reg 23 CA(CSP)(S) Regs
37 The Carer's Assistance (Young Carer Grant and Carer Support Payment) (Miscellaneous Amendment and Saving Provision) (Scotland) Regulations 2025 (draft)
38 Reg 19 CA(CSP)(S) Regs
39 Regs 18A and 18B and Sch 1 tables 1 and 2 CA(CSP)(S) Regs
40 Reg 19 CA(CSP)(S) Regs
41 s56(2)(b) SS(S)A 2018
42 s19(2)(b) WRA 2012

5. **Carer element of universal credit**
43 Regs 29 and 30 UC Regs
44 s19(2)(b) WRA 2012; reg 89(1)(b) UC Regs
45 Reg 29(4) UC Regs
46 s70(7) SSCBA 1992; reg 29(2) and (3) UC Regs

6. **Carer premium and carer addition**
47 **ESA** Sch 4 para 8 ESA Regs
PC Reg 6(6)(a) and Sch 1 para 4 SPC Regs
HB Sch 3 paras 7 and 17 HB Regs; Sch 3 paras 5 and 9 HB(SPC) Regs

7. **Young carer grant in Scotland**
48 Reg 11 CA(YCG)(S) Regs; SSS, *Eligibility for Young Carer Grant*
49 Regs 7(4) and (5) and 10 CA(YCG)(S) Regs
50 Reg 7(3) and (6) CA(YCG)(S) Regs
51 Reg 7(1) and (2) CA(YCG)(S) Regs

Chapter 15

Other financial support

This chapter covers:

Note: you could be entitled to extra help beyond the types set out in this chapter. For example, there are schemes that help with health-related costs (like free prescriptions, dental treatment and hospital travel) and schemes to help with the costs of having children (like Healthy Start, Best Start, Sure Start, help with childcare costs and free school meals).

1. Discretionary housing payment

A discretionary housing payment (DHP) can be made by your local authority to help you with rent or with certain other housing costs. To apply for a DHP, you must be entitled to help with your rent through universal credit (UC) or housing benefit (HB).

DHPs can be made because your UC or HB does not cover your full rent – for example, due to:

- the local housing allowance or bedroom tax;
- deductions being made from your benefit because you live with a non-dependant;
- the benefit cap.

You can also apply for a DHP towards certain one-off costs – eg, if you need a deposit, rent in advance or moving expenses.

Apply through your local authority. Payments are discretionary and are not guaranteed – your council decides based on your situation and its available budget. You might be refused a DHP for budgetary reasons even if you make a strong application, or you might be successful but only receive assistance for a short period. **Note:** if you live in Scotland and are affected by the bedroom tax or the benefit cap, your application for a DHP should automatically be accepted.[1]

A DHP does not count as income for working out your entitlement to means-tested benefits or for the benefit cap.

For more information about DHPs, see CPAG's *Welfare Benefits Handbook* and speak to your local authority.

2. Council tax reduction

You may be able to get your council tax bill reduced under your local authority's council tax reduction (CTR) scheme. In some areas, this is known as council tax support. You can get help whether you rent or own your home.

Check with your local authority whether you qualify for a CTR. In England and Wales, local authorities may devise their own local schemes which must meet minimum requirements. In Wales, if a local authority does not adopt its own scheme, a default scheme applies. In Scotland, there is a national scheme, administered by local authorities.[2]

Note:

- You need to apply for a CTR, usually online or on a paper form from your local authority. If you claim housing benefit for help with rent, it may be possible to claim a CTR at the same time, without filling in a further form. This does not apply when you claim universal credit, so in this situation you must make sure that you put in a separate CTR claim.
- Your income (including entitlement to means-tested benefits) and your capital are generally relevant to your CTR eligibility.
- CTR is not a social security benefit and does not count as income for the purposes of working out your entitlement to means-tested benefits or for the benefit cap.
- CTR is not the same as a council tax discount or exemption – eg, because you live alone or are a student. You might be eligible to be considered for these as well as for a CTR. See CPAG's *Council Tax Handbook* for more details.

3. Budgeting loans and budgeting advances

In some circumstances, you can apply for a repayable loan from the DWP. How you do this depends on which DWP benefits you are receiving.

Universal credit

A budgeting advance is a payment of universal credit (UC) to help you with expenses – eg, buying essential furniture or household equipment. There are rules about your earnings, capital and how long you must have been on means-tested benefits to qualify for a budgeting advance – see gov.uk/guidance/universal-credit-advances#get-a-budgeting-advance.[3] Budgeting advances are discretionary, and if your application is unsuccessful you do not have a right to appeal. Budgeting advances must be repaid, usually by deductions from future payments of your UC and usually over 12 months (24 months for advances taken out from December 2024).

You start an application for a budgeting advance by speaking to your job centre work coach, putting a message on your online journal or calling the UC helpline.

The minimum amount of a budgeting advance is £100. The maximum is:

- if you are single and not responsible for a child, £348;
- if you are in a couple and not responsible for a child, £464;
- if you are responsible for a child and either single or in a couple, £812.

Note: budgeting advances are not the same as 'new claim' advances of UC (see p101).

Other DWP benefits

You may be eligible to apply for a budgeting loan from the DWP if you get pension credit (guarantee or savings credit) or income-related employment and support allowance. You can request a loan to help with several types of expenses – eg, furniture and household equipment, clothes or travelling expenses. The minimum and maximum loan amounts are the same as for a UC budgeting advance (see above). You should apply online at gov.uk/budgeting-help-benefits or in writing on Form SF500, available from gov.uk or the job centre. You can also request that a Form SF500 be posted to you by calling the Social Fund Enquiry Line on 0800 169 0140.

4. Support for mortgage interest

If you have a mortgage, the DWP may offer you a secured loan to help with your mortgage interest payments, known as a support for mortgage interest (SMI) loan.[4] You are only eligible if you are entitled to universal credit, pension credit or income-related employment and support allowance, and you have been getting this benefit for at least three months.

If you accept an SMI loan, payments are usually made directly to your mortgage lender on a regular basis. The amount of each loan payment is calculated using a formula and is not necessarily the amount you are liable to pay.

An SMI loan is not a social security benefit and you normally have to repay it, but there are exceptions. There are more details about SMI loans in CPAG's *Welfare Benefits Handbook*.

Getting advice: support for mortgage interest

It is important to get independent legal and financial advice (eg, from a financial adviser or solicitor) before accepting an SMI loan. The information about the loan you get from the DWP or its agent is *not* independent advice.

5. Local welfare assistance and household support fund

In some circumstances, you can get financial help from a local welfare assistance scheme run by the local council or devolved government. These can provide help, for example, towards immediate short-term needs in a crisis or to ease exceptional financial pressure.

In England, the local scheme is at your local authority's discretion. Check with your local authority to find out what help is available, whether you qualify and how to apply. Note that not all local authorities have a scheme.

In Wales, the Discretionary Assistance Fund offers non-repayable emergency assistance payments and individual assistance payments. You can apply at gov.wales/discretionary-assistance-fund-daf/how-apply.

The Scottish Welfare Fund provides community care grants and crisis grants. The basic rules for the scheme are set by the Scottish government, with each local authority having some discretion. You should apply to your local authority.[5]

The household support fund

The household support fund is a UK government initiative to help people in financial hardship with basic expenses such as food, clothing and energy costs. It was introduced in autumn 2021 and has been extended until 31 March 2026. In England and Scotland, it is administered by local authorities. Application processes and the kinds of financial support offered vary by local authority and it can be a good idea to get information and support from a local advice agency. In some areas, the household support fund has been rolled into the local welfare assistance scheme (see above) but it is also available from local authorities that do not have a local welfare assistance scheme. In Wales, payments from the household support fund are being administered through the Discretionary Assistance Fund (see above).

6. Warm Home Discount

Warm Home Discount is a one-off credit of £150 on your energy bill under the Warm Home Discount scheme. You may be able to get a Warm Home Discount if you get the guarantee credit of pension credit, or you are on a low income and get other qualifying means-tested benefits and meet your energy supplier's criteria. Note that not all energy suppliers take part in the scheme. For further information, visit gov.uk/the-warm-home-discount-scheme and see your energy supplier's website. See also CPAG's *Fuel Rights Handbook*.

7. Food banks

If you are experiencing severe financial hardship (eg, caused by debt or benefit delays), you may be able to get assistance from a food bank. Some food banks operate on a drop-in basis, while others use a voucher scheme. Food bank vouchers are available from many frontline professionals such as doctors, social workers, job centre staff and some charity workers. You can find further information and contact details for many food banks at trussell.org.uk or foodaidnetwork.org.uk/our-members or by contacting your local authority.

You may also be able to get help with food or meals through local community groups which are part of the FareShare network. See more information at fareshare.org.uk.

8. Help to Save

Help to Save is a UK-wide government scheme offering a top-up to working people on low incomes who open a special type of savings account and pay into it regularly. To be eligible, you must be getting universal credit and have earned £1 or more in your last monthly assessment period.[6]

The most you can pay into your account each calendar month is £50, which is £2,400 over four years. In those four years, you can earn up to £1,200 from your savings. See gov.uk/get-help-savings-low-income for more information. You can withdraw money from a Help to Save account at any time, but it will affect the amount of bonus you can get.

9. Help from social services

Local authority adult care and children's services departments have statutory duties and discretionary powers to provide practical and financial help to some families, children, young people, older people, people with disabilities and health conditions, carers, care leavers and asylum seekers. Contact your local authority for information or seek independent advice – see advicelocal.uk.

10. Charities

Many charities provide financial help to people in need. For example, some energy and water companies offer schemes to support customers on low incomes or dealing with debt, through independent charitable trusts. Turn2us has details of charities that can provide financial help on its website turn2us.org.uk. In many cases, you can apply for support directly through the website. If you need assistance with this, you can seek independent advice – see advicelocal.uk.

Notes

1. **Discretionary housing payment**
   1 Scottish Discretionary Housing Payment: Guidance Manual, available at gov.scot

2. **Council tax reduction**
   2 s13A LGFA 1992
   E CTRS(DS)E Regs; CTRS(PR)E Regs
   W CTRS(DS)W Regs; CTRSPR(W) Regs
   S CTR(S) Regs; CTR(SPC)S Regs

3. **Budgeting loans and budgeting advances**
   3 Regs 12-15 SS(PAB) Regs

4. **Support for mortgage interest**
   4 LMI Regs

5. **Local welfare assistance and household support fund**
   5 Welfare Funds (Scotland) Act 2015; The Welfare Funds (Scotland) Regulations 2016 No.107

8. **Help to Save**
   6 Savings (Government Contributions) Act 2017; The Help-to-Save Accounts Regulations 2018 No.87; The Help-to-Save Accounts Regulations 2025 No.327

Part 3

Key topics

Chapter 16

Supporting evidence

This chapter covers:

Key facts

- Supporting evidence about your mental health problem, and how it affects your daily life, can help you to get the right decision about your entitlement to benefits.
- A decision maker can request further evidence before deciding your entitlement, but this rarely happens in practice. It is usually best to provide supporting evidence yourself at the earliest possible chance.
- Useful supporting evidence can include medical evidence (eg, doctors' reports and proof of medication) but also evidence from non-medical professionals (eg, a social care needs assessment), evidence from other third parties (eg, supporting letters from family or friends) and your own evidence about your condition (eg, a diary or personal statement).
- You can usually get free copies of existing documents by making a subject access request to the organisation that holds them. You can also request new supporting evidence.
- How you submit evidence depends on which benefit you are applying for and which stage you are at in the process.
- When deciding your entitlement to benefit, a decision maker will weigh up the available evidence. If there are contradictions in the evidence, you should try to explain why.

1. When you might need supporting evidence

Many of the benefits in this *Handbook* have a health assessment process. This process usually begins with you completing a form to describe your health problem or disability and its impact on your life. For some benefits, this is followed by an assessment with a healthcare professional.

What you write on the form and say in an assessment are both important types of evidence. In some cases, this may be enough on its own for a benefit to be awarded.[1]

However, in practice, claims are more likely to be successful when supported by additional evidence. This can include, but is not limited to, medical evidence.

Supporting evidence can be useful at various stages in the benefit application process, including:

- at the start of a claim – eg, attached to your claim form or questionnaire;
- during an award review or reassessment, to help show that a mental health problem has continued or deteriorated;
- when challenging a decision through mandatory reconsideration, redetermination or appeal;
- to support a request for a remote or home-based assessment (see p256) or a particular type of appeal hearing (see p302);
- to show 'good cause' or 'good reason' for missing a deadline, not attending an assessment, or not taking part in work-related activity.

Although decision makers can request additional evidence themselves, this is rare. You should therefore try to provide your own supporting evidence wherever possible. The situation may be slightly different for disability benefits in Scotland. If you are not able to provide supporting evidence yourself, you can ask Social Security Scotland to gather it on your behalf. You are asked about this when completing the Part 2 form.

If you cannot provide medical evidence, explain why – eg, if your mental health problem has meant that you have not felt able to see your GP or attend appointments. You or someone who knows you well (such as a friend or family member) could write a personal statement to explain this.

What advisers say: supporting evidence

'I read a lot of stuff which suggests that all supporting evidence will be helpful. However, I have seen cases where evidence works against somebody – quite often because, for example, a consultant's clinic letter is very upbeat, telling your GP how well you're doing, focusing on the positives. Even the word 'stable' in that letter can be used by a decision maker as part of their reasoning for refusing your benefit claim. People need to be selective about what evidence they do send.'

'Evidence to show the impact of a person's mental health problem can be really helpful to give a clearer picture of what that person's difficulties are. No two people with the same mental health problem cope in the same way or have the same needs.'

2. Types of evidence and how to get them

Types of evidence

There is a range of supporting evidence you can use to give a full picture of your mental health problem and its impact. The following is not an exhaustive list.

Appointment letter

Benefit forms and leaflets often state that you do not need to provide appointment letters as supporting evidence. However, you might decide to do so if you think the letter is useful – eg, as evidence that you have been referred to a particular professional or for a certain kind of treatment.

Assessment provider's report

Also known as a 'consultation report', this is prepared by either the DWP, a contracted assessment provider on behalf of the DWP or Social Security Scotland (SSS).

As well as your latest assessment report for the relevant benefit, you can get copies of older reports for the same benefit, and reports produced for other benefits. All of these are potentially useful supporting evidence, particularly when different assessors have taken different views about your needs.[2]

You can request copies by making a subject access request (see p248).[3] If your benefit is administered by SSS, you should automatically receive a copy of your assessment report with your determination notice.[4]

Audio recording of a benefit assessment

Many benefit assessments can be audio recorded, but the rules vary depending on the benefit. You often need to request this in advance (see p261, or for adult disability payment in Scotland, see p170).

These recordings can be useful evidence when you disagree with what is written in an assessment provider's report.

Diary

Sometimes, the best way for a decision maker or the tribunal to understand your needs is for you (or someone supporting you) to keep a diary that records your symptoms and the help you need. This can be particularly useful if your symptoms are variable – eg, if you have both good and bad days, or if your symptoms change throughout the day.

Keeping a diary

There is no specific format required for a diary. You can use a notebook, a printable template or a digital document – whatever works best for you. Even a few days of notes can be helpful, but ideally, try to keep a diary for long enough to show a pattern. If you have good and bad periods during the day, try keeping a detailed diary for at least two or three full days. If you tend to have good days and bad days, a period of one or two weeks might be enough to show a pattern. If you tend to have good weeks and bad weeks, you may need to keep a diary for longer to show this.

If keeping a detailed diary feels overwhelming, you might decide to keep a record only of the activities you find most difficult – eg, a 'leaving the house' diary, a 'social contact' diary, and/or a 'showering and dressing' diary.

What advisers say: diary entries

'It is important to use your own words to describe your thoughts, feelings and symptoms. Do not worry if you think it may not make sense to someone else who reads it.'

'Date each diary entry, and be honest and specific. Even brief notes can be powerful.'

Fit note

Also known as a 'statement of fitness for work', this is usually needed as part of the work capability assessment process for universal credit and employment and support allowance, but may not be strong evidence for other benefits. There is more information about getting a fit note on p81.

Friend and family evidence

Some forms include a page which asks for a statement from someone who knows you well. Even if the form does not specifically ask for this, it it can be useful to provide one anyway, especially if you have had limited support from professionals. Your friend or family member may also give spoken evidence at a benefit tribunal hearing (see p303).[5]

What advisers say: friend and family evidence

'There can be a wrong assumption that if you are not in contact with a GP or a community mental health team then your mental health issues can't be that bad, without awareness of how stretched mental health services are and of how long people have to wait (including people who health services may consider to have significant difficulties). A GP honestly may not know that much about how you are affected day to day. That is when the evidence of a close friend or support worker can really count.'

'The person writing the statement should explain how they know you, how often they see you and what they have observed about your needs.'

GP patient summary

You can ask your GP surgery for a printed summary of the records it holds about you, or you can apply for this online.[6] This document is now widely known as a 'summary care record' and can be the easiest medical evidence to obtain. It comes in different formats, ranging from a short summary of your diagnosed problems and medications to a longer record including consultation notes, letters and other documents that your GP holds about you. You may want to ask for a patient summary that includes at least 12 months of consultation notes and documents.

Someone supporting you can make the request on your behalf, with your consent (see p324).

Hospital discharge sheet

This can be useful evidence about when, why and for how long you were admitted to hospital, and any care or treatment plans that have been made on discharge. If you have lost a hospital discharge sheet, ask your GP for a copy (see above) or make a subject access request (see p248) to the relevant hospital trust or health board.

What advisers say: discharge sheets

'Discharge summaries can be especially helpful when they support the need for ongoing care or highlight risks if support is not in place.'

Mental health tribunal papers

If you have been subject to a section (see p25) and applied to a mental health tribunal, various reports might have been prepared that can also be used as supporting evidence for a benefit claim. You can ask the solicitor who represented you for copies. If you were not represented by a solicitor, you could ask the hospital where you were last detained whether it has copies or whether it can tell you where to get copies.

Personal statement

If a benefit form does not give you the opportunity to describe your mental health problems clearly or in a holistic way, you may want to write a separate supporting statement. You have a lot of freedom about what this could contain, but it is best to keep it to one or two pages. You may want to mention the symptoms you are experiencing, how long you have had them, how they vary and the impact of any treatments or medications.

Prescription list

You do not need to be prescribed medication to qualify for health-related benefits, and the type or dose should not be taken as conclusive evidence of your difficulties, but it will certainly be considered as part of the decision-making process.[7]

Report from a specialist doctor

You are normally sent a copy of any report produced by a specialist doctor you have seen – eg, a psychiatrist or psychologist. If you have attended an appointment with a specialist, but do not have a copy of their report, you should be able to get this from your GP or by making a subject access request (see p248).

Report from another medical professional

A report from, for example, a community psychiatric nurse (CPN), an occupational therapist or a child's health visitor may provide more detailed information about the impact of a mental health problem on day-to-day life than a report from a doctor, which is likely to focus on symptoms and treatment.

What advisers say: community psychiatric nurses

'Probably the people I [ask for evidence] most often are CPNs because they have very regular contact with their patients, usually in their homes. If you have been seeing somebody in their home every two or three weeks for six months or more there is a lot you can say about their day-to-day life and their ability to go out.'

Social care evidence

Documents from your local authority's social care department can be very helpful when applying for disability benefits, as they often assess similar day-to-day needs. For adults, this could include a needs assessment or a care and support plan. You can request a needs assessment by calling your local authority, or online at gov.uk/apply-needs-assessment-social-services.

For children, social care evidence could include an education, health and care plan (EHCP) or a statement of special educational needs.

What advisers say: care plans and school reports

'It can be worth looking over care plans and school reports carefully before using them as evidence. [Professionals writing social care plans] may limit themselves to writing about needs and support that the local authority's budget can cover. School reports often want to focus on the positives and ways in which a child does manage to participate and overcome difficulties, without always explaining that the participation may be limited or only be with support and encouragement.'

Supporting letters

In addition to the evidence listed above, you could ask for a *new* supporting letter from anyone with specific knowledge about your mental health problem or about the needs you have as a result. This might include a:

- care co-ordinator;
- CPN;

- counsellor;
- employer;
- family member or friend;
- GP;
- landlord;
- occupational therapist;
- psychiatrist;
- psychological therapist;
- psychologist;
- social worker;
- special educational needs co-ordinator;
- specialist substance abuse worker;
- support worker;
- teacher;
- volunteer – eg, a befriender.

What to ask for in a supporting letter

Ask anyone who writes a supporting letter to comment on the criteria that you are being assessed against. For example, if you are asking your CPN to write a supporting letter for personal independence payment (PIP), give them a copy of the PIP activities and descriptors and ask them to write specifically about these.

Always ask the writer to explain how your condition fluctuates. There are different rules about variability for different benefits, but as a general rule, it is important to explain whether you have good and bad days, times of day, or periods during the year.

The letter must be dated. Ideally, it should say which period the writer is describing – eg, if their letter is dated February but describes symptoms that they know you have had for 18 months.

Different people can comment on different aspects of your mental health problem and needs. You might find that a GP refuses to write about your home life, which they have not observed, while a befriender might not feel comfortable writing about your diagnosis or treatment, because they are not medically trained. It is often best to get evidence from more than one person to build a full picture of your mental health problem and its impact.

Ask that the supporting letter be sent to you, not directly to the DWP, SSS or the tribunal. This gives you the opportunity to review, and ensure you are satisfied with, its contents before submitting it.

Note: some benefit forms and leaflets discourage you from asking for new letters from doctors. It is true that doctors may charge a fee for writing letters and you might get stronger medical evidence by making a subject access request (see p248). However, a new letter can still be useful – eg, especially if you have no recent medical records or you do not have a diagnosis (see p6) and the doctor can confirm your symptoms, or where specific questions have been raised by a decision maker about your treatment plan.

Old, new and undated evidence

Recent evidence is useful because it is most likely to be accepted as up to date. However, there are many reasons why you might not have recent evidence – eg, because your condition is long term and your symptoms and treatment are stable.[8] In this situation, it may be worth providing your older evidence, and you might also consider requesting a new supporting letter from a key professional (see p246).

Sometimes you receive new evidence (eg, a new consultant's report) after a decision has been made. If this relates to symptoms you were already having at the date of the decision, or variability or risks that existed at that time, it can be useful evidence for challenging the decision (see p307 for an example).[9] However, if the evidence is clearly about changes that happened after the date of the decision, it is unlikely to be accepted as supporting evidence when you challenge the decision.[10] You might decide instead to use it as supporting evidence for a new claim or for a supersession request (see p292, or p314 for disability payments in Scotland).

As the date of evidence is so important, you should avoid submitting undated evidence.

Subject access requests

If you need to get hold of an existing document, you can normally do so, free of charge, by making a subject access request to the organisation that holds it or produced it. For example, you can request a consultant's letter by making a subject access request to the relevant hospital trust or health board, or request a copy of your social care needs assessment by making a subject access request to your local authority. Someone supporting you can make a subject access request on your behalf, with your consent (see p324).

How to make a subject access request

Check the organisation's website for specific contact details or an online form for making the request.

Clearly state that you are making a 'subject access request' under the UK GDPR. Be specific about which document(s) you want, if you can.

You should normally receive a response within one month.

Further information is available from the Information Commissioner's Office.[11]

3. Submitting evidence

How you submit supporting evidence depends on the benefit and which stage you are at in the claim or appeal process.

If you are attaching evidence to a claim form or questionnaire, there is usually a freepost envelope provided – this will go to the correct office. However, if you are submitting evidence after returning your form, but before getting a decision, get advice on where to send it – eg, to an assessment provider or to the relevant office of the DWP or Social Security Scotland (SSS).

If you are challenging a decision through a mandatory reconsideration or (for SSS benefits) redetermination request, you should usually send supporting evidence to the address given in your decision letter. For universal credit, you may be able to upload it through your online account.

At the appeal stage, you normally need to send supporting evidence to the appropriate tribunal service. You can do this by post or email. The tribunal service then shares copies of your evidence with the relevant benefit agency, and may resend a copy of this evidence to you.

Dos and don'ts of submitting evidence

Do write your name and national insurance number on each sheet of supporting evidence and include page numbers.

Do not send original documents – only send copies.

Do not delay sending off a form or letter while you wait for supporting evidence if this means missing a deadline. Instead, explain in your form/letter what evidence you are waiting for and ask the decision maker to delay the decision if appropriate.

Do not take supporting evidence to your assessment or appeal hearing if you can provide it sooner. If you take evidence to an assessment, the assessor might not properly consider it – eg, if they do not have the facilities to make a photocopy. If you take evidence to an appeal hearing, the hearing might be adjourned to give the tribunal time to consider it or, exceptionally, the tribunal might decide not to consider it because it is late.[12]

4. Evidence and decision making

A decision maker should consider all of the evidence in your claim, but does not have to treat it all equally. Factors that affect how much weight is given to each piece of evidence include the training or qualifications of the person giving the evidence, how well they know you, and whether what they say is consistent with other evidence.

If you notice conflicting evidence, you should explain the reasons for this. Your explanation can help the decision maker decide which version of events is more accurate.

A decision maker may not have much time to decide your claim. You might get the best decision by submitting a limited amount of high-quality supporting evidence, rather than sending a large volume of evidence, not all of which might be useful – eg, your full medical record. If you have to submit large amounts of evidence (eg, if you need to submit a long report in full), highlight the parts that are most relevant and, if you can, say why.

How the tribunal considers evidence

When deciding your appeal, the tribunal should consider all the evidence available.[13] It should not restrict itself to accepting an assessment provider's report.[14] If there is conflict between what is said in a report and what is written elsewhere (eg, on your claim form), it should not accept the evidence in the report without first listening to what you have to say.[15] The tribunal should be particularly careful not to accept automatically the findings in medical reports produced with the assistance of a computer programme.[16]

Notes

1. **When you might need supporting evidence**
 1 R(I) 2/51

2. **Types of evidence and how to get them**
 2 For example, *GD v SSWP (PIP)* [2017] UKUT 415 (AAC); *SE v SSWP (PIP)* [2021] UKUT 79 (AAC)
 3 For the DWP, you can make an online request at secure.dwp.gov.uk/personal-information-request/name. For SSS, use socialsecurity.gov.scot/contact/subject-access
 4 SSS, *Adult Disability Payment Consultations: what happens after the consultation*, updated 18 September 2023, at mygov.scot
 5 For example, *MA v SSWP (PIP)* [2017] UKUT 351 (AAC)
 6 See nhs.uk/nhs-services/gps/view-your-gp-health-record
 7 For example, *PM v SSWP (PIP)* [2017] UKUT 154 (AAC), as interpreted in PIP AG, para 1.6.36
 8 See, for example, PIP AG, para 1.8.12
 9 R(DLA) 2/01; R(DLA) 3/01; CJSA/2375/2000; *KK v Liverpool City Council (HB)* [2020] UKUT 80 (AAC)
 10 s12(8)(b) SSA 1998; R(DLA) 4/05
 11 ico.org.uk/for-the-public/getting-copies-of-your-information-subject-access-request

3. **Submitting evidence**
 12 CIB/4253/2004; r15(2) TP(FT) Rules; r15(2) FTT(S) Rules

4. **Evidence and decision making**
 13 CDLA/2014/2004
 14 CM/527/1992; CIB/3074/2003; *AP v SSWP (PIP)* [2016] UKUT 416 (AAC); *CF v SSWP (PIP)* [2017] UKUT 356 (AAC)
 15 CIB/5586/1999
 16 CIB/476/2005; CIB/511/2005

Chapter 17

Assessments

This chapter covers:

This chapter covers assessments for personal independence payment (PIP), universal credit (UC) and employment and support allowance (ESA). It does *not* cover other benefit assessments, such as those for adult disability payment in Scotland, which are expected to be far less common. For information about these other assessments, see the chapter about the relevant benefit in this *Handbook*. You might also find useful the general tips in this chapter about preparing for an assessment (see p260), the questions you might be asked in an assessment (p263) and looking after yourself following an assessment (p266).

Key facts

- Most people have an assessment with a healthcare professional as part of the process of claiming PIP, UC or ESA.
- An assessment is not always required, but if you are asked to take part in one, you normally must attend. There are important rules about missing, cancelling or rearranging an appointment.
- Your assessment is not always carried out by a mental health professional.
- There are steps that you can take to make your assessment more accessible (eg, requesting it is carried out at home, by telephone, by video call or in a clinic) and steps you can take to help you feel mentally prepared.
- You can ask in advance to have your assessment audio recorded or ask to make your own recording. The rules are different for PIP assessments and UC/ESA assessments.
- You can be accompanied in the assessment by an independent adviser or someone else who is supporting you.
- There are things you can do before, during and after an assessment to help you manage the impact on your mental health.

1. The assessment provider

Most people have an assessment with a healthcare professional as part of the process of claiming personal independence payment (PIP), universal credit (UC) or employment and support allowance (ESA).[1] Assessments are carried out by the DWP or by private companies on behalf of the DWP. These companies are often known as 'assessment providers' and operate under the umbrella term Health Assessment Advisory Service (HAAS).

Note: assessment providers *do not* make the decision about your benefit eligibility. They carry out the assessment and send a report to the DWP explaining whether they believe you meet the relevant criteria. The DWP then decides your entitlement.

Assessment providers by region

Northern England and Scotland

Assessment provider: Maximus
Website: haas.maximusuk.co.uk
Tel: (PIP) 0800 008 3073; (UC and ESA) 0800 072 0120
Email: Lot1.Customer-relations@haas.dwp.gov.uk

Midlands and Wales

Assessment provider: Capita
Website: haas.capita.co.uk
Tel: 0808 178 8114 or 0808 178 8115 (Welsh language)
Text relay service: 18001 0808 178 8114
Video relay services available via website.
Email: contactus@capita-pip.co.uk

South West and South Central

Assessment provider: Serco
Website: haas-serco.co.uk
Tel: (PIP) 0800 008 3074; (UC and ESA) 0800 072 0257
Text relay service: (PIP) 18001 0800 008 3074; (UC and ESA) 18001 0800 072 0257

South East, London and East Anglia

Assessment provider: Ingeus
Website: haas.ingeus.co.uk
Tel: (PIP) 0800 008 3075; (UC and ESA) 0800 072 0350
Text relay service: (PIP) 18001 0800 008 3075; (UC and ESA) 18001 0800 072 0350
Email: Lot4.CustomerRelations@haas.dwp.gov.uk

If your postcode starts with E5, N2, N3, N4 or N6

Assessment provider for PIP and work capability assessments for UC and ESA: DWP

Tel: (PIP) 0800 121 4433 (UC); 0800 328 5644 (ESA) 0800 055 6688

Textphone: (PIP) 0800 121 4493 (UC); 0800 328 1344 (ESA) 0800 328 1344

Text relay service: (PIP) 18001 0800 121 4433; (UC) 18001 0800 328 5644; (ESA) 18001 0800 055 6688

If you need to contact the DWP about a work capability assessment for UC, you can also use your online journal.

If your postcode starts with B14, B17, B19 and B78

Your assessment provider for PIP only is the DWP. Your assessment provider for UC and ESA is Capita. See the contact details above.

At what stage are you referred?

For UC and ESA, you are referred to the assessment provider after you declare that your disability or illness affects your ability to work (see p81). The assessment provider then issues a UC50 or ESA50 questionnaire. After you return this questionnaire, the provider will decide whether to invite you to an assessment.

For PIP, you are usually referred to the assessment provider only after you return the PIP2 questionnaire to the DWP (see p153).

Knowing at what stage you are referred to the assessment provider can help you know whether to contact the assessment provider or the DWP about particular issues. For example, if you have returned a UC50 and are waiting for an assessment, you may be able to speed up this process by calling the assessment provider, but calling the UC enquiry line might be less productive.

The healthcare professional

Assessments are carried out by healthcare professionals (HCPs) employed and trained by the assessment provider companies. The DWP publishes official guidance for HCPs on how to carry out assessments.[2]

HCPs come from a range of different medical backgrounds and can include doctors, nurses, physiotherapists, occupational therapists, pharmacists and paramedics. Other registered health professionals may conduct assessments, provided they meet DWP standards and have a prior written agreement from the DWP. There is no option to request a particular type of professional for your assessment. You might be assessed by someone with no professional experience of mental health problems and fairly limited mental health training.

If you believe that the person assessing you did not fully understand your mental health problem or ask you relevant questions, this is likely to be grounds for challenging a benefit decision (see Chapter 20) and may also be grounds for a complaint (see p308).

Jo's experience

'The person doing my assessment did not have a clue what my conditions were, which was not helpful.'

When an assessment might not be required

An HCP looks at the evidence you have provided about your mental health problem, including your completed questionnaire, and decides whether they need more information to produce a report for the DWP on your eligibility. If they believe they already have enough information, the HCP reports back to the DWP without the need for an assessment (and the DWP makes its decision).[3] This is sometimes called a 'paper-based review' and only happens in a minority of cases. You will not always be told if this has happened – you may simply receive a decision about your benefit.

You can increase the chances of a paper-based review by providing supporting evidence when you return your questionnaire. Chapter 16 has more information about supporting evidence. It is also important when you fill out the questionnaire to provide contact details for the people and professionals who support you, as the HCP might decide to contact them to fill in any gaps (although you should not rely on this happening).

Caroline's experience

'With PIP I just sent in all the paperwork and they spoke with my CPN [community psychiatric nurse] and I didn't need a further assessment.'

2. In-person, telephone and video assessments

Note: this chapter covers assessments for personal independence payment (PIP), universal credit (UC) and employment and support allowance (ESA). For information about the types of assessment for adult disability payment in Scotland, see p170.

Assessment types

You may be asked to take part in an assessment:[4]

- by telephone; *or*
- online via video call; *or*
- in an assessment centre (often called a 'clinic' appointment); *or*
- at home, with a healthcare professional (HCP) visiting you in person.

The assessment provider will decide which type of assessment to offer you, although you can make a request for a particular assessment type (see p256).

What advisers say: video or telephone appointments

'When you are having a phone or video assessment, make sure you are in a place where you can speak confidentially without being overheard as you're likely to be speaking about lots of personal things.'

Remote assessments

A telephone or video assessment might be more accessible than an in-person appointment, depending on your mental health symptoms and how they affect you. You can join at home or somewhere else.

You can have someone to accompany you in a telephone or video assessment in the same way as for an in-person assessment. They can either join you in person or can be added through a conference calling facility.

There can be some obvious advantages of remote assessments, depending on your difficulties and needs. These advantages include not having to travel and not having to be in the physical presence of an HCP.

There can also be some obvious disadvantages to a remote assessment – eg, if you are not confident with technology, or find it difficult to answer the phone.

Some of the pros and cons of remote assessments are less obvious. For example, in a telephone assessment, you cannot be seen. This might be a disadvantage, because if your mental health problem has visible symptoms, the HCP may miss them. You or someone supporting you may need to try to describe these symptoms throughout the call. On the other hand, if an HCP cannot see you, this removes the risk of them making misleading informal observations (see p265) about your appearance. You might feel that this is an advantage of a telephone assessment.

While video assessments can seem like the best of both worlds, one drawback to a video assessment is that it cannot currently be audio recorded by the DWP, and there are rules about making your own recording (see p261).

Clinic assessments

Venue and travel

If you are asked to attend a clinic assessment, you are not always invited to the assessment centre closest to where you live. However, you should not be asked to travel for more than 90 minutes on public transport to get to an assessment.[5]

It is usually a good idea to arrive 10 to 15 minutes before your appointment is due to start. Your assessment may last an hour or so, but in practice this varies, so try to allow for this when making travel arrangements.

Travel expenses

If you are asked to attend to a clinic assessment, you can get help with travel expenses. You need to fill out and submit an expense form. The assessment provider sends you this with your appointment letter or you can ask for one at the assessment centre reception. You are asked for copies of tickets or receipts.

- **Public transport costs** are reimbursed for the return journey between your address and the assessment centre. Keep your tickets.
- **Car travel costs** can be reimbursed. You can usually claim 25p per mile, plus parking costs if the assessment centre does not provide free parking. Keep parking receipts.
- **Taxi costs** are paid on a case-by-case basis. You must usually show either that there is no public transport for your route or that your condition means you cannot reasonably use public transport for the journey. Request help with taxi fares *before* your appointment by contacting the assessment provider with quotes (see the contact details on p252). Ask the driver or taxi company for receipts.
- **Someone accompanying you** can also have their travel costs reimbursed – eg, if you and they each buy a bus ticket. It is best to request this in advance by contacting the assessment provider.

Assessments at home

An in-person assessment at home is only usually offered if you cannot travel to an assessment centre for health reasons and if a telephone or video assessment is not an effective alternative. You can be accompanied by an independent adviser or someone else who is supporting you.

Asking for a particular assessment type

If a mental health problem affects your ability to take part in certain types of assessment, make this clear as early as possible in your claim. You can write something on the UC50, ESA50 or PIP2 questionnaire explaining why certain venues or formats would not be appropriate. Alternatively, contact the assessment provider as soon as possible after being invited to an assessment (see p258).

Examples

'I have explained that I cannot leave my home alone. My consultant's report confirms this. I do not have anyone who can come with me to a clinic appointment. Please offer a home or video assessment if one is needed.'

'Because of my mental health problem, I do not always answer phone calls. I also find it difficult to express myself by phone. If an assessment is needed, please offer me a face-to-face assessment.'

'I am severely unwell and unable to participate in any type of assessment. I have provided detailed evidence from my consultant, community psychiatric nurse and family members which

gives you a full picture of my difficulties. Please assess me based on that evidence without an in-person or remote assessment.'

It is not guaranteed that a request will be accepted. You may have a better chance of success if you provide supporting evidence (see Chapter 16), but should not be asked to pay for this evidence.[6] For example, if you are asking for a home assessment, you could provide evidence that other professionals visit you at home – eg, your GP, psychiatrist or community mental health team.

If your request for a different format or venue is refused and you do not attend the assessment that is arranged for you, the DWP may decide you are not entitled to the benefit (see p258).

Assessment types and disability discrimination

Under the Equality Act 2010,[7] the DWP and assessment providers have a duty to make reasonable adjustments to the way they carry out assessments to avoid disadvantage to people with disabilities. A failure to make these adjustments is discrimination. (See p5 about the meaning of 'disability'.)

A reasonable adjustment can include a particular venue or format for your assessment. If your request is refused, you may be able to bring a legal challenge against this decision. For example, if your request for a home assessment is refused, you may be able to challenge this using one of the template judicial review pre-action letters available by contacting CPAG's judicial review project at jrproject@cpag.org.uk. Contact an independent advice service if you need support with this step.

Overcoming barriers to attending an assessment

If you are faced with an assessment type or venue that you know you will find difficult, it can help to talk to someone who knows you well about your options.

- Could they, or someone else, accompany you?
- Will requesting a recording (see p261) help you feel any more confident?
- Would it make a clinic appointment more accessible if you had a lift or a taxi arranged in advance?
- Would it help you to manage a telephone or video appointment if a friend or family member took charge of the technology?

3. Missing, cancelling or rearranging an assessment

An assessment is not always needed before a decision can be made about your benefit entitlement, but if you are asked to take part in one, you normally must attend. There are important rules about missing, cancelling or rearranging an appointment.[8] (For the rules for adult disability payment in Scotland, see p170.)

Getting notice of an assessment

You must usually be sent written confirmation of the date, time and location of your assessment at least seven days in advance. This rule does not apply if you accept less notice or notice by phone.[9] See p325 if you have an appointee. If you do not get adequate notice, the usual rules about missing appointments will not apply to you.

Cancelling an assessment

If you have been invited to take part in an assessment, but you believe that this is unnecessary or inappropriate (eg, because you have already provided a lot of supporting evidence about your condition or because you are so unwell that you cannot meaningfully participate in any form of assessment), you can make this case to the assessment provider and ask them to complete a 'paper-based review' instead (see p254). This may only be agreed in exceptional cases.

Rearranging an assessment

You can ask the assessment provider for a different date, time, venue or format for your assessment. Make the request as soon as possible after getting your appointment notification. There is more information about requesting a different venue or format on p256.

Assessment providers only reschedule your appointment once. If you cannot attend the rearranged appointment, your case is returned to the DWP. You can be referred again to the assessment provider if the DWP accepts that you had a good reason (see below) for not attending the second appointment.

Missing an assessment

For universal credit or employment and support allowance

If you miss or are going to miss an assessment for universal credit (UC) or employment and support allowance (ESA), contact the assessment provider as soon as possible to explain why. You are often sent a BF223 form asking why you could not take part in the assessment. Unless you are found to have had good reason/cause, you are likely to be found fit for work.[10]

Good cause (ESA) and good reason (UC)

When deciding whether you have 'good cause' for missing an **ESA** assessment, the DWP must consider all the circumstances, including your state of health and the nature of your mental health problem.[11] Good cause may include being too ill or distressed on the day of the assessment – eg, experiencing a panic attack on the way to the assessment centre or being too anxious to leave the house.

There are no equivalent rules for deciding whether you have 'good reason' for missing a **UC** assessment, but in practice, the same sort of issues should be considered.[12]

To help you demonstrate good reason/good cause, it is often useful to provide supporting evidence (see Chapter 16).

If you are found fit for work because you are considered not to have good reason/ good cause for failing to attend an assessment, it is possible to challenge the decision through mandatory reconsideration and appeal (see Chapter 20). For ESA, you should also get advice about whether a new claim will be possible if your challenge is unsuccessful, or if you will need to claim UC instead.

For personal independence payment

If you miss or are going to miss a personal independence payment (PIP) assessment, contact the assessment provider as soon as possible to explain why. If it is decided that you failed to take part in an assessment without good reason, your PIP claim is likely to be refused and/or your existing award will end.[13]

Good reason (PIP)

When deciding whether you had 'good reason' for missing a PIP assessment, the DWP must consider your state of health and the nature of your mental health problem. The DWP's guidance has several examples in which mental health problems cause someone to miss an appointment with good reason.[14] You might have good reason for missing an assessment if, for example, you were feeling too unwell to attend or the person who normally supports you was unavailable. Being asked to attend an assessment at an unsuitable location can also be a good reason for not attending it.[15] To help you demonstrate good reason, it is often useful to provide supporting evidence.

If you are refused PIP because you are considered not to have good reason for failing to attend an assessment, it is possible to challenge the decision through mandatory reconsideration and appeal (see Chapter 20). You should also get advice about making a new claim in case your challenge is unsuccessful.

If good reason/good cause is accepted

If the DWP accepts that you had good reason/good cause for missing your assessment, it refers your case back to the assessment provider and you are given another appointment. In theory, this can happen multiple times. However, the assessment provider should notice if you are consistently too unwell to attend assessments and might decide to change your assessment venue or format, or to conduct a paper-based review instead. Alternatively, the DWP might refuse to accept good reason/good cause after more than one missed assessment, if it does not find the reasons given plausible.

4. Preparing for an assessment

Assessments can feel daunting. There are steps that you can take to help you feel prepared for an assessment and to help you manage the impact on your mental health. However, preparation itself might also feel overwhelming, particularly when you are faced with lots of information to process at once and lots of different ideas about what you 'should' do or say in the assessment.

When Mind spoke to people about their experiences, many said that they found it helpful to have another person helping them to prepare for an assessment, whether this was a friend, a family member or someone from an advice or advocacy service (see advicelocal.uk).

What to do before the assessment

1. Check the date and time of your assessment. If it is helpful, set reminders on your phone or calendar, or ask someone to remind you.
2. If you are having a clinic assessment, make sure you look up the venue in advance and make arrangements for getting there.
3. Check what you need to do to claim your travel expenses (see p256).
4. If you are having a telephone or video assessment, make sure you feel prepared and confident about the technology involved. Read any joining instructions on your appointment letter and ask for help if you need it.
5. If you would like to be accompanied, make arrangements (someone can accompany you at a remote assessment as well as at an in-person assessment – see p255).
6. Request an audio recording of your assessment if you want one. You must usually ask for this in advance (see p261).
7. Consider and request reasonable adjustments – eg, breaks during your appointment, or a particular room layout (see p328).
8. Make sure you have a copy of your benefit form to read through before the assessment so that you can remember your answers and how you expressed yourself.

9. You might also want to read through the scoring criteria/descriptors for your benefit (see the relevant chapter of this *Handbook*) so that you have an idea what the assessor needs to know.
10. You might find it useful to write down one or two key ideas or phrases that you are worried about forgetting in an assessment – eg, 'what can I do reliably?' or 'what help would I have in an ideal world?' You can take this with you.
11. If you have time, go over some practice questions. See p263 for the kinds of questions you might be asked in an assessment.
12. If you have suicidal feelings or you self-harm, the assessment might be a triggering experience. Talk to someone beforehand about your feelings. It is good to plan in advance how you can take care of yourself before, during and after the assessment to help you manage the impact on your mental health.

Audio recording of your assessment

If you want the assessment provider to make an audio recording of your personal independence payment (PIP), employment and support allowance (ESA) or universal credit (UC) assessment, you must request this in advance. (For Scottish disability benefits, see p170.)

Requesting a recording is usually a good idea because it could positively affect how the assessment is conducted and the accuracy of the assessment report. If there *are* errors in the assessment report, the recording can help you challenge these.

There are different rules about recordings for UC/ESA assessments and for PIP assessments.

For universal credit/employment and support allowance

You must ask the assessment provider in advance if you want a recording of your UC/ESA assessment. The DWP states that this request cannot always be accommodated. You cannot make your own recording of an assessment unless you follow strict rules about the type of equipment you use (laptops and smartphones are not allowed) and make copies that you can physically present to the healthcare professional (HCP) at the end of the appointment.[16]

For personal independence payment

If you want the assessment provider to make a recording of your PIP assessment, you must ask them in advance. The DWP states that this request *will* be accommodated (unless it is a video assessment). You can also make your own audio recording using any equipment you prefer, and you do not have to provide a copy to the HCP.[17] You should inform the HCP in advance that you intend to record the assessment and the HCP will then also record the assessment. This could have a positive impact on how the assessment is conducted and the accuracy of the report.

Missing out on an audio recording

Despite its potential benefits, few people are opting to have their PIP assessment recorded. In June 2024, less than 1.5 per cent of PIP assessments were audiorecorded by the assessor.[18] Advisers should ensure that claimants know their options.

5. **What happens in an assessment**

An assessment typically takes between 20 and 60 minutes. The only people present are you, the healthcare professional (HCP – see p253) and anyone who is supporting you. You are asked questions about your health, difficulties and needs.

Being accompanied

It can be helpful to have someone with you for practical and emotional support. They could help you to travel to a clinic assessment, help you to set up a video call, or give you the confidence to pick up the phone for a telephone assessment.

Sam's experience

'It definitely helps to have someone with you before, during and after the assessment. Having someone with you can make it feel less overwhelming and also has the added bonus of showing the assessor that you need help.'

During the appointment, the person who is supporting you may be able to help if you are having difficulty answering questions – eg, by asking the HCP to slow down or repeat a question. If they know you well, they might be able give the HCP more information about your difficulties. They can also take notes.

If you are having a telephone or video assessment and the person supporting you cannot join in person, they can be added to the call remotely. It is best to contact the assessment provider in advance to arrange this.

If you have an appointee and have been invited to an assessment, see p325.

What advisers say: having someone with you

'It is important where possible to have someone with you, whether that is a professional or a friend or relative, just to give you some kind of support and to act as a witness. If you are being assessed by phone it is worth doing it on speakerphone and having somebody with you.'

Questions

In the assessment, you are likely to be asked about your condition, history and treatment, and about particular difficulties that were covered on the benefit form you completed. To find out more about what you can and cannot do, you are also likely to be asked about:

- what you do in a normal day;
- any hobbies and interests you have;
- whether you use a phone or a computer;
- whether you can drive a car;
- your job (or last job);
- any social activities you take part in;
- how you got to the assessment centre (if relevant).

The HCP is likely to be typing while you are talking. Some people find this rude or off-putting. It can help to remember that the HCP is probably doing this so that they do not forget or miss anything relevant that you tell them.

What advisers say: giving clear answers

'Even if it feels awkward or unnatural, try to avoid saying things like "I'm fine" or "I manage". Don't say "It depends..." without explaining what it depends on, or "I can do that" if you really mean "I try but struggle or need help".'

Are there right and wrong answers?

You might have come across various tips about what you *should* say in an assessment. Some of this advice can be confusing and contradictory. For example, you might have been told:

- not to give away too much information about your day-to-day life in case this is used against you; *but also*
- not to leave gaps in the information you give, in case the person assessing you draws conclusions.

You might have been told:

- to describe your difficulties only as they are on your worst days; *but also*
- to be honest and transparent about your difficulties and not to exaggerate.

It can be overwhelming trying to say the 'right' things in an assessment. Fundamentally, there are no 'wrong' answers. The following are some very basic suggestions.

- Take a breath and a bit of time to think about each question.
- Ask the person assessing you to slow down if they are pushing you to respond too quickly.

- Answer questions honestly.
- Do focus on the negative – what you *cannot* do. This can feel unnatural as many of us are used to trying to focus on the positives and what we *can* do. But being clear about what you struggle with (and when) is what will help you get the right benefit decision.
- Write down one or two key words or phrases before the assessment and take them with you if you are worried about forgetting to mention something.
- For each question, ask yourself:
  - can I do it all the time?
  - can I do it safely?
  - can I do it as often as needed?
  - can I do it in a reasonable time?
  - what help would I get in an ideal world?

What advisers say: giving honest answers

'It is normal to feel anxious about being seen as exaggerating your difficulties. Being honest and open is not exaggerating. Spending time talking about the things you find difficult – rather than trying to brush these off and talking about the positives – is not exaggerating.'

Are there inappropriate questions?

Occasionally, the HCP might ask questions insensitively or ask about things that they do not need to know. You might also hear the HCP using incorrect mental health terminology or feel that they are rushing you to answer questions. You or someone supporting you can challenge this during the appointment. There is more information on p28.

If you believe that an assessment has been carried out inappropriately or in a way that puts your safety at risk, you can make a complaint (see p308).

Self-harm and suicidal feelings

If you have mentioned self-harm (see p21) or suicidal feelings (see p22) in your benefit application, you may be asked about this during an assessment. Talking about self-harm or suicidal feelings during an assessment can be extremely difficult. However, you are not required to share personal or graphic details.

While it may be relevant for you to talk about how your suicidal feelings or self-harm affect your daily life, you do not need to:

- describe how you self-harm;
- show physical evidence of self-harm;
- explain what your suicidal thoughts are and the specifics of any plans or past attempts, unless these details include something particularly relevant to the benefit criteria you are being assessed against;
- justify why you have not acted on sucidial thoughts.

These types of questions can be inappropriate and unsafe, and if asked, you or your supporter can say: 'I'm not comfortable answering that question. Can you explain how this is relevant to the benefit assessment?' or 'I'd prefer to focus on how these feelings affect my day-to-day functioning.'

Informal observations

The HCP may record some 'informal observations' in the assessment report. These are written observations about how you present at the appointment, and are more extensive if you are having an in-person or video assessment. They can include observations about your appearance (eg, how you are dressed, your facial expression), any external signs of distress (eg, sweating, shaking or crying), your ability to make eye contact, the tone of your speech and your ability to build a rapport with the HCP. The observations can only be made between the start and the end of the assessment, and not, for example, while you are in a waiting area.[19] See p27 for some more information about informal observations.

What advisers say: informal observations

'It may be that you have gone to extra lengths to try and make yourself as smart and presentable on the day so that you feel more ready. You may have had a friend help you get ready, got up really early to be ready, and overcome difficulties; timed your medication for the best effects. Do try to explain this to the HCP. Otherwise, it is possible they will assume you look fine and well prepared and not realise just how hard that may have been.'

Participating in the assessment

If you attend an assessment but feel too unwell to participate (eg, because of feelings of anxiety, panic, sadness or anger), you can ask for a short break or, if necessary, you can ask that the assessment be rescheduled. You can make the request partway through the assessment if necessary.

What advisers say: asking for a break

'If you can, explain the difficulties you are experiencing in an assessment, instead of just politely letting things carry on and wishing it could just be over. If you come out and say something, it can be real evidence of difficulties you have that are relevant to the benefit you are claiming.'

If your assessment goes ahead but you do not participate (eg, you do not answer questions, or you behave in a way that means the assessment must end), this can lead to a negative benefit decision. This does not apply if the DWP accepts you had a good reason/good cause for acting as you did because of your state of health or the nature of your mental health problem. There is more information on pp258–60 about good reason/good cause.[20]

Panic attacks

Panic attacks (see p20) can happen during assessments and interviews. If you believe that a panic attack may be likely, you can inform the interviewer or assessor of this beforehand and request reasonable adjustments (see p257).

6. After an assessment

In practice, you might receive a benefit decision between four and eight weeks after having an assessment. See the universal credit, employment and support allowance and personal independence payment chapters of this *Handbook* for information about what happens next.

If you feel an assessment did not go well or if you were asked questions that you believe were inappropriate, it is common to feel upset, angry or vulnerable. It is important to take care of yourself following the assessment to help you manage the impact on your mental health.

After the assessment

Try to plan something distracting or calming for after the assessment. This could be something small, like taking 10 minutes to focus on your breathing, or a bigger plan for the rest of your day if you feel you can manage this. If you would find it helpful, put aside some time to chat about the assessment with someone who knows you well.

If you are an advice worker supporting someone through their assessment, set aside some time after the assessment to answer any questions they might have. The best time for this varies depending on who you are supporting. It can take some people a while to process an appointment, so they might not always have the questions they need to ask right away. Explain clearly the next steps in the process – ie, how long it will be before they receive a decision about their benefit and what happens next.

Complaints

You (or the person accompanying you) can complain about various aspects of the assessment – eg, if you are asked inappropriate questions, if your appointment is held at an unsuitable venue or if other reasonable adjustments are not made. See p308 for how to make a complaint and what it can achieve.

Notes

1. **The assessment provider**

1 **UC** Reg 44(1) UC Regs
ESA Reg 23(1) ESA Regs; reg 19(1) ESA Regs 2013
PIP Reg 9(1) SS(PIP) Regs

2 DWP, *Personal Independence Payment (PIP) Assessment Guide for Assessment Providers*, 25 November 2024, at gov.uk/government/publications/personal-independence-payment-assessment-guide-for-assessment-providers (abbreviated here as PIP AG); DWP, *Work Capability Assessment Handbook: for healthcare professionals*, 6 September 2024, at gov.uk/publications/work-capability-assessment-handbook-for-healthcare-professionals

3 **UC** Regs 43 and 44 UC Regs
ESA Reg 21 ESA Regs; regs 17 and 19 ESA Regs 2013
PIP Reg 9(1) SS(PIP) Regs

2. **In-person, telephone and video assessments**

4 **UC** Reg 44(2) UC Regs
ESA Reg 23(1) ESA Regs; reg 19(1) ESA Regs 2013
PIP Reg 9(1) SS(PIP) Regs

5 **UC/ESA** Confirmed at chdauk.co.uk/find-your-assessment-centre
PIP DWP, *PIP Handbook*, November 2024, at gov.uk/government/publications/personal-independence-payment-fact-sheets/pip-handbook

6 For PIP, see PIP AG, paras 1.6.72-76

7 ss20, 21 and 29 EA 2010 (see also s19)

3. **Missing, cancelling or rearranging an assessment**

8 **UC** Regs 43 and 44 UC Regs
ESA Regs 21 and 23 ESA Regs; regs 17 and 19 ESA Regs 2013
PIP Reg 9(1) SS(PIP) Regs

9 **UC** Reg 44(3) UC Regs
ESA Reg 23(3) ESA Regs; reg 19(3) ESA Regs 2013
PIP Reg 9(3)-(4) SS(PIP) Regs

10 **UC** Reg 44(2) UC Regs
ESA Reg 23(2) ESA Regs; reg 19(2) ESA Regs 2013

11 Reg 24 ESA Regs; reg 20 ESA Regs 2013; interpreted by the DWP at paras 42500-42543 DMG and paras U2500-U2543 ADM

12 Interpreted by the DWP at paras G1128-G1140 ADM

13 s80(4)-(6) WRA 2012; regs 8(3) and 9(2) SS(PIP) Regs; reg 26(2) UC,PIP,JSA&ESA(DA) Regs; *KB v SSWP (PIP)* [2016] UKUT 537 (AAC)

14 Reg 10 SS(PIP) Regs, interpreted by the DWP in Ch P6 ADM

15 *OM v SSWP (PIP)* [2017] UKUT 458 (AAC); *TC v SSWP (PIP) (No.2)* [2018] UKUT 286 (AAC)

4. **Preparing for an assessment**

16 WCAH, para 4.1.3

17 PIP AG, paras 1.6.59-64

18 Response to a Freedom of Information request, 21 August 2024, FOI2024/57343

5. **What happens in an assessment**

19 House of Commons, *Hansard*, Written question 181064, answered 24 April 2023, at questions-statements.parliament.uk/written-questions/detail/2023-04-17/181064

20 **UC** Reg 44(2) UC Regs, interpreted by the DWP in paras G1117-1120 ADM
ESA Regs 23(2) and 24 ESA Regs; regs 19(2) and 20 ESA Regs 2013, interpreted by the DWP in paras 42492-42495 DMG and paras U2492-U2496 ADM
PIP Regs 9(2) and 10 SS(PIP) Regs, interpreted by the DWP in Ch P6 ADM

Chapter 18

Work, work-related requirements and sanctions

This chapter covers:

Key facts

- You can work while claiming most of the benefits covered in this *Handbook*.
- For employment and support allowance (ESA), there are special rules about work.
- If you get universal credit and/or ESA, you might have 'work-related requirements' – eg, requirements to look for or prepare for work.
- If you will struggle to satisfy your work-related requirements because of a mental health problem, you can ask to have them changed, reduced or stopped. The DWP does not have to accept your request but it must comply with equality law and its own policies.
- You cannot always appeal a decision about work-related requirements, but you may be able to challenge it in other ways.
- If you do not comply with a work-related requirement, you could receive a sanction, which means you are paid less or no benefit for a period.
- You can appeal decisions about sanctions and you may also be able to claim hardship payments from the DWP while you are sanctioned.

1. **Benefits and work**

You can claim most of the benefits covered in this *Handbook* while working.

- You can qualify for **universal credit** (UC – see Chapter 5) if you or your partner are in paid work. Your earnings are likely to affect the amount of UC you get (see p74). Managing to do some work may affect whether the DWP accepts that you have limited capability for work or work-related activity (see p80), which can affect the amount of UC you get and whether you have work-related requirements.

- You can qualify for **pension credit** (see Chapter 6) and **housing benefit** (see Chapter 7) while working. Your earnings might affect the amount of benefit you get.
- Work does not prevent you from claiming any of the following benefits, although the tasks you do for work are usually taken into account when assessing your entitlement:
  - personal independence payment (see Chapter 8);
  - adult disability payment in Scotland (see Chapter 9);
  - Scottish adult disability living allowance (see CPAG's *Welfare Benefits Handbook*);
  - disability living allowance (see Chapter 10);
  - child disability payment in Scotland (see Chapter 11);
  - attendance allowance (see Chapter 12);
  - pension age disability payment (see Chapter 13).

There are some benefits that you cannot always get while working.

- You cannot usually claim **employment and support allowance** (ESA – see Chapter 4) if you are working.[1] However, once on ESA, you might be able to do some 'permitted work'. Work that you do for less than 16 hours a week and for which you earn no more than £195.50 a week can usually be permitted work. Earnings from permitted work do not reduce your ESA. You might also be able to get ESA while doing voluntary work or in certain roles – eg, as a councillor or First-tier Tribunal panel member.[2] However, even if work does not stop you getting ESA, the tasks you do for work are usually taken into account in your next work capability assessment and this could affect your future entitlement to ESA.
- You cannot usually get **carer's allowance** or **carer support payment** when you earn more than £196 a week.[3] See Chapter 14 for more information.

Work can have other effects on the benefits you are entitled to. For example:

- if you get UC and have earnings of more than £846 a month, you are exempt from the benefit cap;[4]
- your work history might mean you qualify for contributory benefits like **contributory ESA** or employer-paid benefits like statutory sick pay.

Specialist employment support

If you are keen to find work, but your mental health problem affects the work you can do, you may be able to get specialist employment support through the job centre. For further information, see gov.uk/looking-for-work-if-disabled.

2. Work-related requirements

If you get universal credit (UC) and/or employment and support allowance (ESA), you might have work-related requirements.

Note:

- If you are entitled to UC *and* new-style ESA, you only need to meet one set of work-related requirements – those for UC.[5]
- See CPAG's *Welfare Benefits Handbook* for the rules for new-style jobseeker's allowance (JSA).

Universal credit

The default position is that to get UC you must work or look for work (see p68).[6] However, you should be treated differently if you have a health condition or disability, such as a mental health problem, that restricts your ability to work.

Limited capability for work or work-related activity

If you declare a mental health problem that affects your ability to work, and supply a fit note, you usually have a work capability assessment (WCA – see p80). This is used to decide whether you have limited capability for work (LCW) or limited capability for work *and* work-related activity (LCWRA).

If you have LCWRA, you do not have to meet any work-related requirements to continue getting UC.[7]

If you have LCW, you can be required to:

- take part in work-focused interviews – eg, appointments with a work coach at the job centre or by phone;[8] *and*
- do work preparation – eg, a skills assessment, training and/or a work placement.[9]

Your work coach may also agree voluntary, tailored commitments so you can test out certain activities without risking a sanction.[10]

All work-related requirements

It might be decided that you do not have LCW or LCWRA – ie, that you are 'fit for work'. If this happens, you are usually placed in the all work-related requirements group, sometimes known as the 'intensive work-search group'.

In this group, in order to continue getting UC, you can be required to:

- take part in work-focused interviews – eg, appointments with a work coach at the job centre or by phone;[11] *and*
- do work preparation – eg, a skills assessment, training and/or a work placement;[12] *and*
- look for work – eg, search for and apply to job vacancies and register with employment agencies;[13] *and*

- be available for work – ie, to go to job interviews, and to take up paid work if it is offered to you.[14]

While waiting for a work capability assessment

You are usually put in the all work-related requirements group while you wait for a first WCA. However, your work-related requirements should be tailored to your circumstances during this period (see below).

What advisers say: before a work capability decision

'In the period prior to a WCA decision, work coaches have significant flexibility in terms of whether to, and what work-related requirements, to impose. As always, having someone to accompany you to any meetings (whether it's a CPN, support worker, partner or other family member) is helpful in this regard.'

While challenging a work capability decision

If you have been found fit for work, you are usually put in the all work-related requirements group even if you are challenging the decision (see Chapter 20), but your work coach can and should tailor your work-related requirements.

Adjusting your work-related requirements

The DWP has a lot of discretion about work-related requirements. No matter the outcome of a WCA, your requirements should be adjusted if you are unable to comply with them for mental health reasons. There is nothing to stop you from asking your work coach to review and update your work-related requirements at any time.[15] See Chapter 16 about the kind of supporting evidence that you could use when making a request.

What advisers say: what work-related requirements to expect

'There are huge discrepancies in how claimants are treated depending on who their work coach is and which other job centre staff (see p329) they encounter. This can make it very difficult to advise claimants on what to expect.'

Limitations on work search and work availability

In the all-work related requirements group, you are generally expected to search for work for at least 35 hours a week and to look for work that you can do for at least 35 hours a week. However, if you have a physical or mental impairment (and in certain other circumstances), these hours can be reduced.[16] Most, if not all, mental health problems should be accepted as 'mental impairments'. Additionally, if your condition substantially reduces your ability to do work of a particular type or in particular locations, you do not have to be available for or look for that kind of work.[17]

While you are providing fit notes

If you provide fit notes (eg, because you are waiting for a WCA or because you have a short-term period of sickness), no work search or work availability requirements can usually be imposed on you for the first 14 days. This can apply up to twice in a 12-month period.[18] These rules are not normally helpful for long-term mental health problems. Note the other rules in this section about adjusting your work-related requirements.

Complex needs

The DWP has policies about how it must support people claiming UC whom it considers to have complex needs. This includes giving extra thought to work-related requirements. There is more information on p326.

Easements and reasonable adjustments

If you cannot comply with certain work-related requirements because of your mental health, you can ask your work coach to change, reduce or stop them. These adjustments by a work coach are sometimes called '**discretionary easements**'. The DWP states that these can be applied for a short, medium or long period of time and that they should take account of 'all of [your] individual circumstances'.[19] Easements may include, for example, switching off your work-related requirements during a mental health crisis or pausing your work search requirement for a period while you are unable to comply with it because of your symptoms.

Under the Equality Act 2010,[20] the DWP also has a duty to make '**reasonable adjustments**' to the way it imposes work-related requirements to avoid disadvantage to people with disabilities. A failure to make these adjustments is discrimination. (See p5 about the meaning of 'disability'.) A reasonable adjustment might include changing the type, venue, frequency, length or timing of work-related activity.

Job centre interviews: some types of reasonable adjustment[21]

Changing the location of an interview
Audio recording of an interview
Home visits (in exceptional circumstances)
Private interview rooms or providing a quiet space at the job centre
Changing the time or date of an interview
Involving representatives and other third parties

If a request for an easement or reasonable adjustment is refused, you cannot challenge this through mandatory reconsideration or appeal, but may request a further review of your work-related requirements,[22] complain (see p308) or consider judicial review (p311). For example, if you are being required to attend the job centre every week and this is inappropriate because of your mental health condition, your adviser may be able to challenge this using the template judicial review pre-action letter available by contacting jrproject@cpag.org.uk. Contact an independent advice service if you intend to take this step – see advicelocal.uk.

Examples

Stephen, who experiences anxiety, is assessed as having LCW. He has work-focused interview and work preparation requirements. Stephen can ask to have his work-focused interviews by phone, explaining that visits to the job centre cause him acute anxiety. He can also ask not to be put forward for in-person training in large groups if he would find this unmanageable.

Naima has a long-term mental health condition. On moving from ESA to UC, she has a new WCA and is found 'fit for work'. While appealing the decision, Naima is placed in the all work-related requirements group. She explains her mental health problem to her work coach who agrees to limit her required hours of work-search and work availability. The work coach also agrees that Naima's work preparation requirement can be satisfied through an online course rather than, for example, work experience, because this is something that Naima agrees she can reasonably manage. The work coach does not agree to reduce the frequency of Naima's weekly job centre appointments, despite Naima explaining that she thinks this would be a reasonable adjustment. Although Naima cannot appeal this decision, she may be able to get it changed by asking for a further review of her work-related requirements, making a complaint and/or pursuing judicial review.

Other rules about work-related requirements

Other factors not related to your health can also reduce your work-related requirements for UC – eg, being a carer, being responsible for a child, experiencing domestic abuse or bereavement, or receiving treatment for alcohol or substance abuse. See CPAG's *Welfare Benefits Handbook* for more information.

New-style employment and support allowance

New-style ESA is contributory ESA that 'comes under the UC system', including most awards on new ESA claims made on or after 12 December 2018 (see p52).

If you have LCWRA for new-style ESA, you have no work-related requirements.[23]

If you have LCW for new-style ESA, you can be required to:[24]

- take part in work-focused interviews – eg, appointments with a work coach at the job centre or by phone; *and*

- do work preparation – eg, a skills assessment, training, and/or a work placement.

Note: while you are waiting for a WCA for ESA, or appealing a fit for work decision, you are normally treated as having LCW.[25]

For UC, you can request reasonable adjustments to enable you to meet your work-related requirements (see p272).

Other factors not related to your health can also reduce your work-related requirements for ESA. See CPAG's *Welfare Benefits Handbook* for more information.

Old-style employment and support allowance

Old-style ESA, in practice, covers many ESA awards starting before 12 December 2018, including where you are in the support group and have not claimed UC.

If you have LCWRA for old-style ESA, you have no work-related requirements.[26]

If you have LCW, you can be required to take part in work-related activity that makes it more likely that you will get a job or remain in work.[27] The exact activity is at the discretion of your work coach but cannot include mandatory work experience, being required to apply for jobs, or being required to get medical treatment.[28] See CPAG's *Welfare Benefits Handbook* for more information.

3. Sanctions and hardship payments

Note: see CPAG's *Welfare Benefits Handbook* for the rules about new-style jobseeker's allowance.

Universal credit

Being sanctioned means that your universal credit (UC) payments are reduced or stopped for a period because you have not complied with a work-related requirement. You cannot be sanctioned if you have good reason for not complying.[29]

Good reason is widely defined and may include, for example:[30]

- panic attacks or anxiety that prevent you from travelling to an appointment;
- forgetfulness or confusion as a result of a mental health problem;
- oversleeping, if this is connected with your condition or medication;
- mental health symptoms arising at a particular time – eg, the anniversary of a bereavement;
- a mental health crisis;
- being in hospital or at a medical appointment, although you are expected to give the DWP notice of appointments where you know about them in advance.

The DWP should always check whether you have a mental health problem or other complex needs before referring your case for a sanction decision, and may need to consider a home visit if it cannot get in touch with you. If your case is passed to a decision maker and the evidence shows your work-related requirements were unreasonable at the time you failed to comply with them, the decision maker should accept that you had a good reason and should return the case for your requirements to be reduced.[31]

You may also have good reason if your work-related requirements, or the consequences of not complying with them, were not made clear to you.

Example

Naima (see p273) misses a job centre appointment. She writes a message in her UC journal afterwards explaining that she arrived early for her appointment but had felt acutely paranoid while sitting in the waiting area and had to leave and go straight home. She says that, if needed, she can provide her bus ticket as evidence that she travelled to the job centre. Her work coach accepts that she had good reason for not attending the appointment.

Naima misses her next job centre appointment too. This time, she writes a journal message 45 minutes before the appointment, saying that she feels so unwell she is unable to leave the house. The work coach takes into account what the DWP knows about Naima's mental health problem and again accepts good reason.

If you *are* sanctioned, you can challenge the decision through mandatory reconsideration and appeal (see Chapter 20).[32] There is no time limit for requesting mandatory reconsideration of a sanction. You can challenge a decision on the grounds of good reason, or because you do not agree that you actually failed to comply with a requirement.

What advisers say: challenging a sanction

'It can feel hard to argue against a sanction, [you may] worry that challenging it will only make things worse or that you would do better to take a short sanction on the chin. But sanctions can happen for wrong reasons and decisions can often be reversed if challenged. The trouble with "just accepting" a short sanction is that, should there be another one, it may be for longer as a result.'

You can apply for a reduced-rate payment of UC, called a **'hardship payment'**, if you struggle financially while you are sanctioned. The amount you can get is fixed and you usually have to pay it back.[33]

New-style employment and support allowance

The rules about sanctions for new-style employment and support allowance (ESA) are the same as for UC (see p274).

If you are experiencing hardship while you have a sanction for new-style ESA, you may qualify for a hardship payment of UC (see p275).[34]

Old-style employment and support allowance

Being sanctioned means that your ESA payments are reduced or stopped for a period because you have failed to take part in work-related activity without good cause. Good cause is likely to include many difficulties connected with a mental health problem. You should be given at least five days to show you have good cause before any decision is made to impose a sanction.[35]

You can challenge a sanction decision through mandatory reconsideration and appeal (see Chapter 20).[36] You can also apply for a hardship payment if you struggle financially while you are sanctioned. The amount you can get is fixed and you do not have to pay it back.[37]

Other financial support while sanctioned

When you are sanctioned, applying for a hardship payment (see p275) is a critical step in getting financial support. See Chapter 15 for other help you might be able to get.

Notes

1. **Benefits and work**
1 Regs 40-42 and 44 ESA Regs; regs 37-39 ESA Regs 2013
2 Regs 40, 45 and 88 ESA Regs; regs 37 and 39 ESA Regs 2013
3 s70 SSCBA 1992; reg 8 SS(ICA) Regs
4 Reg 82 UC Regs

2. **Work-related requirements**
5 Reg 42 ESA Regs 2013
6 ss13 and 22 WRA 2012
7 s19 WRA 2012
8 ss15 and 21 WRA 2012; regs 87 and 93 UC Regs; para J3031 ADM
9 ss16 and 21 WRA 2012
10 DWP, *Universal Credit Guidance,* 'No work-related requirements regime', v10.0, and 'Work preparation regime', v19.0, House of Commons library deposited papers, at rightsnet.org.uk/universal-credit-guidance
11 ss15 and 22 WRA 2012; regs 87 and 93 UC Regs; para J3031 ADM
12 ss16 and 22 WRA 2012
13 ss17 and 22 WRA 2012; regs 94 and 95 UC Regs
14 s18(1) and (2) WRA 2012; regs 87 and 96 UC Regs
15 s14(2) WRA 2012
16 Regs 88 and 97 UC Regs
17 s17(4) and (5) WRA 2012; reg 97(4)-(6) UC Regs
18 Reg 99(1), (4), (4ZA) and 4(ZB) UC Regs
19 ADM J3160 and J3250-J3270
20 ss20, 21 and 29 EA 2010. See also s19.

21 DWP, *Universal Credit Guidance*, 'Reasonable adjustments', v5.0, House of Commons library deposited papers, at rightsnet.org.uk/universal-credit-guidance
22 s14(2) WRA 2012; DWP, *Universal Credit Guidance*, 'Claimant commitment not accepted', v6.0, House of Commons library deposited papers, at rightsnet.org.uk/universal-credit-guidance
23 s11D WRA 2007
24 ss11B, 11C and 11F WRA 2007; reg 46 ESA Regs 2013; para U5031 ADM
25 Reg 26 ESA Regs 2013
26 s11D WRA 2007; reg 3(3) ESA(WRA) Regs
27 s13 WRA 2007; regs 3 and 5 ESA(WRA) Regs
28 Reg 3(4) ESA(WRA) Regs; vol 9 Ch 53, para 53073 DMG

3. **Sanctions and hardship payments**
29 **UC** ss26 and 27 WRA 2012; regs 100-114 UC Regs; *JB v SSWP (UC)* [2018] 360 (AAC); *KG v SSWP (UC)* [2020] UKUT 307 (AAC); chs K1-K9 ADM
New-style ESA s11J WRA 2007; regs 50-61 ESA Regs 2013; ch V7 ADM
30 Ch K2 ADM; ADM V7080; *S v SSWP* [2017] UKUT 477 (AAC); *RR v SSWP* [2017] UKUT 459 (AAC); DWP, *Universal Credit Guidance*, 'Failure to attend – good reason', v9.0, House of Commons library deposited papers, at rightsnet.org.uk/universal-credit-guidance
31 paras J3257 and K2054-58 ADM; DWP, *Universal Credit Guidance*, 'Complex needs', v19.0, and 'Home visits', v13.0, House of Commons library deposited papers, at rightsnet.org.uk/universal-credit-guidance
32 s12 SSA 1998; regs 14 and 51 UC,PIP,JSA&ESA(DA) Regs
33 **General** s28 WRA 2012; regs 6 and 115-119 UC Regs; Ch L1 ADM
Recoverability s71ZH(1)(a) SSAA 1992; DWP, *Benefit Overpayment Recovery Guide*, para 5.82 and Chapter 8
34 Reg 112 and Sch 11 UC Regs
35 Regs 61 and 63 ESA Regs; reg 8 ESA(WRA) Regs
36 s12 SSA 1998; regs 3ZA and 28 SS&CS(DA) Regs
37 Regs 2(1), definition of 'hardship payment', and 64A-64D ESA Regs; regs 16A-16C SS(LB) Regs

Chapter 19

In education, hospital, a care home or prison

This chapter covers:

Key facts

- You may be unable to claim means-tested benefits like universal credit if you are in full-time education. If you are studying part time, you are often able to claim these benefits. In either case, student funding can affect how much means-tested benefit you get.
- Being in hospital or in a care home reduces or stops many benefits after a period of time. There are different rules for different benefits.
- Most benefits are affected while you are in prison. Some end, some are suspended and some can only be paid in part.
- If your partner or another member of your household is in education, hospital, a care home or prison, it may affect your benefits.

1. **Education and benefits**

Being in education can affect your entitlement to some of the benefits covered in this *Handbook*. This can apply if you are a student at university, a pupil at school or college, or if you are undertaking a full-time or part-time course.

What happens when you are in education

For more information, including rules about student income, taking time out from your course, and work-related requirements while studying, see CPAG's *Welfare Benefits Handbook*. If you are not sure how these rules apply to you, you can get independent advice – see advicelocal.uk.

Disability benefits

Being in education does not affect your ability to claim personal independence payment (PIP), adult disability payment (ADP), disability living allowance (DLA), Scottish adult disability living allowance (SADLA), child disability payment (CDP), pension age disability payment (PADP) or attendance allowance (AA).

Universal credit

You cannot usually get universal credit (UC) while you count as receiving education.[1] There are exceptions – eg, people who are responsible for children, some people getting PIP, ADP, DLA, SADLA, PADP, AA or CDP (see below), and people waiting to return to a course after taking time out because of illness.[2]

Importantly, not every student or person on a course counts as receiving education. You are *only* classed as 'receiving education' if you are:[3]

- on a full-time course of advanced education – eg, a university degree, postgraduate qualification or HND; *or*
- on any full-time, non-advanced course of study or training for which you receive a student loan or maintenance grant; *or*
- a qualifying young person who is not on a traineeship or a relevant kind of training scheme; *or*
- on any course (full-time or part-time) that is incompatible with your UC work-related requirements. You might argue that this should not apply to you because your work-related requirements are excessive for health reasons (see p270) or because your course should be seen as 'voluntary work preparation' and therefore reduce your work-related requirements.[4]

If none of these describe you, you are not classed as receiving education and can get UC under the same rules as a non-student.

If you have student income, it may affect the amount of UC you get.[5]

Universal credit for students getting disability benefits

You can get UC despite receiving education if:[6]

- you get PIP, ADP, SADLA, DLA, PADP, AA or CDP; *and*
- you are assessed as having, or treated as having, limited capability for work (LCW) for UC (see p80) or employment and support allowance (ESA) (see p57); *and*
- the work capability decision is made *before* the date you start receiving education.

This rule is not always helpful in practice. It can be difficult to get a work capability decision *before* you start a course – eg, because you have not had a long enough break in education to be assessed, or because you did not need to claim UC until after your course began.

Examples

Serena (40) gets UC and was assessed last year as having LCW. She also gets ADP. She enrols on a full-time university course. Although she is now classed as receiving education, her eligibility for UC is not affected because she gets ADP and had her work capability decision before she started her course. The amount of UC she gets might still be reduced by student income.

Isla (21) is already a full-time university student when her mental health problems start. She is able to claim PIP, but cannot claim UC because (a) she counts as receiving education, and (b) she does not come under any of the exceptions that allow someone to claim UC while receiving education. Crucially, she did not get a work capability decision *before* she started studying. If she had, she would have qualified for the exception that allows students getting disability benefits to claim UC.

Billy (19) is enrolled on a full-time, non-advanced life skills course. He has a severe mental health problem and gets PIP. After turning 19, he stops being included in his parents' UC and tries to claim UC in his own right. He is told he does not qualify because he is receiving education and no exceptions apply that allow him to claim UC. Billy and his parents get independent advice and successfully challenge the DWP's decision. They argue that Billy does not meet the definition of receiving education because his course is incompatible with any work-related requirements that could reasonably be set for him, since these would need to be extremely limited due to his severe mental health problem.

Contributory employment and support allowance, pension credit and housing benefit

Being in education does not affect your ability to claim pension credit, pension-age housing benefit (HB) or contributory ESA.

If you are a student, you may only get working-age HB if you meet certain criteria.[7] See CPAG's *Welfare Benefits Handbook*.

2. **Benefits in hospital**

Being in hospital can reduce or stop your benefits after a period of time. There are different rules for different benefits.

What happens when you are in hospital

For more information, including rules about carers, see CPAG's *Welfare Benefits Handbook*. If the rules below will cause you difficulties (eg, you are at risk of losing a tenancy), get independent advice – see advicelocal.uk.

Personal independence payment, adult disability payment, disability living allowance, Scottish adult disability living allowance, attendance allowance and pension age disability payment

These benefits stop being paid when you have been a patient for 28 days, if you were 18 or over when you went into hospital.[8] If you were under 18 when you went into hospital, these benefits continue unaffected.

There is a 28-day 'linking rule' which means that:[9]

- different periods spent as a patient that are separated by 28 days or less are linked together and treated as one period;
- for personal independence payment (PIP), disability living allowance (DLA) and attendance allowance (AA), periods spent as a resident in a care home (or, for PIP, in prison) link with periods spent as a patient if they are 28 days or less apart;
- for adult disability payment (ADP), Scottish adult disability living allowance (SADLA) and pension age disability payment (PADP), a period spent in a care home or in prison links with a period spent as a patient if you transfer directly from one place to the other.

So, for example, if you are in hospital for 14 days, and are then readmitted less than 29 days after discharge, your benefit stops 15 days into your second hospital stay.

There are very limited exceptions to the 28-day rule, such as for people who are terminally ill and living in certain hospices.[10]

You continue to be *entitled* to PIP, ADP, DLA, SADLA and AA or PADP even when they stop being paid. This means you do not need to reapply when you leave hospital. You should notify changes of circumstances to the DWP or Social Security Scotland (SSS) in the usual way, even while you are not being paid.

If you are entitled to one of these benefits, you remain exempt from the benefit cap even after 28 days in hospital.[11]

Child disability payment

You continue being paid child disability payment regardless of how long you are in hospital.[12]

Universal credit

You are automatically treated as having limited capability for work while you are in hospital.[13] In practice, any work-related requirements are likely to be paused.

If you are single, universal credit (UC) continues to be paid while you are in hospital, but the housing costs element stops if your stay in hospital exceeds, or is expected to exceed, six months.[14]

If you have a partner, you are no longer treated as a couple for UC purposes if your stay in hospital exceeds, or is expected to exceed, six months.[15] At this point, you may both need to make new claims as single people.

A child or non-dependant is no longer included in the calculation of your UC award if their stay in hospital exceeds, or is expected to exceed, six months.[16]

Pension credit and housing benefit

These benefits can often continue in hospital, but the amount you get might change. If you get a severe disability premium, it is affected when your disability benefit stops (see above). A disability premium or enhanced disability premium can continue. If you have a partner, you will not usually be treated as a couple after your stay in hospital exceeds 52 weeks.[17]

For pension credit, you are not treated as a couple while one of you is detained under the Mental Health Act 1983 (see p25).[18]

You can usually get housing benefit (HB) or help with housing costs for a maximum of 52 weeks while you are in hospital.[19] However, you cannot get this help if you have permanently left your normal home. Your child or non-dependant is included in the calculation of your HB for a maximum of 52 weeks while they are in hospital.[20]

Contributory employment and support allowance

You are automatically treated as having limited capability for work while you are in hospital.[21] You are not entitled to a work-related activity or support component in your contributory employment and support allowance (ESA) once you have been in hospital for a continuous period of more than 52 weeks.[22]

What counts as being in hospital

If you are getting inpatient treatment in hospital for a mental health problem (see p24), it is likely that you will count as a hospital patient for benefit purposes. You generally count as a hospital patient if:[23]

- you are having medical or other treatment as an inpatient in a hospital or 'similar institution'; *and*
- for PIP, ADP, SADLA and PADP, *any* of the costs of your treatment, accommodation and related services are paid for out of public funds (this usually means they must be paid by the NHS); *or*
- for other benefits except UC and ESA, you are being maintained free of charge (again, usually by the NHS).

Note:

- A care home can sometimes be classed as a 'similar institution' to a hospital.[24]

- If you are detained in hospital while serving a prison sentence, you may be treated as a prisoner (see p286) rather than a patient for benefit purposes.[25]

For UC, you count as being in hospital from the day you are admitted until the day you leave. For HB, the days when you count as a patient depend on which legal rule is being applied. For other benefits, you count as a patient from the day after you enter hospital up to and including:[26]

- for ADP, DLA, SADLA, AA, PADP and, usually, PIP, the day before you leave hospital; *or*
- for the remaining benefits, and for PIP if you go straight on to a care home or prison, the day you leave hospital.

Practical considerations if you go into hospital

If you go into hospital for your mental health, you might be worried about what to do about your benefits. These worries might be affecting your mental health. Remember that being in hospital is likely to count as a 'good reason' for missing benefit deadlines or appointments. While you focus on your wellbeing, you can ask someone else to help manage your benefits. You can ask hospital staff to connect you with someone who can help with this.

- It is important to notify the DWP, SSS, the local authority or any other body that is paying you benefits that you have gone into hospital. Someone can do this for you if you are not able to.
- See Chapter 21 on how someone else can help you manage your benefits while you are in hospital, including information on appointees and third-party representatives.
- Your benefits are not normally affected for the first 28 days in hospital (although you need to be aware of the linking rules above if you have recently come out of hospital and are now being readmitted).
- For UC and ESA, you are automatically treated as having limited capability for work while you are in hospital. In practice, all work-related requirements are likely to be paused while you are in hospital.
- If you need reasonable adjustments, such as changes to how the department paying your benefits communicates with you while you are in hospital, you can ask for them (see p328).
- It is important to clearly tell the departments paying your benefits if your mental health problem has worsened (eg, if this is why you have gone into hospital), as you may now be eligible for a higher rate of benefit.

Example

Ezra (31) is single and admitted to hospital for inpatient treatment for his mental health problem. It is his first time in hospital and stays there for four months. Before going into hospital, Ezra was getting UC (including help to pay his rent) and PIP. While in hospital, his

UC continues to be paid in full, but his PIP stops being paid after the first 28 days. On discharge, his PIP can resume being paid again without Ezra needing to make a new claim. When he is first admitted to hospital, Ezra is too unwell to contact the DWP's PIP and UC departments to let them know about his change of circumstances. His mother contacts them instead and asks to be made Ezra's appointee (see p325) because he is not currently well enough to manage his finances. As Ezra's appointee, his mother receives his benefits on his behalf and can pay his rent and bills. She asks the DWP to end her appointeeship as soon as Ezra is well enough to manage his benefits again.

3. Benefits while staying in a care home

Staying in a care home can reduce or stop your benefits after a period of time. There are different rules for different benefits.

Note:

- Sometimes, while staying in a care home you are classed as a hospital patient (see p282).
- The rules for care homes do not apply to other types of supported or sheltered accommodation, even if you are receiving personal care services there which are provided by your local authority.

What happens while staying in a care home

For more information, including rules about carers, children, non-dependants, savings and Abbeyfield homes, see CPAG's *Welfare Benefits Handbook*. If the rules below will cause you difficulties (eg, you are at risk of losing a tenancy or you are not sure how to pay for your care home), get independent advice – see advicelocal.uk.

Personal independence payment, adult disability payment, disability living allowance, Scottish adult disability living allowance, child disability payment, attendance allowance and pension age disability payment

After 28 days you cannot usually be paid the daily living component of personal independence payment (PIP) or adult disability payment (ADP), the care component of disability living allowance (DLA), Scottish adult disability living allowance (SADLA) or child disability payment (CDP), or any pension age disability payment (PADP) or attendance allowance (AA).[27] You can continue getting the mobility component of PIP, ADP, DLA, SADLA and CDP.

These rules only apply if the costs of your accommodation, board or personal care are met out of public or local funds – ie, not if you are self-funding.[28]

There is a 28-day 'linking rule' which means that:[29]

- different periods spent in a care home that are separated by 28 days or less are linked together and treated as one period;
- for PIP, DLA and AA, periods spent as a resident in hospital (or, for PIP, in prison) link with periods spent in a care home if they are 28 days or less apart.

There are limited exceptions to the 28-day rule, such as for people who are terminally ill and living in certain hospices.[30]

You continue to be *entitled* to PIP, ADP, DLA, SADLA, CDP, PADP and AA even when they stop being paid. This means you do not need to reapply if you move out of the care home. You should notify changes of circumstances to the DWP or Social Security Scotland in the usual way, even while you are not being paid.

If you are entitled to one of these benefits, you remain exempt from the benefit cap even after 28 days in a care home.[31]

Universal credit

If you are single, universal credit (UC) continues to be paid while you are staying in a care home, but the housing costs element stops if your stay exceeds, or is expected to exceed, six months. You cannot get the UC housing costs element for any rent you pay to your care home.[32]

If you have a partner, you are no longer treated as a couple for UC purposes if your stay exceeds, or is expected to exceed, six months.[33] At this point, you may both need to reclaim as single people.

A child is no longer included in your UC claim if their stay in a care home exceeds, or is expected to exceed, six months.[34]

Pension credit and housing benefit

These benefits can often continue when you are staying in a care home, but the amount you get might change. If you get a severe disability premium, it is affected when your disability benefit stops (see above). You may also lose the disability or enhanced disability premium if the only reason you qualified was because you were receiving a disability benefit.

If you or your partner move into a care home permanently, you usually no longer count as a couple. You may both need to reclaim benefits as single people. If you or your partner move into a care home temporarily, you usually still count as a couple for up to 52 weeks.[35]

If you are living temporarily in a care home, you can usually get housing benefit (HB) or help with housing costs on your normal home for a maximum of 52 weeks. You cannot get this help if you have permanently left your normal home. You cannot usually get HB for any rent you pay to your care home.[36]

Contributory employment and support allowance

Contributory employment and support allowance is paid as normal while you are staying or living in a care home.

4. Benefits in prison

Most benefits are affected while you are in prison. Some end, some are suspended and some can only be paid in part.

Note: if you are detained in hospital while serving a prison sentence, you may be treated as a prisoner rather than a patient for benefit purposes (see p282).

What happens while in prison

Except where otherwise stated, these rules apply whether you are serving a sentence or on remand – ie, being held in prison awaiting trial or sentencing.

For more information, including the rules about carers, children and non-dependants, see CPAG's *Welfare Benefits Handbook*. If the rules below will cause you difficulties (eg, you are at risk of losing a tenancy), get independent advice – see advicelocal.uk.

Personal independence payment

You usually stop being paid personal independence payment (PIP) after 28 days in prison, whatever the outcome of the proceedings against you. There is a 'linking rule' which means that different periods spent as a prisoner separated by one year or less are linked together and treated as one period. Periods spent in a care home or hospital are also linked with periods spent as a prisoner.[37] You may be able to resume getting PIP on release without making a new claim, depending on the length of your award, so keep notifying the DWP of changes of circumstances in the usual way even while you are not being paid.

Adult disability payment, Scottish adult disability living allowance and pension age disability payment

You normally stop being paid these benefits after 28 days in prison, whatever the outcome of the proceedings against you. If you are aged 16 or 17, you can get the mobility component of adult disability payment while you are in prison.[38]

Child disability payment

You continue to be paid the care component of child disability payment for the first 28 days that you are in prison, and you continue to be paid the mobility component during any period when you are in prison.[39]

Disability living allowance, attendance allowance, contributory employment and support allowance

When you are in prison awaiting trial or sentencing, these benefits are suspended pending the outcome. If you are given a prison sentence, you are not paid these benefits during your time in prison. If you are not convicted or given a prison sentence, full arrears of any of the benefits that have been withheld are normally payable when you are released.[40]

Universal credit

If you are a single person and you go to prison, you can continue getting the housing costs element in your universal credit (UC) for up to six months, but only if you have not been given a sentence that is expected to extend beyond that six months. You do not get any other elements of UC. Your work-related requirements are switched off during this six-month period.[41]

If you are a member of a couple and you go to prison, your partner can make a UC claim as a single person. If your time in prison exceeds, or is expected to exceed, six months, you no longer count as a couple and your partner's benefit is calculated accordingly. While you do still count as a couple, your and your partner's income and capital are still assessed jointly, even though their UC amount is that for a single person.[42]

A child cannot be included in your UC claim if they are in prison.[43]

Pension credit

Pension credit usually stops immediately if you go to prison. If you have a partner, you are no longer treated as a couple.[44]

Housing benefit

If you are in prison awaiting trial or sentence, you can usually continue to get housing benefit (HB) for your normal home for a maximum of 52 weeks. If you are convicted and given a prison sentence, you can get HB for up to 13 weeks (from the date you went into prison), provided you are unlikely to be away from your home for longer than this.[45]

If you have a partner, you continue to count as a couple for HB while you are in prison, provided you intend to live together again and you are unlikely to be away for substantially longer than 52 weeks.[46]

Notes

1. **Education and benefits**
   1 s4(1)(d) WRA 2012
   2 Regs 13(4) and 14 UC Regs. See also regs 3, 8 and 13(1)-(3) UC Regs
   3 Regs 5 and 12 UC Regs; para H6035 ADM
   4 Reg 95(4) UC Regs; DWP, *Universal Credit Guidance*, 'Students: eligibility, conditionality, student income', v37.0, House of Commons library deposited papers, at rightsnet.org.uk/universal-credit-guidance
   5 Regs 68-71 UC Regs
   6 Reg 14(1)(b) UC Regs
   7 Regs 8(1)(e), 55-58 and 92(7) HB Regs

2. **Benefits in hospital**

8 **AA** Reg 8(4) SS(AA) Regs
DLA Regs 10(6) and (7) and 12B(9A) and (12) SS(DLA) Regs
PIP Reg 30(3) and (4) SS(PIP) Regs
ADP Reg 28(2) DAWAP(S) Regs
PADP Regs 20(2) DAOP(S) Regs
SADLA Regs 23(2) DA(SADLA) Regs

9 **AA** Reg 8(2) SS(AA) Regs
DLA Regs 10(5) and 12B(3) SS(DLA) Regs
PIP Reg 32(4) and (5) SS(PIP) Regs
ADP Regs 28(3) and 31(5) and (6) DAWAP(S) Regs
PADP Regs 20(3) and 23(5) and (6) DAOP(S) Regs
SADLA Regs 23(3) and 26(5) and (6) DA(SADLA) Regs

10 **AA** Reg 8(3)-(5) SS(AA) Regs
DLA Regs 10(3), (6) and (7), 12B and 12C SS(DLA) Regs
PIP Reg 30(2)-(4) SS(PIP) Regs
ADP Regs 29 and 32(2)(b) DAWAP(S) Regs
PADP Reg 21 DAOP(S) Regs
SADLA Regs 24 DA(SADLA) Regs

11 Reg 75F(1)(f) HB Regs; reg 83(1)(h) UC Regs

12 Reg 21 DACYP(S) Regs

13 Reg 39 and Sch 8 para 2 UC Regs

14 Sch 3 para 9 UC Regs

15 s39 WRA 2012; reg 3(6) UC Regs

16 s10 WRA 2012; reg 4(7) and Sch 4 para 11(6) UC Regs

17 **HB** Reg 21(1) and (2) and Sch 3 HB Regs; reg 21(1) and (2) and Sch 3 HB(SPC) Regs
PC Regs 5(1)(a) and (5)(b) and 6 and Schs 1 paras 1(1)(b) and (2)(b)-(ba) and IIA para 6 SPC Regs

18 Reg 5(1)(c)(i) SPC Regs

19 **PC** Sch II para 4(11) SPC Regs
HB Reg 7(16) HB Regs; reg 7(16) HB(SPC) Regs

20 Regs 21(1) and (2) and 74(7)(f) HB Regs; regs 21(1) and (2) and 55(7)(f) HB(SPC) Regs

21 Reg 25 ESA Regs; reg 21 ESA Regs 2013

22 Sch 5 para 13 ESA Regs; reg 63(1) ESA Regs 2013

23 **PIP** s86(2) and (3) WRA 2012; reg 29(2) SS(PIP) Regs; para P3012 ADM
ADP Reg 28 DAWAP(S) Regs
PADP Reg 20 DAOP(S) Regs
SADLA Reg 23 DA(SADLA) Regs
UC Reg 8(3) and Sch 8 para 2 UC Regs
ESA Reg 25 ESA Regs; reg 21 ESA Regs 2013
Other benefits Reg 2(4) SS(HIP) Regs; reg 6 SS(AA) Regs; regs 8 and 12A SS(DLA) Regs; Vol 3 Ch 18, paras 18021, 18028-33, 18041 and 18059 DMG; R(DLA) 2/06
All *White v CAO, The Times*, 2 August 1993, reported as R(IS) 18/94; *Botchett v CAO, The Times*, 8 May 1996, 2 CCLR 121 (CA); *R v North and East Devon Health Authority ex parte Coughlan* [1999] 2 CCLR 285; R(DLA) 2/06; *SSWP v Slavin* [2011] EWCA Civ 1515, reported as [2012] AACR 30

24 Vol 3 Ch 18, paras 18060-63 DMG; s86(2) and (3) WRA 2012; reg 29(2) SS(PIP) Regs; para P3062 ADM; reg 28(4) DAWAP(S) Regs; R(DLA) 2/06

25 **UC** Reg 19(1)(c) and (4) UC Regs
ESA Regs 69(3)-(5) and 160(3)-(4A) and Sch 5 para 12 ESA Regs; reg 96(3)-(5) ESA Regs 2013
PC Reg 8 and Sch 3 para 2 SPC Regs
PIP Reg 31(3) and (4) SS(PIP) Regs
Other benefits Reg 2(3), (4) and (4A) SS(GB) Regs
All CSS/239/2007; *JB v SSWP (IS)* [2010] UKUT 263 (AAC)

26 **AA** Reg 6(2A) SS(AA) Regs
DLA Regs 8(2A) and 12A(2A) SS(DLA) Regs
PIP Reg 32(2) SS(PIP) Regs
ADP Reg 31(2) DAWAP(S) Regs
PADP Reg 23(2) DAOP(S) Regs
SADLA Reg 26(2) DA(SADLA) Regs
ESA Reg 2(5) SS(HIP) Regs; reg 69(2) ESA Regs; reg 63(5) ESA Regs 2013
PC Reg 1 SPC Regs, definition of 'patient'; reg 2(5) SS(HIP) Regs
HB Regs 7(18) and 28(11)(e) HB Regs; regs 7(18), 22(5) and 31(11)(e) HB(SPC) Regs; reg 2(5) SS(HIP) Regs

3. **Benefits while staying in a care home**

27 **AA/DLA** ss67(2)-(4) and 72(8)-(10) SSCBA 1992; regs 7 and 8(1) and (3) SS(AA) Regs; regs 9 and 10(1) and (3) SS(DLA) Regs
PIP s85 WRA 2012; regs 28 and 30(1)-(2) SS(PIP) Regs
CDP Regs 2, 17(2) and 20 DACYP(S) Regs
ADP Regs 2, 27(2) 32(1) and (2)(a) DAWAP(S) Regs
PADP Regs 2 and 19(2) DAOP(S) Regs
SADLA Reg 26(2) DA(SADLA) Regs

28 **AA** Reg 8(6) SS(AA) Regs
DLA Reg 10(8) SS(DLA) Regs
PIP Reg 30(5) SS(PIP) Regs
CDP Reg 17(4) DACYP(S) Regs
ADP Reg 27(4) DAWAP(S) Regs
PADP Reg 19(4) DAOP(S) Regs
SADLA Reg 26(4) DA(SADLA) Regs
All *Steane v CAO and Secretary of State*, 24 July 1996, reported as R(A) 3/96; R(A) 1/02; CA/3800/2006; *CAO v Creighton and Others* [1999] NICA 13, reported as R 1/00 (AA); *SSWP v DA* [2009] UKUT 214 (AAC)

29 **AA** Reg 8(2) SS(AA) Regs
DLA Reg 10(5) SS(DLA) Regs
PIP Reg 32(4)-(5) SS(PIP) Regs
CDP Reg 17(3) DACYP(S) Regs
ADP Reg 27(3) DAWAP(S) Regs
PADP Reg 19(3) DAOP(S) Regs
SADLA Reg 22(3) DA(SADLA) Regs

30 **AA** Reg 8(4) and (5) SS(AA) Regs
DLA Reg, 9(3), (4)(a)-(c) and (5) and 10(6) and (7) SS(DLA) Regs
PIP Regs 28(2)(f), (3)(a)-(b) and (4) and 30(3) SS(PIP) Regs
CDP Regs 17(5) and 21 DACYP(S) Regs
ADP Regs 27(5) and 29 DAWAP(S) Regs
PADP Reg 21(1) DAOP(S) Regs
SADLA Reg 24(1) DA(SADLA) Regs

31 **UC** Reg 83(1)(h) UC Regs
HB Reg 75F(1)(f) HB Regs

32 Sch 3 paras 3(d) and 9 UC Regs

33 s39 WRA 2012; reg 3(6) UC Regs

34 s10 WRA 2012; reg 4(7) UC Regs

35 **PC** Reg 5(1)(1)-(b) SPC Regs
HB Reg 21(1)-(2) HB Regs; reg 21(1)-(2) HB(SPC) Regs

36 Reg 9(1)(k) HB Regs; reg 9(1)(k) HB(SPC) Regs; Sch 3 para 9 HB&CTB(CP) Regs; HB/CTB A20/05

4. **Benefits in prison**

37 s87 WRA 2012; regs 31(1)-(2) and (5) and 32 SS(PIP) Regs

38 **ADP** Regs 3(3), 30 and 32(2)(c) DAWAP(S) Regs
PADP Regs 22 DAOP(S) Regs
SADLA Reg 25 DA(SADLA) Regs

39 Reg 18 DACYP(S) Regs

40 **AA/DLA** s113(1)(b) and Sch 9 para 1 SSCBA 1992; regs 2 and 3 SS(GB) Regs; R(S) 1/71; R(S) 8/79
ESA s18(4)(b) WRA 2007; regs 159-161 ESA Regs; regs 95-97 ESA Regs 2013

41 Regs 2 and 19 UC Regs as interpreted by the DWP at paras E3030 and E3040 ADM. See also DWP, *Universal Credit Guidance*, 'Prisoners', v18.0, House of Commons library deposited papers, at rightsnet.org.uk/universal-credit-guidance.

42 s39 WRA 2012; regs 3(3)(c) and (6), 18, 22(3) and 36(3) UC Regs

43 Reg 4(6)(b) UC Regs

44 Regs 1(2), 5(1)(c), 6 and 7(3) and Sch 2 para 4(11) and (12) SPC Regs

45 Reg 7(13)-(17) HB Regs; reg 7(13)-(17) HB(SPC) Regs; CSH/499/2006; *KdeS v Camden LB (HB)* [2011] UKUT 457

46 Reg 21(2) HB Regs; reg 21(2) HB(SPC) Regs

Chapter 20

Getting a decision changed

This chapter covers:

Key facts

- In some circumstances, a benefit decision can be 'revised'. Usually, this means it is changed with effect from the same date as the original decision.
- In other circumstances, a benefit decision can be 'superseded'. This means that it is changed with effect from a later date, often because of a change of circumstances.
- If you disagree with a benefit decision, you can often challenge it through appeal. Appeals are decided by an independent tribunal.
- Before starting an appeal about a DWP benefit, you usually need to make a request for revision, known as a 'mandatory reconsideration request'.
- The appeal process normally involves submitting an appeal form and written evidence and, in most cases, attending a hearing.
- If you cannot appeal a benefit decision or if an appeal is not effective in resolving your problem, you may decide to make a formal complaint and/or challenge the decision through judicial review.
- There are different rules for challenging decisions made by Social Security Scotland (known as 'determinations').

If you are trying to get a benefit decision changed, it can be difficult to know where to start.

If a benefit decision was right when it was first made but circumstances have changed (eg, you have a personal independence payment (PIP) award but your needs have now increased), see p292 (or p314 for Scottish disability benefits).

If you disagree with a new decision about benefits (eg, a decision finding you fit for work or refusing your claim for PIP), you probably need to start on p294 (or p313 for Scottish disability benefits).

If in doubt, it is always a good idea to seek independent benefit advice – see advicelocal.uk.

1. General rules about revision and supersession

Revision and supersession are the two ways that a benefit decision can be changed.

Revision

Revision is about correcting a decision that was wrong when it was made. When a decision is revised,[1] a new decision is made, usually taking effect from the same date as the original one.[2] There are two types of revision, and the one you use depends on how quickly you challenge the decision.

Note: a revision request is often known as a mandatory reconsideration when it is a required step before you can proceed with an appeal. There is more information about mandatory reconsideration on p294.

'Any grounds' revisions

If you are disputing a recent decision, it is always best to apply for an 'any grounds' revision. In most cases, you must apply within one month of the date the decision was sent, or within 13 months if there are reasons why you could not apply sooner.[3] In practice, revision requests made within 13 months are almost always considered, so do not give up if you have missed the one-month deadline.

You do not need a specific reason to apply for an 'any grounds' revision, you just need to disagree with the decision. The decision maker must take a completely fresh look at the decision. They can only revise a decision based on your circumstances at the time of the original decision, but can consider new evidence or information if it is about those circumstances.[4]

When you make a late request for an any time revision, make sure that you explain why you did not apply sooner. There are some suggestions about relevant factors on p300.

Example

After making a new claim for personal independence payment (PIP), Ava gets a decision stating that she is not eligible. Although she disagrees with the decision, she feels too unwell to do anything about it. A few months later, Ava's sister learns about the decision and encourages her to get advice about challenging it. With her sister's support, Ava books an appointment with a welfare rights adviser, who helps her to submit an 'any grounds' revision request (the adviser refers to this a 'mandatory reconsideration' request – see p298). The request includes reasons for lateness. The DWP accepts the late request on the basis of special circumstances.

'Any time' revisions

If you are disputing a decision that was made some time ago, and you have missed the time limits for an 'any grounds' revision; you need to apply for an 'any time' revision. You can only do this in limited circumstances – you must have specific grounds for disagreeing with the decision. The decision maker may also be restricted in which parts of the decision they can look at again.

Grounds for an 'any time' revision

The main grounds for an 'any time' revision are where there has been:
– an official error;[5] *or*
– a sanction decision;[6] *or*
– an award of a qualifying benefit;[7] *or*
– an appeal against a decision;[8] *or*
– a mistake about, or ignorance of, facts.[9]
See CPAG's *Welfare Benefits Handbook* for more information.

Supersession

Supersession usually happens when a decision was originally right, but has become wrong. When a decision is superseded, a new decision is made, which takes effect from a later date than the original one.[10] The most common ground for supersession is that your circumstances have changed.

You can apply for a supersession even if the decision was made a long time ago, but the arrears of benefit you are paid can be limited. You must usually apply for a revision or appeal instead if you can.[11]

Grounds for supersession

The main grounds for supersession are:
- where there has been a change of circumstances;[12] *or*
- where the decision maker has obtained a new medical report and the decision is about work capability for universal credit (UC) or employment and support allowance (ESA), or is about the disability conditions for PIP;[13] *or*
- for PIP, where you have failed to return the PIP2 questionnaire or attend an assessment;[14] *or*
- where there has been a mistake about, or ignorance of, facts;[15] *or*
- where a decision is legally wrong;[16] *or*
- after a qualifying benefit has been awarded.[17]

When a supersession takes effect

The general rule is that a supersession takes effect from:[18]

- the date you applied for it (or, for UC, from the start of the assessment period in which you applied); *or*
- if you did not apply for it, from the date the decision maker made the supersession decision (or, for UC, from the start of the assessment period in which that decision was made).

There are many exceptions. The following is not a full list. See CPAG's *Welfare Benefits Handbook* for more information.

Reporting a deterioration

If you ask the DWP for a supersession because your health has worsened, and this means you should now get a higher rate of PIP, disability living allowance (DLA) or attendance allowance (AA), you will not start receiving the higher rate immediately. The supersession only takes effect once you have met the benefit's qualifying/relevant period condition (see p129 for PIP, p176 for DLA and p200 for AA).

Getting a qualifying benefit

If you, your partner or a child included in your claim is awarded a qualifying benefit that entitles you to an increase in your means-tested benefit, and arrears of the qualifying benefit are payable, your means-tested benefit can be increased and arrears paid for the same length of time.[19] This applies if, for example, the qualifying benefit entitles you to a premium, an extra element or addition, or if it means you are no longer subject to a non-dependant deduction.

This does not happen automatically, so you must request a supersession (or a revision, depending on the timing). If the DWP fails to increase your award, or does not pay you the arrears you are entitled to, you can challenge this through a mandatory reconsideration request and appeal.

How to request a revision or supersession

It is best to get advice before asking for a revision or supersession of your benefit award. Occasionally, the amount of your benefit might decrease instead of increasing.

It is usually best to make a revision or supersession request in writing. For most benefits, this means sending a letter; however, for UC, it could mean using your online journal for a revision request or the 'Report a change' function on your online account for a supersession request. For housing benefit (HB), revision and supersession requests must be made in writing.[20]

When sending a request by post, keep a copy and ask the Post Office for free proof of posting.

Examples

Scott gets UC and has been found to have limited capability for work. He has a severe episode of psychosis and his dad helps him use the 'Report a change' function on his online account to notify the DWP. The DWP treats this as a supersession request, and Scott is referred for another work capability assessment. This time, he is found to have limited capability for work-related activity. The new decision takes effect from the start of the assessment period in which he reported a change.

Leah applies for PIP and is awarded the standard rate of the daily living component due to her post-traumatic stress disorder. She believes that she should also qualify for the mobility component, because she struggles to go out alone. Leah has a phone appointment with an independent advice worker who explains that, if she asks for a revision, the decision maker will look again at the whole decision, and there is a risk that she could lose the daily living part of the award.

Leah decides to proceed. The adviser helps her to send a written revision request to the PIP section of the DWP. Because the decision was made less than a month ago, the request is accepted as one for 'any grounds' revision.

The decision maker does not change the decision, so the original award (standard rate of the daily living component only) stays the same. When Leah receives the decision notice, she can proceed to appeal if she wants to, because she has satisfied the mandatory reconsideration requirement.

2. Mandatory reconsideration

If you think a benefit decision is wrong when it is made, the first step to challenge it is usually to ask for a revision (see p291). In most cases, you need to do this before you can appeal the decision to the independent tribunal. This requirement is known as 'mandatory reconsideration'.

Note: the terms revision and mandatory reconsideration are often used interchangeably. This happens in the section below and in other parts of this *Handbook*. A mandatory reconsideration is really like any other kind of revision – it is just one that you need to request before you can make an appeal. All the rules about revisions on p291 apply to mandatory reconsiderations.

When to ask for a mandatory reconsideration

You should usually request a mandatory reconsideration within one month of the date of the decision you are challenging, or within 13 months if there are reasons why you could not apply sooner (see p291). You may be able to make a mandatory reconsideration request after more than 13 months but only where you have specific grounds (see p292).

There is *no* mandatory reconsideration requirement – so you can go straight to appeal – if:

- the benefit is housing benefit; *or*
- your appeal concerns an employment and support allowance (ESA) decision that you do not have limited capability for work and you would qualify for payment of ESA pending an appeal against that decision (see p306);[21] *or*
- the DWP does not tell you that you need to apply for a mandatory reconsideration before you can appeal.[22]

How to ask for a mandatory reconsideration

You can make a mandatory reconsideration request yourself or with support from an independent advice service or someone close to you.

In writing

You can apply for a mandatory reconsideration by phone, but it is best to apply in writing (on a form or by letter), if possible, so that there is a clear record of what you have said and when. If you are appealing about universal credit (UC), you can apply on your online journal. In all cases, clearly and prominently state: 'I am requesting a mandatory reconsideration of the decision dated [insert date].'

There are tools for generating mandatory reconsideration request letters on CPAG Welfare Rights. There are also standard DWP forms for requesting a mandatory reconsideration of certain decisions,[23] but you do not have to use these.

When sending a request by post, keep a copy and ask the Post Office for free proof of posting.

It is important to follow up your request to ensure that it has been received and registered.

What advisers say: requesting a mandatory reconsideration

'For UC, discussions via the online journal can be problematic because people often spend a lot of time going back and forth with their work coach about something and never formally challenging a decision. Specify that you are making a "mandatory reconsideration request" as it stops the back and forth and forces an appealable decision to be made.'

Explaining why you think the decision is wrong

In your request, explain why you disagree with the decision. Run through the legal conditions you have to satisfy to get the decision you want (using the relevant chapter of this *Handbook*) and explain how the evidence shows that you meet these conditions. For example, if your appeal is about whether you meet the conditions for an award of personal independence payment, you should run through the descriptors that you believe apply to you, and explain why this is the case, referring to supporting evidence as relevant. You should refer to the decision notice and address specific points that you disagree with – eg, if you think the decision maker has said something that is incorrect.

Providing and asking for evidence

When you send your mandatory reconsideration request, attach copies (never originals) of any additional evidence that supports your case. Label each document clearly and refer to it in your request – eg, 'See enclosed GP letter dated 4 July 2025'. Chapter 16 has more information about supporting evidence.

You should also use the mandatory reconsideration request as an opportunity to ask for a copy of any evidence (such as an assessment report – see p243) that has been used to make the decision.

Giving reasons for lateness

If your request is being made more than one month after the decision date, explain why (see p291).

Providing details of your representative

If someone has helped you to prepare your mandatory reconsideration request, you can mention this in the letter. You can also ask that they are sent a copy of the decision. For this to happen, you need to include written confirmation that the decision maker has your consent to disclose information to that person (sometimes called a 'form of authority'). Chapter 21 has more information about representatives and forms of authority.

The mandatory reconsideration decision

There is no fixed time limit for the DWP to make a mandatory reconsideration decision, and the time it takes can vary widely. In most cases, you can keep getting the benefit you have already been awarded while waiting for a decision (see p306).

Note: the DWP should make a mandatory reconsideration decision within a reasonable time. What counts as 'reasonable' depends on a range of circumstances – eg, whether you are destitute because of the decision. If you think there is an unreasonable delay in your case, you might consider judicial review (see p311).

After considering your mandatory reconsideration request, the DWP should send you a mandatory reconsideration notice telling you the outcome of your application.

If a decision is changed following mandatory reconsideration, you may be eligible for arrears of benefit, also known as 'back pay' (see p305).

If you are unhappy with the mandatory reconsideration decision, you can lodge an appeal (see p297). If you have applied for a mandatory reconsideration, but have not been sent a mandatory reconsideration notice, try to provide evidence to the tribunal that you submitted a request, and that the DWP has considered your application.

3. Appeals

You may be able to appeal against a benefit decision you disagree with. The appeal is decided by an independent tribunal.

You can appeal against most decisions made by the DWP or the local authority. Appeals are heard by the Social Entitlement Chamber of the First-tier Tribunal (Social Security and Child Support) – referred to as 'the tribunal' in this *Handbook*. The administration of tribunals is the responsibility of HM Courts and Tribunals Service (HMCTS).

Before appealing, you might have to satisfy a mandatory reconsideration requirement (see p294).

What advisers say: appeals

'Out of those people who apply for personal independence payment (PIP), are turned down, but go on to win their appeal, more than a third actually get an enhanced PIP component.'[24]

'The DWP does think again at mandatory reconsideration, but it can take something new or compelling to get them to do so. If you can bear to let things go on to appeal – even if you feel that you would not be able to attend – the chances of success can be higher.'

Decisions that can be appealed

Decisions you can appeal include decisions about whether:

- you are entitled to a benefit;
- your claim has been validly made and/or can be backdated;
- you have limited capability for work (LCW) or limited capability for work-related activity (LCWRA);
- you satisfy the disability conditions for a benefit like PIP;
- you should be given a sanction, and whether you had good cause or a good reason for not doing something;
- you satisfy the immigration and residence conditions for a benefit.[25]

Decisions that cannot be appealed

Decisions you cannot appeal include a decision:[26]

- that is discretionary, such as a decision about whether to apply a discretionary easement to your work-related requirements (p270) or whether to give you a discretionary housing payment (see p232);

- to appoint a person as an appointee (see p325);
- to make a short-term advance, a budgeting advance or a payment on account;
- to recover a recoverable overpayment, and the amount of deductions;
- to suspend payment of benefit.

You can still ask for an 'any time' revision (see p292) or a supersession (see p292) of a decision about which you do not have a right of appeal, whatever your reason for thinking it is wrong.[27] However, if the decision maker refuses to revise or supersede such a decision, your only legal remedy is to consider judicial review (see p311).

Advice and representation

You can have a representative to help you make an appeal, prepare your case and/or be with you at the hearing.[28]

Your representative could be a friend or family member, or they could be an experienced welfare rights adviser. Advice and representation may be available in your area from the local authority, a law centre, advice centre or Citizens Advice, and is usually free. Advicelocal.uk can help you find advice services where you live.

If you have a representative, you must provide HMCTS with written notice of their name and address or they must do this on your behalf. You can do this on the appeal form or in a letter or email.[29] Once notified, HMCTS will send all relevant documents to both you and your representative.[30]

Even if you have not previously notified the tribunal that you have a representative, someone can attend the hearing with you (eg, a friend or relative) and act as one, or assist you at the hearing, if the tribunal agrees.[31] Chapter 21 has more information about representatives.

Note: it is usually best to get independent advice before starting an appeal. Appealing a decision means the tribunal looks at the whole decision again. There may be a risk you could lose benefit – eg, if your appeal is about a benefit that can be paid at different rates (eg, PIP), the rate you are awarded could go down.

Appeal process

For a practical guide to preparing for an appeal, see CPAG's *Winning Your Benefit Appeal: what you need to know*.

Mandatory reconsideration

Before you can appeal, you must usually request a mandatory reconsideration (see p294).

Lodging an appeal

Appeal form

You must appeal in writing. You can submit appeals about most benefits using Form SSCS1, or online at gov.uk/appeal-benefit-decision. For housing benefit (HB), send your notice of appeal to the local authority, using its approved form. Keep a copy of your completed form and, if you are sending it by post, get a free proof of postage from the Post Office. Consider attaching supporting evidence (see p248).

The appeal form is an opportunity to mention any special arrangements you need to participate in a hearing – eg, a video or telephone hearing, or a different approach to questioning (see p303).

If you have an appointee, see p326.

Urgent appeals

If you want the tribunal to deal with your appeal quickly (ie, 'expedite' your appeal), make this clear when you appeal, explaining why your case is urgent. For HB, because you have to send your notice of appeal to the local authority, you could write to the tribunal, asking it to intervene. For further information, see the article 'Expediting UC appeals' on p8 of CPAG's *Welfare Rights Bulletin 278.*

Grounds for appeal

The appeal form requires you to give 'grounds' for your appeal – ie, reasons for disagreeing with the decision that you are appealing. These can be brief. If you have already written out your reasons in a mandatory reconsideration request (see p295), you can attach a copy of this to the appeal form and make it clear on the form that these are your grounds for the appeal.

Examples of grounds for appeal

'You say I cannot get personal independence payment daily living component. This decision is wrong because you have not taken into account the amount of help I need to engage in social situations or manage my finances.'

'The decision says that I do not meet the conditions for limited capability for work, but I believe that the difficulties I experience because of my depression have been underestimated and I also do not think that the decision maker has considered whether work presents a "substantial risk" to my health.'

Time limit for appealing

If you had to apply for a mandatory reconsideration before you could appeal (see p294), you must usually appeal within one month of the date of your mandatory reconsideration notice.[32] If you did not have to apply for a mandatory reconsideration, you must usually appeal within one month of the date of the decision you are appealing.[33]

If you miss the one-month deadline, do not give up: your appeal is likely to be accepted up to 12 months after this time limit if you include reasons for lateness on your appeal form.[34] These could include the fact that:

- your mental health condition delayed you reading or dealing with the decision;
- you had to wait to get the assistance you needed to make the appeal;
- you made a reasonable mistake in calculating the time limit;
- you did not receive the decision;
- you posted your appeal in time, but there was a delay caused by the postal service;
- you were given wrong advice or otherwise misled by the DWP (or the local authority).

If you have exceeded the 'absolute' lime limit of 13 months (ie, the one-month normal time limit plus the extension of 12 months), you can only appeal in very exceptional circumstances.[35] Get independent advice if you are in this situation. Your best option may be to make a new claim for benefit or, if you have an ongoing benefit award, make a new request for a supersession (see p292).

Submissions and further evidence

The decision maker's response

After HMCTS has registered your appeal, the DWP or the local authority must prepare a bundle of papers relevant to your appeal – called the 'decision maker's response' – and forward this to the tribunal. This should usually be done within 28 days, but in practice, can take longer.[36] Both you and your representative (if you have one) should be sent a copy.[37] However, check that your representative has received it, as this might not always happen.

The response explains the legal basis for the decision.[38] It must include copies of all written evidence the decision maker has that could be relevant to the appeal.[39] If you think the decision maker may have other relevant evidence (eg, a previous assessment report), you can ask the tribunal to direct them to produce it.

Your submissions

Once you receive a copy of the decision maker's response, you (or your representative) should reply in writing. You should usually do this within one month, but the tribunal may give you longer if it is agreed that you need more time.[40] Clearly label it something like: 'Written submission in support of my appeal'. Send your reply to the tribunal by post or email and it will forward a copy to the decision maker.

This written submission should give details of the legal conditions you have to satisfy to get the decision you want, and explain how the evidence shows that you meet these conditions. For example, if your appeal is about whether you meet the conditions for a PIP award, your submission should run through the activities and descriptors that you believe apply to you, and explain why this is the case, referring to the medical evidence. Use the relevant chapter of this *Handbook* to check the benefit conditions that apply to you.

You can also make specific points about the appeal papers – eg, pointing out something the decision maker or assessor has said that is incorrect.

Ensure that everything you want to say in support of your appeal has been put in writing and that you have sent the tribunal all of the documents and evidence you have that might support your case (see below). You can make more than one written submission if you need to (eg, because you get more supporting evidence or have noticed something else in the appeal bundle that you would like to address), but try to do so in plenty of time before a hearing is arranged.

Supporting evidence

An important part of preparing your appeal is considering the evidence you can provide to support your arguments. This includes medical evidence, but also other forms of written, recorded or filmed evidence, and the oral evidence that you give in a hearing. Chapter 16 considers supporting evidence in detail.

Hearing

Will there be a hearing?

The tribunal makes its decision on your case either:

- at a hearing held in person or remotely – eg, by telephone or video call;[41] *or*
- on the papers only, by looking at what you said on your appeal form, any evidence or other information you provided and the decision maker's response.

You tell the tribunal on your appeal form (or, for HB, on an enquiry form) whether you want to attend a hearing and, if so, the type of hearing you would prefer. If you do not ask for a hearing, you are taken to have agreed to having your case decided on the papers if the tribunal considers it appropriate. A decision 'on the papers' is made by the same panel (see p303) as makes a decision at a hearing.

You can decide whether you want to attend a hearing. You do not have to attend a hearing if it will cause you serious distress or pose a risk to your safety and wellbeing (see p303). Some things to keep in mind when making your decision include the following.

- Unlike hearings in a court, hearings in the First-tier Tribunal are meant to be informal.
- You may be able to participate via video or phone call if attending in person is not possible (see below).
- You can ask (ideally in advance) that the panel members adapt the way they ask questions so that they do so more sensitively (see p303).

- You can request breaks as needed – eg, if you become anxious or overwhelmed during the hearing.
- You can have a representative (see p298) at the hearing. You can also take a friend, relative or support worker with you for support.
- You may be able to get expenses paid, if the cost of going to the tribunal is a concern. You can claim for travel, meals, loss of earnings and childcare costs.[42]
- The tribunal aims to provide a qualified interpreter if you need one.
- You will be able to explain your side of the story in your own words.

What advisers say: appeals

'An appeal is usually the first opportunity for the people making a decision to talk directly with you. Your voice is heard.'

'The sense among advisers is that appeals are often won because tribunals attach more weight to your account of your difficulties as they can ask you about it directly and test it a little bit with questioning.'

Hearings in person or remotely

A hearing can take place in person or by video or telephone call.[43] If you have a video or telephone hearing, you usually stay at home and participate using your mobile phone, landline or computer. The tribunal decides which type of hearing to offer you but considers your needs and preferences, so state these on the appeal form and/or in your written submissions.

What kind of hearing works best is different for everyone. In-person and video hearings mean that the panel sees you when you are answering questions and observes how you are coping. Video and telephone hearings mean that you may be able to participate from somewhere you might find more manageable.

If you have a video or telephone hearing, you can have a representative with you in person, or they can join the call remotely. You can also have a friend, family member or support worker with you.

The date of the hearing

An appeal is usually ready to be given a hearing date (ie, it is 'ready for listing') once the decision maker has sent its response and you have been given a month to reply. In practice, hearings usually take several months after this to be listed.

You must be given 14 days' notice of a hearing unless you agreed to accept shorter notice or exceptional circumstances apply.[44] If you know that you are not available on certain dates (eg, because you have a booked medical appointment or holiday), you should let the tribunal know well in advance.

If you are given a date you cannot attend, contact the tribunal immediately to explain why and to ask for a postponement.[45] The tribunal has discretion over whether to postpone a hearing and is more likely to do so if you give as much notice as possible and have a good reason for being unable to attend. If you have a last-minute emergency (such as a mental health crisis), you can still ask for a postponement.

For information about missed hearings, see p305.

The appeal panel

If your appeal is about attendance allowance (AA), disability living allowance (DLA) or PIP, it is usually decided by a three-person panel. The panel is made up of a judge, a doctor (who is not always a mental health expert) and a person with experience of disability.[46]

If your appeal is about whether you have LCW or LCWRA, it is usually decided by a two-person panel made up of a judge and a doctor (who is not always a mental health expert).[47]

Other appeals are usually decided by one judge on their own.

Who else will be at the hearing?

A **tribunal clerk** is likely to be present in the hearing room. Clerks have an administrative role and do not take part in the hearing.

A **presenting officer** may attend the hearing to represent the decision maker. They are there to explain the reasons for the decision, but may also provide information which helps your case. The tribunal can issue a direction requiring a presenting officer to attend the hearing – eg, if the case is considered complicated. However, presenting officers sometimes attend non-complicated appeals, so there is no need to be concerned if a presenting officer attends your hearing.

You can have a **representative** with you at the hearing (see p298).[48] You can also have another person to accompany you at the hearing without 'representing' you – eg, a **support worker, family member or friend.**[49]

How the tribunal can support you

The tribunal must consider how to help children under 18, vulnerable adults and 'sensitive witnesses' to give evidence. In practice, this includes almost anyone with a mental health problem appealing a decision about a disability benefit or about work capability.[50] The tribunal must consider letting you give evidence by phone or video, or appointing someone with special expertise to help you give evidence, or adopting a less 'robust' style of questioning.

If you need any special arrangements, you or your representative should let the tribunal know as soon as possible in advance of the hearing. The tribunal should note in its record of proceedings that it has considered how to assist you.

What happens at the hearing?

The judge decides how the hearing is conducted – there are no strict rules.[51] The tribunal's overriding objective is that your appeal is dealt with fairly and justly.[52] This includes making sure that you can participate fully.

- The judge should introduce everyone present. The judge and panel members then ask you (and the presenting officer) questions to get the information they need to make a decision. Even if you have a representative, you are usually expected to answer questions for yourself (if you have an appointee, see p326). It is the tribunal's job to help you to say everything you want by putting you at your ease and asking the right questions.
- If you do not understand a question or need to hear it again, say so.
- You can take your time answering the questions. If you think there are errors in the papers, point them out. If you forget to say something when it is your turn to speak, you can add it at the end of the hearing or when you next get the opportunity to speak.

What advisers say: answering questions

'Focus on your difficulties and what you cannot do, even if this is not your natural reaction to the questions. For so many of us it is natural to try and put a positive spin on things.'

- If your appeal is about a health-related benefit decision, the tribunal may ask you specific questions about the medical evidence, including questions about what you wrote in the questionnaire and about what you are reported as saying or doing in your assessment. Try to explain any inconsistencies between different pieces of evidence. The tribunal should not automatically accept what is said in an assessment report, and if there is an inconsistency between the report and your questionnaire, it should not assume that the report is correct without listening to what you have to say (see p250). The tribunal can adjourn the hearing if it is felt more medical evidence is needed.[53]
- In appeals about health-related benefits, it is useful to tell the tribunal whether it is seeing you on a good or bad day, and about any steps you had to go through to get to and participate in the hearing – eg, if you needed to take extra medication, or if you would not have come if a family member had not accompanied you.[54] The tribunal may observe your abilities and behaviour at the hearing and take these into account when making its decision – eg, if your appeal concerns your ability to interact socially.[55] It should not attach undue weight to its observations, and you should usually be given the opportunity to comment on them.[56]
- Sometimes, it can feel as though the panel members are trying to 'catch you out'. Their questioning can be detailed and searching because it is aimed at getting the information needed to make a decision, but the panel should ask questions in an appropriately sensitive way (see p303). If you are becoming overwhelmed or upset during a hearing, try to explain this.
- Your representative, if you have one, may be asked if they have anything to say at the beginning of the hearing and at the end. This is an opportunity for them to summarise your case and to draw out any evidence that they think the

tribunal might have missed. If there is a presenting officer at the hearing, they will be given the same opportunity.

- If a friend, family member or support worker has accompanied you, the panel may ask if they want to say anything at the end about their experience of your difficulties and about the support that they give you. If the panel does not offer this opportunity, you (or the person supporting you) can ask for it.
- The judge makes a record of the tribunal proceedings. This could be a recording of the hearing or a written record.[57] The record is kept for at least six months from the date of the tribunal's decision and you can request a copy.

Missing a hearing

If a hearing has been arranged but you do not attend, the tribunal can go ahead with the hearing if it is satisfied that you were notified of the hearing, or that reasonable steps have been taken to notify you, and it thinks that going ahead is in the interests of justice.[58] However, the tribunal should only go ahead with the hearing if it considers that it has sufficient evidence to decide the appeal fairly,[59] and it should always consider the alternative of adjourning the hearing to give you another opportunity to attend.

If you arrive late, after the tribunal has decided to proceed in your absence, it should consider letting you join in or adjourning to give you another chance to attend.[60]

If you know in advance that you are cannot attend your hearing, you can ask for a postponement (see p302).

Decision and next steps

You may be told the tribunal's decision at the hearing and given a decision notice confirming it. If not (eg, because the panel members need more time to reach a decision), the decision notice is sent to you by post. The same applies if you missed the hearing or asked for a decision to be made on the papers.

The decision notice may contain the tribunal's reasons for the decision. If it does not, you can ask for a 'statement of reasons'.[61] If you disagree with the decision, you may be able to challenge it – eg, by appealing it to the Upper Tribunal. For more information on the next steps if you are unhappy with First-tier Tribunal decision, see CPAG's *Welfare Benefits Handbook* and consider getting independent advice.

When will I get paid?

If you win your appeal, the DWP or local authority should process the tribunal's decision immediately. However, if the DWP or the local authority disagrees with the decision, it might consider appealing against it to the Upper Tribunal. In this case, you are not normally paid while it decides what to do, or (if it decides to appeal) until the Upper Tribunal has made a decision.[62] The First-tier Tribunal can also suspend the effect of a decision if *you* apply for permission to appeal to the Upper Tribunal.

Arrears of benefit ('back pay')

If your appeal leads to a benefit decision being changed, you may be eligible for arrears. This means that you are owed benefit for a period when you were entitled to get it but did not. This is often called 'back pay'. Whether you are eligible for back pay, and how much, depends on the effective date of the new decision (see p291). If you are entitled to back pay, it is usually paid in one lump sum but for some benefits it can be paid in instalments with your consent – eg, if getting a single large payment would put you at risk.[63]

Payments while challenging a decision

Universal credit

If you challenge a universal credit (UC) fit for work decision (ie, a decision that you do not have LCW), you can continue to get UC while your request for a mandatory reconsideration is being considered and while your appeal is pending. However, your award does not include a work capability component during this period, and you may have extra work-related requirements (see p270).

If it has been decided that you have LCW but you challenge the decision that you do not have LCWRA, you can continue being paid UC on the basis of having LCW, including an LCW element if applicable (see p70).

Employment and support allowance

If you appeal against a decision that you do not have LCW for employment and support allowance (ESA) and it is the first such decision you have had, or the first since a previous decision that you have LCW, then once you have appealed and you have submitted a medical certificate, you can usually get ESA until the tribunal makes its decision.[64] However, there are exceptions (see p58) – eg, in some cases where you have failed to return an ESA50 form. You are paid at the assessment rate, which includes your personal allowance and any premiums to which you are entitled.[65] **Note:** in this type of case, you can appeal a decision without going through the mandatory reconsideration process (see p294).

If you are found to have LCW for ESA but you are appealing against the decision that you do not have LCWRA, you continue getting ESA on the basis of having LCW, including an LCW element if applicable (see p56). The usual rules about the length of time you can be paid contributory ESA on the basis of LCW apply (see p54).

Other benefit decisions

While you are challenging a decision about PIP, DLA or AA, you are only usually paid what that decision says you are entitled to. For other benefit decisions, see CPAG's *Welfare Benefits Handbook*.

Example

Mia has an award of the enhanced rate of the daily living allowance of PIP. The DWP reviews her award (see p158) and decides that she is no longer eligible for PIP as she does not score enough points. Her PIP payments stop.

Mia makes a mandatory reconsideration request. She is not paid any PIP while she is waiting for a mandatory reconsideration decision.

On mandatory reconsideration, the DWP decides that Mia qualifies for the standard rate of the daily living component and revises its original decision. Mia is now paid PIP at the standard rate of the daily living component. She is also eligible for back pay (see p306).

Mia is still not happy with the decision and appeals it. She continues getting paid at the standard rate of the daily living component while waiting for a decision. The tribunal decides that she qualifies for the enhanced rate of the daily living component. Only now does she begin to be paid at this rate again. Again, she is eligible for back pay.

If your circumstances change after a decision

If your circumstances change after the date of a decision, the DWP or HMRC cannot take this into account in reconsidering that decision and a tribunal cannot take this into account when deciding an appeal against the decision.[66] In this situation, you may decide to make a new claim or ask for a supersession (see p292) while waiting for a decision on your appeal, to ensure that you get your maximum entitlement from the earliest possible date.

Note:

- The rules may be different for Scottish benefits.[67]
- Evidence about something that happens after the decision with which you disagree could still be relevant to your mandatory reconsideration request or appeal (see p248).

Example

After being found to have LCW for UC, Hana is required to take part in work-related activity. Within a short time, this leads to a deterioration in her mental health. Hana appeals the decision on her work capability and can use evidence about her symptoms getting worse *after* the decision date to show the serious risk that work-related activity posed her health *at* the decision date.

Hana can also (or alternatively) ask the DWP to assess her work capability again while she waits for the appeal to be decided, on the basis that her health has deteriorated since its last decision was made.

4. Making a complaint

Complaints about the DWP and its assessment providers

When to complain

If you are unhappy with the way your benefit claim or award has been handled by the DWP or one of its assessment providers, you can make a complaint. You can do this while challenging a decision through mandatory reconsideration and appeal, or when you have no right of appeal, or when an appeal has been unsuccessful. You might want to complain about:

- a delay;
- poor advice from the DWP;
- your work-related requirements;
- an assessment;
- how the DWP made a decision.

What you can achieve through a complaint

Complaints are often most appropriate when they are about *processes* not being followed properly. Where a *decision* is wrong, your best option is usually to challenge it by asking for a supersession, revision or appeal.

A complaint may lead to an issue being **resolved** – eg, a delayed assessment might be arranged quickly, or your work-related requirements might be changed. However, be aware that the complaints process can be slow and may be ineffective for addressing an urgent issue. See p332 for what to do in urgent cases.

When making a complaint, you can also ask for **compensation** for any financial loss which cannot be made good by a revision or supersession or by backdating your claim. For example, if you did not claim universal credit (UC) for several months because you were misled by the DWP about whether you could get it, and you could not have the benefit backdated for more than one month, you can claim compensation for lost UC income, and ask for an extra amount for lost interest on the arrears and for any extra expenses you had.

You may also receive **consolatory payments** if you are considered to have experienced injustice, hardship or distress. These payments usually range between £25 and £500.

Compensation and consolatory payments are discretionary. The DWP uses a guide, *Financial Redress for Maladministration*, to decide whether and how much you should be paid.[68]

There is also the possibility that following a successful complaint, the DWP will give you an apology, and it might take action to avoid similar mistakes being made in other cases.

How to complain

You can get support to complain, including from independent advice services or from a friend or family member. The complaints process is different for complaints against the DWP itself and for complaints against its assessment providers.

Complaining about the DWP

Start by registering your complaint with the job centre or benefit office responsible for the issue. For example, if your complaint is about how a decision was made, use the contact details on your decision letter to register your complaint, or if your complaint is about a decision made by a work coach, ask to register your complaint with them or with the manager of the job centre.

If this does not resolve the issue, ask for your complaint to go to the DWP Complaints Team. This team should make a decision on your complaint within 15 days of receiving it, or notify you if it is going to take longer. The DWP's full complaints procedure is set out at gov.uk/government/organisations/department-for-work-pensions/about/complaints-procedure.

For UC complaints, the DWP has an online complaints option: makeacomplaint.dwp.gov.uk.

Complaining about an assessment provider

To complain about how an assessment was conducted for UC, employment and support allowance or personal independence payment (PIP), you need to contact the relevant assessment provider and use its complaints procedure.

The issues you can complain about might include:

- how your assessment was conducted;
- not being offered a home or remote assessment when you requested one;
- delays in being offered an assessment appointment;
- evidence or forms that you have provided being lost.

Your appointment letter states which assessment provider was responsible for your assessment, and you can find its contact details and complaints procedure on its website (or see below). Chapter 17 has more information about assessments and assessment providers.

Assessment providers and their complaints procedures

Maximus (Health Assessment Advisory Service/Centre for Health and Disability Assessments)

Complaints procedure: haas.maximusuk.co.uk/feedback-and-complaints

Email: Lot1.Customer-relations@haas.dwp.gov.uk

Address: Customer Relations Team, Health Assessment Advisory Service, Room 4E04, Quarry House, Quarry Hill, Leeds LS2 7UA

Capita

Complaints procedure: haas.capita.co.uk/en/contact-us

Email: PIP: complaints@capita-pip.co.uk;

ESA/UC: lot2.customerrelations@haas.dwp.gov.uk

Address: PIP: PIP Complaints, PO Box 325, Darlington DL1 9P; ESA/UC: ESA Complaints, PO Box 325, Darlington DL1 9PH

Serco

Complaints procedure: haas-serco.co.uk/contact

Address: Customer Experience Team, PO Box 668, Bristol BS34 9NF

Ingeus

Complaints procedure: haas.ingeus.co.uk/contact-ingeus

Email: Lot4.CustomerRelations@haas.dwp.gov.uk

Address: Ingeus, 2nd Floor, Cavendish House, Princes Wharf, Thornaby, Stockton on Tees TS17 6QY

Next steps

Once you have completed the DWP's or assessment provider's complaints procedure, if your issue is still not resolved, you can take your case to the **Independent Case Examiner** (ICE). This is an independent body that deals with complaints about the DWP and its contractors. It can settle complaints by agreement or carry out an investigation and make recommendations on how to settle your complaint.

If you are still not happy after receiving a decision from ICE, you can ask your MP to refer your complaint to the **Parliamentary and Health Service Ombudsman**.

There are also other ways you can involve your **MP** at any stage in the complaints process – eg, by asking them to raise your case with the Secretary of State for Work and Pensions.

Complaints about HM Courts and Tribunals Service or the local authority

You can make a complaint against any government or local authority department and against anyone contracted to provide a service on its behalf. See CPAG's *Welfare Benefits Handbook* for more information.

Complaints about Social Security Scotland

You can complain if you are unhappy about the way you have been treated by SSS or how your claim has been handled. This includes issues such as delays, the behaviour of staff and bad advice.

You should complain by contacting SSS by phone (0800 182 2222; Relay UK service available; if you are a British Sign Language user, via Contact Scotland BSL), in writing (Social Security Scotland, PO Box 10304, Dundee DD1 9FZ), online at mygov.scot/complain-social-security-scotland or via webchat. You should normally make your complaint within six months of the event you are complaining about (or within six months of finding out you might have reason to complain).

SSS should attempt to resolve your complaint and, where it cannot, should provide you with a full response, normally within 20 working days. If this takes longer than this, SSS should keep you updated about how long it will take.

If you are still unhappy after your complaint has been considered by SSS, you can complain to the Scottish Public Services Ombudsman. Usually, you must contact to the Ombudsman within 12 months of the event you are complaining about. Use the online complaint form at spso.org.uk or phone 0800 377 7330.

5. Judicial review

What is judicial review

Judicial review is a form of legal challenge. It can be used in response to a decision, an action or a failure to act. It is generally a challenge to how a benefit decision has been reached, rather than to the decision itself. You can apply for judicial review of any decision of a public nature, which includes benefit decisions made by the DWP, Social Security Scotland or a local authority.

To apply for judicial review, you must have specific grounds. The main grounds are when there has been:

- failure to follow the law; *or*
- failure to make a decision or to make a decision within a reasonable time; *or*
- failure to exercise discretion; *or*
- failure to take into account relevant evidence, or taking irrelevant evidence into account; *or*
- failure to make enquiries; *or*
- failure to follow guidance, or applying unlawful guidance; *or*
- discrimination and breach of human rights; *or*
- irrationality.

Judicial review is a 'remedy of last resort' and usually only available when you do not have an alternative – eg, a right of appeal. It might also be appropriate if you have an alternative remedy which is not 'effective and appropriate'[69] – eg, you have a right of appeal but you will not get a tribunal decision for an unreasonably long time.

Time limits for judicial review

Most judicial review proceedings must be started within three months of the decision you want to challenge.[70]

Sending a letter before action

In England and Wales, before applying for judicial review, you must send a letter before action. This warns the decision maker that you are considering judicial review and contains details of the matter being challenged.[71] You should get a response to a letter before action within 14 days. Where you have a good case, a letter before action will often resolve the problem without you going to court.

It is free to send a letter before action. You do not need a solicitor to help you, but you should get assistance from a welfare rights adviser. There are several template letters before action available by contacting the CPAG judicial review project at jrproject@cpag.org.uk.

In Scotland, this requirement does not apply, but it is still good practice to avoid going to court, and sending a letter before action can achieve this result.

Example

Mark claims universal credit (UC) online. Due to his mental health symptoms, he immediately finds it difficult to keep on top of his online journal and to-do list. He asks his work coach to contact him using letters and phone calls instead, but his work coach says this is not possible. Mark asks to speak to the job centre manager but gets the same response. This refusal causes stress and worsens his mental health. He gets advice and is told that these staff members are not following the DWP's own policies. The adviser adapts a CPAG template letter before action (see p77) and sends it to the DWP's legal team on Mark's behalf. Within 14 days, the DWP responds and resolves the issue in Mark's favour.

Judicial review in the High Court or Court of Session

Always get advice if you are considering going beyond the pre-action letter stage and starting a claim for judicial review. You are unlikely to be successful without the help of a solicitor or welfare rights adviser and there are costs involved. There is more information about judicial review in CPAG's *Welfare Benefits Handbook* and at cpag.org.uk/jr.

6. Getting a Social Security Scotland determination changed

Note: this section covers the rules that apply to Scottish disability benefits – adult disability payment (ADP) (see Chapter 9), child disability payment (CDP) (see

Chapter 11), Scottish adult disability living allowance (SADLA) (see p169) and pension age disability payment (PADP) (see Chapter 13) – which are administered by Social Security Scotland (SSS). It does not apply to the other benefits you can claim while living in Scotland.

Redetermination

If you claim a Scottish benefit correctly and provide any required evidence, SSS makes a 'determination' of your entitlement.[72] In some situations, SSS must also make a 'determination without application' – ie, a new decision on your entitlement which does not follow your making a new benefit claim (see p314).

If you disagree with a determination, you can challenge it by requesting a redetermination.[73] You must request a redetermination before you can appeal.

Note:

- If you request a redetermination, every aspect of the previous determination is considered again. If you have been awarded some benefit, the amount of it could be reduced as a result. Get advice if you have been awarded some benefit and are thinking of requesting a redetermination.
- If SSS has not made a determination, you cannot request a redetermination.[74] Your only options are to complain (see p310) or apply for judicial review (see p311).

Process decisions and appeals

A 'process decision' is a type of decision made by SSS when your claim or redetermination request does not meet specific procedural requirements – eg, you do not complete Part 2 of your claim, or you request a redetermination late, and SSS does not accept that you had a good reason. If a process decision is made, it means SSS has *not* determined or redetermined your benefit claim, usually due to how or when the request was made.

When challenging a process decision, some of the appeal rules are different – eg, you do not have to request a redetermination before appealing.[75] You can appeal directly to the First-tier Tribunal for Scotland at socialsecuritychamber.scot/home/your-appeal/a-process-appeal. If your claim was not determined, you should also claim again.

How to request a redetermination

Check your determination notice carefully to see how to request a redetermination. Usually, you can do this by:

- completing the form which is sent to you with the determination of entitlement; *or*
- online at mygov.scot/disagree-decision/request-redetermination-or-appeal; *or*
- calling 0800 182 2222; *or*
- if you have hearing or speech difficulties, using Relay UK (18001 then 0300 244 4000); *or*

- if you use British Sigh Language, via Contact Scotland BSL.

It is usually best to make your request in writing so that there is a clear record of what you have said and when. See p295 for points to consider when asking for a redetermination.

Time limits

Time limit for requesting a redetermination

Your request for a redetermination must be received by SSS within 42 days of you being notified of the determination.[76] You are normally treated as being notified of the determination two days after it is sent to you.

If you miss the time limit but your redetermination request is received within one year after you were notified of the determination, your entitlement is still redetermined if you have 'good reason' for not making the request sooner.

Time limit for SSS to make a redetermination

Once you have made a valid request for a redetermination, SSS must redetermine your entitlement within 56 calendar days.[77] The time limit normally runs from the day SSS receives your redetermination request, but there are exceptions. If your entitlement is not redetermined within the time limit, you must be informed of this. You then have the right to appeal to the First-tier Tribunal against the original determination (see p315) and, if you choose to, you should do this within 31 days.[78]

Determination without application

'Determinations without application' are similar to certain types of revision decisions and all supersession decisions for other benefits (see p291). If you are entitled to a Scottish disability benefit, a new determination of your entitlement is made if:[79]

- the award is reviewed at the end of the period specified in your previous determination; *or*
- your award was too low due to an official error; *or*
- there is a change in your circumstances that may affect your award; *or*
- your award was too high due to an 'error'; *or*
- the previous determination was made in ignorance of a 'material fact'; *or*
- the amount of DWP benefit you were entitled to before your award began changes.

If you think that one of these situations applies, you can contact SSS and ask for a determination. If SSS makes a determination you do not agree with, you can follow the redetermination process (see p313). If SSS does not make a determination, your only options are to complain (see p310) or apply for judicial review (see p311).

Note: there are complicated rules about the date from which a new determination takes effect. See CPAG's *Welfare Benefits Handbook*.

Appeals

You can only appeal against a determination of entitlement to a Scottish disability benefit after requesting a redetermination (see p313). Appeals are decided by the Social Security Chamber of the First-tier Tribunal for Scotland, part of the Scottish Courts and Tribunals Service. The powers of the First-tier Tribunal, the way that hearings take place, and the steps you should take to try to win your appeal are similar to those for appeals about other benefits, although there are some differences. CPAG's *Welfare Benefits Handbook* has more information.

How to make an appeal

You must appeal in the way required by SSS. An appeal form is sent to you with your redetermination notice or notice that the redetermination time limit has been missed.[80] You must send the completed form to SSS. SSS also currently allows an appeal to be submitted by phone (0800 182 2222). If you have hearing or speech difficulties, you can submit an appeal via Relay UK (18001 and then 0300 244 4000) or, if you use British Sign Language, via Contact Scotland BSL. If you have an appointee, see p326.

Time limits

Time limit for making an appeal

Your appeal must be received by SSS within 31 days of you being notified of the redetermination (or of the redetermination time limit being missed by SSS). You are normally treated as receiving a notification two days after it was sent. If you miss this time limit, but your appeal is received within one year after you were notified of the redetermination (or the redetermination time limit was missed), it can still be admitted. If your appeal is late, you must explain why.

Time limit for SSS to respond to the appeal

Once the First-tier Tribunal decides that your appeal is valid, it informs you and SSS of this in writing. SSS then has 31 days to produce a response to the appeal and send it to the tribunal.[81]

Time limit for the appellant to respond to SSS

You (or your representative) can make written comments or submit evidence in reply to the SSS response. You must do so within 31 days of receiving it. You are treated as receiving the response two days after it was sent.[82]

The appeal hearing

The rules about hearings for Scottish benefits are similar to those for other benefits (see p301).[83] If your appeal is about the impact of a 'physical condition or mental health' on entitlement to a disability benefit, the First-tier Tribunal consists of a legal member, a doctor and a disability expert. In other cases, there is only a legal member.[84]

After an appeal

See CPAG's *Welfare Benefits Handbook* for what to do if you disagree with a First-tier Tribunal decision.

Payments while awaiting a redetermination or appeal

If you are challenging a determination to reduce or stop your entitlement to a Scottish disability benefit, you may be able to claim short-term assistance. This is a temporary payment to help you maintain financial stability while you challenge the decision. The amount of short-term assistance is usually the difference between your payment before the determination that is under review, and your current payment (if any).[85] You apply for short-term assistance by ticking the relevant box on your redeterermination or appeal form, or by calling the SSS helpline.

Note: short-term assistance does not allow someone who cares for you to get carer support payment, the carer element of universal credit or a young carer grant, or increase your entitlement to means-tested benefits in the way that ADP, CDP, SADLA and PADP do. The Scottish government says that if you claim short-term assistance, you or your carer should still be able to later get the relevant benefits/elements/premiums if your challenge is successful. Get advice before claiming short-term assistance if you think that this may affect you.

Notes

1. **General rules about revision and supersession**

1 **HB** Sch 7 para 3 CSPSSA 2000
Other DWP benefits s9 SSA 1998

2 **UC/PIP/new-style ESA** Reg 21 UC,PIP,JSA&ESA(DA) Regs
HB Sch 7 para 3(3) CSPSSA 2000; reg 6 HB&CTB(DA) Regs
Other DWP benefits s9(3) SSA 1998; reg 5(1) SS&CS(DA) Regs

3 **HB** Regs 2, 4(1)(a) and (4) and 5(3)-(6) HB&CTB(DA) Regs
UC/PIP/new-style ESA Regs 2, 3(2), 5(1)(b) and 6 UC,PIP,JSA&ESA(DA) Regs
Other DWP benefits Regs 1(3), 2(b), 3(1)(b) and 4 SS&CS(DA) Regs

4 **UC/PIP/new-style ESA** Reg 5(2)(a) UC,PIP,JSA&ESA(DA) Regs
HB Reg 4(10) HB&CTB(DA) Regs
Other DWP benefits Reg 3(9)(a) SS&CS(DA) Regs

5 **UC/PIP/new-style ESA** Regs 2, 8 and 9(a) UC,PIP,JSA&ESA(DA) Regs
HB Regs 1(2) and 4(2)(a) HB&CTB(DA) Regs
Other DWP benefits Regs 1(3) and 3(5)(a) SS&CS(DA) Regs
6 **UC/new-style JSA&ESA** Reg 14(1)(a)-(c) UC,PIP,JSA&ESA(DA) Regs
Other DWP benefits Reg 3(5C), (6), (6A) and (7CD) SS&CS(DA) Regs
7 **UC/PIP/new-style ESA** Regs 8 and 12 UC,PIP,JSA&ESA(DA) Regs
HB Reg 4(7B) HB&CTB(DA) Regs
Other DWP benefits Reg 3(7) and (7ZA) SS&CS(DA) Regs
8 **UC/PIP/new-style ESA** Regs 8 and 11(1)-(2) UC,PIP,JSA&ESA(DA) Regs
HB Reg 4(1)(c) and (7) HB&CTB(DA) Regs
Other DWP benefits Reg 3(4A) and (5A) SS&CS(DA) Regs
9 **UC/PIP/new-style ESA** Regs 8 and 9(b) UC,PIP,JSA&ESA(DA) Regs
HB Reg 4(2)(b) HB&CTB(DA) Regs
Other DWP benefits Regs 3(5)(b)-(d) and 7A(1) SS&CS(DA) Regs
10 **HB** Sch 7 para 4 CSPSSA 2000
Other benefits s10 SSA 1998
11 **UC/PIP/new-style ESA** Reg 32 UC,PIP,JSA&ESA(DA) Regs
HB Reg 7(4) HB&CTB(DA) Regs
Other DWP benefits Reg 6(3) SS&CS(DA) Regs
12 **UC/PIP/new-style ESA** Reg 23 UC,PIP,JSA&ESA(DA) Regs
HB Regs 7(2)(a) and 7A(4) HB&CTB(DA) Regs
Other DWP benefits Reg 6(2)(a) SS&CS(DA) Regs; Sch 2 para 25A(2) ESA(TP)(EA)(No.2) Regs
All *Wood v SSWP* [2003] EWCA Civ 53, reported as R(DLA) 1/03
13 Reg 26(1) UC,PIP,JSA&ESA(DA) Regs; regs 6(2)(r) and 7A(1) SS&CS(DA) Regs; CIB/4033/2003; R(IB) 2/05
14 s80(5) and (6) WRA 2012; regs 8 and 9 SS(PIP) Regs; reg 26(2) UC,PIP,JSA&ESA(DA) Regs; *KB v SSWP (PIP)* [2016] UKUT 537 (AAC)
15 **UC/PIP/new-style ESA** Regs 24 and 31(a) UC,PIP,JSA&ESA(DA) Regs
HB Regs 4(1)(b) and 7(2)(b) and (d) HB&CTB(DA) Regs
Other DWP benefits Reg 6(2)(b) and (c) SS&CS(DA) Regs
16 **UC/PIP/new-style ESA** Reg 24 UC,PIP,JSA&ESA(DA) Regs
HB Reg 7(2)(b) HB&CTB(DA) Regs
Other DWP benefits Reg 6(2)(b) SS&CS(DA) Regs
17 **UC/PIP/new-styleESA** Reg 23 UC,PIP,JSA&ESA(DA) Regs. For these benefits, although this counts as a change of circumstances, it takes effect differently to most such changes.
HB Reg 7(2)(i) HB&CTB(DA) Regs
Other DWP benefits Reg 6(2)(e) and (ee) SS&CS(DA) Regs
18 **UC/PIP/new-style ESA** Sch 1 UC,PIP,JSA&ESA(DA) Regs
HB Sch 7 para 4(5) CSPSSA 2000
Other DWP benefits s10(5) SSA 1998
19 **UC/new-style ESA** Regs 12 and 23 and Sch 1 para 31 UC,PIP,JSA&ESA(DA) Regs
IS/old-style ESA/PC Regs 3(7), 6(2)(e) and 7(7) SS&CS(DA) Regs
HB Regs 4(7B) and (7C), 7(2)(i) and 8(14) HB&CTB(DA) Regs; CIS/1178/2001
All *BB v SSWP (ESA)* [2017] UKUT 280 (AAC)
20 Regs 4(8), 5(2) and 7(7) HB&CTB(DA) Regs

2. **Mandatory reconsideration**
21 *R (Connor) v SSWP* [2020] EWHC 1999 (Admin)
22 s12 SSA 1998; reg 3ZA SS&CS(DA) Regs; reg 7 UC,PIP,JSA&ESA(DA) Regs; *PP v SSWP (UC)* [2020] UKUT 109 (AAC)
23 Form CRMR1, at gov.uk/government/publications/challenge-a-decision-made-by-the-department-for-work-and-pensions-dwp

3. **Appeals**
24 House of Commons, *Hansard*, Written question UIN 174427, answered 4 April 2023, at questions-statements.parliament.uk
25 *MC and JH v SSWP (ESA)* [2014] UKUT 125 (AAC), reported as [2014] AACR 35
26 **UC/PIP/new-style ESA** Sch 2 SSA 1998; reg 50(2) and Sch 3 UC,PIP,JSA&ESA(DA) Regs
HB Sch 7 para 6(2) CSPSSA 2000; reg 16 and Sch HB&CTB(DA) Regs
Other DWP benefits Sch 2 SSA 1998; reg 27 and Sch 2 SS&CS(DA) Regs

27 **UC/PIP/new-style ESA** Regs 10 and 25 UC,PIP,JSA&ESA(DA) Regs
HB Regs 4(6) and 7(2)(e) HB&CTB(DA) Regs
Other DWP benefits Regs 3(8) and 6(2)(d) SS&CS(DA) Regs
28 r11 TP(FT) Rules; r11 TP(UT) Rules; CIB/1009/2004; CIB/2058/2004
29 r11(2) TP(FT) Rules; r11(2) TP(UT) Rules
30 r11(6)(a) TP(FT) Rules; r11(4)(a) TP(UT) Rules; *MP v SSWP (DLA)* [2010] UKUT 103 (AAC)
31 r11(7) and (8) TP(FT) Rules; r11(5) and (6) TP(UT) Rules
32 r22(2)(d)(i) TP(FT) Rules
33 **HB** r23(2)(a)(i) and (ii) TP(FT) Rules
Other DWP benefits r22(2)(d)(ii) and Sch 1 para 5(a) and (b) TP(FT) Rules
All r12 TP(FT) Rules
34 rr22(8) and 23(5) and (8) TP(FT) Rules
35 *Adesina v NMC* [2013] EWCA Civ 818; *KD v SSWP* [2021] UKUT 329 (AAC); *MZ v SSWP (UC)* [2022] UKUT 292 (AAC)
36 r24(1A) and (1)(c) TP(FT) Rules; Art 6 European Convention on Human Rights; s6 HRA 1998; CH/3497/2005; *MB v Wychavon DC* [2013] UKUT 67 (AAC); Local Government Ombudsman, Complaint 01/C/13400 against Scarborough BC
37 r24(5) TP(FT) Rules
38 *LH v SSWP (PIP)* [2018] UKUT 57 (AAC); *TM v SSWP (PIP)* [2019] UKUT 204 (AAC); *BF v SSWP (PIP)* [2020] UKUT 300 (AAC)
39 r24(4) TP(FT) Rules; *ST v SSWP (ESA)* [2012] UKUT 469 (AAC); *FN v SSWP (ESA)* [2015] UKUT 670 (AAC), reported as [2016] AACR 24; *FI v HMRC* [2018] UKUT 226 (AAC)
40 rr5(3)(a) and 24(6) and (7) TP(FT) Rules
41 r1(3) TP(FT) Rules
42 r21 TP(FT) Rules
43 r1 TP(FT) Rules, definition of 'hearing'
44 r29 TP(FT) Rules
45 r5(3)(h) TP(FT) Rules; r5(3)(h) TP(UT) Rules; *MA v SSWP* [2009] UKUT 211 (AAC); Practice Statement, *Composition of Tribunals in Social Security and Child Support Cases in the Social Entitlement Chamber on or after 1 August 2013*, 31 July 2013, para 10
46 r2 The First-tier Tribunal and Upper Tribunal (Composition of Tribunal) Order 2008 No.2835; Practice Statement, *Composition of Tribunals in Social Security and Child Support Cases in the Social Entitlement Chamber on or after 1 August 2013*, 31 July 2013
47 *CH v SSWP (ESA)* [2017] UKUT 6 (AAC)
48 r11 TP(FT) Rules; CIB/1009/2004; CIB/2058/2004
49 r11(7) and (8) TP(FT) Rules
50 Practice Direction, *Child, Vulnerable Adult and Sensitive Witnesses*, 30 October 2008; *SW v SSWP (DLA)* [2015] UKUT 319 (AAC); *LO'L v SSWP (ESA)* [2016] UKUT 10 (AAC), reported as [2016] AACR 31; *RT v SSWP (PIP)* [2019] UKUT 207 (AAC), reported as [2020] AACR 4; *JE v SSWP (PIP)* [2020] UKUT 17 (AAC). Cases like *GJ v SSWP (PIP)* [2022] UKUT 349 (AAC) highlight the limitations of this.
51 Practice Statement, *Composition of Tribunals in Social Security and Child Support Cases in the Social Entitlement Chamber on or after 1 August 2013*, 31 July 2013, para 12
52 r2 TP(FT) Rules
53 *MA v SSWP (PIP)* [2017] UKUT 351 (AAC)
54 R(DLA) 8/06
55 r25(2) TP(FT) Rules
56 R(DLA) 1/95, qualified by CM/2/1994; *GL v SSWP* [2008] UKUT 36 (AAC); *ID v SSWP (PIP)* [2015] UKUT 692 (AAC); *KMN v SSWP (PIP)* [2019] UKUT 42 (AAC)
57 Practice Statement, *Record of Proceedings in Social Security and Child Support Cases in the Social Entitlement Chamber on or after* 31st March 2022, 31 March 2022; *MK v SSWP (CI)* [2014] UKUT 323 (AAC)
58 r31 TP(FT) Rules; *WT v SSWP (DLA)* [2011] UKUT 93 (AAC); *PS v SSWP (ESA)* [2017] UKUT 55 (AAC); *KD v SSWP (ESA and IS) and KD and HMRC (TC)* [2020] UKUT 9 (AAC)
59 *LR v SSWP (ESA)* [2017] UKUT 412 (AAC)
60 *AK v HMRC (TC)* [2016] UKUT 98 (AAC)
61 r34(2) and (3) TP(FT) Rules; CCS/1664/2001
62 **UC/PIP/new-style ESA** s21 SSA 1998; reg 44 UC,PIP,JSA&ESA(DA) Regs
HB Sch 7 para 13 CSPSSA 2000; reg 11 HB&CTB(DA) Regs
Other DWP benefits s21 SSA 1998; reg 16 SS&CS(DA) Regs
All r5(3)(l) TP(FT) Rules

63 Reg 21ZA SS(C&P) Regs
64 Reg 30(1) and (3) ESA Regs; reg 26(1) and (3) ESA Regs 2013
65 Reg 5(4) ESA Regs; reg 6(5) ESA Regs 2013 provides that the assessment phase applies, pending the First-tier Tribunal's decision
66 **HB** Sch 7 para 6(9)(b) CSPSSA 2000
Other DWP benefits s12(8)(b) SSA 1998; R(DLA) 4/05
67 SS(S)A 2018 contains no provision equivalent to ss8(2)(b) and 12(8)(b) SSA 1998

4. **Making a complaint**
68 gov.uk/government/publications/compensation-for-poor-service-a-guide-for-dwp-staff

5. **Judicial review**
69 *Glencore Energy UK Limited v Commissioners of HMRC* [2017] EWHC 1476 (Admin), para 42
70 **England and Wales** r54.5(1) and 54.7A(3) CPR
Scotland s27A Court of Session Act 1988
71 gov.uk/guidance/pre-action-protocol-for-judicial-review

6. **Getting a Social Security Scotland determination changed**
72 ss37 and 40 SS(S)A 2018
73 s41 SS(S)A 2018
74 s41(1) SS(S)A 2018
75 s61 SS(S)A 2018;
76 **ADP** Reg 54(1) DAWAP(S) Regs
CDP Reg 37(1) DACYP(S) Regs
PADP Reg 46(1) DAOP(S) Regs
SADLA Reg 49(1) DA(SADLA) Regs
77 **ADP** Reg 54(2) DAWAP(S) Regs
CDP Reg 37(2) DACYP(S) Regs
PADP Reg 46(2) DAOP(S) Regs
SADLA Reg 49(2) DA(SADLA) Regs
78 ss43(3) and 46 SS(S)A 2018
79 **ADP** Regs 45-50 53 DAWAP(S) Regs
CDP Regs 28-33 DACYP(S) Regs
PADP Regs 37-42 DAOP(S) Regs
SADLA Regs 40-45 DA(SADLA) Regs
80 ss44(1)(b), 45(1)(b) and 47 SS(S)A 2018
81 r21(1)-(4) FTTSSSC(P) Rules
82 rr1(2) and 21(6) and (7) FTTSSSC(P) Rules
83 rr23-27 FTTSSSC(P) Rules
84 Regs 2-3 First-tier Tribunal for Scotland Social Security Chamber and Upper Tribunal for Scotland (Composition) Regulations 2018 No.351
85 **All** s36 and Sch 10 SS(S)A 2018
ADP Sch 2 Part 1 DAWAP(S) Regs
CDP Sch Part 1 DACYP(S) Regs
PADP Sch Part 1 DAOP(S) Regs
SADLA Sch 1 Part 1 DA(SADLA) Regs

Chapter 21

Support, escalation and third parties

This chapter covers:

Key facts

- You can give permission for someone (eg, an adviser or family member) to deal with benefit agencies or the tribunal on your behalf. This person is sometimes known as a 'third-party representative'.
- A third-party representative must show that they have your consent to act on your behalf. There are different consent rules for different benefits.
- If you cannot manage your benefits at all, someone else can become your 'appointee'. This person takes on all your rights and responsibilities in respect of your benefits. This is a greater commitment than being a third-party representative.
- There is extra support within the benefits system that you should be offered if you need it – eg, reasonable adjustments and recognition for complex needs.
- You should be able to escalate an urgent benefit issue to someone more senior if it is not getting resolved.

1. Representatives and consent

You can give permission for someone (eg, an adviser or family member) to deal with benefit agencies or the tribunal on your behalf. This person is sometimes known as a 'third-party representative' or an 'intermediary'.

Giving consent is not always straightforward because public bodies have data protection duties and are cautious about discussing your personal details with anyone who is not you. There are different rules on consent for different benefits.

Consent rules

Universal credit

To deal with the universal credit (UC) division of the DWP on someone else's behalf, you need that person's **explicit consent**.[1] This means that the person needs to tell the UC division who you are and what you have permission to discuss on their behalf. They can do this:

- in a message on their online journal;
- by post using an authority form (see p324);
- by phone;
- in person – eg, at a job centre appointment.

They should specify your name, organisation (if relevant) and contact details, and what you have their permission to do. They should also try to specify what information you need from the DWP and why.

Explicit consent is usually time limited. It lasts until a specific issue is resolved or, when this does not apply, until the end of the following assessment period. If you are supporting someone long term, you might need to renew explicit consent regularly – eg, with monthly journal notes.

There is no equivalent of implicit consent (see below) for calls to the UC helpline.

Other DWP benefits

The following rules apply to DWP-administered benefits other than UC – eg, personal independence payment (PIP) and employment and support allowance (ESA).

If you are writing a letter to the DWP on behalf of someone you are supporting, attach an authority form (see p324) and ask to receive a copy of any response to the letter.

If you are calling a benefit helpline and the person you are supporting is not with you, you have two options. If you have already written to the DWP (about that benefit) with an authority form, you can ask the call handler to find this on file and speak to you on this basis. Otherwise, start the call by explaining that you would like to discuss the claim under **implicit consent** (also known as an '**alternative enquiry**').

For this option, you should be asked a series of questions about the person you are supporting and their benefit(s). If you answer enough of these questions correctly, you can then discuss details of the claim. However, even if you answer enough questions correctly, the call handler has some discretion about which details to share with you.

Examples of questions for implicit consent

National insurance number
Date of birth

Full address (including postcode)
Date of last payment
Which other benefits does this person get?
Which bank is their benefit paid into?

If a call handler refuses to accept implicit consent, you can ask to add the person you are supporting to the call through a conference calling or call merge facility so that they can confirm you have their permission to proceed.

You cannot usually, as a third party, report a change of circumstances on behalf of the person you are supporting (eg, a change of address or a deterioration in health) unless the person you are supporting is also on the call and gives verbal consent first.

What the DWP says: non-UC benefits[2]

'Customers have the right to ask a representative to help them conduct their business with the [DWP] and it is important that the DWP balances this with our duty to protect the personal information we hold. (...)

'Where there is no valid written authority, or the customer is not present to confirm permission verbally, (...) staff must ask questions and use judgement based on the answers in order to determine whether or not the caller is a genuine representative, and alternative enquiry can be assumed. (...)

'The information we can disclose to a representative must be limited, current, and focused to the relevant enquiry. (...) For example: information about the progress of the claim; how benefit or payment has been calculated; how a particular payment is made up; rates of specific benefits in payment; why a particular benefit, premium or allowance has been allowed or disallowed; what factors have been taken into account in reaching a decision; [and] what future action is likely to be taken on the claim. (...)

'Where written authority is held, all possible steps should be taken to inform the representative at the same time as the customer is informed.'

Social Security Scotland benefits

Adult disability payment (ADP), Scottish adult disability living allowance (SADLA), pension age disability payment (PADP) and child disability payment (CDP) are administered by Social Security Scotland (SSS).

If you need to discuss someone else's ADP, SADLA, PADP or CDP with SSS, that person generally needs to give explicit consent first. This can be done by phone or by post using an authority form. SSS has its own preferred authority form which you can download at mygov.scot/third-party-authorisation-form. Alternatively, you can use another authority form (see p324) but it must clearly state that it applies to SSS benefits. If you are supporting someone long term, you may need to update this consent regularly.

In the future, it might be possible to use implicit consent (see p321) in some cases.[3]

What Social Security Scotland says[4]

'A third party representative can:

- support a person in making an application
- ask how an application is going
- make phone calls
- receive copies of Social Security Scotland notifications
- ask for an explanation of a person's entitlement and how it was decided
- help with a redetermination or appeal'

Housing benefit

If you write to the local authority about someone else's housing benefit (HB), you need to attach an authority form (see p324). Although not essential, it can be worth asking whether your local authority has a preferred authority form template and whether you can send the form by email instead of post if this will save time.

If you want to discuss someone else's HB by phone, it is likely that you will need to send written consent in advance or have the person you are supporting with you on the call. Alternatively, you might be able to discuss the HB in person at a local authority office. The person you are supporting must usually be present or you must have their written authority.

The tribunal

HM Courts and Tribunals Service

Most benefit appeals are dealt with by HM Courts and Tribunals Service (HMCTS) – but see below for Scottish benefit appeals. You can be added as a representative when the person you are supporting is making their appeal. They should provide your details in the representative section of the appeal form. You can also be added as a representative later in the appeal process. Make this request in writing by email or post, attaching an authority form (see p324). When you are a representative in someone's appeal, you should be sent copies of all the correspondence that they receive.[5]

See p297 for more information about HMCTS and appeals.

Scottish Courts and Tribunals Service

The Scottish Courts and Tribunals Service (SCTS) deals with appeals about ADP, SADLA, PADP and CDP. The person you are supporting can notify SCTS at any stage in the appeal process that you are supporting them as a representative. You should then be sent copies of all correspondence that they receive. **Note:** the SCTS rules do not explicitly allow you to make an appeal on someone else's behalf, so the person you are supporting should always sign their own appeal form.[6]

See p315 for more information about SCTS and appeals.

The NHS (for medical evidence)

You can request medical evidence from the NHS on behalf of the person you are supporting. You need that person's written consent – ie, an authority form.[7] Chapter 16 has more information about requesting medical evidence.

Producing an authority form

An authority form is a short written statement confirming that you agree to someone else acting on your behalf in relation to your benefits.

It should contain your full name, date of birth, national insurance (NI) number and address. It should state clearly the name of the person whom you authorise to act on your behalf and spell out what you agree for them to do – eg, 'act on my behalf in all benefit matters'; 'discuss my personal independence payment with the DWP and contact the NHS to request medical evidence on my behalf'; 'write to my local authority about my housing benefit'. It must be signed and dated.

Most advice organisations have their own templates.

Example authority form

I, ... (name, date of birth, NI number)

of .... (address)

authorise the disclosure of information to .... (name, role/relationship, and where relevant organisation)

by the DWP, local authorities and HMCTS in relation to all benefit matters including benefit appeals and by the NHS in respect of my medical records.

I authorise this person/organisation to act on my behalf in relation to all benefit matters including benefit appeals and in making a subject access request to any public body.

Signed: ....

Dated: ....

Note: for UC, you might need to include more detail about which information you want the DWP to disclose and why it is needed, to ensure that an authority form satisfies the DWP's explicit consent rules (see p321).

An authority form might not be accepted if it is considered too old. If you are being supported by someone long term, it can be a good idea to sign a new form every three or six months (or monthly for UC). You can withdraw consent at any time by contacting the relevant benefit department or NHS team by phone or in writing.

2. Appointeeship

If you cannot claim or manage benefits for yourself (eg, because of a severe mental health problem), someone else can be authorised to act on your behalf.[8] This person is called an 'appointee'. The support they give you goes further than the support you can get from a third-party representative; the appointee takes on all of your rights and responsibilities as a claimant, including receiving payments.

An appointee can be, for example, a family member, friend, solicitor or representative of your local authority. **Note:** if someone is already legally appointed to take care of your finances (eg, a deputy or someone who has lasting power of attorney), you are unlikely to need an appointee.

DWP benefits

For DWP benefits, an appointee must be over 18. To apply, the potential appointee should contact the helpline for the relevant benefit. The DWP arranges for someone to visit and assess whether an appointee is needed, and to make sure the proposed appointee is suitable. The application form (Form BF56) can be completed by the visiting officer during the assessment. If the DWP agrees with the application, it sends Form BF57 to the appointee, confirming their appointment.

The appointeeship continues until you are clearly able to manage your affairs or the appointee no longer wishes, or is no longer able, to act for you. It can also be stopped if the appointee is not acting properly.[9] If you want an appointeeship ended, contact the relevant benefit department using its helpline or by post.

Appointeeship and assessments

If you have an appointee, they should be the one contacted by an assessment provider if you are required to take part in an assessment (see Chapter 17). However, the appointee cannot simply attend on your behalf. You also need to be there and the expectation is that you answer the questions yourself. If this is not appropriate in the circumstances, your appointee should ask that your claim be decided without the need for an assessment (see p256). **Note:** you must never be assessed on your own if you have an appointee.[10]

Social Security Scotland benefits

If you are 16 or over, you can have an appointee (who must also be 16 or over) if you are incapable within the meaning of the Adults with Incapacity (Scotland) Act 2000, with no guardian acting or appointed under that Act and no other person who has the power to act on your behalf and is willing to do so. In future, you may be able to have an appointee if you are not legally 'incapable' but you have agreed to the appointeeship.

For child disability payment (CDP), a person aged 16 or over can only act as an appointee if there is no adult who lives with, and has responsibility for, the child and is willing to act on their behalf. So, in most cases, a parent or guardian would act on the child's behalf and would not need to be made an appointee unless unusual circumstances apply.

An appointeeship may be ended at any time by Social Security Scotland. A request can be made to end an appointeeship by the child or adult it concerns, by another person with an interest in their welfare or financial affairs, or (for CDP) by someone with parental responsibility.[11]

Housing benefit

If no one has been formally appointed to look after your affairs (eg, as a deputy), the local authority can make someone aged over 18 your appointee. This person can write to the local authority to ask to be your appointee.

An appointee can resign after giving four weeks' notice. The local authority may also end their appointeeship at any time. If someone is given a formal legal appointment, that person automatically takes over from the person appointed by the local authority.[12]

The tribunal

An appointee can submit a benefit appeal and discuss it with HM Courts and Tribunals Service or the Scottish Courts and Tribunals Service on your behalf.[13] If you have an appointee, it may not be appropriate for you to be required to attend an appeal hearing or give evidence.[14] Your appointee can participate in a hearing and their evidence will be weighed like any other evidence (see p250). You can attend your appeal hearing if you want to. Chapter 20 has more information about appeal hearings.

3. Support within the benefits system

If you need support to claim or manage benefits, you may be able to get it from friends or family, charities, your local authority or other organisations. See advicelocal.uk as a starting point to find out what help is available.

There is also support you should be offered *within* the benefits system – ie, extra support from the DWP and the other public bodies that pay benefits.

Complex needs guidance

'Complex needs' is a term often used by the DWP, and sometimes by other agencies, to describe additional support needs – eg, as the result of a mental health problem, another health issue or disability, domestic abuse, a life event such as bereavement, or sometimes due to factors like age or parenthood.

This term can be frustrating because often we feel our needs are not complex at all, but are simply not being noticed, listened to or understood. Another term used often is 'vulnerability', which has its own problems as a catch-all term.

The DWP and other benefit agencies have internal guidance about recognising complex needs/vulnerability and offering the appropriate support. This guidance often tells staff to offer reasonable adjustments (see p328) and to consider whether someone has good reason for failing to meet certain requirements – eg, see p83 for universal credit (UC) and employment and support allowance (ESA), and p155 for personal independence payment (PIP). There is also DWP guidance about carrying out home visits in certain circumstances before stopping your payments (see p329).

In practice, it is clear that complex needs are not always recognised or acted on appropriately. Much is left to the discretion of individual work coaches and decision makers who might lack the time, knowledge or confidence to take the right steps.

What the DWP says: complex needs

For UC: 'When a claimant with complex needs contacts DWP, their customer journey must be equal in quality and outcome to those whose needs are not complex.'[15]

For PIP: 'In the PIP journey, [some] claimants are considered to require additional support from DWP and elements of the PIP claims process have been adapted to provide further support for this group.'[16]

For PIP assessments: '[Healthcare professionals should] consider the needs of vulnerable claimants. A vulnerable claimant is defined as "someone who has difficulty in dealing with procedural demands at the time when they need to access a service".'[17]

Communicating complex needs

You have probably told the DWP, Social Security Scotland (SSS) or the local authority quite a lot about your diagnosis or symptoms, but this does not guarantee that they understand what support you need to claim benefits. For example, mentioning your mental health problem when claiming UC does not mean that your work coach automatically understands the arrangements you need for job centre appointments. You may therefore decide to send a clear 'alert' to the DWP or other benefit agency, clearly stating how your condition affects your ability to cope with the benefits system and the additional support you might need while claiming benefits. It is often best to do this in writing – eg, in a short letter or on your UC journal. You can do this at any point. Some advice agencies have a template that you can use.

Complex needs markers

Once you have told a benefit agency about your complex needs, it should record this information appropriately and use it to give you consistent support.

For UC, DWP staff should record information about complex needs in the profile notes within your UC records. DWP staff viewing your file should routinely check this section.[18]

Guidance also suggests that a mental health flag can be used on the DWP's medical services referral system, the portal between the DWP and assessment providers for **UC and ESA assessments.**[19]

For **PIP**, the DWP can add an 'additional support marker' to your records if you have a mental health problem. This should then be considered throughout the PIP claim process and throughout your PIP award. It should also be taken into account by assessment providers.[20]

Reasonable adjustments

Under the Equality Act 2010,[21] public bodies and assessment providers have a duty to make 'reasonable adjustments' to avoid disadvantage to people with disabilities, and a failure to make these adjustments is discrimination. (See p5 about the meaning of 'disability'.)

A reasonable adjustment might include:

- sending you information about your benefit in a particular format;
- letting you claim UC by phone if you cannot manage an online claim (see p76);
- changes to job centre appointments and other work-related requirements (see p272);
- offering a particular venue or format for an assessment (see p256);
- alternative payment arrangements (covered in the relevant benefit chapters of this *Handbook*).

In practice, if you need a reasonable adjustment, it usually falls to you to request it (see p327 about communicating your needs). If your request is refused, you may be able to bring a legal challenge against this decision. Get specialist advice if you are considering this.

What the DWP says: universal credit[22]

'DWP has a duty under the Equality Act to offer reasonable adjustments to claimants with disabilities and/or health conditions. DWP staff also have a duty to provide extra support to claimants suffering from mental health conditions.

'It is important to talk, and actively listen, to the claimant to find out what support they need and their preferred communication method. ... Be flexible – there is no one size fits all approach.'

Special rules about returning forms

DWP guidance states that if you have been identified as having a 'mental or cognitive impairment' (which can include a mental health problem), and/or you have an 'additional support marker' (see p328), your **PIP** claim should not be affected if you fail to return a 'How your disability affects you' questionnaire. You should simply be referred straight on for an assessment.[23]

Guidance also suggests that the DWP may refer you straight for an assessment if you fail to return a **UC50** or **ESA50** form and are known to have a mental health problem.[24]

Home visit before payments are stopped

If you are recognised as having complex needs or being vulnerable, the guidance sets out situations when the DWP must make a home visit before stopping your UC or ESA payments – eg, due to a sanction or because you have failed to attend an assessment.

Note: this does not apply in every case where payments are stopping. It is unlikely to apply, for example, if you lose your entitlement to ESA because you are found fit for work after attending an assessment.

What the DWP says: home visits

For UC: 'A claimant may have complex needs and or a health condition that affects their ability to understand their requirements and the consequences of not doing what is required of them. A sanction must not be considered until at least two attempts have been made to complete a home visit.'[25]

For ESA: 'If DWP knows that a claimant has a condition that could affect their ability to understand or comply with their obligations or conditionality, or to understand the implications of not so complying, a core visit to their home must be considered prior to any sanction or disallowance decision being made.'[26]

The tribunal

There is guidance the tribunal must consider when hearing your benefit appeal if you are recognised as vulnerable (see p303).

Specialist staff members and teams

If you are trying to navigate the benefits system but are having difficulties related to your mental health, and frontline staff (eg, work coaches or helpline call handlers) are not providing the answers or support you need, one of the following might be able to help.

Disability employment advisers (DWP)

'The disability employment adviser (DEA) is an enabling role, supporting job centre work coaches and other colleagues to develop their skills to effectively support claimants with a health condition or disability. DEAs can also provide direct support to claimants requiring additional help to move into or closer to work. Job centre employer advisers can consult with a DEA if support is needed to help a claimant or employee retain employment due to a health condition or disability.'[27]

How to contact: a work coach or employer adviser raises your case with the DEA. You cannot self-refer, but you can ask your work coach or employer adviser to approach the DEA. 'There are flexibilities within the process to allow for a claimant to request a DEA referral.'[28]

Work psychologists (DWP)

'Work psychologists in DWP have specialist training in the field of occupational psychology and are employed by DWP to support the department's aim of [helping] individuals with complex health and disability needs to progress into and sustain employment. They provide guidance to individuals, front-facing staff members, employers, internal and external stakeholders through case management advice, case conferencing and designing and delivering one-to-one/group interventions to assess the employment related support needs of job seeking customers who are socially excluded, vulnerable or otherwise disadvantaged. (...) Referral and participation in work psychology appointments is always voluntary.'[29]

How to contact: you cannot self-refer. You are usually referred by a work coach or DEA (see above).

Partnership managers (DWP)

Local partnership managers (LPMs) are based at the job centre. Their role is to build relationships with organisations external to the DWP – eg, health bodies, the local authority and advice agencies. If your case needs specific attention (eg, because an issue is not being resolved through the usual channels), one of these organisations may be able to raise it with a partnership manager.

How to contact: an organisation supporting you may be able to raise your case with the partnership manager.

What advisers say: local partnership managers

'If there's a serious delay or lack of response from DWP staff, it can be beneficial to contact an LPM. They don't usually deal with individual claimants directly but may intervene behind the scenes when an external organisation raises a concern.'

Vulnerable claimant champions (DWP)

There is limited public information about vulnerable claimant champions (VCCs). They appear to work in some, but not all, DWP benefit centres (ie, DWP's administrative and decision-making offices) to provide guidance and support to other DWP staff. If your issue is with a benefit like PIP that is not typically dealt with in the job centre, a VCC might be better positioned to help with your case than the job centre-based staff members above.

What the DWP says: vulnerable claimant champions

'The vulnerable claimant champion role is to assist DWP staff in the disability services area where additional advice is required to support a vulnerable customer. Referral routes are via internal channels only – ie, external organisations cannot refer a customer, and customers cannot self-refer.'[30]

How to contact: you cannot refer your own case to a VCC, but you might be able to ask a DWP staff member to do so – eg, ask a helpline call handler to refer you, or send a written request to the benefit centre.

Visiting officers (DWP)

The DWP has a visiting service for benefit claimants who need extra support with benefits – eg, because of complex needs and/or a disability. If the DWP agrees that you are eligible, it can send a visiting officer to visit you at home, in hospital or in another setting.

How to contact: see gov.uk/support-visit-benefit-claim.[31]

Advanced customer support senior leaders (DWP)

'DWP has a network of advanced customer support senior leaders (ACSSLs) across England, Scotland and Wales. ACSSLs do not work directly with benefit claimants; they offer a consultancy service to support DWP staff where it has been identified that the customer is at risk and normal business interactions are not mitigating the risk. They work closely with all DWP benefit areas, local authorities and other partners to achieve multi-agency solutions.'[32]

How to contact: you cannot refer your own case to an ACSSL, but you might ask a DWP staff member to refer your case, or ask your local authority/advice agency if it can make a referral.

Independent advocates (SSS)

In Scotland, if you have any kind of disability and are making a claim for a Scottish disability benefit, you have a right to be assisted by an **independent advocate**. The advocate is not an adviser but helps you to communicate – eg, to complete forms, ask questions and understand information. You can have someone to support you (see p320) as well as having an independent advocate.[33]

How to contact: use the SSS helpline or webchat and ask to be referred to the independent advocacy service.

Local delivery client support advisers (SSS)

You can get additional support with Scottish disability benefits (including in-person support) from the SSS local delivery service. You are offered an appointment with a client support adviser. They can answer benefit questions, take you through application processes and forms, and give advice about supporting evidence.

How to contact: use the SSS helpline or webchat and ask for a local delivery appointment.

Local delivery relationship leads (SSS)

SSS employs local delivery relationship leads for each region in Scotland. Their role is to build relationships with external organisations – eg, health bodies, the local authority and advice agencies. If your case needs specific attention, one of these organisations can raise it with a local delivery relationship lead.

How to contact: through an organisation that is supporting you.[34]

4. Urgent cases

Sometimes, a benefit issue needs to be resolved urgently to prevent a serious risk such as destitution, harm or neglect. For example, a delayed decision or payment might leave you with no income, or you might urgently need an appointeeship to be ended because the person acting as your appointee is not spending your money to meet your needs. You should be able to escalate an urgent benefit within the benefits system if it is not getting resolved through the usual routes.

There is no single policy about how to escalate a case within the DWP. The best option from the following list is likely to depend on the situation. It is not usually recommended that you pursue more than one of them at once. You might:

- ask to escalate the issue to a job centre line manager or to discuss it with your job centre's disability employment adviser (see p329), particularly if the issue has started because of action taken by a work coach; *or*
- ask that the case be referred to the regional vulnerable claimant champions, advanced customer support senior leaders or the visiting service (see p329); *or*
- make a complaint, involve your MP and/or consider judicial review (see Chapter 20). **Note:** the complaints process can be slow, so complaining is unlikely to be enough on its own to resolve an urgent issue.

Ask an advice worker to help with any of these steps, and to use any additional contacts they have – eg, a partnership manager (see p330).

What advisers say: escalation

'My escalation contact is absolutely fantastic for supporting people with mental health problems and particularly who might be at risk of suicide and self-harm issues.'

For benefits administered by Social Security Scotland, the starting point is to raise the issue through the helpline on (0800 182 2222) or by webchat. If this is unsuccessful, you might:

- request an appointment with the local delivery service (see p331); *or*
- make a complaint, involve your MP and/or consider judicial review (see p310). **Note:** the complaints process can be slow, so complaining is unlikely to be enough on its own to resolve an urgent issue.

Ask an advice worker to help with these steps and to use any additional contacts they have – eg, a local delivery relationship lead (see p332).

For **housing benefit**, local authorities can have their own escalation and complaints processes. It is often worth speaking to an advice worker (if possible, one employed by the local authority) for guidance on how to escalate an issue.

5. Safeguarding

Safeguarding in the benefits system

Safeguarding is the process of protecting people's health, wellbeing and human rights. Certain public bodies and organisations (eg, local authorities) have a safeguarding duty that means they need to make sure people are free from harm, abuse and neglect.[35]

The DWP does not currently accept that it formally has this type of safeguarding duty. However, the DWP has guidance about how it should work with people it classes as having complex needs or being vulnerable (see p326), including guidance about what it should do if you fail to return a benefit form (see p328) or are at risk of being sanctioned (p329).

The DWP also has guidance about proactive disclosure – ie, disclosing information about you without your consent, including in the interests of your safety.

What the DWP says: proactive disclosure [36]

'Where it is clear that a claimant with complex needs, or a child, faces clear and significant risks to their welfare or safety, DWP staff are explicitly empowered to proactively disclose information to the relevant body without the claimant providing explicit consent. (...) DWP staff are explicitly empowered to take any reasonable steps felt necessary in order to address these risks. This includes concerns about the risk of injury; ill treatment; neglect; physical or sexual abuse; [or] exploitation. These are examples and not a complete list.'

The DWP also has a six-point plan detailing the steps staff should take when someone says that they intend to attempt suicide or self-harm.[37]

Safeguarding someone you are supporting

If you have a safeguarding concern about someone you are supporting with their benefits, you can contact their local authority safeguarding adults board. If your concern falls under the Care Act 2014, the local authority has a duty to respond and provide support. See the Mind website for more information on safeguarding from local authorities.

If you work or volunteer for an organisation that supports people with benefits claims, make sure you are aware of the safeguarding policy for your organisation. Seek support and advice from someone within your organisation if you are concerned about someone's wellbeing.

In an emergency, such as when someone's life is at immediate risk, call 999.

Notes

1. Representatives and consent

1 DWP, *Universal Credit Guidance*, 'Consent and disclosure including when to share with third parties', v27.0, at rightsnet.org.uk/universal-credit-guidance

2 DWP, *Working with Representatives: guidance for DWP staff*, 17 December 2021, at gov.uk/government/publications/working-with-representatives-guidance-for-dwp-staff

3 SSS, 'Acting on behalf of someone applying for benefits', 24 March 2025, at mygov.scot/acting-on-behalf-of-someone-applying-for-benefits; SSS, *Client Representative Guidelines - Part 7: third party representatives*, October 2023, at socialsecurity.gov.scot/guidance-resources/guidance/client-representative-guidelines. See also s59 SS(S)A 2018.

4 SSS, 'Acting on behalf of someone applying for benefits', 24 March 2025, at mygov.scot/acting-on-behalf-of-someone-applying-for-benefits

5 r11 TP(FT) Rules; r11 TP(UT) Rules; CIB/1009/2004; CIB/2058/2004; *MP v SSWP (DLA)* [2010] UKUT 103 (AAC)

6 r9 FTT(S) Rules; these do not contain an equivalent provision to r11(5) TP(FT) Rules

7 NHS, 'Accessing GP services for someone else, with proxy access', at nhs.uk/nhs-services/gps/gp-services-for-someone-else-proxy-access

2. Appointeeship

8 **UC/PIP/new-style ESA** Regs 57 and 58 UC,PIP,JSA&ESA(C&P) Regs
Other DWP benefits Regs 30 and 33 SS(C&P) Regs
CDP/PADP/SADLA/ADP ss85A and 85B SS(S)A 2018
HB Regs 82 and 94 HB Regs; regs 63 and 75 HB(SPC) Regs

9 **UC/PIP/new-style ESA** Regs 57 and 58 UC,PIP,JSA&ESA(C&P) Regs
Other DWP benefits Regs 30 and 33 SS(C&P) Regs

10 PIP AG, paras 1.15.14-19; DWP, *Work Capability Assessment Handbook: for healthcare professionals*, 6 September 2024, para 3.1.3, at gov.uk/government/publications/work-capability-assessment-handbook-for-healthcare-professionals

11 ss85A and 85B SS(S)A 2018

12 Reg 82 HB Regs; reg 63 HB(SPC) Regs

13 **UC/PIP/new-style ESA** Reg 49 UC,PIP,JSA&ESA(D&A) Regs
Other DWP benefits Reg 25 SS(D&A) Regs
CDP/PADP/ADP ss85A(5) and 85B(9) SS(S)A 2018
HB Sch 7 para 6(3) and (6) CSPSSA 2000
14 HMCTS, *Senior President of Tribunals' Practice Direction on Child, Vulnerable Adult and Sensitive Witnesses*, at judiciary.uk

3. **Support within the benefits system**
15 DWP, *Universal Credit Guidance*, 'Complex needs overview', v19.0, and see also 'Mental health', v4.0, House of Commons library deposited papers, at rightsnet.org.uk/universal-credit-guidance
16 PIP AG, para 1.12.4
17 PIP AG, para 1.3.12
18 DWP, *'Spotlight on: Using the claimant profile to record complex needs'*, October 2020. See freedom of information response FOI2021/18134 at whatdotheyknow.com
19 DWP, *Universal Credit Guidance*, 'Mental health', v4.0, House of Commons library deposited papers, at rightsnet.org.uk/universal-credit-guidance
20 PIP AG, paras 1.12.1-6
21 ss20, 21 and 29 EA 2010. See also s19
22 DWP, *Universal Credit Guidance*, 'Mental health', v4.0, House of Commons library deposited papers, at rightsnet.org.uk/universal-credit-guidance
23 PIP AG, para 1.1.7; parliamentary answer UIN 142830, 21 February 2023, at questions-statements.parliament.uk
24 DWP, *Guidance: capability for work questionnaire*, disclosed to CPAG in response to freedom of information request FOI2022/102752, 6 January 2023
25 DWP, *Universal Credit Guidance*, 'Home visits', v13.0, House of Commons library deposited papers, at rightsnet.org.uk/universal-credit-guidance
26 DWP, *Core Visits – ESA guidance*, published in response to freedom of information request FOI2020/40120, 17 December 2020, at whatdotheyknow.com
27 DWP External Stakeholder Engagement team, email to CPAG, 22 February 2023
28 DWP, Response to freedom of information request FOI2023/17658, 24 March 2023, at whatdotheyknow.com
29 DWP External Stakeholder Engagement team, email to CPAG, 22 February 2023
30 DWP External Stakeholder Engagement team, email to CPAG, 22 February 2023
31 For UC, see also DWP, *Universal Credit Guidance*, 'Home visits', v13.0, House of Commons library deposited papers, at rightsnet.org.uk/universal-credit-guidance
32 DWP External Stakeholder Engagement team, email to CPAG, 22 February 2023
33 s10 SS(S)A 2018; reg 2 SS(ASS)(S) Regs; Social Security: *advocacy service standards*, at gov.scot/publications/social-security-advocacy-service-standards
34 List of contact details at socialsecurity.gov.scot/guidance-resources/resources/local-delivery-relationship-leads-june-2023

5. **Safeguarding**
35 See mind.org.uk/information-support/legal-rights/health-and-social-care-rights/safeguarding-in-social-care
36 DWP, *Universal Credit Guidance*, 'Consent and disclosure including when to share with third parties', v27.0, at rightsnet.org.uk/universal-credit-guidance
37 DWP, *Universal Credit Guidance*, 'Suicide and self-harm DWP six point plan framework', v10.0, at rightsnet.org.uk/universal-credit-guidance (but not only relevant to UC)

Appendix 1

Glossary of terms

Alternative payment arrangements
Non-standard arrangements about when or where your benefit is paid. For example, universal credit might be paid twice a month or directly to a landlord.
Appeal
When you ask an independent tribunal to look at a benefit decision and consider whether it should be changed.
Appointee
Someone authorised to claim and receive your benefit on your behalf, when you are unable to manage it yourself.
Backdated
When you can get a benefit from a date before the date on which you actually claimed it.
Bedroom tax
A reduction in the maximum amount of housing benefit you can get, or the maximum housing costs element you can get in your universal credit, if you live in social housing and are regarded as having any spare bedrooms.
Benefit cap
The maximum yearly amount of benefits that someone can receive. Not all benefits are included and not all people are affected.
Capital
This includes (but is not limited to) savings, shares, certain lump-sum payments and most property that is not a person's main home.
Care component
Part of disability living allowance and child disability payment paid if someone needs supervision or assistance because of a disability or health condition.
Claimant commitment
A document setting out what someone must do while claiming universal credit, and the possible penalties if its terms are not met.
Contributory benefit
A benefit for which entitlement depends on having paid a certain amount of national insurance contributions.

Daily living component
Part of personal independence payment and adult disability payment paid if someone has difficulties with certain daily living activities.
Descriptor
A statement describing your ability to carry out one of the activities in the work capability assessment or the personal independence payment assessment.
Discretionary housing payment
A payment that can be made by a local authority to top up universal credit or housing benefit to help with rent or some other housing costs.
Habitual residence
When someone has a settled intention to stay in the UK, and has usually been living here for a period.
Healthcare professional
A doctor, nurse, paramedic, physiotherapist or occupational therapist who carries out assessments.
Journal
An online record for your universal credit claim.
Judicial review
A way of challenging the decisions of government departments, local authorities and some tribunals against which there is no right of appeal.
Mandatory reconsideration
The requirement to have a decision looked at again by the DWP before you can make an appeal.
Means-tested benefit
A benefit that is only paid if someone's income and capital (eg, savings) are low enough.
Mixed-age couple
A couple in which one partner has reached pension age and the other has not.
Mobility component
Part of some disability benefits paid if someone has difficulties getting about, including for mental health reasons.
Non-dependant
An adult, other than a partner, who lives with the person claiming benefit – eg, a grown-up daughter or son. There are some special rules about who is included.
Non-means-tested benefit
A benefit that is paid regardless of the amount of someone's income or capital such as savings.
Overpayment
An amount of benefit that is paid which is more than a person's entitlement.
Pension age
This is currently 66 and rising to 67 between 2026 and 2028.

Person subject to immigration control
Someone who requires leave to enter or remain in the UK but does not have it, or who has leave to remain but is prohibited from having recourse to public funds, or has leave to remain in the UK on the basis of a sponsorship agreement.
Qualifying benefit
In general, any benefit which gives you entitlement to another benefit, or makes another benefit payable at a higher rate.
Revision
A method of changing a benefit decision, (usually) effective from the date it was originally made.
Right to reside
A social security test, mainly affecting European Economic Area nationals, which must be satisfied in order to claim certain benefits.
Sanction
A reduction in benefit for failing to meet work-related requirements without a good reason or because of a benefit offence.
Specified accommodation
Accommodation from a relevant body also providing care, support or supervision, or temporary accommodation provided because of domestic abuse.
Supersession
A method of changing a benefit decision some time after it was made, often because of a change in circumstances.
Temporary accommodation
Certain types of homeless accommodation where payments are made to a local authority or a social housing provider.
Two-child limit
A restriction on the number of child elements included in universal credit. There are exceptions – eg, if a child is adopted or for multiple births.
Work allowance
The amount of earnings ignored before a person's universal credit award starts to be reduced. The amount depends on personal circumstances.
Work capability assessment
An assessment of whether, because of a health condition or disability, someone has limited capability for work/work-related activity.
Work-focused interview
A job centre appointment to discuss issues related to work – eg, future work opportunities and barriers to work.
Work preparation
Carrying out activities to prepare for a future return to work, such as training or CV writing.
Work-related requirements
Activities connected with finding or preparing for work that some people must undertake to receive universal credit or employment and support allowance.

Appendix 2

Information and advice

Benefits independent advice and representation

If you want advice or information on a benefit issue, the following organisations may be able to assist.

- Advicelocal (advicelocal.uk) has details of advice organisations in your area.
- Citizens Advice. You can find out where your local office is from the Citizens Advice website at citizensadvice.org.uk (England and Wales) or cas.org.uk (Scotland).
- Law centres. You can find your nearest law centre at lawcentres.org.uk.
- LawWorks (lawworks.org.uk) has details of local legal advice centres that give free advice.
- Housing association welfare rights services for tenants.
- Local authority welfare rights services.
- Local and national organisations for particular groups of claimants may offer help. For instance, there are unemployed centres, pensioners' groups and organisations for people with disabilities.

Advice from CPAG

Unfortunately, CPAG is unable to deal with enquiries directly from members of the public. If you are an adviser you can phone or email for help with advising your client.

Advisers in England, Wales and Northern Ireland can call from 10am to 12pm and from 2pm to 4pm (Monday to Friday) on 020 7812 5231. Email advice is limited to enquiries that are specifically about universal credit and child benefit. Our email address is advice@cpag.org.uk. For more information, see cpag.org.uk/advisers.

Advisers in Scotland can call from 10am to 4pm (Monday to Thursday) and from 10am to 12pm (Friday) on 0141 552 0552, or email advice@cpagscotland.org.uk.

CPAG's Upper Tribunal assistance project can support advisers who are helping claimants to challenge tribunal decisions. See cpag.org.uk/upper-tribunal-assistance-project. We also provide training and advice to support advisers to pursue judicial review remedies. See cpag.org.uk/jrproject.

CPAG takes on a small number of test cases each year. We focus on cases that have the potential to improve the lives of families with children in poverty. If you are an adviser and would like to refer a test case to us, please see cpag.org.uk/test-case-referrals.

Finding help online

Information about benefits, including a selection of leaflets and forms, is available on the gov.uk and mygov.scot websites.

CPAG Welfare Rights is an information and solutions platform for advisers. It includes a digital version of some CPAG publications, fully searchable and updated throughout the year. See cpag.org.uk/welfare-rights.

The *rightsnet* website (aimed at advisers) at rightsnet.org.uk provides information on new welfare rights legislation, caselaw and guidance. It also provides updates on developments in other areas of social welfare law and has a discussion forum where advisers can discuss particular cases.

Most Acts and regulations can be found at legislation.gov.uk.

You can find commissioners' and Upper Tribunal decisions at gov.uk/administrative-appeals-tribunal-decisions.

Other CPAG publications

Other CPAG *Handbooks*

Benefits for Migrants Handbook (online subscription available)
Child Support Handbook
Council Tax Handbook
Debt Advice Handbook (available free at CPAG Welfare Rights)
Debt Advice Scotland Handbook (available free at CPAG Welfare Rights)
Fuel Rights Handbook
Welfare Benefits Handbook (online subscription available)
Benefits for Students in Scotland Handbook (available free online at CPAG Welfare Rights)
Children's Handbook Scotland (available free online at CPAG Welfare Rights)

CPAG guides

Financial Help for Families: what you need to know
Personal Independence Payment: what you need to know
Universal Credit: what you need to know
Winning Your Benefit Appeal: what you need to know

CPAG Welfare Rights Digital+

CPAG's full digital package, which includes the full content of the *Welfare Benefits Handbook* and *Benefits for Migrants Handbook* updated throughout the year, the *Welfare Rights Bulletin* and decision-making tools and appeal letter generators. See cpag.org.uk/subscriptions for details.

Appendix 3

Abbreviations used in the notes

AAC	Administrative Appeals Chamber
AACR	Administrative Appeals Chamber Reports
AC	Appeal Cases
All ER	All England Law Reports
Art(s)	Article(s)
CA	Court of Appeal
CC	County Council
Ch	chapter
CSIH	Court of Session, Inner House
DC	Divisional Court
EWCA Civ	England and Wales Court of Appeal (Civil Division)
EWHC	England and Wales High Court
HL	House of Lords
HLR	Housing Law Reports
LB	London Borough
para(s)	paragraph(s)
QBD	Queen's Bench Division
r(r)	rule(s)
Reg(s)	Regulation(s)
s(s)	section(s)
Sch(s)	Schedule(s)
SSWP	Secretary of State for Work and Pensions
UKSC	United Kingdom Supreme Court
UKUT	United Kingdom Upper Tribunal
Vol	volume
WLR	Weekly Law Reports

Acts of Parliament

CSPSSA 2000	Child Support, Pensions and Social Security Act 2000
EA 2010	Equality Act 2010
HRA 1998	Human Rights Act 1998
IAA 1999	Immigration and Asylum Act 1999
ITT(OI)A 2005	Income Tax (Trading and Other Income) Act 2005
JSA 1995	Jobseekers Act 1995
LGFA 1992	Local Government Finance Act 1992
PA 1995	Pensions Act 1995
PA 2014	Pensions Act 2014
SPCA 2002	State Pension Credit Act 2002
SS(AP)A 2023	Social Security (Additional Payments) Act 2023
SS(S)A 2018	Social Security (Scotland) Act 2018
SSA 1998	Social Security Act 1998
SSA(F)A 1997	Social Security Administration (Fraud) Act 1997
SSAA 1992	Social Security Administration Act 1992
SSCBA 1992	Social Security Contributions and Benefits Act 1992
WRA 2007	Welfare Reform Act 2007
WRA 2012	Welfare Reform Act 2012
WRWA 2016	Welfare Reform and Work Act 2016

Regulations and other statutory instruments

Each set of regulations has a statutory instrument (SI) number and a date. You can find them all at legislation.gov.uk.

CA(CSP)(S) Regs	The Carer's Assistance (Carer Support Payment) (Scotland) Regulations 2023 No.302
CA(YCG)(S) Regs	The Carer's Assistance (Young Carer Grants) (Scotland) Regulations 2019 No.324
CB&GA(Admin) Regs	The Child Benefit and Guardian's Allowance(Administration) Regulations 2003 No.492
CTR(S) Regs	The Council Tax Reduction (Scotland) Regulations 2021 No.249
CTR(SPC)S Regs	The Council Tax Reduction (State Pension Credit) (Scotland) Regulations 2012 No.319
CTRS(DS)E Regs	The Council Tax Reduction Schemes (Default Scheme) (England) Regulations 2012 No.2886
CTRS(DS)W Regs	The Council Tax Reduction Schemes (Default Scheme) (Wales) Regulations 2013 No.3035 (W303)

CTRS(PR)E Regs	The Council Tax Reduction Schemes (Prescribed Requirements) (England) Regulations 2012 No.2885
CTRSPR(W) Regs	The Council Tax Reduction Schemes and Prescribed Requirements (Wales) Regulations 2013 No.3029 (W316)
DACYP(S) Regs	The Disability Assistance for Children and Young People (Scotland) Regulations 2021 No.174
DAOP(S) Regs	The Disability Assistance for Older People (Scotland) Regulations 2024 No.166
DAWAP(S) Regs	The Disability Assistance for Working Age People (Scotland) Regulations 2022 No.54
DAWAP(TPMA) (S) Regs	The Disability Assistance for Working Age People (Transitional Provisions and Miscellaneous Amendment) (Scotland) Regulations 2022 No.217
ESA Regs	The Employment and Support Allowance Regulations 2008 No.794
ESA Regs 2013	The Employment and Support Allowance Regulations 2013 No.379
ESA(TP) Regs	The Employment and Support Allowance (Transitional Provisions) Regulations 2008 No.795
ESA(TP)(EA) (No.2) Regs	The Employment and Support Allowance (Transitional Provisions, Housing Benefit and Council Tax Benefit) (Existing Awards) (No.2) Regulations 2010 No.1907
ESA(WRA) Regs	The Employment and Support Allowance (Work-Related Activity) Regulations 2011 No.1349
ESAUC(MA) Regs	The Employment and Support Allowance and Universal Credit (Miscellaneous Amendments and Transitional and Savings Provisions) Regulations 2017 No.204
FTT(S) Rules	Schedule to The First-tier Tribunal for Scotland Social Security Chamber (Procedure) Regulations 2018 No.273
HB Regs	The Housing Benefit Regulations 2006 No.213
HB(SPC) Regs	The Housing Benefit (Persons who have Attained the Qualifying Age for State Pension Credit) Regulations 2006 No.214
HB&CTB(CP) Regs	The Housing Benefit and Council Tax Benefit (Consquential Provisions) Regulations 2006 No.217
HB&CTB(DA) Regs	The Housing Benefit and Council Tax Benefit (Decisions and Appeals) Regulations 2001 No.1002

JSA Regs	The Jobseeker's Allowance Regulations 1996 No.207
JSA Regs 2013	The Jobseeker's Allowance Regulations 2013 No.378
LMI Regs	The Loans for Mortgage Interest Regulations 2017 No.725
PIP(TP) Regs	The Personal Independence Payment (Transitional Provisions) Regulations 2013 No.387
SCP Regs	The Scottish Child Payment Regulations 2020 No.351
SP Regs	The State Pension Regulations 2015 No.173
SPC Regs	The State Pension Credit Regulations 2002 No.1792
SPC(CTMP) Regs	The State Pension Credit (Consequential, Transitional and Miscellaneous Provisions) Regulations 2002 No.3019
SS(AA) Regs	The Social Security (Attendance Allowance) Regulations 1991 No.2740
SS(ASS)(S) Regs	The Social Security (Advocacy Service Standards) (Scotland) Regulations 2020 No.115
SS(C&P) Regs	The Social Security (Claims and Payments) Regulations 1987 No.1968
SS(CCPC) Regs	The Social Security (Contribution Credits for Parents and Carers) Regulations 2010 No.19
SS(Cr) Regs	The Social Security (Credits) Regulations 1975 No.556
SS(DLA) Regs	The Social Security (Disability Living Allowance) Regulations 1991 No.2890
SS(GB) Regs	The Social Security (General Benefits) Regulations 1982 No.1408
SS(HIP) Regs	The Social Security (Hospital In-Patients) Regulations 2005 No.3360
SS(ICA) Regs	The Social Security (Invalid Care Allowance) Regulations 1976 No.409
SS(LB) Regs	The Social Security (Loss of Benefit) Regulations 2001 No.4022
SS(ME) Regs	The Social Security (Medical Evidence) Regulations 1976 No.615
SS(NCC) Regs	The Social Security (Notification of Change of Circumstances) Regulations 2001 No.3252
SS(OB) Regs	The Social Security (Overlapping Benefits) Regulations 1979 No.597
SS(OR) Regs	The Social Security (Overpayments and Recovery) Regulations 2013 No.384

SS(PAB) Regs	The Social Security (Payments on Account of Benefit) Regulations 2013 No.383
SS(PAOR) Regs	The Social Security (Payments on Account, Overpayments and Recovery) Regulations 1988 No.664
SS(PIP) Regs	The Social Security (Personal Independence Payment) Regulations 2013 No.377
SS(RB) Regs	The Social Security (Recovery of Benefits) Regulations 1997 No.2205
SS&CS(DA) Regs	The Social Security and Child Support (Decisions and Appeals) Regulations 1999 No.991
SSB(CE) Regs	The Social Security Benefit (Computation of Earnings) Regulations 1996 No.2745
ST(TL) Regs	The Scottish Tribunals (Time Limits) Regulations 2016 No.231
TC(Imm) Regs	The Tax Credits (Immigration) Regulations 2003 No.653
TP(FT) Rules	The Tribunal Procedure (First-tier Tribunal) (Social Entitlement Chamber) Rules 2008 No.2685
TP(UT) Rules	The Tribunal Procedure (Upper Tribunal) Rules 2008 No.2698
UC Regs	The Universal Credit Regulations 2013 No.376
UC(CP)(S) Regs	The Universal Credit (Claims and Payments) (Scotland) Regulations 2017 No.227
UC(ERSD) Regs	The Universal Credit (Energy Rebate Scheme Disregard) Regulations 2022 No.257
UC(MMP&MA) Regs	The Universal Credit (Managed Migration Pilot and Miscellaneous Amendments) Regulations 2019 No.1152
UC(TP) Regs	The Universal Credit (Transitional Provisions) Regulations 2014 No.1230
UC,PIP,JSA&ESA (C&P) Regs	The Universal Credit, Personal Independence Payment, Jobseeker's Allowance and Employment and Support Allowance (Claims and Payments) Regulations 2013 No.380
UC,PIP,JSA&ESA (DA) Regs	The Universal Credit, Personal Independence Payment, Jobseeker's Allowance and Employment and Support Allowance (Decisions and Appeals) Regulations 2013 No.381
WHACYP(S) Regs	The Winter Heating Assistance for Children and Young People (Scotland) Regulations 2020 No.352

WRA(No.21)O	The Welfare Reform Act 2012 (Commencement and Transitional and Transitory Provisions) Order 2015 No.33
WRA(No.23)O	The Welfare Reform Act 2012 (Commencement No.23 and Transitional and Transitory Provisions) Order 2015 No.634
WRA(No.31)O	The Welfare Reform Act 2012 (Commencement No.31 and Savings and Transitional Provisions and Commencement No.21 and 23 and Transitional and Transitory Provisions (Amendment)) Order 2019 No.37
WRA(No.32)O	The Welfare Reform Act 2012 (Commencement No.32 and Savings and Transitional Provisions) Order 2019 No.167

Other information

ADM	*Advice for Decision Making*, vols A1-V8
CBTM	*Child Benefit Technical Manual*
DMG	*Decision Makers' Guide*, vols 1-14
PIP AG	*PIP Assessment Guide for Assessment Providers*, 21 July 2022, available at gov.uk/government/publications/personal-independence-payment-assessment-guide-for-assessment-providers
SSS DMG	Social Security Scotland, *Decision Making Guide*, available at socialsecurity.gov.scot/guidance-resources/guidance/decision-making-guide
WCAH	*Work Capability Assessment Handbook: for healthcare professionals*, 10 October 2022, available at gov.uk/government/publications/work-capability-assessment-handbook-for-healthcare-professionals

Index

How to use this Index

Entries against the bold headings direct you to the general information on the subject, or where the subject is covered most fully. Sub-entries are listed alphabetically and direct you to specific aspects of the subject.

H

I

J